# Unmaking Race, Remaking Soul

# Unmaking Race, Remaking Soul

*Transformative Aesthetics and the Practice of Freedom*

*Edited by*

Christa Davis Acampora
and
Angela L. Cotten

State University of New York Press

Published by
State University of New York Press, Albany

© 2007 State University of New York

All rights reserved

Printed in the United States of America

No part of this book may be used or reproduced in any manner whatsoever without written permission. No part of this book may be stored in a retrieval system or transmitted in any form or by any means including electronic, electrostatic, magnetic tape, mechanical, photocopying, recording, or otherwise without the prior permission in writing of the publisher.

For information, contact State University of New York Press, Albany, NY
www.sunypress.edu

Production by Christine Hamel
Marketing by Michael Campochiaro

**Library of Congress Cataloging-in-Publication Data**

Unmaking race, remaking soul : transformative aesthetics and the practice of freedom / edited by Christa Davis Acampora, Angela L. Cotten.
    v. cm.
    Includes bibliographical references and index.
Contents: Joy A. James, "'tragedy fatigue' and 'aesthetic agency,'" Christa Davis Acampora, "on making and remaking: an introduction" — Resisting imagination — Ritch Calvin, "writing the xicanista : Ana Castillo and the articulation of chicana feminist aesthetics" — Kelly Oliver, "everyday revolutions, shifting power, and feminine genius in Julia Alvarez's fiction" — Christa Davis Acampora, "authorizing desire : erotic poetics and the aesthesis of freedom in Morrison and Shange " — Body agonistes — Martha Mockus, "meshell ndegéocello : musical articulations of Black feminism" — Kimberly Lamm, "portraits of the past, imagined now : reading the work of Lorna Simpson and Carrie Mae Weems" — Eduardo Mendieta, "the coloniality of embodiment : Coco Fusco's postcolonial genealogies and semiotic agonistics" — Changing the subject — Ruth Porritt, "pueblo sculptor Roxanne Swentzell : forming a wise, generous, and beautiful 'I am'" — Phoebe Farris, "the syncretism of Native American, Latin American, and African American — Women's art : visual expressions of feminism, the environment, spirituality, and identity" — Nandita Gupta, "dalit women's literature : a sense of the struggle" — Home is where the art is : shaping space and place — Ailsa I. Smith, "the role of 'place' in New Zealand Maori songs of lament" — Katherine Wilson, "theatre near us : librarians, culture, and space in the Harlem Renaissance" — Jaye T. Darby, "into the sacred circle, out of the melting pot : re/locations and homecomings in native women's theater".
ISBN 978-0-7914-7161-6 (hardcover : alk. paper)
ISBN 978-0-7914-7162-3 (pbk. : alk. paper)
1. Aesthetics. I. Acampora, Christa Davis, 1967– II. Cotten, Angela L., 1968–

BH39.U56 2007
111'.85—dc22
                                                                    2006032684

10  9  8  7  6  5  4  3  2  1

*For Christa's brave and creative mother, Frances,*
*and*
*Angela's wise and generous mother, Mary*

# Contents

| | | |
|---|---|---|
| | List of Illustrations | ix |
| | Foreword: "Tragedy Fatigue" and "Aesthetic Agency"<br>*Joy James* | xi |
| | Acknowledgments | xv |
| | On Making and Remaking: An Introduction<br>*Christa Davis Acampora* | 1 |

## I. RESISTING IMAGINATION

| | | |
|---|---|---|
| 1 | Writing the Xicanista: Ana Castillo and the Articulation of Chicana Feminist Aesthetics<br>*Ritch Calvin* | 21 |
| 2 | Everyday Revolutions, Shifting Power, and Feminine Genius in Julia Alvarez's Fiction<br>*Kelly Oliver* | 47 |
| 3 | Authorizing Desire: Erotic Poetics and the *Aisthesis* of Freedom in Morrison and Shange<br>*Christa Davis Acampora* | 59 |

## II. BODY AGONISTES

| | | |
|---|---|---|
| 4 | MeShell Ndegéocello: Musical Articulations of Black Feminism<br>*Martha Mockus* | 81 |
| 5 | Portraits of the Past, Imagined Now: Reading the Work of Carrie Mae Weems and Lorna Simpson<br>*Kimberly Lamm* | 103 |

6   THE COLONIALITY OF EMBODIMENT: COCO FUSCO'S
    POSTCOLONIAL GENEALOGIES AND SEMIOTIC AGONISTICS    141
    *Eduardo Mendieta*

## III. CHANGING THE SUBJECT

7   PUEBLO SCULPTOR ROXANNE SWENTZELL:
    FORMING A WISE, GENEROUS, AND BEAUTIFUL "I AM"    161
    *Ruth Porritt*

8   THE SYNCRETISM OF NATIVE AMERICAN, LATIN
    AMERICAN, AND AFRICAN AMERICAN WOMEN'S ART:
    VISUAL EXPRESSIONS OF FEMINISM, THE ENVIRONMENT,
    SPIRITUALITY, AND IDENTITY    181
    *Phoebe Farris*

9   DALIT WOMEN'S LITERATURE: A SENSE OF THE STRUGGLE    197
    *Nandita Gupta*

## IV. HOME IS WHERE THE ART IS: SHAPING SPACE AND PLACE

10  THE ROLE OF "PLACE" IN NEW ZEALAND
    MĀORI SONGS OF LAMENT    213
    *Ailsa L. Smith*

11  THEATER NEAR US: LIBRARIANS, CULTURE,
    AND SPACE IN THE HARLEM RENAISSANCE    231
    *Katherine Wilson*

12  INTO THE SACRED CIRCLE, OUT OF THE
    MELTING POT: RE/LOCATIONS AND HOMECOMINGS
    IN NATIVE WOMEN'S THEATER    247
    *Jaye T. Darby*

    WORKS CITED    265

    ABOUT THE CONTRIBUTORS    283

    INDEX    287

# Illustrations

| | | |
|---|---|---|
| FIGURE 1.1 | Ana Castillo, "Ourselves" | 22 |
| FIGURE 1.2 | Ana Castillo, "Spirituality" | 44 |
| FIGURE 5.1 | Carrie Mae Weems, "Mirror, Mirror" (from *Ain't Jokin'*) (1987–1988) | 104 |
| FIGURE 5.2 | Lorna Simpson, "Twenty Questions (A Sampler)" (1986) | 106 |
| FIGURE 5.3 | Carrie Mae Weems, "You Became Playmate to the Patriarch" from *From Here I Saw What Happened and I Cried* (1995–1996) | 113 |
| FIGURE 5.4 | Carrie Mae Weems, "And Their Daughter" from *From Here I Saw What Happened and I Cried* (1995–1996) | 114 |
| FIGURE 5.5 | Lorna Simpson, "Three Seated Figures" (1989) | 119 |
| FIGURE 5.6 | Lorna Simpson, "Portrait" (1988) | 121 |
| FIGURE 5.7 | Lorna Simpson, "Stereo Styles" (1988) | 123 |
| FIGURE 5.8 | Lorna Simpson, "Five Day Forecast" (1988) | 125 |
| FIGURE 5.9 | Lorna Simpson, "Untitled (Prefer, Refuse, Decide)" (1989) | 130 |
| FIGURE 5.10 | Carrie Mae Weems, "Van and Vera with Kids in the Kitchen" from *Family Pictures and Stories* (1978–1984) | 133 |
| FIGURE 5.11 | Lorna Simpson, "Details" (1996) | 139 |
| FIGURE 6.1 | Coco Fusco and Guillermmo Gómez-Pena, "Two Undiscovered Amerindians" | 150 |
| FIGURE 6.2 | Coco Fusco, "Stuff" | 152 |

| | | |
|---|---|---|
| FIGURE 6.3 | Video still, Coco Fusco, "The Incredible Disappearing Woman" (2003) | 157 |
| FIGURE 7.1 | Roxanne Swentzell, *Making Herself,* 2000 | 171 |
| FIGURE 7.2 | Roxanne Swentzell, *Pinup, 2000* | 175 |
| FIGURE 7.3 | Roxanne Swentzell, *Soaking in the Sun, 1990* | 177 |
| FIGURE 7.4 | Roxanne Swentzell, *Window to the Past, 2000* | 178 |
| FIGURE 11.1 | "Party for Langston Hughes on roof of 580 St. Nicholas Avenue, Harlem" (1924) | 235 |
| FIGURE 11.2 | "Scene from Harlem Experimental Theater production of Climbing Jacob's Ladder by Regina Anderson Andrews" (1924) | 237 |

# Foreword

## *"Tragedy Fatigue" and "Aesthetic Agency"*

---

Last spring, preparing to leave for a University of California conference on "black thought in the age of terror," I tuned into the local public radio station and heard a BBC report on "tragedy fatigue" in Australia. The reporters narrated, among news of varied atrocities on aboriginal lands committed by aboriginal men, the stitching together of an infant following a rape (the mothers of the victims, I was told, were out drinking when the assaults occurred).

Make a face.

Our very horrors function as infomercials and markers of our limitations, and currency for the entertainment of trauma tourists, and justification for corporate-state punitive cultures to expand in their violence.

We are inundated by trauma sites and tragedies—from invasions, occupations, and failed democracies punctured by insurgencies' improvised explosive devices (or IEDs) to reflections on shoot-to-kill edicts that dictate to conscientious (black) mothers to first obtain bullet proof vests before securing bottled water, baby formula, and pampers for those abandoned by the state in post-Katrina New Orleans. (A survival guide that addresses black female expendability might prove a very useful cultural handbook.)

Those who create and perform in the academy are indeed indebted to those outside or those who "straddle" to theorize and make theory into politics as aesthetic agency that counters empire.

Christa Acampora writes in the introduction to the volume, a tribute to Gloria Anzaldúa, of *aesthetic agency* as social and political progress engendered not only by conventional intellectual or cognitive development but also by sensibilities that hone perceptions or critiques and inspire creative political acts.

Such aesthetic agency likely creates a resting place, a haven for struggle to continue. A "home" of sorts. Where else would *transformative aesthetics exist in the practice of freedom* if not in our lives at home, beyond the closets of corporatist or statist academia.

Cultural production that creates a breathing space, or momentarily stops breath, allows us to pause to catch our thinking and move in a different way in pursuit of freedom. Such work is both necessary and alienating. Some domiciles, particularly those for most (black) women of color, often pose the inverse of the dominant cliché cemented in sentimental family values: in which "A man's home is his castle" becomes "A black woman's home is her bomb shelter."

Would it matter if the poor or rich (white) man's castle has less or more resale value than the rich or poor woman's bomb shelter (once she has removed all black family photos for the prospective buyers)? Labor to culturally produce is necessary because everyone must shelter. But perhaps the necessary labor is to no longer seek culture as reified real estate, to improve on property values by aspiring to some developer's fantasy of gated community.

"Tragedy fatigue" manifests not only among the invaded and colonized, among the impoverished or caged in penal sites that double as trauma sites. It is the hallmark of imperial ambitions and the corporate, statist, militarist, or academic agents that further or counter those ambitions.

Exhausted by struggle, captivated by the idea of freedom, seeking relief and an alternative to the reality of empire—where the breaking of souls and bodies is routine, as patriotism, patriarchy, (hetero)sexism, or racism—some create an altered reality through aesthetic production and political action. Such production might enable us to pass from this current reality of growing police powers and concentrations of wealth and avarice to another imagined or fabricated existence.

We can ask the price of the ticket to travel beyond a cultural and political morass marked by terror in which state violence and domestic violence seem to have an uncontested marriage in conventional thought. But then, after inquiries, we balk at the cost for an altered reality: the struggle of liberation that ensues from loving when one has gone beyond one's limits—beyond fatigue and beyond tragedy—to create something revolutionary. Some, beyond their limits, perform in streets, such as Daisy or "Miss Prissy" in David LaChappelle's documentary *RIZE*. Through their "Krump" dancing, they create new art forms and manifestations of fused female identity and black identity in Los Angeles zones designated as expendable, yet home to ecstatic or trance performances that transport while remaining connected.

The cultural productions of those discussed in this volume frame shelters. It is likely the making of shelters through cultural production, not the structure itself, that offers some promise of protection, that unmakes the stultified spaces that ban oxygen. Some labor in the service of agency is alienated/alienating because its very intensity and relentlessness breed exhaustion: its own form of fatigue to counter tragedy.

All homes are not created equal. The castle has keep, serfs, servants, slaves. Employees service edifices that buttress empire. The "castle," like the academy, presumes a stability and presence, a production of culture tied to the reproduction of dominance in the form of "nation" and "family" and "culture" and their "values," guarded by fortress walls and policing apparatuses shaped by white supremacy, class, and warfare against queerness—all have agency to destabilize what threatens and to promote impermanence as permanent in an ongoing siege.

What is a resting place for an "academic homemaker"? Is it a domicile from which to speculate and participate in struggle? Is it a space of perceived freedom and presumed mobility distant from street fighting and artistic production in nonelite communities? And what constitutes such "freedom" as cultural production or interrogation or affection or agency? The labor intensity of shape shifting the academy into a politically relevant residence is the homemaker's private and public joke, distorting her face into something beyond grimace. The satire of some cultural productions should leave us laughing, with the subversion inspired by the creation.

To this tribute to Gloria Anzaldúa, I add mine and also celebrate, with affection, the aesthetic agency of other (soon to be) ancestors: Barbara Christian, Octavia Butler, Toni Cade Bambara, June Jordan, Nina Simone. At Eleggua's crossroads, their offerings of aesthetic agency permit our passage to cross over with brilliance, breath, and wry humor.

*Joy James*

# Acknowledgments

We wish to thank Jane Bunker and her assistants for guidance of this project from its first draft to its last. Two anonymous reviewers made many helpful suggestions that improved the organization of the volume generally and specific contributions particularly. The SUNY Women's Studies program and its co-sponsors generously supported a symposium in 2003 that made possible a gathering of several of the contributors, which inspired spirited exchanges and buoyed us toward completing this book. The Hunter College Philosophy Department and the Philosophy Program at the CUNY Graduate Center provided some support for the manuscript preparation. Acting Dean Judith Friedlander and Acting Provost Vita Rabinowitz, both at Hunter, provided funds that made it possible to include images from the Schomberg Center of the New York Public Library. We are grateful for this assistance. Most of all, we wish to express gratitude to our contributors and the very many artists who inspired such lively critique and discussion.

Photo of Ana Castillo "Ourselves" appears courtesy of Ana Castillo.

Photo of Ana Castillo "Spirituality" appears courtesty of Ana Castillo. Photo by Margaret Randall.

Photos by Lorna Simpson appear courtesy of Sean Kelly Gallery, New York.

Photos by Carrie Mae Weems appear courtesy of Carrie Mae Weems.

Photos and video stills of Coco Fusco appear courtesy of Coco Fusco.

Photos of sculptures by Roxanne Swentzell appear courtesy of Roxanne Swentzell.

Photo of "Party for Langston Hughes" appears courtesy of the New York Public Library.

Photo of Regina Andrews, "Climbing Jacob's Ladder" appears courtesy of the New York Public Library.

*This is the story of a house. It has been lived in by many people. Our grandmother, Baba, made this house living space. She was certain that the way we lived was shaped by objects, the way we looked at them, the way they were placed around us. She was certain that we were shaped by space. From her I learned about aesthetics, the yearning for beauty that she tells me is the predicament of heart that makes our passion real. A quiltmaker, she teaches me about color. Her house is a place where I am learning to look at things, where I am learning how to belong in space. In rooms full of objects, crowded with things, I am learning to recognize myself. She hands me a mirror, showing me how to look. The color of wine she has made in my cup, the beauty of the everyday. Surrounded by fields of tobacco, the leaves braided like hair, dried and hung, circles and circles of smoke fill the air. We string red peppers fiery hot, with thread that will not be seen. They will hang in front of a lace curtain to catch the sun. Look, she tells me, what the light does to color! Do you believe that space can give life, or take it away, that space has power? These are the questions she asks which frighten me. Baba dies an old woman, out of place. Her funeral is also a place to see things, to recognize myself. How can I be sad in the face of death, surrounded by so much beauty? Dead, hidden in a field of tulips, wearing my face and calling my name. Baba can make them grow. Red, yellow, they surround her body like lovers in a swoon, tulips everywhere. Here a soul on fire with beauty burns and passes, a soul touched by flame. We see her leave. She has taught me how to look at the world and see beauty. She has taught me "we must learn to see."*
(hooks 1990, 103)

# On Unmaking and Remaking

*An Introduction
(with obvious affection for Gloria Anzaldúa)*

CHRISTA DAVIS ACAMPORA

Our title for this volume makes obvious reference to Gloria Anzaldúa's magnificently rich collection of writings by feminists of color titled *Making Face, Making Soul/Haciendo Caras* (1990). Her recent death is a loss for all of us, and her passing warrants memorializing. In addition to her two coedited collections, including *This Bridge Called My Back: Writings by Radical Women of Color* (1981), Anzaldúa authored her own essays and poetry, a book combining poetry and critical analysis titled *Borderlands/La Frontera: The New Mestiza* (1987), and several works in children's literature. A common theme in her work is the significance of linguistic expression and how it is central to the formation of one's sense of self and the possibilities for community. Her *Borderlands* explores the cultural spaces between geographic, sexual, spiritual, and economic borders drawn specifically to distinguish, isolate, and exclude those who are deemed deviant from the dominant cultural interests. Although this book was well underway prior to Anzaldúa's death, we hope that it will serve in some small way as a tribute by advancing the aims of her writings and editorial labors.

In the introduction to *Making Face, Making Soul/Haciendo Caras*, Anzaldúa describes "making face/*haciendo caras*" as an expression of feeling (as in what one conveys when one "makes a face"), a kind of sharing and communicating with others, a way of relating to them. Making face can also carry political import in the form of "the piercing look that questions or challenges, the look that says, 'Don't walk all over me,' the one that says, 'Get out of my face'" (Anzaldúa 1990, xv). Many of the cultural productions discussed and presented in this volume incorporate both of these senses in their meditations on the nature of community and social justice.

Anzaldúa further observes that the face at the body's surface is also the site for inscriptions of social structures in which, "We are 'written' all over [. . .] carved and tattooed with the sharp needles of experience" (1990, xv). A major premise of this book is that one of the ways in which persons of color, but especially *women of color*, have effected an *un*making of the face that marks them as female and gives them racial particularity is through their cultural productions in which they aesthetically transform the values that have been used to stain them as inferior, deficient, and defective. Cultural productions such as those considered here constitute efforts to elude and transform the "gaze" that constitutes such faces and to remake oneself according to one's own aesthetic sensibilities and aspirations. This way of "looking back" locates women's political resistance in places not often recognized as legitimate sites of political contestation. And yet it is, in part, because women are excluded or shunned from more traditional venues of political organization against racial and class oppression (specifically because of their gender) that they seek these alternative modes and media of expression.

The facts that women have complicated and compromised access to outlets for organized resistance and that their oppressors refuse to recognize them as legitimate contestants in the public sphere partly—but *only partly*—explain why so many women have consciously sought transformative social change through less traditional channels. Another reason is that the kind of transformation or remaking sought *requires* different modes of expression. Many find they do not have the language to simply rewrite the inscriptions that mark the faces of racism and sexism, or they find that writing alone is insufficient for their task. Thus, women of color have been leading innovators in remaking a variety of media in the formal arts as well as in creative practices that lie outside those dominant categories. Women working in the traditional arts have also sought to blend or bend standard genres, developing novel forms such as choreopoetry (as in the case of Ntozake Shange 1981a). They also utilize approaches that several contributors here describe as *syncretic*. Syncretism involves drawing upon and incorporating a variety of traditions in the making of something new that is nevertheless authentic and respectful of traditions.

Syncretism is particularly significant as a strategic response to problems faced by women of color especially, as numerous authors here indicate. Persons of color who endeavor to inhabit and nurture cultural spaces outside of the traditions that define them as "other" and "outsider" face a dilemma: they can cling to romantic notions of a cultural past from which they are geographically and historically separated, or they can strive to invent a culture anew. The former prong of this dilemma is often organized around an essentialized and static conception of culture generally, and the latter seems too readily dismissive of the ways in which meanings emerge from historical and situated contexts and are not simply the freewheeling inventions of individuals. The denial of metaphysical essentialism (often used as the basis for the subjection of others) differs from recognition of "situational differences" insofar as the features that are defined and used as the basis for "constructed" differences are understood as having real material consequences with durable legacies. The contributors to this volume and the artists they discuss are mindful of this distinction and emphasize the constellation of interests and desires that inform and shape their lived experiences.

This fact is relevant to the classical aesthetic concept of 'disinterestedness,' which was so prominent in European-centered conceptions of aesthetics in the nineteenth and early twentieth centuries and which served as a criterion for the possible contemplation of true, genuine, or "high" art. Disinterestedness—the idea that aesthetic objects are necessarily disengaged from practical concerns—has fallen out of favor, at least overtly, as a criterion for worthy aesthetic contemplation, although it lives on with more subtlety in the ongoing debate about whether political art can be appreciated primarily for its aesthetic qualities (see Mullin 2003).

The aesthetic transformations of women of color are anything but disinterested; indeed, they are often connected to lived, everyday experience, the practical realm of interests that comprise the social institutions that limit and define their possible ways of being in the world. The artists discussed here are concerned with *exposing* the (often hidden) racist, patriarchal, and economic interests of others and of shaping and *remaking* a form of interest or desire that is redemptive of the value of their experiences and aspirations. We are, all of us, informed by a great variety of traditions and cultural values, and our conceptions of the lives we want as *ours* are shaped by these forces, which are often in conflict. Early theoretical formations of racial/ethnic oppression, including constructions of the colonial in both postcolonial theory and anticolonial nationalism, tended to elide gender differences in the experience of oppression. Many feminist critics have shown, however, that gender was deployed strategically in imperial and colonial practices and that women suffered at least two layers of oppression relating to their colonized and gendered bodies (McClintock 1995, Suleri 1992, Mohanty 1991, Spivak 1995, Wallace

1979). By the same token European and North American feminists (white and nonwhite alike) have sometimes misrepresented the problems and interests of women in developing nations by analyzing their situations using theoretical models that are blind to the very differences that define their particular situations (Oyewumi 2003, Mohanty 1991, hooks 1984). For many of the authors and artists whose contributions and works are discussed here, what is meant by "making" and "remaking" soul involves grappling with these challenges: a kind of critical relationality, which "means negotiating, articulating and interrogating simultaneously a variety of resistant discourses relationally and depending on context, historical and political circumstances" (Davies 1994, 47).

The cultural productions of many artists, writers, and musicians featured here can be read as their *homes*. As hooks puts it: these repositories of personal transformation and visions of beauty, art, and human possibility shelter and provide ground for the cultivation of new aesthetic sensibilities, new ways of relating to others and to the world, and thus new possibilities for building community and organizing resistance (e.g., 1994a, 1994b). The very subtitle of this collection, *Transformative Aesthetics and the Practice of Freedom*, echoes a subtitle by bell hooks—*Teaching to Transgress: Education and the Practice of Freedom*. In many of her writings, hooks connects aesthetics and education to an ethic or practice of freedom that enables and activates a resistive form of agency. Her writings explore in a variety of ways how educating the senses (drawing out and cultivating them, as the Latin relative of the word *education*, *educere*—to lead forth, suggests) and nurturing sensibility enable intellectual, moral, and spiritual growth, activism, and community formation. In her essay "An Aesthetic of Blackness: Strange and Oppositional," hooks heralds a radical aesthetic to be sought by progressive African Americans, which would provide "vital grounding that helps make certain work possible, particularly expressive work that is transgressive and oppositional" (hooks 1990, 110; compare and contrast with texts central to the Black Arts Movement of the 1960s and 1970s [Baraka 1966, Fuller 1967, Gayle 1971, Sell 2001], which played a prominent role in the establishment of black studies).

۞

Each part of the book is comprised of chapters motivated by and explicitly oriented toward the idea that social and political progress requires not *only* what is traditionally considered intellectual or cognitive development but also expansion of the sensibilities that both sharpens our perceptual capacities and fuels creativity activity. We call this "aesthetic agency." In designating this capacity for action "aesthetic," we do not imply a strict contrast with what the so-called western tradition allegedly considers to be moral agency and its typical rational basis and ideal of autonomy (we write "allegedly," because there is a tradition stretching back to Kant and further to Plato that connects morality and aesthetics). Yet the exclusivity and presumed primacy of these conditions for action (rationality, autonomy) are challenged in a variety of ways by the women whose works are discussed in this volume. The importance of individuality for identity, the conception of freedom as independence or freedom from restraint, and the ideal of a universal intelligence are questioned here without simply renouncing everything conceived as emblematic of Euro-centered culture, including theory and its applications. The core idea of aesthetic agency is that integral to our understanding of the world is our capacity for making and remaking the symbolic forms that supply the frameworks for the acquisition and transmission of knowledge.

Thus, this new sensibility does not simply pertain to what is generally conceived as sheer emotional energy or what the western tradition might designate (and, at times, *denigrate*) as mere "feeling." Aesthetic sensibility cultivates the senses, including that of sight: it nurtures a different way of seeing. For many of the authors here, such "seeing" grounds a different cognitive perspective, a different way of understanding the world, one's place within it, and how the world might possibly be negotiated and reorganized. Thus, aesthetic agency is liberating in a broad sense to include the expansion not only of our capacity for joy but also our capacities to know, to judge, and to act.

One of the purposes of this volume is to allow the distinctive ways of seeing and feeling of women artists to become available for others to experience. We have conceived the designation of "artist" broadly so as to include those working in a variety of cultural media, including artistic practices other than those exercised in the formal arts. (This same interest motivates our companion volume titled *Cultural Sites of Critical Insight* 2007.) To accomplish our aim, we have selected scholarly and theoretical works that provide numerous illustrative examples, and we have included visual reproductions of several works of art, most of which are not widely accessible. This way of organizing the material and developing themes distinguishes this book from others, which either focus particularly on literature and literary theory (e.g., Bobo 2001), a particular cultural tradition (e.g., Martinez 2000), primarily the productions of men (e.g., Gayle 1971, Powell 1997), or relevant issues of theory that nonetheless do not explicitly consider the cultural innovations and reformations that are advanced in the kinds of works discussed here (e.g., Gordon and Gordon 2006). These other volumes make their own significant contributions, so we recommend them for those wishing to further develop ideas raised in this text.

Many of the anthologies treating feminist aesthetics and the cultural productions of women include only a few pieces that focus on the experiences, theoretical perspectives, and self-consciously creative practices of women of color (as an exception, see Shohat 1998). This is not to say that the fine collections available, including a special issue of *Hypatia, Women, Art, and Aesthetics* (Brand and Devereaux 2003), include *no* essays that are relevant to, by, or about women of color (see also Hein and Korsmeyer 1993, Brand and Korsmeyer 1995, Allan 1995, and Ecker 1985); but often their perspectives remain marginal or sparse. Our volume aims to make the works and distinctive concerns of women of color more prominent, to spur and supplement the growing body of work in this area. Anthologies that are devoted primarily or exclusively to the works and ideas of women of color, such as James' and Sharpley-Whiting's *The Black Feminist Reader* (2000), Bobo's *Black Feminist Cultural Criticism* (2001), Brown and Gooze's *International Women's Writings: New Landscapes of Identity* (1995), and Wisker's *Post-Colonial and African-American Women's Writing* (2000), generally include only previously published materials, are focused on theoretical perspectives, or are written chiefly by literary theorists. Our volume includes only new material written specifically for this book by scholars and artists who work in a variety of disciplines and media and who utilize interdisciplinary methods. Our collection explicitly develops the relation between (and challenges the binary of) the theoretical and the practical as it illuminates theoretical revisions that emerge from the cultural productions of women of color, and it accomplishes this through works that emerge from a variety of cultural perspectives. Each of the related works mentioned above fills gaps left open in the prior literature. They are highly recommended to those who wish to further pursue themes raised here.

An original plan for the book called for its organization along the lines of the kinds of arts or cultural productions under discussion, so, for example, we planned a section on literature, one on performance art, and others on visual and material arts. As we prepared our manuscript for review and publication, however, we realized that our original scheme was problematic. Virtually all of the artists discussed here work in multiple media or in media that cannot be easily classified, and they often challenged the very distinctions such an organizing principle would utilize. It soon became clear that a different scheme for arrangement would be more appropriate and perhaps more helpful to the reader. Thus, we have grouped the essays here along the lines for four broad themes: those developing a crucial precursor (and product) of aesthetic agency—imagination; those focused on issues relating to the body, particularly as its morphological features provide the material for both discrimination and recreation of meaning; those investigating the connection between aesthetic productivity and the formation of new or specific identities both personal and cultural; and those concerned with issues of space and place, the transformation of the conditions in which we live and our relations to geographic and spiritual domains. As writers in the first part argue, there are certain powers of imagination that people must cultivate in order to be able to exercise the human form of creativity that characterizes the production of culture and its reformation; there is, as Kelly Oliver describes, a kind of psychic space that must be claimed in order to have the resources to imagine a different life one would want to call one's own. Aesthetic experience and imaginative activity are bidirectional: aesthetic experience can ignite imaginative activity, and the latter enhances and further facilitates the likelihood of the former. This basic feature of aesthetic agency has immediate applications for the transfiguration of the body, its articulations in the productions of dominant and oppressive cultures, and resistive practices that form the basis for political action. Chapters in the second part of the book specifically focus on this idea. The third part considers specific formations of identity that are enabled by a remodeled sense of body and spirituality, particularly as such are enabled through engagement in aesthetic productivity in material, visual, and literary arts. The fourth and final part considers the aesthetic dimension of relations to earth, home, community, and nation as it relates to place making. The chapters here consider aesthetic agency as a way of *dwelling* in a sense that permeates ordinary lived experience and conditions the extraordinary sense of connection to others. In many ways, each chapter addresses or is relevant to each of these themes, too, although the present arrangement allows grouped chapters to bring out more subtle commonalities as well as differences and complementary perspectives.

Part One includes chapters that aim to articulate the kind of imagination that is engaged in the process of creativity and how it bears on the development of a kind of political imagination that is crucial for resistance. Artists considered include Ana Castillo, Julia Alvarez, Ntozake Shange, Audre Lorde, and Toni Morrison. Ritch Calvin's chapter, "Writing the Xicanista: Ana Castillo and the Articulation of Chicana Feminist Aesthetics," provides a point of entry for the collection, since one of Calvin's claims is that Castillo endeavors to create a new discourse entirely—one that is not preoccupied with the need for translation and thus operates on its own terms—but that is concerned with *communication*, thus engaging the norms and customs of formal discourse that predominate institutions of power such as academia. Calvin persuasively argues that Castillo's writing is misunderstood when viewed only as an example of the genre of magical realism. The *real* magic of her works, as he describes them, lies in her transformation of language, her reformation of identity, and her development of prepatriarchal models for Xicanista ontology that are deeply rooted in lived experience. Calvin intelligently describes the peculiar position and dilemma of Xicanistas, who find the need to simultaneously resist colonial identities as well as the patriarchal elements of resistance movements and who, nevertheless, as a legacy of colonialism, find themselves at a considerable distance from indigenous models of world making that might supply the cultural and creative resources for engaging in such transformative resistance. As Calvin traces the strategies that Castillo deploys throughout her vast body of writing, he particularly notices how Castillo's Xicanisma discourse incorporates as well as subverts traditional Anglo discourse, including academic models. In this regard he finds Castillo's work distinctive. What emerges is a form of Xicanista subjectivity that is defined in and on its own terms, but which is also interactive with other forms of subjectivity and alternative ways of structuring and ordering experience. It also redefines the very terms of subjectivity, shifting it away from an account of distinctive individual identity to one that is first and foremost rooted in community and social relations.

Kelly Oliver, in "Everyday Revolutions, Shifting Power, and Feminine Genius in Julia Alvarez's Fiction," focuses on the ways in which the fault lines of oppressive power structures are reconfigured according to race, class, and gender. She considers how gendered power in particular can be manifest in the exploitation of tensions and cross-currents within and among these structures by illuminating how Alvarez depicts scenes in which we see, for example, "shifting power relations": "class privilege has given way to gender privilege, and then the relation between gender hierarchy and class hierarchy is reversed again." Oliver provides examples of the ways in which one form of privilege can be played to undermine another or turned against itself. Two other features of gendered power are explored in Oliver's essay, including the idea of the female genius, borrowed from Julia Kristeva, and the significance of the everyday and ordinary struggles that are faced by the characters in Alvarez's novels. Although the figure of the genius might appear to stand far apart from the ordinary, Oliver shows how the characters in Alvarez's volumes often show themselves to be geniuses of the ordinary, "in which the very trappings of femininity, womanhood, and motherhood can be used against patriarchal values and institutions in order to open up a space for women's resistance to domination." A particularly potent feature of Alvarez's writing, as Oliver describes it, is its exercise of imagination, which "enriches our own sense of possibility and freedom."

In the final section of her chapter, Oliver focuses on Alvarez's novel *In the Name of Salomé*, in which the main character battles depression and struggles to recapture her creative imagination. Oliver focuses upon this character to underscore the ways in which oppression can diminish the capacities for sublimation and imaginative activity that are crucial for women's psychic lives and exercise of agency. This very problem is at the center of Christa Davis Acampora's "Authorizing Desire: Erotic Poetics and the *Aisthesis* of Freedom in Morrison and Shange." Instead of describing the problem in terms of sublimation, Acampora considers how oppressive power structures diminish and redirect desire so as to cut one off from both the resources to create and the imagination of free ends toward which one might direct creative action. Acampora shares Oliver's interest in what constitutes psychic freedom and emphasizes how it is predicated, at least in part, upon certain kinds of aesthetic experiences. In pursuit of this thesis, Acampora draws on an existential framework to elaborate how existential freedom is dependent upon opportunities for creative activity, particularly in the production of meanings. She looks to Frantz Fanon's work to expose some problems with early existential views, and to the choreopoetry of Ntozake Shange for further elaboration of the particular situation faced by men and women of color and the potency of aesthetic experiences for addressing these problems. Highlighting Audre Lorde's conception of erotic power, Acampora further underscores the importance of the aesthetic basis of freedom in consideration of the deformations of desire illustrated in Toni Morrison's *Beloved*.

Part Two focuses on issues of embodiment and the transformation of the meaning of the body through aesthetic creativity. Martha Mockus heads her chapter, "MeShell Ndegéocello: Musical Articulations of Black Feminism," with an epigraph in which bassist/singer/songwriter Ndegéocello emphasizes her sense of rhythm that is informed by the invisible materiality of the body: "the pulses of the rivers of blood that flow through my body." This is how she describes her sense of the divine, her belief in things that are not visible. Mockus' chapter takes its cue from Ndegéocello's interest in "the epistemological power of music," which is often ignored in a culture that is driven primarily by the visual and literary. Using what Mockus describes as an alternative and defiant "acoustic logic," Ndegéocello challenges her listeners to tap that unseen but *felt* power in order to rethink and redefine what they believe they know about freedom. This is further reflected in her lyrics addressing capitalism, racism, sexism, and homophobia particularly in African American culture. Although Ndegéocello herself has resisted describing her work as feminist—largely because she associates feminism with the interests of white middle-class women—Mockus reveals how her compositional process, her use of musical formations, and her lyrics are compatible and in dialogue with feminist analyses along the lines of those advanced by bell hooks and Angela Davis.

A different approach to transforming our sense of the visual and literary, particularly as it relates to representations of the body, is taken by Kimberly Lamm in her "Portraits of the Past, Imagined Now: Reading the Work of Carrie Mae Weems and Lorna Simpson." Lamm describes how both Simpson and Weems explore and exploit the "'bizarre axiological ground'" (determinations of value that ground meaning and significance), borrowing a phrase from Hortense Spillers, from which the lives of African American women and their families emerge. Lamm's focus on portraiture is significant, since the portrait is a good index of the historical axes of individuality, dignity, and respectability (particularly among whites), which define and regulate norms of beauty and propriety and thereby control or contain the (especially black) body. Portraiture is thus a potent medium for resistance as well as a site against which resistance must be mounted.

Weems' and Simpson's portraits of women also draw on their complicated place in their homes, their immediate communities, and the larger social order that presses upon and endeavors to define, regulate, and control the other spheres. As mentioned near the outset of this introduction, women of color face particular difficulties when endeavoring to claim, craft, or create positive models for subjectivity from such a considerable historical distance to models they might regard as legitimate expressions of their own cultural traditions. Lamm does an especially good job of elaborating the pitfalls of endeavoring to find such models simply through reappropriation of what is cast as marginal or negative. She helpfully describes how the works by Weems and Simpson depict—offer a portrait of, that is, constitute a way of *looking at*—the lives of women in ways that recognize their perceived status as marginal and imagine an alternative set of values and norms in which their concerns might be central.

A poignant mindfulness of the impact of *being seen*, the gaze, is a central concern for Eduardo Mendieta in "The Coloniality of Embodiment: Coco Fusco's Postcolonial Genealogies and Semiotic Agonistics." Mendieta looks to the vast array of productions of Coco Fusco to consider how she crafts a perspective that challenges and undermines the colonizing and racializing gaze that endeavors to make her "other." He is especially interested in how Fusco accomplishes this sort of "looking back" through what he calls "semiotic agonistics"—a deliberate and self-conscious entrée to the public sphere that aims to destabilize and transform signifiers and the construction of what is signified. Mendieta argues that Fusco engages this struggle of meaning (that is "semiotic agonistics") in body performance, which contributes to and reconfigures the meaning of the body itself and how the body serves as a creative site of meaning ("somatic semiology"). For Mendieta, Fusco's work exemplifies both "performance *of* the body and the body *in* performance."

Mendieta draws on a broad and somewhat unexpected range of theoretical perspectives in his analysis, including Heidegger's conception of "worlding" and Foucault's conception of genealogy. He characterizes Fusco's work as "arting" the body, which is to say she quite consciously highlights how bodies are bearers of meaningful signs and how they are used in the transmission of culture, and she performs her body in ways that trace, interrogate, and challenge the genealogies of producing colonial and postcolonial subjectivities. Mendieta provides illuminating examples of precisely how this is accomplished by Fusco, particularly in his discussion of her performance work "Two Undiscovered Amerindians," with Guillermo Gómez-Peña, to mark the five hundredth anniversary of the "discovery" of the "New World."

Mendieta's chapter provides an excellent segue to part Three, which is focused on the nature of agency and identity as they are produced through artistic and aesthetic enterprises that take a variety of cultural forms. The chapters in this section consider the remaking of self and the making of agency not just in terms of disassembling or erasing but rather as a practice that replaces the face of race with the pleasure and joy of soul. They envision a truly creative enterprise that *vivifies* and transforms rather than simply masks or re-masks. What is found here is an effort to develop a poetics of soul and community that challenges the self-contained individualism of most western, Enlightenment-based cultures. Extreme individualism underwritten by late capitalism in these cultures keeps us from recognizing our connections with others and the natural world. Many Native American women writers critique this ontology and express alternative visions of harmony and wholeness between the individual, community, environment, and cosmos (Allen 1991). Ruth Porritt finds such a view in Pueblo Tewa cosmology and in the contemporary sculpture of Roxanne Swentzell. Porritt's "Pueblo Sculptor Roxanne Swentzell: Forming a Wise, Generous, and Beautiful 'I Am'" describes how Swentzell's sculptures convey a sense of self as first and foremost rooted in a community that complements an array of talents while nurturing and balancing a variety of needs. The agent as emotional energy is also of concern to Swentzell, and she is particularly interested in how the communal ties mentioned above can provide a basis for healing and growth. Calling herself "a sculptor of human emotions," Swentzell endeavors to expand emotional capacities for expression and healing and to provide a sense of *felt-form* to augment our more familiar senses of visual form. Her work is stirred by a deep recognition of human suffering and responsibility and a candid exploration of the role of sadness in our lives.

Drawing on the writings and works of Kay WalkingStick, Oscar Howe, and Nancy Hartsock, Porritt argues that Swentzell's works engage what she describes as "standpoint emotional integrity." Standpoint emotional integrity, as Porritt defines it, draws on the concept of 'standpoint epistemology' that is developed in the work of Hartsock (1983). Porritt highlights both the cognitive and ethical character of the emotions in standpoint theory as she describes "a sensitive individual's perceptive consciousness of intercultural and intracultural differences, particularly as discrepancies in values or beliefs are carried by emotional recognitions." But this is not simply an exchange of empathy: standpoint emotional integrity also clarifies and neutralizes aggressive and divisive intentions, replacing them with "a strong sense of wonder and hope." It involves the agent in thoughtful and reflective creative action in which "the individual manifests a talent for forming an undivided—if emotionally complex—whole." That practice of making whole provides a formal basis for community building and regenerative healing from the scarring effects of racism and sexual discrimination. Porritt emphasizes the way in which standpoint emotional integrity "is specifically embodied; the sensations which signal our emotions arise out of our bodies as physical responses to our experiences with other people and our environment." Through analysis of numerous illustrated examples Porritt describes precisely how Swentzell brings this forth in her works.

Gaining a sense of community in the wake of colonialism and the cultural discontinuity that stems from practices of forced migration and cultural terrorism is addressed by Phoebe Farris in "The Syncretism of Native American, Latin American, and African American Women's Art: Visual Expressions of Feminism, the Environment, Spirituality, and Identity." Farris describes the art-making activities of Native American, African American, and Latin American women as practices of syncretism. Syncretism involves utilizing and adapting various symbols and traditions from both ancient and modern cultural practices, and it allows these artists to explore possibilities for generating their own norms and values in the context of the vast network of relations and affiliations (both voluntary and otherwise) that characterize modern life and their lived experiences. Of particular concern to those producing syncretic works is a rejection of the strict notion, pressed from both inside and outside their own cultures, to deploy "traditional" forms of expression as the only way to be truly "authentic" or to realize some essential kind of agency. Farris explicitly rejects this way of conceiving authenticity and cites numerous ways in which it is directly challenged by the women artists she studies: "Any insistence that Indian art remain 'traditional' as a way of preserving culture is a form of cultural discrimination because cultures are dynamic, not static." The artists Farris cites draw upon the ideas and philosophical perspectives of a variety of communities, including those organized around political movements found in feminism and environmentalism, especially for their emphases on human dignity, relational and communal agency, and the connections between human beings and the places in which they live and from which they draw their sustenance. Virtually all of these artists consider art to have curative powers that can heal psyches, communities, and intercommunal relations on a global scale. This art dissolves the high/low distinction as it challenges the categories of the authentic and naïve/traditional in pursuit of new forms of human expression in the production of ethnic heritage. Farris reviews a stunning array of women artists and vast collections of works to illustrate just how pervasive these ideas are.

The roles and challenges of women in the context of broader liberation movements are explored by Nandita Gupta in her "Dalit Women's Literature: A Sense of the Struggle." In particular, Gupta focuses on the distinctive character of the voices of women writers, how they depict the aims of the movements of which they are a part, and the ways in which women characters figure in their literary productions. A special feature of this contribution is its use of materials that are difficult to acquire. Gupta traces the development of agency in the writings of women throughout the Dalit movement, and she underscores the difficulties of the tensions between women of different castes.

The volume concludes with a group of chapters that explicitly addresses a theme raised in the epigraph to this volume in which bell hooks describes a house, more properly a "home," that is a living space that is shaped by and shapes within those who dwell there (the notion of 'home' stands in contrast with 'house' in the sense invoked in Audre Lorde's famous "The Master's Tools Will Never Dismantle The Master's House" [1984]; compare a new sense of theoretical 'house' in Gordon and Gordon 2006). Such practices of shaping that are found in the production of that home are *aesthetic*. The home-making that organizes and animates such an aesthetic instills what bells hooks describes as "a yearning for beauty," which is "the predicament of the heart that makes our passion real" (hooks 1990, 103). The chapters in this part of our volume explore in a variety of ways the connections between place, particularly the home or homeland, and a kind of yearning that draws one out of oneself, that serves as the basis for a kind of *ecstasy*—or standing out—from the ready-made personas created by the objectifying gaze of the dominant culture. Such ecstasy is what makes the spaces in which we find ourselves *live*, and in that living, our aspirations, wants, and desires—our passion—is given direction, meaning, and purpose, which makes it real.

The emotional charge of place and its role in shaping a sense of community and cultural continuity are emphasized in Ailsa Smith's "The Role of 'Place' in New Zealand Māori Songs of Lament," which is a fascinating study of Māori songs of lament collected, recorded, and written by her great-grandfather during the nineteenth century. These songs are especially important for cultural recovery and identity formation for Smith herself, and for other Māori peoples, since colonial invasion resulted in a sense of dislocation among the self, the land, and language. Smith explores the oral tradition's role in helping to sustain some sense of identity under colonialism. She considers the ways in which the songs were used to convey and preserve tribal information, including practical knowledge about food sources and environmental features. She also reveals how their formal organization provides a rhythmic mnemonic for ideas that shaped distinctive ways of thinking about place, time, history, and community. Smith elaborates this in the context of a discussion of *wā*, which indicates the circumstances of an event that emphasizes the interconnectivity and inseparability of people and place in an ongoing and relational process. Women participated in the composition of songs of lament, and Smith notices that such activities provided powerful outlets for the assertion of agency and the acquisition of respect within the community. Since the Māori community, particularly the Taranaki tribe, which is the focus of Smith's investigation, defined itself in terms whose significances were written in the landscape, its fundamental concepts were particularly durable but also contingent upon rights and access to the lands in which those meanings were inscribed through song. Smith skillfully illuminates this in her discussion of the historical example of the Treaty of Waitangi and how the European presence in New Zealand, facilitated by Māori acceptance of that document, led to the loss of land that was so often the theme of the songs of lament she studies.

Through an exploration of the complicated and fascinating history of the development of the Harlem Experimental Theater in the basement of the public library on 135th Street in Harlem, Katherine Wilson highlights the cultural production of spaces of knowledge and creativity in her "Theater Near Us: Librarians, Culture, and Space in the Harlem Renaissance." While works by and about black artists were featured in a variety of theatrical venues during this time, as Wilson notes the productions staged in the public library basement were among the first that represented the character of black experience both depicted and staged in the places where African Americans actually lived. Instrumental in bringing about this opportunity was the effort of Regina Andrews, whose story as a woman of mixed racial ancestry striving to achieve professional success and institutional reform is interesting in its own right. Entwined in this history of giving the Harlem Experimental Theater its home is an analysis of the library as the home of the space of knowledge, accessible to women because of its association with "an extension of the (bourgeois) home" in which "library discourses identified librarians literally as 'hostesses.'" Wilson's chapter provides a fascinating example of the ways in which social and cultural transformation is manifest in the unmaking and remaking of public space.

The making of home and the recovery of the idea of homecoming in Native American theater is thematized in the final contribution to the volume, "Into the Sacred Circle, Out of the Melting Pot: Re/Locations and Homecomings in Native Women's Theater" by Jaye T. Darby. Darby draws on the works of Paula Gunn Allen, a Laguna Pueblo/Sioux scholar and writer, in her articulation of how homecomings are variously represented and achieved in the works of three modern women playwrights: Marcie Rendon (White Earth Anishinabe), Diane Glancy (Cherokee), and Daystar/Rosalie Jones (Pembina Chippewa). A variety of themes and challenges are explored in their works, including the tensions between urban life and traditional spirituality, the ways in which cultural narratives that form oral histories can seem alien to younger generations more comfortable with the modern vernacular; and how dance, song, and story can form the basis for the restoration of cultural memory and social transformation. Each play considered explores the liminal spaces lying between the modern situation of cultural and geographic isolation and dispossession and the promise of spiritual renewal in cultural making or coming home.

⁂

This book admits of a variety of approaches to enjoying and appreciating its contents. Those wishing to pursue the themes that characterize feminist aesthetics generally—issues relating to imagination, the body, agency, and place—might very well find that reading the book from beginning to end gives them a helpful perspective on these broader issues, especially in the context of thinking about how women of color particularly encounter and approach them. Since most authors also discuss and/or draw upon better known theoretical frameworks, including those generated by women of color, a course that considers the cultural productions of women of color as sites of resistance and social transformation might fruitfully utilize this book alongside readings of important theorists, collections of which are mentioned above. Still others might enjoy exploring the specific works described and illustrated herein, deciding to pick and choose among the chapters without concern for reading the them in any particular order. Each chapter was written in order to open up a distinctive perspective in its own right; each endeavors to illuminate and articulate a sense of the unmaking and remaking that taps the transformative power of women's aesthetic agency. Each reader is encouraged to engage in an imaginative dialogue in order to make it her or his own.

# Part I
Resisting Imagination

# 1

## Writing the Xicanista

### Ana Castillo and the Articulation of Chicana Feminist Aesthetics

RITCH CALVIN

---

> What happens when we refuse learned associations, dualisms, metaphors? We may begin to introduce unimaginable images and concepts into our poetics.
> —Ana Castillo, *Massacre of the Dreamers*

Of all the writers to whom Ana Castillo is compared, perhaps the most frequent are Colombian Gabriel García Márquez and Chilean Isabel Allende, arguably the two best-known proponents, or practitioners, of "magical realism." García Márquez's *Cien años de la soledad* (One Hundred Years of Solitude), which was originally published in 1967 and has become synonymous with "magical realism," contains the following passage, in which Remedios the Beauty ascends into the skies:

> She had just finished saying ["I never felt better"] when Fernanda felt a delicate wind of light pull the sheets out of her hands and open them up wide. Amaranta felt a mysterious trembling in the lace on her petticoats and she tried to grasp the sheets so that she would not fall down at the instant that Remedios the Beauty began to rise. Úrsula, almost blind at the time, was the only person who was sufficiently calm to identify the nature of that determined wind and she left the sheets to the mercy of the light as she watched Remedios the Beauty waving good-bye in the midst of the flapping sheets that rose up with her, abandoning with her the environment of beetles and dahlias and passing through the air with her as four o'clock in the afternoon came to an end, and they were lost forever with her in the upper atmosphere where not even the highest flying birds of memory could reach her. (García Márquez 1970, 222–23)

FIGURE 1.1. Ana Castillo, "Ourselves"

In Isabel Allende's first novel, *La casa de los espíritus* (The House of the Spirits), which was first published in 1982 and has become synonymous with "feminist magical realism," Allende describes one of the daughters of the Trueba family:

> Her gaze rested on Rosa, the oldest of her living daughters, and, as always, she was surprised. The girl's strange beauty had a disturbing quality that even she could not help noticing, for this child of hers seemed to have been made of a different material from the rest of the human race. Even before she was born, Nívea had known she was not of this world, because she had already seen her in dreams. This was why she had not been surprised when the midwife screamed as the child emerged. At birth Rosa was white and smooth, without a wrinkle, like a porcelain doll, with green hair and yellow eyes—the most beautiful creature to be born on earth since the days of original sin, as the midwife put it, making the sign of the cross. (1985, 5–6)

Ana Castillo's third novel, *So Far from God*, published in 1994, has become synonymous with "Chicana magical realism." It contains a passage that narrates the funeral service of the three-year-old Loca, during which the child is "resurrected" and "ascends":

> The lid had pushed all the way open and the little girl inside sat up, just as sweetly as if she had woken from a nap, rubbing her eyes and yawning. "¿Mami?" she called, looking around and squinting her eyes against the harsh light. Father Jerome got hold of himself and sprinkled holy water in the direction of the child, but for the moment was too stunned to utter so much as a word of prayer. Then, as if all this was not amazing enough, as Father Jerome moved toward the child she lifted up into the air and landed on the church roof. "Don't touch me, don't touch me!" she warned. (1994, 22–23)

Each of these passages contains "characteristics" of "magical realism," which Patricia Hart defines as a narrative wherein the real and the magical are juxtaposed; this juxtaposition is narrated matter-of-factly; the apparently impossible event leads to a deeper truth that holds outside the novel; conventional notions of time, place, matter, and identity are challenged; and the effect of reading the fiction may change the reader's prejudices about what reality is (Hart 1989, 27). Furthermore, all three passages exhibit significant similarities in content: all three represent an unusually beautiful female character; all three have some religious content or allusions; and two of them represent an "ascension."

Despite these apparent similarities of form and content, however, Castillo has categorically denied any connection with magical realism:

"Someone always asks me about 'magic realism.' But people who know see the sources for my 'magic.' Like in *So Far from God*—the women are literally saints. I read *The Dictionary of Saints* as background research. [. . .] 'Magical realism' is just another name for the imagination of Latino Catholics" (Rose 2000). In other words, what we see here is an example of critics attempting to read one author through a critical lens developed for other writers, from different countries, from different cultures, and with different aims. By simply noticing some superficial similarities and then lumping these three texts together, I would contend, critics are misreading Castillo's text. While magical realism developed as a literary aesthetic within a particular cultural and political history, that same aesthetic does not apply to *So Far from God*, despite superficial similarities. Castillo, from her perspective, is not juxtaposing the magical with the real. But rather, she is representing the *real*. Furthermore, although Castillo has consequently come to be synonymous with Chicana magical realism, the only place in which these apparent similarities exist in any consistent degree is the novel *So Far from God*. Therefore, categorizing Castillo by misreading the content of a single novel reduces her work to a single characteristic and marginalizes it by placing it within an "exotic" categorization. Furthermore, focusing on a higher profile characteristic such as "magical realism" diverts attention from other more relevant and more pressing aspects of this text, in particular, and of her body of work, in general. Instead of imposing a critical framework developed by and for other writers onto Castillo's work, I propose examining Castillo's body of work in the terms of her philosophical articulation in order to develop a model of interpretation of her work.

Castillo's collections of poetry include *Otro Canto* (1977), *The Invitation* (1979), *Women Are Not Roses* (1984), *My Father Was a Toltec* (1988), *My Father Was a Toltec and Selected Poems 1973–1988* (1995), and *I Ask the Impossible* (1998). Her novels include the epistolary novel *The Mixquiahuala Letters* (1986); the sprawling *Sapogonia* (1990); the Chicana *telenovela*, *So Far from God* (1993); and her most recent novel, *Peel My Love Like an Onion* (1999). Her single collection of short stories appeared under the title *Loverboys* (1996), and her single collection of critical essays was published as *Massacre of the Dreamers* (1992). In addition to her own work, Castillo cotranslated (with Norma Alarcón) Anzaldúa and Moraga's anthology *This Bridge Called My Back* under the title *Esta Puente, Mi Espalda* (1988) and coedited (with Norma Alarcón and Cherríe Moraga) a collection of essays entitled *The Sexuality of Latinas* (1991). Finally, Castillo edited and introduced a collection of writings by various Latinas and Latinos on the figure of the Virgin of Guadalupe, entitled *Goddess of the Americas/La diosa de las Américas* (1996).

Of the popular and critical attention Castillo has received, nearly all of it has been directed at two texts: *The Mixquiahuala Letters* and *So Far from God*. In fact, after a search through the MLA bibliography, one might arrive at the conclusion that they are the only two books Castillo ever wrote. While both of these novels are interesting, entertaining, and provocative, they constitute only a fraction of her work. And while they also exhibit many of the same concepts and tropes that appear elsewhere in her work, those concepts and tropes are more fully developed throughout her corpus. Criticism on Castillo's writing has tended to focus on "magical realism," ethnography (Quintana 1991; Bennett 1996), border writing (Yarbro-Bejarano 1992), religiosity (Delgadillo 1998), or sexuality (Álvarez 1995; Alarcón 1989). While most of these examples are worthy of detailed examination and are important elements of her writing, they certainly do not exhaust the possibilities of her texts. Taken at a macroscopic level, however, they all—with the exception of the analysis of "magical realism"—contribute to Castillo's articulation of Xicanisma (which, according to Castillo, is a homophone of Chicanisma), or Chicana feminism.

An important element of developing an aesthetic of Ana Castillo's Xicanisma is the level of discourse. Castillo is able to utilize and manipulate many types of discourse, including traditional (Anglo) academic discourse, something that another prominent Chicana writer, Gloria Anzaldúa, refused to do. In *Borderlands/La frontera*, Anzaldúa's most "academic" and "critical" work, she still avoids standard academic diction and syntax. Her "prose" is filled with poetic turns of phrase, grammatical errors, and multiple levels of diction, including poetic, familiar, and colloquial versions of several languages. In addition, her choice of material to footnote (or not) is often ironic and intended to undermine the academic tradition. This stands in contrast with *Massacre of the Dreamers* in which Castillo writes in a traditional academic discourse. She writes, for example, "What phallocentric ego could imagine this suicidal strategy as the basis of a religious ideology?" (1995a, 99). Furthermore, the essays included in *Massacre* are more meticulously footnoted than are those in *Borderlands/La frontera*, signaling, at the very least, a willingness to engage Anglo academic culture on its own terms. As Castillo says in an interview with Cinander and Finch, "because of the commitment that I have to contributing to social change, I did the serious research and analysis that academia demands" (Cinander and Finch 2000).

This position becomes something of a paradox for Castillo. While attempting to negotiate a position for herself, and, by extension for Chicanas, within a liberal, academic discourse, Castillo suggests that leftists and liberals are also often complicit in the oppression of "others" and that they are unaware of the ways in which they have benefited from that oppression. Meanwhile, mestizas and mestizos are advised and expected to "assimilate" into mainstream culture, which Castillo insists is a form of "genocide" (Castillo 1995a, 22). In an interview with Cynthia Rose, Castillo states, "If Latina writers choose to embrace 'white writing,' then we may well limit our perceptions" (Rose 1996). In other words, the very language that Chicanas are compelled to adopt in order to participate in liberal, academic discourse contributes to their disappearance. And for creative writers, the adoption of Anglo standards of literature is, similarly, an element of the annihilation of Chicana literature. The alternative would be to develop and foster standards that are products of the culture—or, in other words, an autochthonous discourse and an autochthonous feminism.

However, the simple rejection of hegemonic language and standards has its own consequences. In the short story "Being Indian, a Candle Flame and So Many Dying Stars," Castillo writes, "'It is moments like this, watching that story about the Chamulas, that I know that I am Indian,' I said in my own language and not in this one that I am speaking to you now because if I don't, like the Chamulas, my story will be annihilated and not heard" (1996, 96). And to silence so "*annihilated*" is another form of genocide. So, in her academic writing, Ana Castillo adopts a traditional (Anglo, masculine) discourse in order to be heard, in order to re-vision institutions of machismo and patriarchy, and in order to have that revision read and considered. However, in her short stories and novels, Castillo maintains an autochthonous Chicana discourse and aesthetic.

Castillo's theory and feminist goals appear most explicitly in her collection of essays, *Massacre of the Dreamers*. Through this series of interconnected and occasionally overlapping essays, Castillo attempts to establish a historical, philosophical, and religious/spiritual foundation for her feminist practice. By then examining her novels, short stories, and critical essays, that is, through examining her *practice* of her writing, we can further articulaate her theoretical model of a localized or autochthonous feminism. As we will see, Castillo demonstrates a great deal of theoretical and philosophical consistency over the course of her career and across the various types of writing. In other words, the themes she develops in her (academic) critical essays are also expressed in her (creative) short stories and her novels.

In developing a model of autochthonous feminism, like Anzaldúa, Castillo situates herself and her writing in relation to two movements: Anglo feminism and *El Movimiento* (the Chicano movement). And like Anzaldúa, she attempts to distance herself from both of these movements. As for the former, she argues that Anglo feminism had very little influence on her. As a Chicana growing up in the barrios of Chicago, her existence was informed by working-class Chicano culture and not middle-class Anglo culture. "I had no idea what white feminists were thinking of in spheres far from my life in those asphalt, slush-covered streets of working class Chicago" (Castillo 1995a, 122). In fact, Castillo grew up thinking of herself as a Mexican, even though she was born in Chicago and did not visit Mexico until she was ten years old (Castillo 1995a, 24). Furthermore, in *Massacre of the Dreamers*, she argues that contemporary feminist writing, among which she includes such contemporary standards as Susan Faludi's *Backlash* (1991), Naomi Wolf's *Beauty Myth* (1991), and Camille Paglia's *Sexual Personae* (1990), is centered on Anglo perspectives (Castillo 1995a, 1–2). Consequently, Castillo attempts an articulation of feminism that is not Anglocentric.

Just as Castillo positions herself in relation to Anglo feminism, she spends even more time and energy positioning herself in relation to *El Movimiento*, if only because it has had a larger and more direct impact on her own life. In her analysis of the antiwoman and antifeminist bias within *El Movimiento*, she explores the two "doctrines" or ideologies that structure it: Marxism and Catholicism (Castillo 1995a, 85). Castillo argues that the Chicana feminist and Xicanisma cannot merge the doctrines of feminism and Marxism because, for one thing, a Chicana activist is not necessarily a feminist, and, for another, the social stigma attached to "socialism" and "communism" causes Chicana activists to shy away from the ideology (1995a, 85). Simultaneously, Catholicism has had a profound impact on *El Movimiento* and those involved in it. Castillo argues that the historical longevity of Catholicism (relative to Marxism) gives Catholicism greater claims over people's lives and social structures. In fact, for Castillo, "Catholicism is synonymous with Mexican society" (Castillo 1995a, 86). However, since *El Movimiento* was engaged in a struggle with the government for civil rights, it was represented as antidemocratic, and therefore, communistic.

Castillo argues, then, that the exclusion of the feminine principle within Marxism and Catholicism prohibits women from fully participating in Chicano society and *El Movimiento*. "More precisely, omission of the feminine principle in society prohibits true social transformation" (Castillo 1995a, 87). So, if society, Marxism, and Catholicism—and by extension, *El Movimiento*—are all informed by a masculinist perspective, Xicanisma and Xicanistas need to turn elsewhere for inspiration and guidance. "By recalling the long forgotten ways of our Amerindian heritage, we will be led back to a view that all things created in the universe are sacred and equal" (Castillo 1995a, 87).

Xicanistas, however, find themselves in a dilemma. While Anglo feminists draw on the myths, religions, and traditions of Europe and feel both comfortable and entitled to do so, the Xicanista feels less comfortable and less entitled to look to the myths, religions, and traditions of her Mexic Amerindian ancestors because she is so far removed from that society and because she is also likely to consider herself Christian/Catholic. Since Anglo society and Christian doctrine have long urged her to reject her indigenous roots, practices, and identity (Castillo 1995a, 87), the Xicanista often finds herself in between her political consciousness and her society (religion and family) (Castillo 1995a, 89).

Castillo argues for a return, then, to prepatriarchal models and examples. Despite the fact that a "conservative viewpoint" argues that matriarchal societies did not exist, she argues that they *did* exist and that they can serve as an example for an autochthonous feminism and for a nonpatriarchal society. "For too long we have been told what we are and why we are as women: mujeres mestizas (sino descendientes de sangre Europea, somos indias sin razón), católicas (sino ahora protestantes o pecadoras), definitions embedded in a history that has subordinated the female gender [sic]" (Castillo 1995a, 104). However, unlike Anzaldúa, whose work conveys a kind of optimism and, at times, uncritical acceptance of prepatriarchal models, Castillo is less sanguine about access to such models because of the pervasiveness of patriarchy in Anglo *and* Mexican societies.

For Castillo, then, the Xicanista response develops "in the acknowledgement of the historical crossroad where the creative power of woman became deliberately appropriated by the male society. And woman in the flesh, thereafter, was subordinated. It is our task as Xicanistas, to not only reclaim our indigenismo—but also to reinsert the forsaken feminine into our consciousness" (Castillo 1995a, 12; cf. also 189). The key for Castillo is the transition from celebrating the feminine creative spirit and body to a masculine creative power that resides in the intellect and not the body. "Spirituality is an acutely personalized experience inherent in our ongoing existences. Throughout history, the further man moved away from his connections with woman as creatrix, the more spirituality was also disconnected from the human body" (Castillo 1995a, 13). In other words, for Ana Castillo, the *telos* for the Xicanista is reintegration of the feminine, the creative, and the spiritual into society, and the model for such a society exists in the prepatriarchal societies of the pre-Aztec Mexic Amerindians.

Ana Castillo's first large work of fiction was the epistolary novel *The Mixquiahuala Letters*, which narrates the travels and relationships of two women, Teresa and Alicia, through Teresa's letters *to* Alicia. Since the novel develops solely from Teresa's perspective, she acknowledges that they are *partial* and biased and that they may not reflect Alicia's perceptions of their history together. As Letter Sixteen begins, "i doubt if what i'm going to recall for both our sakes in the following pages will coincide one hundred percent with your recollections" (Castillo 1986, 53). Furthermore, the letters are not a strictly chronological narrative of their "adventures." Instead, Castillo presents the reader with a number of choices about how to approach reading the letters/novel. The table of contents reads, "Dear Reader: It is the author's duty to alert the reader that this is not a book to be read in the usual sequence. All letters are numbered to aid in following any one of the author's proposed options." What follow are three proposed schemes for reading the letters: "For the Conformist," "For the Cynic," "For the Quixotic." Each of the three proposals lists a series of numbers corresponding to the forty letters that constitute the novel and suggests which letters to read and which to omit and the order in which they should be read. Finally, she writes, "For the reader committed to nothing but short fiction, all the letters read as separate entities."

Nevertheless, the question of structure remains. If Castillo neither deliberately employed nor parodied the structure of "Boom" writer Cortázar, then why employ the fractured and nonunitary narrative structure? One of Castillo's stated objectives was to include poetic elements in a novelistic form; for the poet Castillo, the rigidity of the novel form was limiting. Furthermore, Castillo contends that playing with language is an important aspect of her cultural and familial background. The narrative structure, however, has two other effects. For one, it actively draws the reader into the reading process, foregrounding the fact that meaning is also produced in the act of reading. In this, Castillo falls within a tradition of "experimental" writers, like those of the Latin American "Boom" and the French *nouveau roman*, and of cultural theorists such as Roland Barthes.

Perhaps more important, the fragmented and nonunitary structure of her novel formally thematizes a nonunitary subjectivity of the Chicana.

While Chicano artists such as Guillermo Gómez-Peña have represented the ways in which Chicano subjectivity fragments in Anglo society, Castillo represents the effects of a patriarchal, Anglo society on a specifically Chicana subjectivity. As Yvonne Yarbro-Bejarano writes, "In Castillo's writing Chicanas struggle to understand themselves in relation to what Alarcón calls a 'multiplicity of others'—the individual women and men of their culture and of other cultures as well as entire racial, class and cultural groups" (1992, 66). In part, then, *The Mixquiahuala Letters* becomes the performance of Gloria Anzaldúa's conceptualization of a borderlands subjectivity. As Yarbro-Bejarano points out, Teresa exists in the space among numerous cultures and crosses several national borders. Furthermore, Teresa exists in the borderlands of race, class, and sexuality, all of which separate her from Alicia and prevent "the establishment of real intimacy between the two women" (1992, 67). And rather than rejecting such a fragmentary identity, the novel validates it by refusing to accept any single reading. Instead, the reader can chose or reject any of the possible readings offered by the author, which leaves Castillo in a quandary. On the one hand, the novel's content argues that patriarchal society threatens and limits possibilities for Teresa and Alicia and that the racial/ethnic rift prevents the two women from connecting in a more meaningful way. On the other hand, the novel's form accepts the fragmentation of subjectivity, arguing instead for a nonhegemonic, nonpatriarchal model of reading.

In other words, one of Castillo's aims is to articulate and explore nonhegemonic and prepatriarchal modes of representation. Here, Teresa and Alicia enact Castillo's philosophical search for prepatriarchal models of human relations in Mexico. Indeed, Teresa and Alicia encounter some of the same obstacles that Ana Castillo encountered in her own search for those models in Mexico: "Unfortunately the writings of mestizos, criollos, Spaniards, and Anglos from the nineteenth century up to [1979] did not reveal anything more than stereotypes. At best I found ethnographic data that did not bring me closer to understanding how the Mexic Amerindian woman truly perceives herself" (Castillo 1995a, 7).

Castillo's second novel, *Sapogonia*, raises some of the same theoretical arguments. While the narrative of *Sapogonia* revolves around three primary characters, the central character, Máximo Madrigal, leaves his family and homeland of Sapogonia to "conquer" new territory in the United States. *Sapogonia* is Castillo's only work to feature a male protagonist.

Máximo becomes involved with the singer/songwriter Pastora Velásquez Aké, although she refuses to be conquered by Máximo; Pastora is involved with Perla, although the two women, like Teresa and Alicia, are never able to establish "real intimacy."

In order to thematize the distancing and fragmenting effects of culture on identity, Castillo again employs a nontraditional narrative structure, specifically through multiple narrative voices. Although the use of multiple viewpoints is not necessarily novel, either, Castillo's combination of first-person, second-person, and third-person narrators is relatively uncommon (though see, for example, Carlos Fuentes's *The Death of Artemio Cruz*). Close reading of the novel reveals that there are actually several third-person narrators, none of whom is necessarily reliable. Writers such as James Joyce have also employed nontraditional narrative structures, and Joyce also uses the narrative technique to signal a destabilization of personal, ethnic, and national identity. His use of the narrative strategy, however, derives from the specificity of the modernization of Great Britain and Europe and the relationship between England and Ireland, among other things. For Ana Castillo, Elsa Saeta concludes, "The structure and narrative strategy of the novel thus serve to reinforce one of the novel's major themes: the tenuous relationship between the real and the unreal, between reality and illusion, between historical fact and narrative fiction" (1994, 71).

While the narrative strategy undermines the reliability of the reader's perceptions, Castillo also attempts to draw the reader into the process, just as she does in *The Mixquiahuala Letters*. As an epigraph, Castillo writes, "This is the story of make-believe people in a real world; or, if you like, the story of real people in a make-believe world." Through this literary device, Castillo invites the reader to question the relationship between the characters and reality. If the characters are fictional but the world is real, then Perla and Pastora's inability to establish "real intimacy" and the kinds of violence enacted upon Pastora are a part of *our* world. If the characters are real but the world is fictional, then there are, in fact, two women who have not been able to establish "real intimacy" and a woman who has been murdered by a man who cannot break her.

Furthermore, Castillo ruptures the narrative through discontinuities in the chronology. While much of the novel progresses chronologically, the novel also introduces multiple chronological shifts. For example, the very first chapter occurs at the very end of the narrative chronology, and, in fact, the characters and circumstances involved in Chapter One do not become clear until the very end. The narrative uncertainty of the opening chapter signals the narrative instability and unreliability to the reader. Máximo's frequent references to his dreams further undermine the narrative stability. In Chapter Two, the third-person narrator says, "All my life has been divided into two realities: dreams of revelation and prophecy, and those dreams that manifest my present" (Castillo 1990, 11). The effect is that the reader does not know whether the narrative being read is a dream, a reality, or a prophecy of things to come. In both *The Mixquiahuala Letters* and *Sapogonia*, then, the fragmentation of the narrative coincides with the fragmentation of Chicanas in society and culminates with the murder of one of the female protagonists.

In her third novel, *So Far from God*, Castillo once again employs various narrative strategies in order to represent formally the destabilization of patriarchal forms. *So Far from God* narrates the lives of five women, Sofía and her four daughters, La Loca, Caridad, Fe, and Esperanza, although various boyfriends, fiancés, stalkers, and husbands float in and out of the text, as well. In weaving together the narratives of these five women, Castillo draws upon numerous genres, including allegory, religious texts, folk tales, *dichos* ["maxims"], *telenovelas* ["soap operas"], and cookbooks. As all five women find themselves in the borderlands among various religions, cultures, men, and languages, they are all too often the victims of neglect or abuse.

On the one hand, the novel assumes characteristics of an allegory. Castillo models her female protagonists on women in *The Dictionary of Saints*, and the names of the characters only serve to accentuate their allegorical status: the mother Sofía (Wisdom), the eldest daughter Esperanza (Hope), the daughters Fe (Faith) and Caridad (Charity), and the youngest, La Loca (the Crazy One). In addition, Doña Felicia (Lady of Happiness) and Esmeralda (Emerald—who is natural, nurturing, and feminine, much like the earth to which she will return)—figure prominently in the novel. Castillo's aim here is to undermine narrative forms by subverting the allegory and by turning these stereotypical feminine roles on their heads. The Faith, Hope, and Charity of the three oldest daughters have traditionally characterized "good" women in Mexican culture, and the Madness of the youngest daughter has traditionally characterized "irrational" women. Castillo, then offers a subversion of traditionally accepted Christian, Mexican values. Despite being the holders of positive cultural values, Fe, Esperanza, and Caridad all meet unfortunate ends. But Castillo offers La Loca, the holder of negative cultural values, as a positive model. Only she embodies the values of community, and only she remains connected to the values and members of the community.

In employing multiple hegemonic forms, Castillo subverts them by defying the reader's expectations of the form or by transforming them into something "other." For example, the traditional form of a religious pilgrimage, here in the form of the annual trek to Esquipúlas, ends, not in a renewal of faith in Jesus but, instead, in an encounter between two women. Their meeting resembles the traditional tale of Juan Diego who first encounters the Virgin of Guadalupe on the hillside. As Castillo suggests: "Obviously, one does not only undermine the status quo by stating it, but you undermine it by virtue of the language that you've chosen to write in, and by your acts. [. . .] My language is not white standard English. It doesn't matter if you claim to be Chinese American or Mexican American or African American and put in all the familiar cultural motifs if you're still using the language that is acceptable by the status quo. And I've not done that" (Saeta 1997, 141). So, apart from subverting the "status quo" of the allegory, Castillo also subverts received literary traditions through her use of language. For one, Castillo argues that her language is an important element: "If my novel was instead written in White standard English, I'm doing nothing more than writing a White standard novel with an ethnic motif" (Romero). Consequently, Castillo writes *So Far from God* using a regional dialect, which includes Spanish words and phrases that are rarely translated and turns of phrase that are peculiar to New Mexico, such as multiple double negatives. For Castillo, then, both the content and the language must reflect a Chicana consciousness, which undermines and revises received, patriarchal literary traditions. In this regard, Castillo is even more radical than someone like Gloria Anzaldúa. Although Anzaldúa makes liberal use of Spanish (in its many forms) throughout *Borderlands/La frontera*, she almost always translates the Spanish into English, providing access to nonnative speakers. Conversely, Castillo rarely translates any Spanish into English, leaving the nonnative speaker of Spanish either to participate actively by learning Spanish or to be left in the dark.

Thematically, the protagonists in all three of these novels find themselves confronted with, threatened by, and generally oppressed by Anglo *and* Mexican patriarchy. Many of the characters are oppressed by various manifestations of Anglo patriarchy, and they struggle with the means to escape, or at least withstand their oppression. Sometimes, they are oppressed by Chicanos within the Anglo culture, and within *El Movimiento*, in particular. In order to combat, or subvert, these patriarchal forces, Castillo's characters often seek a prepatriarchal model. However, the combination of oppressive elements overwhelms the characters, leaving them wondering where or how to begin their struggle. If they reject Anglo patriarchy and turn toward Mexican culture, they are often confronted by a Mexican patriarchy that can be every bit as oppressive and threatening. For example, in *The Mixquiahuala Letters,* in order to escape an Anglo patriarchy, Teresa joins the Chicanos and *El Movimiento.* However, such a move brings its own frustrations. As Teresa writes,

> The eloquent scholars with their Berkeley Stanford
> seals of approval
> all prepped to change society articulate the
> social deprivation of the barrio
>        starting with an
> Anglo wife, handsome house, and a Datsun 280Z in the driveway
>    they were our new brothers. (Castillo 1986, 43)

If Anglo culture is unacceptable, and if Chicanos are unacceptable, then another alternative might be a Mexican man. However, in Letter Sixteen Teresa struggles with her relationship with Alvaro Pérez Pérez, a Mexican living in the United States. They meet in Mexico, while he is home with his family. Alvaro obviously courts her, introduces her to his family, and attempts to seduce her, and Teresa finds him difficult to resist. "This was a woman conditioned to accept a man about whom she has serious doubts concerning his legitimate status with the human race" (Castillo 1986, 54). When Teresa spurns his sexual advances, he leaves in a rage, only to return later in a drunken state, leaving Teresa and Alicia both afraid of him. "We, like a pair of dogs, huddled at the foot of the bed" (58). Or, when she writes, "*Saved you again?* Like the night when we escaped gang rape at that university auditorium or earlier that night, when searching for you, i drove up with Jesús to that pitched black lover's hide-away at a pier and you jumped out of Eric's car where he threatened to take you at the point of a gun" (92). It seems, then, that the journey to Mexico has not provided the answer for which they were looking.

 Unlike the slender volume, *The Mixquiahuala Letters, Sapogonia* sprawls over three continents and several lives. Like its predecessor, *Sapogonia* features two female characters who struggle against the men and masculine institutions in their lives. The male protagonist, Máximo Madrigal, an egocentric and misogynistic man, emigrates from the fictional country Sapogonia to the United States. Máximo callously rapes a young local girl in Sapogonia. "I hardly knew why I took that girl by force. It wasn't as if I couldn't have had any other girl that I wanted without a struggle" (13). When he is told that he will marry Marisela, his grandmother says: "aunque en este caso, tal vez sería preferible si te murieras" ("although, in this case, perhaps it would be better if you were dead") (14). However, Marisela metaphorically emasculates Máximo. The first time they have sex, she wipes away the semen as if in disgust. When Máximo asks if she enjoyed making love, she replies, "'Your friend is much better than you'" (14). In his rage, Máximo nearly kills her and decides to leave Sapogonia that night. In Paris, he believes he may have gotten a young woman, Catherine, pregnant but does not demonstrate the least remorse or concern for her life. In New York City, he begins a sexual relationship with Hilda Gálvez, only to cast her aside for the more attractive La China. In Chicago, he forces himself upon a young Polish woman, Josephine—whom he finds disgusting—on the very same day he meets his wife-to-be, Laura Jefferson, a wealthy woman with connections in the art world. He cannot, however, maintain his relationship with Laura because he feels emasculated by her wealth and influence. In order to ameliorate his feelings of emasculation, Máximo must break her control and take her by force. At the moment when she finally submits, he says, "'Marry me'" (158). Even then, it is not a question, but rather an imperative. Despite conquering and marrying Laura, he has numerous sexual liaisons with other women. Finally, he deliberately seduces Maritza Marín-Levy, who is affianced to Chicago's first Chicano mayoral candidate, Alan García.

One of those women with whom Máximo has a sexual relationship is Pastora Velásquez Aké, a singer, songwriter, musician who sings only protest songs. When Máximo first encounters Pastora, he finds her physical beauty frustrating because he cannot dominate her in the ways he has dominated and broken every other woman he has known. He is "bothered" by the way that Pastora will not surrender herself to him (Castillo 1990, 127). When she walks out of his studio on his first crude attempt to seduce her, he writes, "She didn't know what that kind of rejection did to a man. [. . .] It was hard on a man to be told so unabashedly that he wasn't appealing" (132). As he reflects on how Pastora dominates him, he writes of himself, "You're a selfish wimp, no more willful than that kind of pussy-whipped husband with a yoke about his neck that you detest so much as to laugh aloud in the poor sucker's face. [. . .] Admit it, Máximo Madrigal, Pastora Velásquez Aké has you by the balls, los puros huevos. [. . .] Face it. Max, she's got you whipped" (172). Perhaps what galls Máximo the most is that "[s]he wasn't insecure enough to worry about the faithless lover. She did as she damn well pleased" (173–74). Her autonomy in the face of his dependence is more than he can bear. The final chapter makes clear what begins in Chapter One. While awaiting Maritza's return from Brazil, Máximo pays another visit to Pastora, and they make love repeatedly. When he awakens from sleep, he discovers that he is with Pastora in an unfamiliar room, one that is filled with domestic touches—which is wholly uncharacteristic of Pastora. Máximo picks up a pair of scissors from the sewing table and approaches the bed.

> In one thrust his clenched fist holding the scissors from her sewing table comes down to pierce the hollow spot between the lumps of nippled flesh. Her eyes open and are on him. Her face is wild as she inhales with the thrust and exhales when he pulls the scissors out.
>
> His hands are wet and drip red,
> he wipes the sweat from his brow
> mixed with tears.     ¿Estás muerta ya, puta? (8–9)

However, the reader remains uncertain about whether the murder occurs or not. The epilogue represents a happy and domestic Pastora with her husband, Eduardo, and their son. Unlike the preceding 307 pages, Pastora narrates, and she says, "Life goes on, Máximo Madrigal." Was chapter 59 a fantasy or reality? Was it one of Máximo's dreams? And if a dream, was it a dream of prophecy? In either event, the brutal murder of the woman who possessed him represents his murderous intent in the face of Pastora's autonomy and unwillingness to be broken by her lover.

Although the artist Máximo Madrigal appears to be the central character, the singer Pastora Velásquez Aké also plays a pivotal role. In the beginning of the novel, Pastora lives above Perla and her two roommates, Jesús and Francisco. Perla is a mother with twin sons. Her family holds against her the fact that she never married. When Perla discovers that her boyfriend has another woman, Perla physically attacks them both in a cafeteria. Pastora invites Perla over to comfort her, and the two begin a strong, supportive relationship. Because the two women begin living together and openly support one another, many assume that they are lesbians (25). "During their first months together they were not too unlike a pair of newlyweds, blissful within the tight cocoon they had woven for themselves" (69). A friend, Fabiola, tries to discover whether or not they are lovers. "The only factor that Fabiola could tell was not in the relationship was sex. Everything else was obvious: companionship, financial interdependency, as well as individual independence" (70).

The two grow apart, eventually, in no small part because of Máximo and his obsession with Pastora. Perla, who has her own intense and intimate feelings for Pastora, envies Pastora's obsessive lover and decides to find a man who will be obsessed with her. Perla eventually marries a materialist Anglo, and Perla fully assimilates into a materialist lifestyle, substituting a relationship with money for her relationship with Pastora. Pastora regrets losing Perla; Máximo, the cause of their estrangement, however, remains.

Chapter Nine of *Massacre of the Dreamers*, "Toward the Mother-Bond Principle," attempts to explain the possibilities of the relationship between Pastora and Perla, a relationship that Carroll Smith-Rosenberg calls "homosocial bonding" and Adrienne Rich calls the "lesbian continuum." In Mexican and Chicano culture, the special friend may well be a "comadre." "[C]omadres may be a splendid source for companionship, spiritual uplifting, positive affirmation. By comadre I am not limiting the definition to solely the woman who has baptized our child or vice versa, but to mean close friend" (Castillo 1995a, 191). However, in *Sapogonia* and *The Mixquiahuala Letters*, Castillo seems to argue that the presence and intervention of men prevents the formation of comadres, of female intimacy.

Because Pastora is a strong woman who is also spiritual, Máximo often calls her a witch and equates her with the pagan goddess, Coatlicue. When Máximo calls Pastora a witch, she responds that "Latino men always thought that a woman who allowed herself to be thought of sexually and denied any reason to feel shameful of it and had none of the inhibitions or insecurities with relation to commitments as it was considered a woman should—had to be a witch" (Castillo 1990, 125). He also belittles her devotion to the spiritual world, calling her a weak-willed woman for her "common" "weakness" (159). However, Pastora continues to pray: "To Santa Clara, she relayed the precariousness of her recent behavior. She had been too frivolous and materialistic. Santa Clara had no objections to material gain, but Pastora had forsaken those guides who watched out for her welfare for the sake of tentative things" (164).

In Pastora, Castillo develops a strong Chicana who refuses to be dominated by men or by their institutions. She refuses to accept the materialism of Anglo society and the values and practices of that society that have produced injustice and oppression. At the Colloquium of U.S. Latinos with the newly elected Chicano Mayor García, Pastora calls for child-care reform for working-class women and men. However, when both the mayor and his associate, Maritza Marín-Levy, dismiss her pleas, she rejects liberal reforms. In other words, she understands that "the master's tools will never dismantle the master's house." Or, as Pastora says, "'I'll be damned if I can understand why [Chicanas are] so determined lately to emulate the values of the white people in this city who created the problems we have to begin with!'" (281). For Pastora, no patriarchal, liberal, reformist model will suffice.

*So Far from God* differs from *The Mixquiahuala Letters* and *Sapogonia* in that the characters do not necessarily go anywhere; nevertheless, they all find themselves in a different place. In the opening chapter, La Loca "dies" at the age of three, but is "resurrected" days later, during her funeral. From that moment on, she shuns all human contact, except with her mother, and prefers the contact of animals. Following her miraculous resurrection, La Loca turns her back on the Church and Father Jerome. As Theresa Delgadillo argues, "This striking scene suggests that Castillo is engaged in revisionism on a small scale, substituting a Chicana resurrection for Christ's resurrection, and accordingly creating an alternate religious history or perhaps a new myth" (1998, 895–96). In other words, La Loca rejects the patriarchal institution of the Catholic Church *and* its masculine representatives. The resurrected Loca remains psychically and spiritually connected to her sisters. La Loca "cures" her sister Caridad following her brutal rape and mutilation; she speaks to her sister Esperanza while she is "lost" in Saudi Arabia and the army cannot locate her. By rejecting patriarchal culture and the Church, La Loca establishes powerful and otherworldly connections to the other women in her family.

The fourth sister, Esperanza, also escapes from patriarchal culture into another space. Esperanza, the oldest of the daughters, attended college (and earned a BA in Chicano studies), where she met numerous men, had some affairs, and went through a Chicano activist stage. However, Esperanza realizes that there is no place for her within *El Movimiento*. Eventually realizing that her Chicano-activist boyfriend, Rubén, uses her, she becomes a journalist, moves to Houston and then goes to Saudi Arabia, where she "disappears." After La Llorona informs La Loca that Esperanza "is died," Esperanza makes frequent appearances. She appears near the river, lays down with her mother, and discusses the U.S. war policy in the Middle East with Caridad.

Ana Tomek suggests that while feminists might expect that Esperanza would be redeemed, if not fulfilled, through her attainment of her high-profile, Anglo career, Castillo rejects such values. "Esperanza feels that her search for career success will bring meaning to her life; instead it brings only death" (Tomek). She further suggests that, for Castillo, the importance of Esperanza as a La Llorona figure is her reintegration into the family unit, which she had left for her career. "[P]erhaps Castillo wants us to feel that Esperanza has triumphed in her reconciliation with the family she left behind. She is not 'just dead' as is her sister Fe later on; she lives on in a truly intangible (perhaps liberated?) form" (Tomek). Once again, as in the case of Fe, Esperanza's assimilation into the patriarchal values of the materialist Anglo world, and the simultaneous rejection of Chicano values and a Chicano family, brings death. Although noncorporeal, Esperanza rejoins the family.

For Castillo, Fe represents what happens to those who whole-heartedly accept Anglo values. Fe (a.k.a. "la Gritona" [the Screamer]) had the perfect life, working in a bank and engaged to be married. However, Fe's fiancé jilts her, and she responds by screaming for weeks. When she finally stops screaming, her voice has suffered permanent damage, and no one can understand her. She eventually marries her first cousin, Casimiro de Nambe. After the wedding, Fe leaves her job at the bank because the management did not like her "handicap" (her speech impediment) and because she and her husband want more money. At this point, Fe begins to express her dissatisfaction with her family and her culture, and she begins to distance herself (physically and emotionally) from both of them. Instead, she goes to work at a local factory, which pays large bonuses, and she and her husband begin to accumulate all the material goods they had ever wanted. For Fe, however, the cost of abandoning her family and culture—of acculturating into Anglo materialism—is sickness and death. The management of the factory uses toxic chemicals without fairly notifying its employees, and Fe contracts cancer and dies only a year after her wedding.

Like her sisters, Caridad rejects patriarchal culture. Initially, Caridad works in the hospital. She likes to frequent bars and pick up men. Eventually she gets pregnant by Memo but has an abortion with the help of La Loca. One night she is found badly beaten, her breasts bitten off. Eventually, La Loca "prays real hard" (Castillo 1994, 38) for Caridad, and completely restores her to her former physical self. Once restored, Caridad has moments where she "goes away." What she "sees" in these trances always proves true, and her father capitalizes on her foresight and renews his gambling. In other words, after the *malogra* ["evil spirit"] that rapes and brutalizes her "takes advantage" of her, her father does, too. As Delgadillo suggests, the "beast" that attacks Caridad "metaphorically describes the force of the institutionalized patriarchal relations that foster disregard for women at every level of society" (1998, 907).

Eventually, however, Caridad and her horse, Corazón ("Heart"— though also "core" or a term of endearment), move outside of town to a small trailer that Doña Felicia owns. With the help of Doña Felicia, Caridad begins her training as a *curandera* (healer). Caridad, rejecting the patriarchal culture that has taken advantage of her, escapes the company of men and joins the community of women. One day, while visiting the shrine of the black Christ from Esquipúlas, she sees a woman, Esmeralda, and falls in love. The encounter with Esmeralda, and Caridad's compelling attraction to her, unsettles Caridad so completely that she goes to the hot springs for a bath. She disappears for an entire year, which she spends living in a cave, another feminine-coded space. When several young men "discover" her, she is proclaimed a saint. However, during this period of self-reflection and reconnection with the natural world, Caridad has become so strong that the young men are unable to lift her and carry her out of the cave.

Caridad's infatuation with Esmeralda deepens; however, Esmeralda already loves another woman. When Caridad and Esmeralda go up on the mesa to consult another clairvoyant, they hear the voice of the spirit Tsichtinako calling them, and they run over the cliff together and are taken away. In Castillo's terms, the fact that Caridad and Esmeralda hear the voice of a prepatriarchal spirit is crucial. According to Delgadillo "Tsichtinako or Tse che nako [. . .] is Thought Woman in the Keres cosmology, the female spirit and intelligence that is everywhere and is everything" (1998, 904). In addition, *this* "ascension," unlike that of La Loca, subverts the patriarchal model. As Enid Álvarez suggests, "la ascensión. ¿No sería mejor decir el descenso? En un giro paródico se invierte el mito de la ascensión pues en lugar de subir a los cielos, ella baja a integrarse a la tierra" ("ascension? Wouldn't it be better to say 'descent?' In a paradoxical turn, the myth of ascension is inverted; instead of rising into the heavens, she descends to be reintegrated into the Earth") (1995, 145). For Caridad and her "lover," Esmeralda, escape from the oppressions of a patriarchal society leads them to a prepatriarchal voice, to a prepatriarchal cosmology, to the loving and nurturing embrace of a feminine-coded earth.

Through the characters of Caridad and Esmeralda, Castillo explores a long-standing theme for women writers: What space can women occupy outside of the patriarchal order? For example, Kate Chopin thematizes the question in her 1899 novel, *The Awakening*. When Edna Pontillier rejects the patriarchal order, the space left for her is, presumably, drowning in the sea. A similar situation arises in the film *Thelma and Louise* when the two title characters, faced with certain capture and return to the masculine order, drive over the cliff, clutching each others' hands. The scene from the film appears remarkably similar to Castillo's scene in which Caridad and Esmeralda leap over a cliff while holding hands. However, in the film, the characters are completely without any alternative.

They are faced with the choice of returning to the patriarchal order, or not, and their choice leads them into oblivion, into the gaping void of the canyon. With Caridad and Esmeralda, their escape from the patriarchal order, in the person of the male stalker, signals a return to a prepatriarchal order. Instead of a descent into oblivion, theirs is an "ascent" into another signifying system.

Perhaps the clearest positive example of Castillo's concept of the 'Xicanista' lies in the mother figure, Sofía (more commonly called "Sofi"). She is a hard-working woman who runs a butcher shop, the Carne Buena Carnecería, and raises her children as a single mother. Her husband, Domingo, abandoned her and the children long ago, although he returns after a twenty-year absence, walking in the front door as if nothing had happened, as if no time had passed. Two days after her fifty-third birthday, and fed up with Domingo's laziness, Sofía decides to run for mayor of Tome and fix the things that need fixing. She is tired of outsiders moving into their hometown and exploiting them, is tired of being a "conformist" (Esperanza's term), and wants to work for "community improvement." She sells shares of her Carnecería and creates a food cooperative. As Sofía becomes more and more independent and more and more self-assured, Domingo begins to feel more and more emasculated. For example, she tells him, "And don't call me 'silly Sofi' no more neither," and, "Do I look like a silly woman to you, Domingo?" (Castillo, 1994, 109–10). Eventually Sofi, La Abandonada (The Adandoned Woman) kicks her husband out for good.

Through Sofi's initiative and the hard work of the women of the cooperative, they are able to sustain two dozen women and their families. The women who are mothers are able to bring their children to work with them, are able to earn college credits, and are able to produce inexpensive and environmentally safe fruits and vegetables. While Sofi and the other women had been socialized to believe that they had to rely on men to sustain and support the family, they begin to move outside the patriarchal order. They establish a new social order, built upon a nonpatriarchal ideology, which is nonmaterialistic and serves the interests of all the community instead of exploiting the community for the benefit of a few. According to Castillo, Sofía had many forebearers. Early Christian mythology appropriated the Greek goddess Sofía and "her daughters and turned them into martyrs." However, Castillo reappropriates the mythological goddess in order to represent a woman who resists fate: "She takes over. She doesn't submit to that point in history when patriarchy took over her authority" (Saeta 1997, 147).

The lessons of *So Far from God* seem brutal: leave the community, assimilate into Anglo society, rely on men, remain vulnerable to a patriarchal system, and death awaits. In the end, although Sofía loses all four of her daughters, she emerges as a strong, confident, and productive subject. As Delgadillo argues, Castillo's Sofía represents the possibilities for a new "Chicana subjectivity that defines itself within the context of community and in league with the struggles of others attempting to overcome marginality, subordination, and silence" and that the novel "attacks the individualism that fuels a chaotic live-for-the-moment mentality by showing us how that individualist ethic harms women, communities, and the environment" (1998, 912–13) In other words, the "wise" Sofía becomes the embodiment of Castillo's concept of the Chicana feminist, the Xicanista.

As Ana Castillo develops her concept of the Xicanista and Xicanisma through her first three novels, *The Mixquiahuala Letters*, *Sapogonia*, and *So Far from God*, she also develops her theoretical conception in *Massacre of the Dreamers*, where she argues that many writers and activists are moving away from the term *Chicana* because they see it as "an outdated expression weighed down by the particular radicalism of the seventies" (Castillo 1995a, 10). In its stead, Castillo employs two distinct terms: *Mexic Amerindian* and Xicanista. She differentiates between the two, depicting the former as the articulation and assertion of "indigenous blood" and "the source, at least in part, of our spirituality" (Castillo 1995a, 10). For Castillo, 'Mexic Amerindian,' an "ethnic and racial" term, describes people from a certain area. 'Xicanista' describes an individual who is an activist, an individual who actively seeks to improve the lives of women within the Chicano community, who actively seeks alternative ontologies within a patriarchal order. Just as people are reacting to the once-powerful and current term 'Chicana' as a sign of activism, Castillo argues that people are reacting against feminism itself, which she views as an outdated movement from a specific historical and cultural moment, and an ideology relegated to academic classrooms. Her hope is to get Xicanisma out of conference rooms and classrooms and into the work place and the home (Castillo 1995a, 11).

Castillo writes that Xicanisma is formed "in the acknowledgement of the historical crossroad where the creative power of woman became deliberately appropriated by the male society. And woman in the flesh, thereafter, was subordinated. It is our task as Xicanistas, to not only reclaim our indigenismo—but also to reinsert the forsaken feminine into our consciousness" (1995a, 12). For Castillo, matriarchy is not the opposite of patriarchy, and the goal of the Xicanista should not be the appropriation of all masculine ideals and behaviors. Instead, Xicanisma aims at the reintegration of the feminine creative powers back into society and is closely connected with "selected aspects of the traditional woman's role in Mexican/Latin American society (such as the virtues of patience, perseverance, commitment to one's children), while rejecting the negative stereotypes of women that emanate from mainstream machismo" (Milligan 1999, 28).

Similarly, just as Castillo does not suggest the supplanting of patriarchy with matriarchy, she does not suggest that Xicanisma, nor a Xicanista epistemology, should supplant any other epistemology: "[W]e are not asserting that our perspective is the only legitimate one, that it is superior to or should replace, repress, or censure others. What we are conscious of is that our reality is vastly different from that of the dominant culture and by any measure worth considering" (1995a, 5). The goal is a community that understands and accepts alternative modes of knowing and integrates feminine and masculine principles into society. For Ana Castillo, the goal of Xicanisma entails creating a nonmaterialistic and nonexploitative society, in which feminine principles of nurturing and community prevail. That society incorporates spirituality as a daily lived experience and therefore overcomes any division between mind and body.

The theories Castillo develops in *The Massacre of the Dreamers* appear in her fiction. For example, in her first novel, *The Mixquiahuala Letters*, Teresa and Alicia confront the objectification and violence in their relationships, traits they associate with the patriarchy. The two find themselves unable to establish "real intimacy" because of the competitive relationship patriarchy engenders. In Castillo's second novel, *Sapogonia*, the relationship between Pastora and Perla also dissolves in a brew of patriarchy and materialism. By novel's end, Pastora rejects the possibility of liberal reforms and seeks a nonpatriarchal model.

In her third novel, *So Far from God*, Castillo develops the prototype for the Xicanista, the "wise" Sofía. From the beginning of the novel, Sofi, trapped within the traditional patriarchal order, with an irresponsible husband who drinks and gambles away their money (and, eventually, the deed to the house), must raise her four daughters alone. One by one, they each reject the family, reject the community, and succumb to materialist Anglo values. Sofía, however, emerges from her ordeal a strong, active woman, who has brought together an entire community of women who are now able to support themselves, without men, and without the mate-

FIGURE 1.2. Ana Castillo, "Spirituality"

rialist values of Anglo society. Sofi escapes the patriarchal order and produces a new Xicanista ontology, one that is no intellectual exercise but rather a lived experience. Perhaps, then, the physical journey to Mexico is an unnecessary one, and the Xicanista can find non- or prepatriarchal models without leaving home.

# 2

## Everday Revolutions, Shifting Power, and Feminine Genius in Julia Alvarez's Fiction

KELLY OLIVER

Julia Alvarez uses the conventions of domestic femininity, womanhood, and motherhood to resist patriarchal authority both at the level of private family life and in public institutions, including government. These uses simultaneously demonstrate that resistance to domination involves shifting power dynamics and strikingly underscore sexual difference in relation to power, resistance, and genius. Alvarez's fiction powerfully portrays how shifting power relations are gendered and are inflected by race and class.

### EVERYDAY REVOLUTIONS

Alvarez's first novel, *How the Garcia Girls Lost Their Accents* (1991), documents various everyday struggles of women and girls against restrictive traditions. The novel tells the stories of four sisters—Yolanda, Sandy, Carla, and Fifi—who are exiled from the Dominican Republic along with their parents because their father was involved in an attempt to overthrow the dictator Trujillo. In a chapter entitled "A Regular Revolution," Alvarez suggests that revolution is a matter of "constant skirmishes" on a mundane level (1991, 111). She compares the four daughters' revolt against their parents' authority and against patriarchal authority to their father's participation in the revolt against the Trujillo dictatorship. The girls plot their revolution using the accepted patriarchal codes for chaperones, and for young ladies' proper behavior, against those very codes. Alvarez shows how the patriarchal traditions are turned against themselves in order to undermine patriarchal authority. She imagines how everyday practices of domination also open up everyday modes of resistance, how power is not only the power to dominate, but also the power to resist.

In "A Regular Revolution" three of the sisters, Carla, Yolanda, and Sandi, are trying to rescue the fourth, Fifi, from getting pregnant and stuck marrying their very traditional, sexist island cousin Mundín. Here, Mundín is called a "tyrant" and the girls are staging a "revolution," "a coup on the same Avenida where a decade ago the dictator was cornered and wounded on his way to a tryst with his mistress" (1991, 127). The girls use traditional restrictions on girls and women to their advantage when they insist that their cousin and chaperone, Manuel, take them home early without the lovers Mundín and Fifi. They use Manuel's responsibility for them to combat the "male loyalty" that "keeps the macho system going" (127). Manuel is forced to take them home without the lovers, which blows their cover. The "first bomb" explodes on the women's side of the patio when the girls report that Fifi is with Manuel and then "there is an embarrassed silence in which the words her reputation are as palpable as if someone had hung a wedding dress in the air" (129). The girls use the patriarchal convention that girls are not to be left alone without their chaperone to expose the breach of another convention that girls are not to be left alone with their *novios*. Their motives, however, are not to protect their sister's reputation or virginity but to protect her from the oppressive patriarchal culture that would demand and circumscribe marriage, family, and subservience to her husband.

The central plot of Alvarez's third novel, *In the Time of the Butterflies* (1994), revolves around revolution, specifically the four sisters Mirabal—Dede, Patricia, Minerva, Maté—and their involvement in the underground revolution against Trujillo. Again feminine revolution and resistance are not painted in the broad strokes of bloody battles and guerilla uprisings but in the mundane makeup of femininity. Alvarez's story of the Mirabal sisters' revolution against Trujillo is as much about their own everyday revolutions against the restrictions of patriarchy as it is about a rebellion against the restrictions of dictatorship. In fact, the dictator's authority is depicted as founded on the macho image of a patriarch who has his ways with women.

Like *How the Garcia Girls Lost Their Accents*, *In the Time of the Butterflies* describes how patriarchal conventions are used to undermine patriarchal values and institutions and how the trappings of femininity are used to fuel revolution—this time political as well as personal revolution. The church, crucifixes, and praying become forms of rebellion (1994, 237). The sisters use the script they learned from the nuns for writing out Bible passages to list the ammunition in their hiding places (168). The sisters' mental and physical discipline while in prison is compared to keeping a baby on a feeding schedule (235). Maté uses her long hair and hair ribbons to smuggle news stories to other prisoners and secret notes detailing the human rights' abuses of the Trujillo regime to the Organization of American States' representatives when they visit the prison (246, 252). A young woman's diary becomes incriminating evidence against the dictatorship's human rights' abuses. The election of "Miss University" becomes the promise of democratic elections; Minerva tells Maté that "this country hasn't voted for anything in twenty-six years and it's only these silly little elections that keep the faint memory of democracy going" (136).

For the Mirabal sisters, love, family, and revolution are inseparable. Passion between lovers feeds passion for revolution, and the common struggle against the dictator fuels personal passion. For example, the struggle for freedom keeps Minerva and her husband, Manolo, together through difficult personal times. Maté falls in love with Leandro when she meets him delivering ammunition for the revolutionaries. She sees the revolution as her chance for personal independence from a family that treats her like a baby. More than that, she realizes that her looks and easy manner with men can serve the revolution. She writes in her diary, "[N]ow I can use my talents for the revolution" (143). Patricia becomes involved after her church group witnesses young guerillas attacked by Trujillos soldiers. She sees the face of her own son Nelson in the face of a dying young guerilla and from that moment on is committed to saving her family by fighting Trujillo. All the while that these women are fighting against the national patriarch, Trujillo, they are also fighting against their own local patriarchs at home. They all have various skirmishes with their father and their husbands in order to assert themselves against patriarchal conventions.

If, as Minerva Mirabal says of the dance that cures her headache, "one nail takes out another," then she is the hammer (97). She knows how to strike one nail of patriarchy against another in order to get what she needs. When her father will not let her leave the farm to go to law school, and when El Jefe (Trujillo) wants to make her his mistress, she eventually convinces Trujillo to allow her go to law school to be near him in the city (1994, 98). She pits the authority of Trujillo against her father's authority. When Trujillo suggests private meetings, she uses the patriarchal conventions of propriety and honor to argue that it would not be honorable of her to meet him alone (111). One nail of patriarchy takes out another.

Alvarez's novel describes the ways in which femininity and women's restricted and stereotypical roles as guardians of the family and of religion are put into the service of revolution—revolution against the dictatorship and revolution against patriarchy. Confessional diaries become means not only for personal therapy and self-surveillance but also for testimonies of injustice and suffering. The trappings of femininity, such as beautiful long hair, become means to deliver secret messages to the outside world. Alvarez's *In the Time of the Butterflies* shows some of the ways in which the very trappings of domination can be used to resist that domination. In her fictional account of the Mirabal sisters' participation in the resistance to the Trujillo dictatorship, Alvarez imagines resistance not only to the patriarchal power of the dictator but also to a more mundane patriarchal power that subordinates women in their everyday lives.

## SHIFTING POWER DYNAMICS

In addition to showing how women's revolution happens through everyday resistance, Alvarez's novels also show how power dynamics are fluid and change according to shifting gender, race, and class positions. In one sense, Alvarez's first novel, *How the Garcia Girls Lost Their Accents*, is a study in mobile and transitory points of resistance and shifting power dynamics that fracture unity and affect regroupings. Throughout this novel, Alvarez shows how power relations among race, class, and gender are dynamic. For example, in the first chapter, "Antojos," Yolanda Garcia returns to the Dominican Republic after five years without a visit and ventures into the countryside to pick fresh guavas. This chapter opens with the narrator describing the color coding of class hierarchy: old aunts in greys and blacks of widowhood, cousins in bright colors, nursemaids in white uniforms, and kitchen help in black uniforms (3). This chapter, and the book as a whole, repeatedly recounts the deferential gestures that signal power relations among race, class, and gender. When scolded for not having matches on hand to light the candles on the cake, one of the maids, Iluminada, makes a pleading gesture with her hands clasped against her breast (4). When another maid, Altagracia, is asked to explain the word "antojo" to Yolanda, she "puts her brown hands away in her uniform pockets" and "says in a small voice. You're the one to know" (8). These deferential gestures signal class and race hierarchy and the differential power relation in terms of class and race privilege.

Later in this chapter when Yolanda is picking guavas, and she gets a flat tire, gender hierarchy displaces class hierarchy, and the power dynamics shift. Alone with her car, Yolanda is terrified when two men appear out of the grove with machetes hanging from their belts. She considers running, but she is paralyzed with fear and rendered speechless (19). The narrator describes her repeating the same pleading gesture of Illuminada, hands clasped on her chest (20). Yolanda's class privilege in relation to the maid, and in relation to the young boy, Jose, who has taken her to pick the guavas, changes in relation to these two men whose gender privilege is threatening to Yolanda. Now she is the one using deferential gestures.

The power dynamics again suddenly shift in this scene when she begins speaking in English, and the two men conclude that she is American. At this point, they are "rendered docile by her gibberish," and when she mentions the name of her aunt's rich friends, the Mirandas, "their eyes light up with respect" (20–21). This scene captures the fluidity power relations—class privilege has given way to gender privilege, and then the relation between gender hierarchy and class heirarchy is reversed again. In the end, when Yolanda tries to confirm her class privilege and express her gratitude by paying the men, they refuse and look at the ground, as the narrator tells us, with the same deferential gestures of Illuminada and the little boy Jose (22). The chapter ends with Jose returning from the Mirandas slapped, shamed, and accused of lying when he tells the guard that a woman is out picking guavas alone. Even Yolanda's dollar bills cannot cheer him. The collusion of rigid gender and class structures results in Jose's punishment, which is only intensified when Yolanda offers him money. Even in her attempts to make Jose happy, Yolanda reaffirms her class dominance over him.

Although the novel is full of this type of power reversal and shifting power dynamics, I will mention just one more example of fluctuating relations among race, class, and gender from chapter 10, "Floor Show." As the novel moves back in time, this chapter takes place in New York when the Garcia girls are young, shortly after their family has fled the Trujillo dictatorship. Here, the Garcias have been invited to join Dr. Fanning and his wife for dinner at a restaurant. Dr. Fanning arranged the fellowship that allowed "Papi" Garcia to take his family to New York and was trying to help Papi get a job. For days "Mami" gave the girls instructions on how to behave, and the evening of the dinner she dressed them in binding braids and tights in the hopes of disciplining not only their behavior but also their bodies. The dinner scene is very tense because the Garcias, used to having class privileges in the Dominican Republic, are financially beholden to the Fannings. In their presence both Mami and Papi Garcia display deferential gestures and repeatedly look down at the floor.

This chapter displays several reversals among race, class, and gender hierarchies. First, because Mami Garcia studied in the United States as a girl, her English is better than Papi's, which gives her more power than him in social situations: "Mami was the leader now that they lived in the States. She had gone to school in the States. *She* spoke English without a heavy accent" (176). The gender dynamic between mother and father is reversed by the power of linguistic access. Class dynamics shift when the Garcias, struggling to make ends meet in the United States, no longer have class privilege. Papi no longer has the honor of paying for dinner. The Fannings, who appeared in the Dominican Republic as silly-looking tourists speaking bad Spanish, now make the Garcias look small (184). Gender dynamics shift when Mrs. Fanning kisses Papi Garcia on the way to the bathroom. In this context his class and race deference to Mrs. Fanning make him powerless to object to her flirtations. Power dynamics change again when Sandi, who witnessed the kiss, uses what she saw to blackmail her father into allowing her to get a doll that they cannot afford and for which the Fannings end up paying. Also in this chapter Sandi recognizes the value of passing as a white American when she studies her fair skin and blue-eyed beauty in the mirror after she has seen the power Mrs. Fanning exercised over her father with the kiss.

Fluid power dynamics are also central to *In the Time of the Butterflies*. Here, there is a scene similar to the *Garcia Girls* "Floor Show" where a daughter becomes more powerful than her father when he wants her to keep a secret from her mother. When Minerva Mirabal discovers that her father has a secret second family, she gains power over her father; gender and generation power relations shift. In the end, it is this second, illegitimate family, much poorer and less powerful than the first, that smuggles letters and care packages back and forth between the girls in prison and their family at home; the class dynamic is reversed when the lower-class family has access to the guards in a way unavailable to the upper-class family. And, as we have seen, Alvarez's fiction brings to life various ways in which women and girls resist domination by turning patriarchal restrictions to their advantage by using "one nail" of domination against another.

Alvarez's fiction exemplifies mobile and transitory sites of resistance that reconfigure shifting power relations. These novels show some of the ways in which individuals are furrowed by intersecting axes of power, cut up and remolded and marked by their various positions in shifting power relations that constantly regroup them in terms of race, class, and gender, among other alliances. Alvarez's novels make clear that the differential norms for masculinity and femininity within patriarchal cultures circumscribe power relations differently for men and women. Alvarez is sensitive to how women's subject positions within patriarchal cultures affect their sense of their own agency both in terms of their subjection to patriarchal restrictions and in terms of their resistance to those restrictions.

For Alvarez, fiction shows us something about life that history cannot; it speaks to the heart in a way that "immerses" readers in an epoch and helps them to "understand" it. This understanding is not intellectual but affective. Fiction helps us to understand the effects of colonization, domination, and oppression on the affects of those oppressed. Alvarez's fiction gives us especially powerful portraits of the effects of domination on women's psyches and affects and how anger and pain can be turned into resistance. Indeed, in the postscript to *In the Time of the Butterflies* she tells us that "a novel is not, after all, a historical document, but a way to travel through the human heart" (324) and that an epoch of life "can only be understood by fiction, only finally be redeemed by the imagination" (324).

In the same postscript, Alvarez also says that she presents neither the real Mirabal sisters of fact nor the Mirabal sisters of legend, but she tries to demythologize their courage by describing ordinary people. She presents their genius as everyday genius. More than this, she presents their genius as *feminine* genius, the genius of penmanship, hair ribbons, feeding schedules, and girls' diaries. Alvarez's portrait of these heroines who gave their lives and their freedom for their beliefs paints a picture of ordinary women doing what is necessary for themselves and their families. By opening our imaginations to everyday genius Alvarez's genius enriches our own sense of possibility and freedom.

## FEMININE GENIUS

Alvarez's fiction thrives on what Julia Kristeva calls "female genius" (2001). Although Kristeva does not fully develop a theory of female genius when she valorizes three great women writers in three volumes (Hannah Arendt, Melanie Klien, Colette), she does introduce her female trilogy with some suggestions about female genius that have implications for genius and psychic life in general. She suggests that genius and geniuses are necessary for psychic life: we need geniuses to validate the exceptional within our own lives, which is as true for women as it is for men. Psychic life is dependent upon a sense of validation and legitimization of the possibility of creativity and greatness for all of us. We need to idealize geniuses and identify with them. But, in order to imagine idealization as identification, we also need to conceive of genius as a type of social phenomena and the product of the lives of ordinary people who do extraordinary things.

Implicit in Kristeva's analysis are two types of female genius: one that is documented by the creative and intellectual writings of great women and another that is not documented or even appreciated, the everyday genius of ordinary women, which speaks to the singularity of each individual. Both forms of female genius have been and continue to be devalued within our culture, which continues to be controlled by patriarchal values. As I argue elsewhere, female genius in both of these forms is an antidote to the colonization of psychic space and social melancholy that result from a lack of accepting social support (Oliver 2004).

The figure of "the genius" opens up the imagination to the possibility of one's own genius and creativity in at least two respects. The idealization of female geniuses and women's contributions to culture provide positive images of women and role models that support women's and girls' positive sense of self. Genius in this traditional sense of an extraordinary accomplishment (such as Kristeva's examples of Arendt, Klein, and Colette) provides women geniuses to idealize and with whom to identify. Another way in which the figure of "the genius" opens imaginative possibilities is through the recognition of genius as the extraordinary within the lives of ordinary women. This opens up the social space for an imaginary identification with the possibility of creativity and the extraordinary within everyday lives, promoting the sublimation of repressed affects into signification. The notion that genius demonstrates the possibility of the extraordinary—creativity and sublimation—within the ordinary shows girls and women that they too are capable of sublimation that gives meaning to their lives and to their experiences as girls and women. Both forms of female genius promote the idealization and sublimation necessary to resist patriarchal restrictions that hamper women's creativity and to overcome women's depression insofar as it is caused by women's oppression. Women need their own geniuses, heroines of the spirit, in order to find value in their own everyday genius.

Alvarez's fiction presents both types of feminine genius and displays the relations between consecrated, culturally recognized genius and the genius of the ordinary lives of women; in her work these two types of feminine genius are always intertwined. Through the genius of the everyday, her heroines turn patriarchal restrictions and domination against themselves in order to initiate revolutions that resonate throughout all levels of experience. The revolutions of Alvarez's heroines are not monumental actions that overthrow governments but everyday struggles with authority that enable and empower resistance. Rather, they display the ways in which the very trappings of femininity, womanhood, and motherhood can be used against patriarchal values and institutions in order to open up a space for women's resistance to domination.

In her latest novel, *In the Name of Salomé* (2000), Alvarez again imagines the world of everyday genius along with the ways in which ordinary people are invested in, and rely on, the figure of genius in their midst. The novel alternates between the life of one of the Dominican Republic's most acclaimed nineteenth-century poetesses, Salomé Ureña, and the life of her daughter, Camille Henríquez, a literature professor in New York. Salomé dies when Camille is only three years old, and throughout the novel Camille is searching for the remembrance of her mother. The novel makes it clear that Camille strongly identifies with her mother to the point of imagining that "she were somehow resurrecting her mother in her own flesh" (2000, 121), and yet she feels inadequate to her mother's memory, in the shadow of her greatness, and the heir to maternal depression. Childless and unmarried, Camille wanders through the novel unable to sustain intimate attachments and mourning the loss of her mother. She feels guilty for her mother's death because as the novel suggests it is Salomé's pregnancy with Camille on top of her tuberculosis that kills her (2000, 325). Camille identifies with her dead mother, even the corpse of her mother, and she is unable to separate herself from her mother. As a little girl she imagines her mother lives inside her because she has her mother's name. She imagines that she is both Camille and Salomé: "Salomé Camilia, her mother's name and her name, always together! . . . 'Here *we* are,' she [Camille] calls out" (2000, 331).

Camille cannot find the words with which to express the pain of her loss. Her identification with her lost mother results in the loss of herself. She desperately attempts to identify with her mother's creativity, with her poetry, and to become a poet herself, but she is inhibited by the maternal corpse that (as Julia Kristeva might say) she keeps locked up in the crypt of her psyche. While her brother Pedro is able to sublimate the loss of his mother and like Salomé create through writing, Camille's creativity is stifled by cultural expectations for a woman, by the loss of her mother, and in particular by her brother's criticisms. While he has the social support necessary to find signifying practices through which to discharge maternal affect, she is expected to conform to the role circumscribed for her as a woman. Although Camille is a depressed character, her life is not without its own revolutions. She refuses to marry but maintains a life-long friendship with a lesbian lover, Marion. She gives up her teaching position at Vassar to work for the revolution in Cuba. In her work toward literacy in Cuba, Camille realizes, "The real revolution could only be won by the imagination. When one of my newly literate students picked up a book and read with hungry pleasure, I knew we were one step closer to the patria we all wanted" (347).

For the women in Alvarez's novels, creative revolt or revolt of imagination operates as a counterweight to depression, in particular the depression that results from women's oppression within patriarchal culture; as I argue elsewhere, women's depression can be diagnosed as "social melancholy" that results from oppression (Oliver 2004). The opposition between depression and creativity is perhaps most apparent in Alvarez's character Salomé. The everyday expectations of her as a wife and mother and her duties to her country as a woman take their toll. She gives up writing poetry for the sake of these duties, and the result is depression, disease, and ultimately death. With her poetry she found a way to sublimate her depression. She repeats in the novel that "tears are the ink of the poet"; rather than waste them by crying, she turns these painful affects into art. Through poetry she finds a means by which to discharge affects and sublimate bodily drives and sensations. Without that means these affects, drives, and sensations become symptoms that manifest themselves in her body now unable to express itself. When she sacrifices her creative genius in order to take up roles traditionally assigned to women, she suffocates.

As she does in *In the Time of the Butterflies*, Alvarez presents Salomé's genius as part of an ordinary life, more particularly a woman's life troubled by the restrictions of patriarchy. There are several points in the novel when Salomé reflects on the irony of fighting for national liberation while she suffers the double standards and sexism of that nation: "Here she was—enslaved to her family's smallest demands and fighting for these larger freedoms" (2000, 151). She recognizes that "there was another revolution to be fought if our patria was to be truly free" (145)—a domestic revolution to free women from patriarchal oppression, a revolution that Alvarez suggests can only be won by the imagination. Revolt against patriarchal institutions and values is one of imagination not only because it is necessary to change the ways in which we imagine ourselves as men and women but also because oppression takes its toll on the imagination and on the ability to imagine and create value and meaning in one's own life. In her novels, Alvarez not only describes this imaginary revolt in the lives and thoughts of her characters, but she also opens up the possibility of imagining otherwise, of imagining strong women capable of agency and making meaning for their own lives, of imagining women engaged in everyday revolts, through her own creativity as a novelist.

Without creativity and revolt, women lack the ability to sublimate, which is crucial for psychic life and the ability to find and create meaning in life and language. Oppression undermines the possibility of sublimation and thereby leaves women feeling empty, depressed, and passive, without a sense of their own agency. Through sublimation bodily drives and their attenuating affects become discharged in signifying practices; and insofar as signification is dependent upon the discharge of drives, we could say that through the process of sublimation drives become signification. The meaning of language is dependent upon the process of sublimation of drives and affects into words. Infants enter language by virtue of sublimating their drives or bodily needs into forms of communication; their early means of communication can be seen as primordial modes of sublimation. At the other end of the spectrum, the depressive gives up on words because of a breakdown in the process of sublimation such that drives and affects are no longer discharged in language. When drives and affects become cut off from words, the result is depression (Cf. Kristeva 1989). As I argue elsewhere, in its most severe forms, depression is the inability to sublimate (Oliver 2004).

*In the Name of Salomé* can be read as a lesson in the importance for women's psychic life of maintaining the space of creativity and sublimation. As we have seen, Camille's poetic voice is stifled by patriarchal restrictions and expectations placed on women. And, without the creative revolt provided by her poetry, Salomé suffers what her son calls "moral asphyxiation" (2000, 281). Although her husband, Pancho, falls in love with Salomé's poetry and image as the national poetess, once they marry Salomé's duties to her him and his sense of her duties to the nation (which includes opening a school rather than writing poetry, particularly love poetry), and her duties to her children, overtake her passion for poetry. Her poetry is what keeps her alive, and when that is taken from her by the demands and expectations of patriarchal culture, she dies exhausted and depressed. Indeed, throughout the novel, poetry serves as an antidote to depression: "'Tears are the ink of the poet,' Papá had once said. But I was no longer writing, I could waste them now on my own sadness" (259). By sacrificing her voice for the sake of her family and her nation, in the end she sacrifices herself. Ultimately, the everyday revolts that sustain psychic life through creativity and imagination are essential forms of resistance against women's oppression that results in depression and psychic (if not physical) death. If depression is one symptom of oppression, a symptom with a female face, then resistance, particularly everyday revolt and feminine genius, is a prescription for psychic freedom.

# 3

## Authorizing Desire

*Erotic Poetics and the* Aisthesis *of Freedom in Morrison and Shange*

CHRISTA DAVIS ACAMPORA

---

>  oppression/makes us love one another badly/makes our
>      breathing
>  mangled/while i am desperately trying to clear the air/
>  in the absence of extreme elegance/
>  madness can set right in like
>  a burnin gauloise on Japanese silk.
>  though highly cultured/
>  even the silk must ask
>  how to burn up discreetly.
>        —Ntozake Shange, "a photograph: lovers in motion"

Oppression has at least two existential characteristics: (1) it aims to reduce the oppressed to the status of an object, and (2) it excludes the oppressed from the community of those regarded as having the capacity and the authority to make meanings and establish values. In *The Ethics of Ambiguity*, Simone de Beauvoir specifically identifies manipulation of desire as a primary mechanism through which oppression is exercised and finds its most destructive effects. If desire, or *passion* as Beauvoir and Sartre call it, is important for the realization of freedom, incapacitating it—extinguishing desire or mutilating it in some way—would have detrimental consequences for the pursuit of making a life of meaning and purpose. Similar ideas are advanced and further developed in the work of Drucilla Cornell (1998 and 1995), who, as discussed later, makes the case for what she describes as *imaginative agency*. This chapter develops the outlines of a theoretical framework for considering the relation between freedom and desire for applications in investigations of artistic practices of resistance that aim at producing transgressive expressions of desire and what I shall describe as the *aisthesis* (or felt quality) of freedom. The poetics of desire, or erotic poetics, provide a vehicle for formulating an answer to the question, What would it be good for me (or for us) to *want*? rather than address the question, What should I (or we) *do*? which is the context in which imagination has been explored most often in the area of moral psychology. Erotic poetics allows us to conceive, formulate, and reformulate affiliations that enhance our participation in a social eroticism, an economy in which our energies are oriented toward forging significant relations with each other and striving together toward creating a social order that cultivates and enhances capabilities. (See also Ferguson 1989 on social eroticism.)

To illustrate some cases in point, I open a discussion of Ntozake Shange's choreopoem "Spell #7" and Toni Morrison's *Beloved*. Both works exemplify concern with the problem of revaluing what oppression denigrates. Both seek meaningful agency emerging out of a situation that is affectively incapacitating. I read Shange's work in particular as endeavoring to open different possibilities for loving—as producing an erotic poetics—and I look to Morrison's work for insights relevant to moral psychology and for an invitation to contemplate what difference it makes in having experience (or a lack thereof) of the *felt quality* of freedom.

## DESIRE AND FREEDOM IN BEAUVOIR

In *The Ethics of Ambiguity*, Beauvoir casts her own light on the situation of human existence—neither god nor thing, we live as liminal creatures who often find themselves drawn toward one or the other end of this pole. Sartre, of course, names that desire—longing to be either god (for Sartre, pure transcendence, absolute subjectivity) or thing (pure immanence, absolute objectivity)—bad faith. For Sartre, the temptations of bad faith are numerous, nearly ubiquitous, and it becomes difficult to see how we are anything but damned or how a meaningful social existence is possible. Beauvoir is similarly wary of bad faith. Her *Ethics of Ambiguity* operates largely within a Sartrean ontological framework, but for her the trap of bad faith is not inevitable: she distinguishes the desire to disclose being from the wish to possess or coincide with the object of desire.

According to both Sartre and Beauvoir, projects of bad faith fundamentally aim at fleeing our freedom. We pursue it in order to mollify anxiety in the face of freedom and to avoid the metaphysical risks involved in what Sartre describes as "making ourselves a lack of being" or exercising transcendence. Beauvoir also recognizes this tendency, which she describes as a desire to flee freedom that stems from our nostalgia for the security and cheerfulness of childhood.

The child's world is a serious one, but it is one for which she or he bears no responsibility. The serious world, characterized by what both Sartre and Beauvoir identify with the "spirit of seriousness," is one comprised of ready-made values. The child in the serious world considers the world as given, values as inherent, and the adults who structure their lives as having pure being. One may live in such a world playfully because "the domain open to his subjectivity seems insignificant and puerile in his own eyes" (Beauvoir 1948, 35). And one may pursue some measure of freedom within it only insofar as one seeks the realization of those values and traverses the path toward being that is worn by those beings one takes to be complete. This is not to say that children live in bad faith, of course, since children are not yet aware of their subjectivity and do not have a sense of inhabiting the world in any other way. (Beauvoir thinks it is conceivable that eighteenth-century slaves and "the Mohammedan woman enclosed in a harem" [1948, 38] have a similar existence.) However, once one matures in one's subjectivity and becomes acquainted with one's freedom, then the nostalgia for the serious-but-carefree world of the child, the desire to trade freedom for security, and the resignation or outright denial of one's responsibility, constitute bad faith.

If Sartre sees this desire as ultimately damning, Beauvoir does not. It is not the desire itself that is dangerous, but rather the mistaken notion that desiring is terminable, that it aims at a satisfaction of completion. It is not possession of the object itself that desire genuinely seeks, Beauvoir claims, but rather *the process of disclosure itself* (cf. Ferguson 1989, 73–74 and 77–99). What desire as passion celebrates is the disclosive character of human existence, an idea more akin to Heidegger's view than Sartre's. In other words, Beauvoir sees human beings as realizing their existence in disclosing possible ways of being and bringing forth their meanings. She characterizes it thus: Human existence has its being in "vitality, sensitivity, and intelligence," which are not themselves "ready-made qualities, but a way of casting oneself into the world and of disclosing being":

> Every man casts himself into the world by making himself a lack of being; he thereby contributes to reinvesting it with human signification. He discloses it.

> And in this movement even the most outcast sometimes feel the joy of existing. There is vitality only by means of free generosity. Intelligence supposes good will, and inversely, a man is never stupid if he adapts his language and his behavior to his capacities, and sensitivity is nothing else but the presence which is attentive to the world and to itself. The reward for these spontaneous qualities issues from the fact that they make significances and goals appear in the world. They discover reasons for existing. They confirm us in the pride and joy of our destiny as man. (Beauvoir 1948, 41–42)

Beauvoir describes our living out this destiny as "living warmth," or passion, and she associates it with love and desire. It is a kind of loving that invests human activity with meaning, a kind of loving that bestows human existence itself with value. Such desire is directed by ends, no doubt, but its pleasure is not sustained by acquiring those ends. The pleasure of desire, desire's delight, unfolds in the perpetual pursuit and recreation of those ends. And this is what grounds our pursuit of freedom for others, according to Beauvoir. We desire the freedom of others to multiply these possibilities. The freedom of the other provides an opening to the social in which the meanings that we make take on their significance.

These ideas become somewhat clearer in Beauvoir's discussion of oppression, which emphasizes the significance of the freedom of others for us and elaborates the crucial role of desire in the exercise of freedom and the realization of its ecstasies. In the situation of oppression, the oppressed is both reduced to pure facticity, regarded as an absence of human transcendence, and explicitly denied opportunities for meaningful transcendence insofar as the oppressed is excluded from participation in the production of social meanings. Obviously, a person cannot be stripped of her metaphysical freedom since human existence is radically free according to the existential framework. But it can happen that in the situation of oppression, the possibilities of the joyful exercise of freedom can be diminished insofar as the prospects for meaningful transcendence are minimized or eliminated. Beauvoir writes: "As we have already seen, every man transcends himself. But it happens that this transcendence is condemned to fall uselessly back upon itself because it is cut off from its goals. That is what defines a situation of oppression. Such a situation is never natural: man is never oppressed by things" (1948, 81). In other words, there exists a social reality that provides the context in which one's ability to make meanings, one's participation in the production of values, meaningfully occurs. Excluded from that community, incapacitated for such participation, one is unable to make the movements of desire that freedom requires. Beauvoir continues:

> As we have seen, my freedom, in order to fulfill itself, requires that it emerge into an open future: it is other men who open the future to me, it is they who, setting up the world of tomorrow, define my future; but if, instead of allowing me to participate in this constructive movement, they oblige me to consume my transcendence in vain, if they keep me below the level which they have conquered and on the basis of which new conquests will be achieved, then they are cutting me off from the future, they are changing me into a thing. (1948, 82)

And one need not be actively and repeatedly excluded from this process in order to be oppressed. Perversions of desire that draw one toward fruitless endeavors and mechanical gestures are sufficient for cultivating in the oppressed a desire that *wills one's own exclusion* from the meaningful creation of the future. Beauvoir continues:

> Life is occupied in both perpetuating itself and surpassing itself; if all it does is maintain itself, then living is only not dying, and human existence is indistinguishable from an absurd vegetation; a life justifies itself only if its effort to perpetuate itself is integrated into its surpassing and if this surpassing has no other limits than those which the subject assigns himself. Oppression divides the world into two clans: those who enlighten mankind by thrusting it ahead of itself and those who are condemned to mark time hopelessly in order merely to support the collectivity; their life is a pure repetition of mechanical gestures; their leisure is just about sufficient for them to regain their strength; the oppressor feeds himself on their transcendence and refuses to extend it by a free recognition. The oppressed has only one solution: to deny the harmony of that mankind from which an attempt is made to exclude him, to prove that he is a man and that he is free by revolting against the tyrants. In order to prevent this revolt, one of the ruses of oppression is to camouflage itself behind a natural situation since, after all, one can not revolt against nature. (1948, 82–83)

Diminish desire and the oppressed effect their own exclusion since they do not want to participate in the pursuit and recreation of ends that afford the ecstatic life, the life of metaphysical risk, of "being thrown dangerously beyond" ourselves, the stakes of which are the very meanings of our lives.

For Beauvoir, the world that oppression erects is one plagued by the spirit of seriousness. It affirms the oppressive order as "a natural situation," a world that one cannot change and against which one cannot hope to successfully revolt. One cannot know the joy of the "destiny" of human existence caught within a world of ready-made values. There is a kind of existential retelling of the story of the Judeo-Christian "Fall of Humankind" at work in this idea: Just as the mythical first human beings traded paradise for the pleasures and pains of knowledge, the existentialist sees the human condition as characterized by a brokerage of the pleasures of lacking responsibility (for the meaning and significance of one's life) for the anxieties of subjectivity and its joyful possibilities. The only escape from the serious world is revolt, a thoroughgoing rebellion. One cannot merely make modest modifications in such world: "[T]he oppressed can fulfill his freedom as a man only in revolt, since the essential characteristic of the situation against which he is rebelling is precisely its prohibiting him from any positive development; it is only in social and political struggle that his transcendence passes beyond to the infinite" (Beauvoir 1948, 87).

## THE DILEMMA OF REVOLT: FANON'S CASE

But precisely how does one undertake such a revolt? The logic of rebellion that Beauvoir heralds appears to require a revaluing of precisely that which grounds the oppression of the other. It demands that "the essential characteristic of the situation" (Beauvoir 1948, 87) be challenged. In his *Black Skin, White Masks*, Fanon contemplates his possibilities for revolt within an existentialist framework, and he struggles to apply it to the particular situation of the colonized, who are subjugated and marked by "the fact of blackness."

Fanon scrutinizes Sartre's assessment of the attempted revaluation of "blackness" in the poetics of "negritude," which aims to affirm and positively define the very difference that serves as the basis of exploitation for the colonizers. In his 1948 preface to *Black Orpheus*, Sartre claims:

> In fact, negritude appears as the minor term of a dialectical progression: The theoretical and practical assertion of the supremacy of the white man is its thesis; the position of negritude as an antithetical value is the moment of negativity. But this negative moment is insufficient by itself, and the Negroes who employ it know this very well; they know that it is intended to prepare the synthesis or realization of the human in a society without races. Thus negritude is the root of its own destruction, it is a transition and not a conclusion, a means and not an ultimate end. (xl; cited in Fanon 1967, 133)

But Fanon himself questions whether any movement can be authentic if regarded as merely a turn in a larger historical process. How can one possibly regard one's sense of one's own worth in such terms? When one's very life is on the line, when what one endeavors is the poetic transformation of the meaning of one's very own existence and future possibilities, how could one simultaneously hold the new valuation as a mere means to yet another end, the "real" or legitimate one that differs from what one had taken as one's poetic aim? Sartre essentially claims that a poetics of blackness, insofar as it seeks to valorize the fact of blackness, simply reverses the very terms against which it aims to rebel. It inverts the content (i.e., what was bad is now good) without obliterating the form, and hence it fails to escape what it aims to overthrow, the terms of valuation itself. If this is so, what remains for the colonized to do; whence comes liberation from oppression of this sort? Whence comes a legitimate black identity? Can there be a black voice that authorizes meaning and writes its own significance? What direction of desire could be liberating? *What should the colonized want?* Fanon laments, "I *wanted* to be typically Negro—it was no longer possible. I *wanted* to be white—that was a joke. And, when I tried, on the level of ideas and intellectual activity, to reclaim my negritude, it was snatched away from me. Proof was presented that my effort was only a term in the dialectic" (1967, 132; emphasis added).

If the poetics of blackness cannot escape failure, what is to be done to escape what physically cannot be fled, namely, the facticity that serves as the basis of the oppression, the abiding fact of blackness? The revaluation of blackness seems the only available way out. Fanon writes immediately following Sartre's assessment cited above, "When I read that page, I felt that I had been robbed of my last chance" (1967, 133). He later explains, "And so [as Sartre sees it] it is not I who make a meaning for myself, but it is the meaning that was already there, pre-existing, waiting for me. It is not out of my bad nigger's misery, my bad nigger's teeth, my bad nigger's hunger that I will shape a torch with which to burn down the world, but it is the torch that was already there, waiting for that turn of history" (1967, 134). He continues, "[M]y shoulders slipped out of the framework of the world, my feet could no longer feel the touch of the ground. Without a Negro past, without a Negro future, it was impossible for me to live my Negrohood. Not yet white, no longer wholly black, I was damned" (138). If the poetics of negritude fail, at least in cases in which they constitute reversals of the values they aim to reject, what then can serve as the basis of revolt in situations of racialized oppression? Perhaps, one might claim, Fanon's account better reveals an inherent contradiction in existential thought than it does a fatal flaw in black poetry. Perhaps we can resolve the dilemma articulated by Fanon by simply rejecting the existential account of meaning and human existence. Fanon himself is not wholly willing to do so, and I do not think this contradiction that

Fanon forcefully illuminates necessarily requires us to throw out the baby with the bathwater.

The existential framework sketched above from Beauvoir's work fails to account for one very important idea. In the summary of Beauvoir's discussion of the frivolity of the child in the serious world, I indicated that Beauvoir claims that one who is childlike lives playfully in the serious world (that is a world of ready-made values) until one becomes familiar with the nature of human subjectivity as fundamentally and radically free. Beauvoir indicates, without elaborating, the importance of imagination for envisioning a possible future when she writes that "the goal toward which I surpass myself must appear to me as a point of departure toward a new act of surpassing. Thus a creative freedom develops happily without ever congealing into unjustified facticity" (1948, 27–28).

But what propels one toward taking those goals? What enables one to *see* as one must in order for "a point of departure toward a new act of surpassing" to in fact *appear*? (Beauvoir 1948, 27). It seems that what is necessary, as Beauvoir claims, is "an apprenticeship of freedom" (1948, 37). Precisely how does one become apprenticed in freedom? What leads us to that knowledge such that it animates an entire form of life? *What makes freedom our familiar?* Without an account of this, it seems to me, a tremendous chasm is left in the existential view. To describe it merely as consciousness raising does not seem sufficient. After I become aware of injustices in the serious world that would keep me its subject, how do I acquire the sense that there is something to be done about it, and that I am the one (perhaps together with others who share my situation) to do it? What directs my own way out of the serious world? And if the serious world is the only one I have known and the only one I have previously thought possible, whence comes my direction for conceiving its alternatives?

## OPENINGS TO OTHERNESS: THE IMAGINARY DOMAIN

Although she is not writing in response to these questions as I have posed them, Drucilla Cornell articulates a conception of the imaginary domain and its fundamental significance for the realization of subjectivity that is relevant. Cornell describes a conceptual space in which one exercises the freedom to do the work of conceiving the world as other, of imagining a world one wants as one's own, of pursuing other modes of disclosure, and of revealing other forms of reality. What she describes as "the imaginary domain" is "that psychic and moral space in which we [. . .] are allowed to evaluate and represent who we are" (Cornell 1998, x; cf. Cornell 1995). Cornell discusses the imaginary domain specifically in terms of sexual desire and sexuate being, but it could apply to desire generally and other specific ways of being. Cornell further describes the imaginary domain as what "gives to the individual person, and her only, the right to claim who she is through her own representation of her [sexuate] being. Such a right necessarily makes her the morally [and legally] recognized source of what [the] meaning [of her sexual difference] is for her" (1998, 10).

Having access to the imaginary domain activates the possibility for change—insofar as different forms of existence emerge as options to pursue or reject—and hence the imaginary domain facilitates a more rigorous exercise of our agency. Cornell writes that "the imaginary domain is the space of the 'as if' in which we imagine who we might be if we made ourselves our own end and claimed ourselves as our own person" (1998, 8). Simply put, the imaginary domain is that space in which not merely *what* we desire—or what we take to be the good—is derived but also the *shape* of desire is given its form in terms of *how* desire unfolds, *how* its ends might be pursued. Cornell describes the kind of freedom exercised in the imaginary domain as "freedom of personality." It "is valuable because it is what lets us make a life we embrace as our own" (1998, 62).

Cornell's work significantly enhances and fills out the framework of freedom and desire I have drawn from Beauvoir and that I have made more complex and problematic by engaging Fanon, but it would be useful to see it in action, to get a sense of a concrete application of the utilization of an imaginary domain. And Cornell's view still leaves what I perceive as a gap—namely, some account of what other resources one might need to flourish in that space. We need to know what allows for the experimentations of subjectivity the imaginary domain affords. For better appreciation of these considerations, I shall turn to Ntozake Shange whose choreopoem "Spell #7: geechee jibara quik magic trance manual for technologically stressed third world people" explicitly thematizes the nature of poetic power and considers how one might tap it.

## ACTING OUT: THE ECSTASIES AND AGENCY OF SHANGE'S EROTIC POETICS

Shange's "Spell #7" focuses on the lives of a group of black actors and their friends who struggle to negotiate their oppressive situation. "Betinna," an actress, describes her experience in the (white) world that determines and constructs her as *being black* when she says of herself, "I am theater" (Shange 1981b, 24). To *be black* is to be already defined, to already have a role, to be a reluctant actor on a white stage. Betinna also recognizes that her possibilities for transcending that role (living out the "fact" of blackness) lie in *acting out* of it. At best, she and the other characters in the play are socially invisible, unrecognized as legitimate candidates for living a human life; at worst, they are despised, devalued, and even physically and mentally destroyed. Their possibilities for *acting out* are limited, since access to many of the ordinary means of such transcendence is prohibited to them.

What they need is magic, "blk magic" [sic], that will allow them not merely to be satisfied with themselves but to be *loved*—to become subjects enabled by "loving perception," a perspective that invests what it perceives as potent and full of possibilities, possessed with the capacity for transfiguration. (The concept of 'loving perception' figures prominently in certain works in feminist and Africana literature. It is initially defined in Frye 1983. Cf. Lugones 1987 and Gordon 1997.) The characters in "Spell #7" need a magic space in which they can conjure the creative energy necessary for exercising meaningful agency. And they need an opportunity to *practice* magic: they need to somehow acquire the means to engage in transforming the negative values they have been given by others into those they can affirm as beautiful and significant. I take it this is another way of envisioning the tasks and possibilities of a poetics of negritude mentioned above.

In the context of existential literature, magic appears to be significantly related to desire. One might say that magic seeks to transform the impossible, to render it within the realm of possibility. Translated into the language of the existentialists with whom I began this chapter, magic aims at the conversion of facticity to transcendence; magic seeks to open as a candidate for otherness (as a candidate for legitimate longing-to-be-other) what has been confined to the realm of brute facts. I think Toni Morrison's *The Bluest Eye* provides a rich basis for a more thorough exploration of how the desire to practice magic constitutes an effort to conjure "an imaginary domain." But such desire is not always creative, not always truly enabling, as one witnesses in the case of Pecola, as I shall discuss in the section that follows. In Shange's "Spell #7" "blk magic" is also risky: the play opens with the magician "lou" recounting how his own father retired from magic when lou was just a child. One of lou's young friends asked his father to practice his magic by making him white. "All things are possible," lou recalls, "but aint no colored magician in his right mind/gonna make you white" (Shange 1981b, 8). Lou and his father practice magic for the purpose of "fixin you up good/fixin you up good & colored" (8). They aim at making black life good and desirable. When the child asked for whiteness instead, the blk magician's practice was entirely undermined and drained of all its potentency.

Poetry and dance are the means through which the characters of "Spell #7" attempt to bring their work to fruition. One of the characters, a poet named Eli, claims that "whoever that is authorizing poetry as an avocation/is a fraud/put yr own feet on the ground" (1981a, 25). Creating poetic expression is described as "authorizing"—drawing on senses of both being an author ("authoring") and granting or grounding legitimacy ("authorizing"). Being a creator is simultaneously granting power, sanctioning, and providing sufficient grounds for the values and worldviews it establishes. To do so in a way that considers the activity as merely a hobby, to write poetry recklessly, is fraudulent. Grounding the significance of one's life is an endeavor that requires a kind of serious energy, but some things break a spirit of that capacity and diminish its possibilities for creative activity, for *poiesis* (the practice of poetry broadly conceived in terms of articulating and reshaping meaningful significances in one's life and one's community). As the choreopoem unfolds, the characters strive to reach the place in which that rift can be transcended, in which magic, specifically "blk magic," can happen. The choreopoem represents Shange's effort to conceive a formal structure that is specific enough to succeed in defining meanings and values that can take hold and yet flexible enough to offer others transformative possibilities.

In her foreword to the collection in which "Spell #7" is published, Shange indicates that her work aims to provide an alternative to the "artificial aesthetics" of a "european framework for european psychology" (1981a, ix). She is specifically concerned to amplify possibilities for communication beyond the verbal, claiming that in her choreopoems, "music functions as another character" (1981a, x). The choreopoem is a poetic amalgamation that draws its elements from choreography, theater, and a variety of meters and musical rhythms. It is a novel dramatic, poetic framework aimed at generating and giving shape to alternative forms of creative expression and producing transformative manifestations of desire. In these works, the "person/body, voice & language/address the space as if [they] were a band/a dance company & a theater group all at once, cuz a poet shd do that/create an emotional environment/felt architecture" (1981a, xi).

Shange's use of language, which some have seen as an effort to destroy the English language as such, is more creative than destructive. Although Shange does regard "the King's English" as a straightjacket that supports oppression and limits creative expression, she is not merely seeking to destroy it by using it recklessly. In an interview Shange explains that "language will allow us to function more competently and more wholly in a holistic sense as human beings once we take hold of it and make it say what we want to say" (Shange and Lester 1990, 727). And a number of her characters struggle to achieve precisely that aim. Choreopoetic structure opens spaces ordinarily closed by other dramatic forms by giving a more prominent place to the full sense of lived embodiment through movement and by tapping the emotive qualities of music. When language fails or cannot reach its aim, music and dance step in. But these elements are not merely surrogates for speech, and narrative wholeness does not loom over the work as the ideal for which the characters should strive and in light of which they are deficient. Rather, the nonlinguistic elements are themselves in a supralinguistic dialogue: music and dance do not merely stand in for speech, they also serve to produce the psychic space in which new articulations and new conceptualizations might occur. The opening scene in which the magician lou sings, dances, mimes, performs, boasts, offers a speech, whispers secrets, and addresses both the audience and the characters works to conjure a specific place—an imaginary domain—in which *what is impossible* in the serious white world in which the actors are thrown *is bracketed out, disabled, or suspended*. It is that transformation of impossibility to possibility—to realize an acting out that is not dependent upon, relative to, or bound by the terms defined by whiteness—that constitutes the practice of lou's magic.

Shange's characters' use of language reflects not only their attempts to make it speak their own voice but also the fact that they are "constricted" and "amputated" characters (xiii), whose movements and musical vocalizations both mirror their dismemberment and mark their efforts to poetically transform and transcend them. The limits of their desire have been defined in terms of two equally impossible directives—*either* desire to be a slave (in other words, desire to have your desire wholly determined by another) *or* desire to be white (in other words, desire to renounce all desire insofar as *being* anything would require you to give up that process of *becoming* described earlier as the direction of desire toward disclosing being). Shange challenges her characters and her audience to sing and dance their way out of this false dilemma in the absence of a liberative narrative framework in which they might insert themselves.

Shange claims that "literature, if it does nothing else, should stimulate one's imagination to know that there is more—maybe not more 'out there,' but more inside of us that we can use for our own survival" (Shange and Lester 1990, 729). Shange's choreopoetry aims to engage that imagination. It seeks to provide openings for the direction of imaginative *re*-membering (both a drawing on the past and a reconstitution of a meaningful world in which one can be a full participant) and the circulation of affirmative desire. It opens new and different circuits for loving—in the sense of valuing—that enable the transformation of desire that has been distorted by oppression. This is the practice of authorizing that is realized in erotic poetics.

Similar conceptions of poetic power and its social applications are advanced in Audre Lorde's well known "Uses of the Erotic: The Erotic as Power." And one finds in Toni Morrison's work, particularly *Beloved*, connections drawn among the *feeling* of power, the development of human agency, and the materialization of freedom. I conclude by briefly considering both of these works in order to elaborate how the *aisthesis* of freedom—the *feeling* of oneself as free and rich with possibilities—is linked with the creative power of being a maker of meaning and pleasure, and how erotic poetic practice—the engagement of desire enabled for authorizing—affords the creative resources for transgressive resistance.

## POETIC POWER AND THE *AISTHESIS* OF FREEDOM

In her well-known "Uses of the Erotic: The Erotic as Power," Audre Lorde articulates and distinguishes a sense of the erotic as a form of loving that draws one out of oneself. It is tied to the creative power of producing meanings and determining worthy goals, and it provides a significant form for resistance. She recognizes that one way in which oppression operates and incapacitates its victims is through the manipulation of desire: "In order to perpetuate itself, every oppression must corrupt or distort those various sources of power within the culture of the oppressed that can provide energy for change" (Lorde 1984).

Lorde vividly describes the relation between the erotic and a sense of power connected with expressive feeling (contrasted with mere sensation). She explicitly connects this desire to creative production (e.g., writing poetry, dance) and aesthetic experience in everyday life (e.g., "moving into the sunlight against the body of the woman I love"). She describes how the erotic opens aesthetic possibilities and creates a "clearing" for joy:

"Another important way in which the erotic connection functions is the open and fearless underlining of my capacity for joy. In the way my body stretches to music and opens into response, hearkening to its deepest rhythms, so every level upon which I sense also opens to the erotically satisfying experience, whether it is dancing, building a bookcase, writing a poem, examining an idea." Lorde envisions an erotic poetic practice that affords transgressive resistance. It is transformative and generates a basis for political resistance that is not merely reactionary. What Lorde's erotic poetics aim at is activation and engagement of the *aisthesis* of power—a capacity that is not contingent upon the acquisition of power over others but that is lived out through effective action *with others*, bodied forth in the world.

The creative activity of art reflects a way of organizing the world (or a part thereof). As we experience the work of art, we experience that structuring, that organization. Aesthetic experiences similarly organize us by taking us through a variety of organized structures. Art effects how we experience ourselves (our own form and its possibilities), our relations with others, and how we encounter and make sense of our worlds. Our experience of the *shaping* that happens in art *shapes* us. Our engagement of different aesthetic qualities in art makes us different, too—it *en*forms us with a sense of shaping itself, of what it means to actively give shape and form. Works of art *work* in and through us. It is in this way that aesthetic experience is transfiguring and transformative.

Both words *transfiguration* and *transformation* indicate reshaping, remolding, and rearranging. They suggest a further development, an imposition of a new form, a stage, or a process of forming. Insofar as aesthetic experience provides opportunities for transformation and transfiguration, it provides (quite literally) an exercise of imagination that is vital not only for our appreciation of art but also for projecting ourselves as other than what we are at any given moment. John Dewey has argued that it is this very aspect of art that makes it "the chief instrument of the good," "more moral than moralities" (1987, 350). Citing Shelly, Dewey describes the significance of the power of imaginative projection thus: "'The great secret of morals is love, or *a going out of our nature* and the identification of ourselves with the beautiful which exists in thought, action, or person, not our own. A man to be greatly good must imagine intensely and comprehensively.'" Imaginative projection, ignited by love (or what I have described here as the erotic), aims at a kind of standing out of ourselves (ecstasy), a way of being drawn out of our nature, and allows us to transgress the boundaries that appear to be drawn between ourselves and others. To imagine ourselves as other is absolutely crucial for our growth as individuals: for setting goals, imagining the kinds of persons we want to become, and devising a route to get there.

And imagining ourselves as other is an important way in which we build communities. Such imagination leads us out of ourselves, enhancing our capacity to set aside our own particular interests in order to recognize the needs of others or what would be required for us to pursue a common ideal. Dewey identifies this power as unfolding in the redirection of desire and purpose, the first intimations of which are of necessity imaginative (1987, 352). That redirection of desire and purpose potentially presents us with opportunities to pursue new and different possibilities, opening up what Homi Bhabha calls "liminal spaces," which are sites for the production of cultural hybridities (1994). Such imagination facilitates dynamic manifestations of social agency, garnering the resources to participate in the *production* of political, cultural, or ethnic identities. (This contrasts quite markedly with the conception of identity as linked to some essential or static entity. On the way in which linguistic community and autonomy of expression are relevant to this process, see Cornell 2000, ch. 8, and Anzaldúa 1990, ch 5.) Imagination enables us to better understand how our actions and our decisions affect others, to see ourselves in-relation-to-others. And it heightens our capacity for compassion in the sense of *feeling with* others, what Kundera describes as "the maximal capacity of affective imagination, the art of emotional telepathy [. . . which] in the hierarchy of sentiments . . . is supreme" (1984, 20; cf. Willett 2001, ch. 7, on erotic power and understanding the "individual in relationship-to-others").

Aesthetic engagement potentially activates imaginative resources that enable the realization of agency. This strikes me as crucial at a time when it is argued not only that one must become a moral agent in order to be free but also that one must at least play a role in *determining* the means and meaning of that endeavor as such. This is the very predicament faced by the characters of Toni Morrison's *Beloved*: they are (eventually) "free men" before the law but are at sea when it comes to realizing how that freedom might meaningfully animate their lives. Lacking what I describe as the felt quality of freedom—the feeling of themselves as free—they are without the imaginative resources to envision lives of meaning and purpose that they might seek as their own (for a similar discussion of these ideas in a different context, see Acampora 2006).

The experience of the enslaved body generates a mutilated aesthetic. The theft of slavery commits a dual crime—not merely a theft of the property of one's labor, slavery manipulates and disciplines the slave's erotic resources to serve the master's material interests. Bodies whose senses are anesthetized by an economy that treats them as commodities to be bought, bartered, and broken by others struggle to see themselves as human beings with possibilities to be sought, shaped, and shared. They emerge from slavery with transmogrified desire—the phenomenon of "slave breaking" bears witness to the necessity of the transformation of desire in the maintenance of the institution of slavery—and an impaired sense of the erotic they might otherwise engage in bringing forth beauty, bringing about a world imbued with meanings and pleasures they participate in defining.

In Morrison's *Beloved* we encounter a story about a community of former slaves and their children. Some of them had their freedom from slavery purchased for them, others escaped, and others were literally born in the passage between. Part mystery, part history, part psycho-biography, *Beloved* depicts the specters of slavery, its perversions of desire, and the struggle to realize freedom when emerging from a condition of bondage. It poignantly illustrates the crippling effects of a mutilated aesthetic resulting from the experience of the enslaved body. Much of *Beloved* focuses on attempts (most of which fail) to engage that sense of the erotic and to become aesthetically empowered. Consider, as merely one example, Baby Suggs' "call" in the clearing in which she endeavors to enliven those gathered there by a sense of the erotic that is explicitly tied to seeing one's own body as a source of meaning (both loving and lovable) and value (in social and aesthetic, not merely economic, terms). Such enlivening aims at making a new perspective possible—it facilitates "loving perception," a way of seeing the world such that one seizes upon and finds one's ecstasies in the *possibilities* of what one perceives.

Shortly following Sethe's escape from slavery, her former master finds her at the house she is sharing with her mother-in-law in Ohio, Baby Suggs. When the master arrives at the house, designated only by its number "124," Sethe retreats to a shed. There she decides that she and her children would be better off dead than be slaves. Before she can take her own life, the master bursts through the door only to find the baby dead and the other children lying crying nearby. That she would murder her own children is evidence enough that Sethe is "tainted," and she is viewed as unfit even for life on the plantation. She spends a little time in jail and then returns to 124.

But things are not the same. Once a place where former slaves met, laughed, talked, and tried to heal, 124 is now as anesthetic as its name.

Years later the space, no longer invested with the significances of a *place*, becomes haunted by a baby's ghost. The ghost has violent outbursts and mercilessly taunts the inhabitants until a fellow exslave, Paul D., takes up residence with Sethe and kicks the ghost out of the house. The ghost then appears in the form of a live human being. "Beloved" is all *crave*: for sugar, for complete attention, for life. We are told that "Sethe was licked, tasted, eaten by Beloved's eyes" (Morrison 1987, 57). She had "A touch no heavier than a feather but loaded, nevertheless, with desire. [. . .] The longing [Sethe] saw there was bottomless" (58). Beloved is quite literally the personification of exorcised desire, and she can find no satisfaction.

Baby Suggs has lost her will to live: "Her faith, her love, her imagination and her great big old heart began to collapse twenty-eight days after her daughter-in-law arrived" (89). It is as if at the very moment that Sethe, Baby Suggs, their family, and their friends finally began to experience the first moments of genuine freedom—described earlier by Baby as a kind of self-granted grace—the shadow of slavery darkened the sky. Before Sethe's ruinous encounter with the master in the shed, Baby Suggs occasionally presided over a gathering of former slaves in a clearing in the wood near her home, issuing a "Call." The Call is not a sermon, we are told (177), rather it brings the people together as a community and draws them toward pursuing a hitherto unknown love. She tells them that "in this here place, we flesh; flesh that weeps, laughs; flesh that dances on bare feet in grass. Love it. Love it hard." The love she evokes is a kind of erotic that would enable them to have the imaginative resources for grace: "She told them that the only grace they could have was the grace they could imagine. That if they could not see it, they would not have it" (88–89). Desiring a route to revaluing their bodies the former slaves laugh, cry, dance, and weep.

Cynthia Willett, in her *The Soul of Justice* (2001), describes this event as a chiefly cathartic moment. I am less inclined to see it as a purging of something that has been constrictive in the past. Baby Suggs' "calling" is a creative exercise or communal practice aimed at the imagination of self- and communal making; it seeks not a release from the past but a reaching toward the future. The difference, as I understand it, is potentially significant: the kind of freedom that would be gained from the removal of impediments or impurities (as *catharsis* suggests) is insufficient for understanding what the meaningful *exercise* of freedom is. In identifying freedom with a communal practice as opposed to an accomplishment of a lone autonomous subject, I follow Willett, but I also think it is crucial to investigate the resources required to *engage* such a practice. My argument here has been that these resources are significantly, if not exclusively, aesthetic, hence my emphasis on creative and imaginative appropriation rather than purgation. Willett's emphasis on catharsis occludes our sight of expressions of desire (and its failures) to engage a most imaginative and creative activity as it is expressed in Morrison's work. It is the *dis-*orderings and attempted reorderings of desire that seem most vividly at play in *Beloved.*

In *Beloved,* we witness the poverty of aesthetic experience in the lives of many characters. "Color" literally and figuratively evaporates from their lives. Baby Suggs, for example, "was so starved for color. There wasn't any except for two orange squares in a quilt that made the absence shout.... In that sober field, two patches of orange looked wild—like life in the raw" (Morrison 1987, 38). After Sethe kills her child and goes to jail, Baby tells "Stamp Paid" that she's just going to lay down and think about color for the rest of her life (177). Sethe does not notice, but color disappears from her life, too: "[T]he last color she remembered was the pink chips in the headstone of her baby girl. After that she became as color conscious as a hen.... It was as though one day she saw red baby blood, another day the pink gravestone chips, and that was the last of it" (39). Being severed from a kind of desire that would enable them to creatively and imaginatively live their lives as free and full of possibilities, the characters repeatedly exhibit failure and frustration.

*Beloved's* characters seem to be disabled in ways that their ancestors, who were born in Africa but were enslaved in the United States, were not. What Sethe remembers of her childhood was watching those other slaves transform themselves, if only temporarily. They became enraptured not with fantasies of becoming like white people and not with a kind of nostalgia that can lead to paralyzing resentment. Rather, transported by dancing and singing, they practiced *shape shifting.* Sethe recalls:

> Of that place where she was born (Carolina maybe? or was it Louisiana?) she remembered only song and dance. Not even her own mother, who was pointed out to her by the eight-year-old child who watched over the young ones—pointed out as the one among many backs turned away from her, stooping in a watery field. [...] Oh but when they sang. And oh but when they danced and sometimes they danced the antelope. The men as well as the ma'ams, one of whom was certainly her own. They shifted shapes and became something other. (31)

It is the capacity to imaginatively project oneself as other—to envision one's body as a live, creative, dynamic, and powerful form—that slavery seems to have stripped from most of the characters in *Beloved*, and it is this same legacy the characters of "Spell #7" endeavor to overcome. Without such power—lacking a form of desire that authorizes and facilitates imaginative transfiguration—they are unable to envision a future that does not resemble the past, unable to sketch before themselves possibilities that differ from the present, unable to give shape to lives that they can come to think of as their own.

Willett emphasizes what happens when the erotic core at the heart of a person is assaulted. The cases she cites strike me as ruptures, breaks in the social bonds. I have focused on what I have characterized as erotic perversions, the ways in which slavery effects a kind of incapacitating desire, desire that is organized for hatred and self-loathing (e.g., that which is exemplified in Toni Morrison's *The Bluest Eye* and theorized as *ressentiment* in Nietzsche's *On the Genealogy of Morals*) or rendered impotent through direction toward the impossible or other-wordly (e.g., what Baby Suggs explicitly resists and what Beauvoir discusses in her *The Ethics of Ambiguity*). The characters of *Beloved* love—each other, themselves, and their possibilities—badly in the way suggested by Shange in the epigraph to this chapter. Morrison's and Shange's works provide profound examples not only of how we can become severed from the erotic that draws us into transfiguration but also of how vital it is that we gain access to that kind of power in order to see ourselves as free, loving and loveable, and full of possibilities. This is not to say that the characters completely fail to attempt or even have marginal successes in transfiguration. As an example of Sethe's aesthetic revaluation, see her conversion of the scars she has on her back into "her tree." Paul D. will see the same as "the decorative work of an ironsmith too passionate for display," while Amy (the white indentured servant Sethe meets during her escape) will see the marks as "tiny little cherry blossoms" (Morrison 1987, 17). Willett argues convincingly that the modern conception of autonomy is ill equipped to "protect the person from violations of his meaningful relationships" (2001, 210). I would add that this includes aesthetic meaning—the felt quality of experience as such. The aesthetic is the ground upon which, with which, and out of which the symbolic order is organized, reformed, and shaped anew. *Beloved* ends with the collective forgetting of Beloved's miraculous apparition and subsequent disappearance (Morrison 1987, 274–75). She is "disremembered," which calls to mind the difficulties of "rememory" Sethe experiences. One of the stories "laid down" in that work and in Shange's "Spell #7," perhaps one that *is* to be passed on, is the story of *Eros* (rather than Prometheus) bound, the story that shapes the many stories witnessed in these texts that mark the binding or constriction of the very desire that is necessary for the pursuit of meaningful freedom.

Making significances and goals appear in the world, discovering reasons for existing, manufacturing joy—these are the goods of the passion, the eros, that animates human existence. Our acquaintance with these activities is what the space of the imaginary domain is supposed to enable. It provides entrée to an apprenticeship in freedom insofar as it serves as a place that we make our own through the imaginative refiguring of our relations to others, ourselves, and our capabilities. It is precisely that facility that is required to make the movements of desire that Beauvoir associates with human vitality and joyful possibilities: to see each goal of our desire not simply as an end in itself but rather as an opening, "a point of departure" (Beauvoir 1948, 28), to new possibilities. It is what enables one to cast oneself into the world in such a way as to disclose its possible meanings and bring forth its desirable qualities. Fanon, Lorde, Shange, and Morrison explore how such bringing forth, or *poiesis*, is relevant for the realization of freedom. For Fanon, the passion Beauvoir describes needs to be able to *burn* if it is to sufficiently fuel revolt against the serious world: it must enable one "to shape a torch with which to burn down the world" (1967, 134). That flame is to be utilized not simply to destroy in the name of vengeance or to be destructive for its own sake. Rather one raises such a torch to blaze a trail out of the serious world that fixes the significance of "the fact of blackness" and determines the horizon of goals that follow from it. At the same time, this fire can be used to ignite a passion that stimulates others to burn. It is the multiple ways in which poetic power is a propellant and accelerant that I have emphasized in the works of Lorde, Shange, and Morrison. Loving, in the form of willing, and authorizing in the sense of creating and sanctioning, are what erotic poetics seek to exercise and make available to others. Aesthetic experience can draw us into this process and help us make it our own. It provides us with a tangible experience of the *aisthesis*— the felt quality—of freedom. Thus enlivened, we are enabled to claim and exercise our authority as makers of meaning and pleasure with others and for ourselves.

# Part II
Body Agonistes

# 4

# MeShell Ndegéocello

*Musical Articulations of Black Feminism*

Martha Mockus

---

> To some, god is the light that leads them to believe that they see and know everything . . . I sway to the pulses of the rivers of blood that flow through my body, because I believe in things that you cannot see. I believe in things I cannot see.
> —MeShell Ndegéocello, "Akel Dama (Field of Blood)"

> The most arousing thing to me is sound. Even the sound of bodies when they're touching just wears me out, or the sound of breath, or the sound of wetness.
> —MeShell Ndegéocello, interview with Rebecca Walker, 1997

What does it mean to "believe in things we cannot see"? How is wetness audible? In western cultures, sight and vision dominate conceptualizations of knowledge, power, aesthetics, and sexuality. The epistemological power of music (sounding and listening) is often marginalized, cast in the shadow of visual and literary culture. In American popular music, bassist/singer/songwriter MeShell Ndegéocello privileges sound over sight in order to address some of the most critical problems in contemporary society. Her daring intelligence and musical creativity render her one of the strongest voices, male or female, in popular music today, yet the only published feminist analysis of Ndegéocello (Burns and LaFrance 2002, 133–67) focuses on just one of her songs ("Mary Magdalene" 1996). This chapter aims to fill a serious gap in the literature and to highlight the powerful aesthetics created in Ndegéocello's remarkable works.

Ndegéocello's music is rooted in 1970s funk but also blends stylistic features of soul, jazz, and hip hop. For her virtuosity, musical energy, and sexual candor many critics have compared her to Prince (York 1993, Harrington 1994, Seigal 1994, Darling 1994, Powers 1996, Sanders 2001, Jackson 2002), yet she also names Toshi Reagon and Sweet Honey in the Rock as important models (Rogers 1996, Harrington 1994). Unlike Prince, Ndegéocello has an audience comprised of mostly young women of color and queer women; her music is played rarely, if at all, on mainstream radio. She offers her listeners an unusually politicized musical experience of sensuality that reaffirms the need for personal passion and feminist transformation.

In June 2002, Ndegéocello released her fourth album entitled *Cookie: The Anthropological Mixtape.* Three months earlier in an interview with *Essence* she said, "I call it an anthropological mixtape because it's a musical excavation of my own journey, one that I hope others will relate to" (Bandele 2002, 99). In later interviews she explained this more fully:

> This record is about digging up our past in order to understand where we are going; it is about me evaluating my musical journey from [Washington] D.C. and go-go to being a jazz musician to a funk and soul singer to a hip hop lover; it is about critiquing the music industry, programmed radio and my own participation in that industry. I don't believe in pointing fingers in one direction, so the album is definitely as much of a self-critique as a critique. Beyond these themes, I just tried to be funky and collaborate with amazing vocalists, musicians and icons to create an intergenerational dialogue on identity and transformation. (Waring 2002; Cline 2002, 46)

If some of the constitutive binaries of anthropology have been self/other, civilized/primitive, colonizer/colonized, and speaker/spoken for, Ndegéocello turns anthropology on its head. Much like the work of her literary predecessor Zora Neale Hurston, Ndegéocello's "anthropological mixtape" emanates from a cultural insider seeking to explain her own worldview by locating herself as a black, queer female musician and assessing the state of black America at the start of the twenty-first century. Central to her musical ethnography are her political convictions about the search for freedom and the struggles against capitalism, racism, sexism, and homophobia in African American cultural history. I want to argue that Ndegéocello's music embodies many of the same feminist critiques offered by Patricia Hill Collins, bell hooks, and Angela Davis, and it is their work that informs and inspires my analyses. I also include the voices of Lorraine Hansberry, Alice Walker, Audre Lorde, and Cheryl Clarke, whose passionate ideas about economic justice and sexual freedom resonate deeply with those of Ndegéocello.

In her groundbreaking book *Black Feminist Thought*, Collins writes, "Developing Black feminist thought also involves searching for its expression in alternative institutional locations and among women who are not commonly perceived as intellectuals. [. . .] Black women intellectuals are neither all academics nor found primarily in the Black middle class" (2000, 14). Collins then identifies who we might turn to as additional, fully legitimate sources of Black feminist theories and knowledges: "Musicians, vocalists, poets, writers, and other artists constitute another group from which Black women intellectuals have emerged. Building on African-influenced oral traditions, musicians in particular have enjoyed close association with the larger community of African-American women constituting their audience" (2000, 17). Although Ndegéocello identifies herself as neither intellectual nor feminist, I welcome Collins's invitation to engage her music as spirited articulations of black feminist thought. Likewise, Ndegéocello's use of the term *anthropological* in the subtitle of *Cookie* prompts a more imaginative understanding of anthropology: its methods and goals need not be defined solely by professional academics in the university. Collins also analyzes the importance of lived experience and everyday life in black feminist epistemology as practiced by academics, activists, and artists alike. Similarly, Ndegéocello identifies everyday life as her primary muse (Waring 2002, Cline 2002, Orloff 2002, Thomas 2002). In addition to Collins's framework, bell hooks' critical phrase "white supremacist capitalist patriarchy"—one she uses repeatedly throughout her works—is especially useful because it sets up race, class, and gender as intertwining forms of identity *and* as interlocking sites of oppression and resistance.

I.

> Since so many black folks have succumbed to the post-1960s notion that material success is more important the personal integrity, struggles for black self-determination that emphasize decolonization, loving blackness, have had little effect. As long as black folks are taught that the only way we can gain any degree of economic self-sufficiency or be materially privileged is by first rejecting blackness, our history and culture, then there will always be a crisis in black identity.
> 
> —hooks, *Black Looks*

In "Dead Nigga Blvd," the opening track on her anthropological mixtape, Ndegéocello fiercely interrogates white constructions of black stereotypes and condemns the conflation of freedom with capitalist consumption.

> you sell your soul like you sell a piece of ass
> slave to the dead white leaders on paper
> and welfare cases
> rapists and hoes
> all reinforced by your tv show
> exotic and beautiful videos
> a jail's a sanctuary for the walking dead
> it fucks with your head
> when every black leader ends up dead

On one level, the title of her song refers to the pattern of naming streets—usually in the ghetto—after Martin Luther King Jr. and Malcolm X. On another level, Ndegéocello includes those "dead niggaz" whose sense of self and freedom has been killed off by capitalist exploitation and some of black nationalism's essentialist notions of black identity. For example, in the chorus she declares, "you try to hold on to some africa of the past/one must remember it's other africans that helped enslave your ass." In her essay, "Eating the Other," bell hooks argues:

> Resurgence of black nationalism as an expression of black people's desire to guard against white cultural appropriation indicates the extent to which the commodification of blackness (including the nationalist agenda) has been reinscribed and marketed with an atavistic narrative, a fantasy of Otherness that reduces protest to spectacle and stimulates even greater longing for the "primitive." Given this cultural context, black nationalism is more a gesture of powerlessness than a sign of critical resistance. [. . .] When young black people [today] mouth 1960s' black nationalist rhetoric, don Kente cloth, gold medallions, dread their hair and diss the white folks they hang out with, they expose the way meaningless commodification strips these signs of political integrity and meaning, denying the possibility that they can serve as a catalyst for concrete political action. As signs, their power to ignite critical consciousness is diffused when they are commodified. Communities of resistance are replaced with communities of consumption." (hooks 1992, 33)

Assimilation is also a false notion of freedom. In the first verse of "Dead Nigga Blvd" Ndegéocello claims, "somebody said our greatest destiny is to become white, but white is not pure and hate is not pride." This resonates with bell hooks' critique of some of the weaknesses of civil rights' ideology. According to hooks:

Since freedom for black folks had been defined as gaining the rights to enter mainstream society, to assume the values and economic standing of the white privileged classes, it logically followed that it did not take long for interracial interaction in the areas of education and jobs to reinstitutionalize, in less overt ways, a system wherein individual black folks who were most like white folks in the way they looked, talked, and dressed would find it easier to be socially mobile. [. . .] Unfortunately, black acceptance of assimilation meant that a politics of representation affirming white beauty standards was being reestablished as the norm." (1994b, 176–77)

Musically, "Dead Nigga Blvd" is a medium tempo funk tune built on a two-measure groove in the bass and drums. Guitars and keyboard are used rhythmically for their percussive colors rather than melodically. In the chorus, as the lyrics move around past, present, and future, Ndegéocello uses her voice as echo, so that each alternating line of lyric is heard twice. However, we hear the "distant" echo first, followed by the "nearer" initial vocalization (noted below in italics), which creates a *reverse* echo effect—a stunning sonic enactment of rebellion and confrontation.

(while we) campaign for every dead nigga blvd
*so y'all young motherfuckers can drive down it in your fancy cars*
you try to hold on to some africa of the past
*one must remember it's other africans that helped enslave your ass*
cuz everybody's just trying to make that dollar
*remember what jesse used to say? i am somebody*
no longer do i blame others for the way that we be
*cuz niggas need to redefine what it means to be free*

Defying acoustic logic, the jarring effect of her reverse echo challenges the listener to rehear, rethink, and as Ndegéocello demands, "redefine what it means to be free."

At the last line of the final chorus, the music is abruptly redefined as the drums, bass, and guitar disappear behind the ethereal chords of the keyboards. (In her liner notes, Ndegéocello playfully refers to this as "Chocolate Spaceship Keys" [Ndegēocello, 2002]) We hear a sample from Dick Gregory's speech "Human Rights and Property Rights": "Understand young folks, when you put property rights ahead of human rights—understand you're tampering with nature. Hmm. That's right. You see, property rights is controlled by man, and human rights is controlled by nature" (1971). Added effects of wind and upward *glissandi* on the "spaceship keys" convey a floating sense of suspension as Ndegéocello leaves us to ponder the deeper distinctions between the material and the conceptual.

"Dead Nigga Blvd" protests assimilation, separatism, the commodification of blackness, and leaves open this question of freedom. Meanwhile each of the following songs on the album addresses more specifically the various shapes freedom ought to take: economic freedom (an end to capitalism), sexual freedom (an end to homophobia), spirituality (freedom from religious dogmatism), and self-definition. But none of these freedoms can come about without revolution, especially revolutionary art.

## II.

> MAMA: Son—how come you talk so much 'bout money?
> WALTER: (*With immense passion*) Because it is life, Mama!
> MAMA: (*Quietly*) Oh—(*Very quietly*) So now it's life. Money is life. Once upon a time freedom used to be life—now it's money. I guess the world really do change . . .
> —Lorraine Hansberry, *A Raisin in the Sun*

In *Cookie's* next tune, "Hot Night," we hear Ndegéocello's compositional process informed by her burning desire to reinvigorate the concept of 'revolution,' but at the same time she is fully aware of how easily revolutionary ideas, such as hers, are coopted by the entertainment industry. "Hot Night" begins with the voice of Angela Davis in an excerpt from her speech *The Prison Industrial Complex*: "I was a member of the communist party. I'm not a member of the communist party, anymore—but I still consider myself very much a socialist. So we'll get to that later. One of the reasons why the war in Vietnam was able to happen as long as it did was because this—of this fear of communism. And people pointed to the Vietnamese as their enemy. As if somehow or another, if the country defeated the communist enemy in Vietnam, things were gonna be okay at home" (1999). Accompanying Davis is a sample of a two-measure horn riff from "La Fama" (1974) by Hector Lavoe, a well-known Puerto Rican salsa singer and bandleader. Musically, the salsa horn sample forms the groove for this piece, setting the tempo and harmonic flavor and providing the only truly melodic material. After the second cycle of the horn sample, Ndegéocello adds hip hop drums and bass line, accentuating the groove and defining the lower range left open by the trebly brass. In the salsa horn riff, the last two beats are unmarked—and in that space one hears Ndegéocello's creativity as a bass player, filling it in and taking us to the next downbeat, occasionally punctuated by a well-placed grunt. Politically, the combination of these two samples—Davis and Lavoe—creates a sonic realm in which both Vietnam and Puerto Rico are located as sites of American imperialism.

Furthermore, Angela Davis's vocal presence functions in two very important ways. First, her voice begins and ends this piece, forming a vocal frame around the rest of the music and clarifying its structure. She initiates the political dimension in global terms (Vietnam), and she concludes in local terms, with her indictment of the devastating effects of "welfare reform" on poor women in the United States. Second, sampling Davis also works as a musical tribute to her own long-term commitment to black women in music, culminating in her book *Blues Legacies and Black Feminism* but also apparent in many related articles prior to that book (Davis 1984, 1990, 1995).

Ndegéocello's own lyrics examine "the plight of a revolutionary soul singer" who struggles against a "romanticized idea of revolution/with saviors prophets and heroes" and laments that

> we all living in a world built upon
> rape, starvation, greed, need, fascist regimes
> white man, rich man, democracy
> suffer in a world trade paradise hear me now

In the second verse, Talib Kweli (of Black Star) attacks capitalism head-on in his rap filled with humorous rhymes and clever wordplay, and performed at breakneck speed. Kweli exposes the commodification of music and the need to confront a music industry interested only in markets and profit. Ndegéocello shares this view but knows that working as a musician—even as a "revolutionary soul singer"—in the larger machine of commerce is fraught with contradictions. In an interview with *Bass Player* magazine, Ndegéocello talks about visiting the plant of a company that wanted her to endorse their basses. She says that "they wouldn't send me one that worked, I knew I'd be their only black endorser, and when I went down to the plant there were all these older black women doing all the painting. I know I seem like I'm a fist-in-the-air rah-rah-rah activist, but it was hard for me" (Leigh 2002, 81). (Mark Anthony Neal also quotes from this interview but does not a pursue a specifically feminist analysis of Ndegéocello's music [Neal 2003].) Likewise, Angela Davis in her work has documented the recording industry's exploitation of African American women blues musicians, as well as their efforts to assert artistic and economic control. Thus, in "Hot Night" Ndegéocello creates and shares musical space with a like-minded activist and revolutionary soul singer passionately concerned with economic strife. Sonically and conceptually, each woman amplifies and clarifies the other's feminist voice, especially as we arrive at the end of this piece and Ndegéocello's phrase, "soul singer," embellishes Davis's words: "And now of course, that the welfare system has been disestablished and there are no jobs, so to speak, for women who are told that if they don't work, that's just too bad. They can only get welfare for a certain period of time and then they have to find a job. Now, they haven't had the opportunity to go to an institution like this [college]. They may not have the skills. Where are they going to find a job? And if they have children, how are they going to pay for childcare, in order to guarantee the conditions which will allow them to work?" (Davis, 1999).

### III.

> It was this, Meridian thought, I have not wanted to face, this that has caused me to suffer: I am not to belong to the future. I am to be left, listening to the old music, beside the highway. But then, she thought, perhaps it will be my part to walk behind the real revolutionaries—those who know they must spill blood in order to help the poor and the black and therefore go right ahead—and when they stop to wash off the blood and find their throats too choked with the smell of murdered flesh to sing, I will come forward and sing from memory songs they will need once more to hear. For it is the song of the people, transformed by the experiences of each generation, that holds them together, and if any part of it is lost the people suffer and are without soul. If I can only do that, my role will not have been a useless one after all.
> —Alice Walker, *Meridian*

Although a small handful of artists in popular music celebrate queer sexuality, very few (if any) have directly challenged homophobia. (One notable exception is Linda Tillery's song, "Don't Pray For Me," which openly condemns Anita Bryant's homophobic campaign of the mid-1970s [Tillery 1977].) Ndegéocello's "Leviticus: Faggot" rails against parental homophobia as legitimized by narrow interpretations of Christianity. This was a song she wrote and recorded on an earlier album entitled *Peace Beyond Passion* (1996), a critically acclaimed concept album exploring the tension between religious dogma and spiritual quest. Leviticus, of course, is the Old Testament book listing the instructions for religious ceremonies and ritual cleanliness, including a set of sexual prohibitions. Leviticus 18:22 states: "No man is to have sexual relations with another man; that is a hateful thing," and the punishment appears in 20:13: "If a man has sexual relations with another man, they have committed an abomination, and both shall be put to death. Their blood will be on their own heads." These are the two quotations commonly used in our culture to justify homophobia, violence against queers, and antigay sentiment in general. (Historically, counterdemonstrators at queer rallies or marches make consistent use of these two passages from Leviticus, waving them on their signs and banners.)

In Ndegéocello's song "Leviticus: Faggot" a gay son is violently rejected by his father, while his mother claims an unsympathetic piety, praying to Jesus to "save him from this life." Her other line is "The wages of sin are surely death." As Judith Casselberry notes in her insightfully detailed analysis of the lyrics, "Not only do sexism, racism, homophobia, and classism permeate our society, they invade our individual homes and psyches" (1999, 107). At age sixteen, the son is kicked out of their house, turns tricks on the street for money, and winds up beaten to death. "Faggot" is used initially by the father to refer to his son, but later we learn that the son's name is Michael. Such naming humanizes and dignifies the gay man, directing our empathy toward him, while his parents remain generic—Daddy and Mama—depicting this family tragedy as commonplace rather than isolated or unusual.

> *Verse 1:*
> Hey Faggot better run, run, learn to run cuz Daddy's home
> Daddy's sweet little boy just a little too sweet
> And every night the man showed the faggot what a real man
>     should be
> But the man and the faggot will never see
> For so many can't even perceive a real man
> Tell me
> It's not that the faggot didn't find a woman fine and beautiful
> He admired desired their desires
> He wanted love from strong hands
> The faggot wanted the love of a man

Michael's story unfolds in third-person narration. Ndegéocello's vocal performance of the lyrics creates an interesting dramatic portrayal of each of the parents. Ndegéocello delivers both verses by speaking or chanting the text. Sung melody is reserved for the mother, and her role in the drama lies almost entirely in the chorus with her prayer to "save him from this life." Ndegéocello's voice is overdubbed in two-part harmony to evoke a church choir sound.

*Chorus:*
His mother would pray
Save him, save him, save him from this life

However, at the bridge, Ndegéocello shifts from third-person narrator into first person, adopting the persona of "the faggot" and therefore aligning herself with Michael's oppression. At this shift the music also changes: the texture thins out considerably, the lead guitar disappears, the groove is less funky; piano and strings are more prominent. Ndegéocello as Michael asks, "[W]ho will care for me? [W]ho will love me?" The most remarkable moment arrives in the extended coda (entirely in Michael's narrative voice) in which Ndegéocello quotes from and expands the spiritual "Swing Low, Sweet Chariot":

Swing low, my sweet chariot
Let me rise above my fear
Let me rise above my sadness
Let me rise above my tears
Swing low, my sweet chariot
Let me rise
Let my conscience be clear as I rise, as I rise

During slavery, spirituals were collective musical articulations of hope and freedom. As Angela Davis, James Cone, and others have shown, the spirituals utilized the vocabulary of Christian suffering and redemption to cloak the more subversive messages of insurrection and escape—messages that went undetected by white slave owners who only heard the surface-level Christian meaning (Davis 1984, Cone 1972). Davis writes: "But even when the spirituals were not linked to specific actions in the freedom struggle, they always served, epistemologically and psychologically, to shape the consciousness of the masses of Black people, guaranteeing that the fires of freedom would burn within them. [. . .] The spirituals have directly influenced the music of other people's movements at various moments in the history of the United States. [. . .] [T]he 'freedom songs' of the Civil Rights movement were spirituals whose lyrics were sometimes slightly altered in order to reflect more concretely the realities of that struggle" (1984, 202–03). Ndegéocello's appropriation of a spiritual in the service of an antihomophobic message continues this tradition, extending the subversive appropriation of Christian rhetoric and reclaiming this aspect of black musical culture more specifically for black queers.

Some listeners to "Leviticus: Faggot" will undoubtedly hear a connection to the end of Parliament's "Mothership Connection (Star Child)" from 1975, which also quotes "Swing Low Sweet Chariot." Indeed, Ndegéocello often identifies Parliament's music as inspirational to her, especially Bootsy Collins on bass. I would argue, however, that Parliament's quotation of "Swing Low" serves a rather different purpose—one more interested in partying than in protesting homophobia. Ndegéocello claims that "Leviticus: Faggot" is a reference to Funkadelic's "Jimmy's Got a Little Bit of Bitch in Him" from their 1974 album *Standing on the Verge of Getting It On* (Powell, 1996). "Jimmy" is a playful, flamboyant tune about the unconventional gender traits of a gay man. However, the political courage and lyrical-musical complexities of "Leviticus: Faggot" far surpass those of "Jimmy."

"Leviticus: Faggot" and other songs I will discuss later inevitably raise the question of Ndegéocello's own sexuality. Since the earliest days of her recording career she has granted interviews with mainstream newspapers, the popular music press, the African American press, and the lesbian/gay press in which she has spoken openly about her relationships with dancer-choreographer Winifred Harris and author-activist Rebecca Walker. Over the years she has referred to herself as gay, bisexual, lesbian, and "a femme in a butch body" (Phoenix 1994, 33). Arguably, such a collection of terms might render her an apt representative of "queer" and its boundary-crossing inclusiveness, but to the best of my knowledge, Ndegéocello has never used that term about herself in public. Instead, she has emphatically criticized the white male connotations of "gay" (Darling 1994, Charles 1996, Moore 2002, Thomas 2002, Fullwood 2002, Watts 2002). She has repeatedly complained that mainstream images of "gay life . . . [are] patterned off of a white gay male aesthetic" (Moore 2002, 42), which is produced and circulated by popular music, film, and television and which erases the lives and ideas of queer people of color. In a parallel vein, Ndegéocello has decried the limits of musical categories, lamenting that the marketing interests of record labels, radio stations, and music stores want black musicians to fit easily into the genres of jazz, rock, funk, rhythm and blues, soul, hip hop, and so on (McDonnell 1994–95, Powell 1996, Powers 1996, Walker 1997, Johnson 2001, Thomas 2002). Ndegéocello is a creative musician and songwriter who draws from all of these traditions (as do many other artists). The categories of sexual identity *and* musical genre frustrate her because they both erase difference and deny complexity. That said, I am less concerned with a precise definition of Ndegéocello's own sexuality and more interested in how she articulates a feminist politics of sexuality (including homosexuality and homophobia) in her music.

### IV.

> The erotic is a measure between the beginnings of our sense of self and the chaos of our strongest feelings. It is an internal sense of satisfaction to which, once we have experienced it, we know we can aspire. For having experienced the fullness of this depth of feeling and recognizing its power, in honor and self-respect we can require no less of ourselves. [. . .]
>
> In touch with the erotic, I become less willing to accept powerlessness, or those other supplied states of being which are not native to me, such as resignation, despair, self-effacement, depression, self-denial.
>
> —Audre Lorde, "Uses of the Erotic: The Erotic as Power"

On the anthropological mixtape, Ndegéocello examines homophobia in yet another context. In her tune "Barry Farms," homophobia is rooted not so much in biblical condemnation but in teenage peer pressure to conform to heterosexual norms even when sexual experimentation violates those norms. "Barry Farms" describes Shorty, a seventeen-year-old straight woman who becomes sexually involved with a queer woman, MeShell, and needs to keep it secret. (Here I use "MeShell" to refer to the narrative persona in this song, distinct from Ndegéocello as composer-performer.) Ndegéocello sings from the lesbian perspective, exposing Shorty's sexual objectification of MeShell and her homophobic betrayal. In the chorus, Ndegéocello claims, "She couldn't love me without shame, she only wanted me for one thing." Indeed, according to Shorty, sex with MeShell is superior to sex with her boyfriend. However, MeShell refuses to be Shorty's girl-toy and retorts, "you can teach your boy to do that."

"Barry Farms" belongs to the genre of go-go music, an off-shoot of funk that emerged in Washington, D.C., in the late 1960s and was popularized in the 1980s by bands such as Experience Unlimited, Rare Essence, and Little Bennie and the Masters. Go-go is typically characterized by a "loping, percussion-driven shuffle beat" (Leigh 2002, 46). The title, "Barry Farms" is the name of a large housing project in a predominantly black section of Washington, D.C. Thus, in both the song's title and the use of go-go music, Ndegéocello essentially locates the drama in a black urban context, thereby identifying lesbianism and homophobia as real and relevant to African Americans and making a crucial intervention into the overwhelming whiteness that has defined much of queer politics and popular culture in the United States.

The opening bars of "Barry Farms" set up the peculiar tension that permeates this piece on several levels. First, we hear the voice of Kiggo Wellman, a virtuoso drummer well known for his work in go-go music, and it is he who plays the drums and other percussion in this tune. He introduces the song by announcing, "go go music is party music." Second, shortly after Wellman establishes the groove, we hear Ndegéocello's voice: a hissing whisper, almost as if she is mimicking the cymbals on the hi-hat. Her whisper ("slice 'em on up"), both seductive and ominous, indicates that we are about to enter a world of secrets. The complexity of this world is suggested musically by the sharp contrast between the drums and the harmonic palette. While drums and percussion form the center of the mix, providing the groove's energy and elasticity, harmonically, the g-sharp minor chords are relentless, never straying until the very end of the piece.

As the narrative of shame, betrayal, and pain unfolds, Wellman's "go go music is party music" is rendered ironic—this is go-go, but it certainly is not "party music." Ndegéocello then shifts into her signature vocal style of speaking and singing, but later on in the piece's climactic moment, she returns to that whisper, this time *a cappella*, to deliver the words Shorty cannot bring herself to speak out loud: "can't nobody eat my pussy the way that you do."

In the chorus, MeShell ultimately rejects Shorty, and the power of her confrontation is marked by the shift from third person "she" to direct address—"you." In addition, the strings (a synthesizer meant to sound like strings) play an ascending melodic line, strengthening that assertion and in a sense asking us to sympathize with MeShell, not Shorty. The dissonance of that line's A-sharp against the G-sharp minor harmony intensifies the conflict inherent in MeShell's confrontation.

> *Verse 2:*
> now word had been gettin' around town that shorty and I
> we was a little bit more than just friends
> and see, she wasn't really feeling that
> so she stopped calling me
> then one day i ran into her
> she was hanging out with this young boy that liked to take her
>     around and buy her things

and you know how we like material things
and then she walked over, licked her lips
and whispered in my ear and she said,
*"you know i've missed you baby"*
I said, *"cool"*
and I said, *"tell me, tell me what do you miss?"*
she said, *"can't nobody eat my pussy the way that you do"*

*Chorus:*
she couldn't love me without shame
she only wanted me for one thing
but you should teach your boy to do that
can you love me without shame?
I need you when I feel pain
but now you like to fuck around

In his book, *Songs in the Key of Black Life*, Mark Anthony Neal discusses "Barry Farms" (along with most of the other tunes on *Cookie*), observing that this song "highlights how even lesbian sex does not necessarily translate into a feminist politics that rejects the objectification of black female sexuality or resist[s] a heterosexist paradigm" (2003, 19–20). I agree with Neal's claim, but he misses an even more fundamental issue: lesbian sex, enjoying lesbian sex, does not challenge homophobia, let alone eradicate it. This goes for participants as well as voyeurs of lesbian sex, hence the long historical tradition of straight men who consume lesbian images in pornography but could care less about the well-being of "real" lesbians. Furthermore, Neal fails to acknowledge that in "Barry Farms," it is the lesbian voice in charge of the narrative, the lesbian as active subject who condemns Shorty's homophobia. When listened to in this way, we actually hear a very old feminist politics at work in "Barry Farms," namely, its function as an "advice song," a common strategy of the women's blues music from the 1920s and 30s (Davis 1998). Ndegéocello initially addresses "all the Shorties in the house" warning them not to treat other women as their secret girl toys. Simultaneously, she reminds queer women what they can expect if they become involved with the proverbial Shorty. In *Blues Legacies and Black Feminism*, Angela Davis argues convincingly that the public identification of taboo "private" issues such as male violence against women, the myth of marital bliss, lesbian sexuality, and homophobia were central to the work of blues women, including none other than Ma Rainey and Bessie Smith. According to

Davis, addressing these issues openly in their music (both in live performances and on recordings) was a way of removing them from the secrecy of the private sphere and exposing them as social problems requiring political attention, much the way the second-wave feminist movement would do forty years later (Davis 1998, 28). Similarly, Ndegéocello continues this tradition of feminist resistance to heteropatriarchy by creating a space in which she names homophobia as a social problem worthy of public discourse and asks her listeners to think critically about homophobia beyond the realm of the personal.

Patricia Hill Collins, Evelyn Hammonds, Jackie Goldsby, and bell hooks have thoroughly documented the ways black female sexuality—lesbian or not—is always constructed as deviant and excessive (Collins 2000, Hammonds 1997, Goldsby 1993, hooks 1992). Ndegéocello is less interested in repeating that analysis and more concerned with claiming subjectivity and sexual agency for black women in particular and for queer women for whom the scenario portrayed in "Barry Farms" is more common than not.

The music at the end of "Barry Farms" undergoes a dramatic change of character. The static, trapped G-sharp minor harmony expands to a more fluid four-chord progression (played on keyboards/organ) that moves farther afield, and the bass comes alive, reaching into the upper register with energetic fills. This change in harmonic motion, timbre, and groove evokes a libratory transformation—freedom from the oppression of secrecy—signaled by the message of honesty and truth in the lyrics. The four-note melody in the keyboards is taken up by the synthstrings. As the music fades, Kiggo Wellman's voice returns: "When I play, I watch the crowd. I watch the women—women party—chain reaction." Like "Hot Night," Ndegéocello employs a vocal frame to mark the beginning and ending of this piece. The effects are rather different, though. The samples of Angela Davis are quite lengthy, and the power of her ideas forms the central source of the political potency of "Hot Night.'" Wellman's brief words seem odd and barely related to the queer emotional intensity of "Barry Farms." Nevertheless, the music continues without pause as this song segues into "Trust," and Ndegéocello moves from the pain of homophobic hypocrisy to the pleasures of sexual intimacy. As to the particular type of sexual intimacy (homo, hetero, bisexual), this song certainly invites a number of interpretations. While the lyrics alone do not specify a male or female beloved, and the phrase "you're so hard" suggests a heterosexual encounter, there is no palpable male presence in the music. Therefore, I pursue a lesbian reading of "Trust." (Had soul/rhythm and blues vocalist Maxwell agreed to sing on this song as originally planned, "Trust" would not sound nearly as queer to me.) Caron Wheeler, black British vocalist well-known for her work with Soul II Soul, joins Ndegéocello on "Trust," and the sound of both women singing to one another effectively decenters a heterosexual reading of the lyrics:

*Verse 1*
put your tongue in my mouth
make me wet
run your hands down my back
grab my ass
lay me down
spread my legs
tell me what it's like

*Chorus*
inside me
inside me
oh yeah
inside me

*Verse 2*
you're so hard
so warm baby
so deep
deep
let me hold you closer baby
i won't let go
let me stroke you with my warmth
make you come

In verse 1, the lyrics initiate a frank carnality issued as a series of commands to the beloved who then responds in the first chorus. Verse 2 describes the lover's perceptions of her partner and how she aims to please her beloved. The second chorus is elongated, adding an emotional component to the erotic in the form of questions and answers:

inside me
inside me
yeah, does it feel good?
inside me
can't you feel my sadness?

> inside me
> can't you feel?
> so deep

Here, the erotic double meanings of the words "inside me" and "feel" express both physical and emotional intimacy.

In "Trust," Ndegéocello assembles an incredibly sensuous combination of tempo, timbres, and textures to convey erotic seduction and ecstasy. The piece begins with a spare accompaniment and sultry pace: a basic drum pattern that simply marks the beat while a short melodic riff in the keyboards repeats in each measure. The bass outlines a two-measure harmonic progression that does not change throughout the song. The harmonic cycle is enhanced by the piano and doubled on synth-violin in a repeating two-measure melodic motif that gracefully stretches over the bass line. Though the notes of this melodic motif fall directly *on* the beat, emphasizing the slow tempo, the shimmering piano-violin timbre adds a delicate tenderness to the overall emotional soundscape. Drums, bass, piano, and synth-violin maintain the harmonic and rhythmic stability (much like an *ostinato*) around which the changes in timbre and texture arise. The magnificent guitar solo (at 3:32), for instance, introduces another timbral shift but lends melodic cohesion by borrowing directly from the keyboards' opening riff.

Ultimately, the erotic energy of "Trust" lies in the vocal interplay between Ndegéocello and Wheeler. Ndegéocello sings the first verse in her characteristically deep, husky voice, staying mostly in the alto range. Wheeler's voice is quite different: lighter and revealing a beautifully florid agility in the upper range. Her performance does not conform to the role of "back-up singer." Even though she sings a smaller portion of the lyrics, sonically she is an equal partner in the vocal texture. Wheeler sings the refrain ("inside me") and embellishes the word "deep" in the second verse. Both women share the extended second chorus as they exchange lines of lyrics and Wheeler answers Ndegéocello's questions:

> CW: inside me
> MN: yeah, does it feel good?
> CW: inside me
> MN: can't you feel my sadness?
> CW: inside me
> MN: can't you feel?
> CW: yeah, yeah
> [etc.]

Wheeler and Ndegéocello respond to one another with more immediacy as the temporal distance between each utterance shortens and their voices gradually overlap, thus intensifying their vocal intimacy. The sounds of breathing become more audible. The pleasure of the moment is enhanced by the musical accompaniment's avoidance of both harmonic resolution and rhythmic closure. After the guitar solo, Ndegéocello's voice fades away, yielding to Wheeler, who abandons words altogether and continues singing in long phrases of nonverbal syllables. The bass and trap set drop out to make room for an abundant rhythmic texture of maracas/shakers, xylophone, cowbell, and hand drums. The passionate intensity of this musical transformation is breathtaking. Wheeler's wordless vocalizations join the timbrally rich percussion to produce a kind of textural ecstasy—a musical *jouissance*.

### V.

> Mary Magdalene's palm leaf to you, dearest whore.
> Flash it across your sex back and forth like a
> shoe shine rag more gently with as much dedication
> while I (and the one you sleep with tonight instead
> of me) watch and wait for the miracle
> weave it into a cross pray to it
> wear it as headband and wristband
> tie your ankle to the bedpost with it
> tongue of the holy ghost
> palm leaf of Mary Magdalene.
> —Cheryl Clarke, "palm leaf of Mary Magdalene"

"Barry Farms" and "Trust" are not Ndegéocello's first foray into the complexities of nonnormative black female sexuality. On *Peace Beyond Passion*, "Mary Magdalene" is an exquisite lesbian fantasy in which Ndegéocello queers the Bible story of Mary Magdalene's encounter with Jesus, casting her as a misunderstood sex worker completely worthy of dignity, love, and respect. Ndegéocello not only appropriates the savior role of Jesus but further sexualizes that role as a black woman openly desiring the "undesirable" Mary, audaciously subverting a number of oppressive binary oppositions within patriarchy: white/black, male/female, hetero/homo, sacred/secular, and virgin/whore.

> *Verse 1:*
> I often watch you the way you whore yourself
> *You're so beautiful*

*You flirt and tease* enviously *I wish you'd flirt with me*
Perhaps I'm enticed by what you are
I imagine us jumpin' the broom foolish I know
*that's not the life you live*
*You live alone in a crowded bed* never remembering faces
    conversations
just a body for the lonely
*Spend one night with me satisfy me for free*
*and I'll love you endlessly*
You always tell them you'll give them what they want
So give me what I want
*Chorus:*
*Tell me I'm the only one*
*I want to marry you*
Tell me I'm the only one

In their extremely detailed analysis of "Mary Magdalene," Mélisse LaFrance and Lori Burns argue that in this song "Ndegéocello's compositional strategies subvert and displace many operative sites of both white and masculine supremacy" (2002, 134), and she successfully "challenges many regimes of the normal" (2002, 147). Burns's musical analysis focuses on "attributions of power" that alternate between Ndegéocello and Mary. The ground bass, harmonic, rhythmic, and melodic elements perform important structural and dramatic roles, but Ndegéocello's vocal delivery best articulates the circulation of power and desire. Her combination of speaking and singing works to distinguish desiring subject from desired object, potentially containing Mary in the "fixed" position of other. However, Burns argues:

> [T]he musical presentation lends the Other her own potential for dramatic "movement." The subject's reflections are presented in spoken form, while the Other is presented in an elaborated melodic form. The Other is, in that context, not in a "fixed" position after all. This second conception of the Other (imbued with the power of movement) might be understood as a contradiction of the former image (in a "fixed" position). However, I would prefer to privilege neither one, but rather to explore the potential of each and to celebrate the equal distribution of dramatic-musical power between subject and object that results. I believe that this is a musical representation of the revised conception of the sexual "gaze" discussed earlier. (Burns and LaFrance 2002, 154)

For instance, the text of the sung phrases (noted above in the lyrics marked in italics) address Mary directly, and the melodic patterns

Ndegéocello sings rarely coincide rhythmically with the ground bass pattern, granting an active independence to Mary's persona and erotic power. Burns concludes that this "song develops a sexual gaze in which the object is not only permitted but encouraged to assume a position of strength.... [Ndegéocello] succeeds in creating a distinct subject and object by associating each with her own musical domain; that is, the subject can celebrate her own discursive power in the domain of rhythm and meter, while the object is granted power in the domain of melody and counterpoint.

The musical ascription of power to both subject and object comprises a significant revision of a conventional construct, the sexual gaze" (Burns and LaFrance 2002, 166–67). I agree with this reading, but I also detect additional dimensions of the sexual politics at work in "Mary Magdalene." The first emerges at the narrative level—a queer woman's desire for a prostitute—and alludes to the "historical sisterhood" between lesbians and prostitutes. In her essay, "Lesbians and Prostitutes: An Historical Sisterhood," Joan Nestle identifies the myriad ways western culture has demonized women who are lesbians, prostitutes, or both (1987). Likewise, Evelynn Hammonds historicizes the links between black female sexuality and prostitution (1997). The discourses of language (especially slang), religion, medicine and psychiatry, laws and politicians, police and prisons have historically constructed lesbians and prostitutes as deviant, damaged, diseased—or not women at all. As sexually outlawed women, their histories of resistance and survival have sometimes overlapped, particularly in the creation of working-class subcultures. Nestle and Hammonds each points out that certain middle-class corners of the feminist movement have shunned both lesbians and sex trade workers as undesirable others.

Ndegéocello herself has admitted to a certain fascination with sex workers, and her interactions with them probably inspired her to write "Mary Magdalene." In her interview with Rebecca Walker, she says:

> What turns me on is if I can get close enough to them [erotic dancers] so they tell me what they feel when they're doing that. I want to know what *they're* thinking. [. . .]
>
> When I was in high school, I used to hang out in Dupont Circle and watch prostitutes. There was always one that I thought was absolutely beautiful. I was fascinated by her demeanor, her rudeness. She was, like, "Come on, tell me what you want me to do." And I was, like, Damn, come tell *me* that!
>
> I guess I'm still trying to figure out why the woman goes to jail. What about arresting the man? And I always wonder, do they receive any kindness, or are they just beat to the pavement from giving their bodies? I like talking to them because I don't pose a threat to them, and they don't know who I am, and that makes for some of the best conversations I've ever had. (1997, 82)

In "Mary Magdalene" Ndegéocello recasts both the dyke and the whore as fully human, restoring their sexual power and agency in a fantasy of sweet romance. This song is a musical illustration of Nestle's and Hammonds's observations, this time located in an interracial context.

In addition, I hear a butch-femme dynamic in the two musical domains of Burns's analysis. First, in terms of the narrative, Ndegéocello claims the masculine subject position (and its attendant power and privilege) by appropriating the role of Jesus and reinventing that role as MeShell, a butch lesbian who desires Mary Magdalene. (Here again I distinguish between "MeShell" as the narrative persona in the song and Ndegéocello as composer/performer.) In the lyrics Mary is described as "beautiful," she "flirts and teases" and wears a dress, revealing some of her femme traits. Second, and even more compelling, is Ndegéocello's vocal portrayal of MeShell and Mary as butch and femme. As Burns points out, spoken text and its rhythmic intricacies are associated with MeShell, while sung text and melodic elaboration connote Mary's power. I wish to queer Burns's analysis further. Ndegéocello performs a butch MeShell by pitching her speaking voice in the lower range, a vocal space normally inhabited by tenors and baritones. Whenever I play "Mary Magdalene" for students, friends, or colleagues, they usually respond to Ndegéocello's voice by saying "that sounded like a guy . . . I didn't realize this was a woman until she *sang*." Her deep speaking voice and clipped rhythms avoid the effusiveness of melody and evoke a studly restraint in her tale of longing. By the same token, the allure of Mary's femmeness is characterized by the higher-pitched melodic phrases, always sung *legato*, and—like makeup or jewelry—made fancier by the overdubbing in the chorus.

The sound of a butch-femme dynamic in "Mary Magdalene" is meaningful for at least two reasons. First, critical work on butch-femme has focused almost exclusively on visual components—the sartorial, gestural, and behavioral characteristics of lesbian masculinity and femininity. These are very important features, of course, if one accepts that lesbian visibility is intimately connected to cultural intelligibility and political legitimacy. However, this line of inquiry has muted other questions of how butch-femme is constructed and/or perceived through sound, music, voice. Thus, Ndegéocello's performance in "Mary Magdalene" invites a reconsideration of music as a significant space of butch-femme desire. Second, butch-femme has been studied and theorized almost entirely by white, lesbian writers (mostly academic), yet the larger field (historical and contemporary) of butch-femme life reveals great diversity. In "Mary Magdalene," Ndegéocello joins Jewelle Gomez, Gladys Bentley, Mabel Hampton and Lillian Foster, Cheryl Clarke, Mildred Gerestant, and many other artists to remind us of black women's varied and spirited participation in butch-femme.

To conclude, I have argued that Ndegéocello employs a feminist sensibility in her compositional process—how she goes about assembling music and texts and the sensory effects of her choices. However, she expresses an ambivalent relationship to feminism. In an interview from 1994, she claims a contradictory position: "I'm not a feminist, [. . .] Feminism is a white concept for white, middle-class women who want to have the same opportunities as their white, male counterparts. We can fight our men, or we can fight the system. [. . .] To me, an issue is all the women—black and white—who are on welfare" (Seigal 1994, F-1). In a later interview from 1997, when asked, "How do you feel about the word 'feminist'?" she offers a more flirtatious reply: "I don't know what a feminist is. If I see a beautiful woman, I stare. Is that not being a feminist?" (Jamison 1997, 161). Part of the problem here is that "feminism" is not defined in popular press interviews with Ndegéocello (or with other women musicians in general), which inadvertently sets up feminism as something to dismiss or avoid. In more recent years "feminism" and "feminist" are completely absent from popular press coverage of Ndegéocello. Certainly her rejection of feminism as white and middle class is shared by many women of color across generations who have encountered racism and/or classism from white women active in the mainstream women's movement or who self-identified as feminist. Yet, many of Ndegéocello's concerns about class, racism, homophobia, and the limits of identity politics are indeed *feminist* issues. She resists the *term* feminist but not necessarily the ideals of feminism, especially those that encompass a more complex vision of liberation and address the differences *between* women in productive ways. In this sense, she is in concert with a community of American feminists of color who understand themselves variously as "mestiza," "sister outsider," "woman warrior," or "womanist" (Anzaldúa 1987, Lorde 1984, Kingston 1977, Walker 1983, Sandoval 2000). Their works—as poetry, fiction, memoir, and academic feminist theory—have clearly demonstrated the need to conceptualize gender and the category "woman" *in terms of* race, class, and sexuality, because each of those systems casts "woman" differently in a "white supremacist capitalist patriarchy" (hooks 1992). Ndegéocello makes a compelling musical contribution to this very same project, challenging her listeners to hear the connections and inviting us to enjoy it in the process and to think harder about how her music participates in feminist struggle.

# 5

## Portraits of the Past, Imagined Now

### Reading the Work of Carrie Mae Weems and Lorna Simpson

KIMBERLY LAMM

Carrie Mae Weems' *Mirror, Mirror* (1987–88, figure 5.1), from her *Ain't Jokin'* series, is a photograph of a black woman holding up a mirror that does not reflect her image. Her face is turned away, and her eyes are cast downward. Her expression suggests a melancholy shadowed by exhausted disgust. In the place of her reflection, we see the image she responds to: a light-skinned or white woman shrouded in white gauze. As if to emphasize how the mirage of whiteness registers itself in the assumed actuality of black skin, Weems has photographed the black woman in a sleeveless night dress with thin shoulder straps, exposing the skin of her arm, neck, and back, which contrasts sharply with the white gauze and its blurry, billowing effect. With fingers converging behind a rough, silvery starfish that stains the mirror's surface, the woman in the mirror seems to be casting a spell. Moreover, Weems has reconfigured *Snow White's* most famous lines and placed them beneath the photograph: "Looking into the mirror, the black woman asked, 'Mirror, Mirror on the wall, who's the finest of them all?' The Mirror says, 'Snow White, you black bitch, and don't you forget it!!!'" This cruel call-and-response shapes our reading of *Mirror, Mirror* and reveals how the mythologies of white femininity produce visual codes that depend upon racist negations. An image of woman split along racial lines, *Mirror, Mirror* corresponds to, but also complicates, Lorraine O'Grady's analysis of Western culture's racial division of the female body: "The female body in the West is not a unitary sign. Rather, like a coin, it has an obverse and a reverse: on the one side, it is white; on the other, not-white or, prototypically, black. The two bodies cannot be separated, nor can one body be understood in isolation from the other in

FIGURE 5.1. Carrie Mae Weems, "Mirror, Mirror" (from *Ain't Jokin'*) (1987–1988)

the West's metaphoric construction of 'woman.' White is what woman is; not-white (and the stereotypes not-white gathers in) is what she had better not be" (O'Grady 1992, 152).

*Mirror, Mirror* exposes the racism within white femininity's perceptual and cultural syntax. That is, the piece depicts white women's dependence upon black women for their embodiment of "what woman is." Furthermore, Weems's revision of *Snow White*'s lines reveals the severity with which this division is policed. While this punitive interpellation announces and insists upon strict divisions among "black" and "white" women, the grays and continuum of tones Weems renders in this photograph suggest otherwise. Moreover, it is significant that Weems places the white woman—not the black woman—on the imaginary side of the mirror. In other words, *Mirror, Mirror* is not another representation of the black woman constructed in the cultural eye of whiteness but instead reveals the image of white femininity haunting the history and self-perceptions of black women. This is how, *Mirror, Mirror* argues, white femininity's proprietary claim to beauty continues to impinge upon black women's self-portrayals. *Mirror, Mirror* exposes grim realities, but the multiple framings and deliberate constructedness of the image do suggest the possibilities of undoing, reimagining, and remaking the scene it depicts.

Less explicitly but no less critically, Lorna Simpson's *Twenty Questions (A Sampler)* (1986, figure 5.2) also reveals how the imbricated ideologies of racism and sexism make beauty the property of white femininity. *Twenty Questions (A Sampler)* is a series of four circular black-and-white photographs depicting the back of a black woman's head. The woman in the photograph wears a sleeveless white cotton shift that falls just below her neck. Shot from behind rather than head-on, the photographs focus on the woman's hair. Somewhere between a straightened style and a natural curl, the woman's hairstyle brings the cultural symbolism and political resonance of black women's hair into the work's questioning of beauty. The engraved plastic plaques, which Simpson has placed beneath and between the photographs, are crucial to the multiple levels of questioning at work in *Twenty Questions (A Sampler)*. The first plaque asks, "Is she pretty as a picture," a quaint and old-fashioned question, which corresponds to the photographs' circular shapes and their evocation of a cameo's antique charm. This slight invocation of charm is quickly undercut as the plaque begins a series of clichéd questions that reveal the malevolent racial valences working within the hierarchical codes of feminine beauty. The second and third plaques evoke the

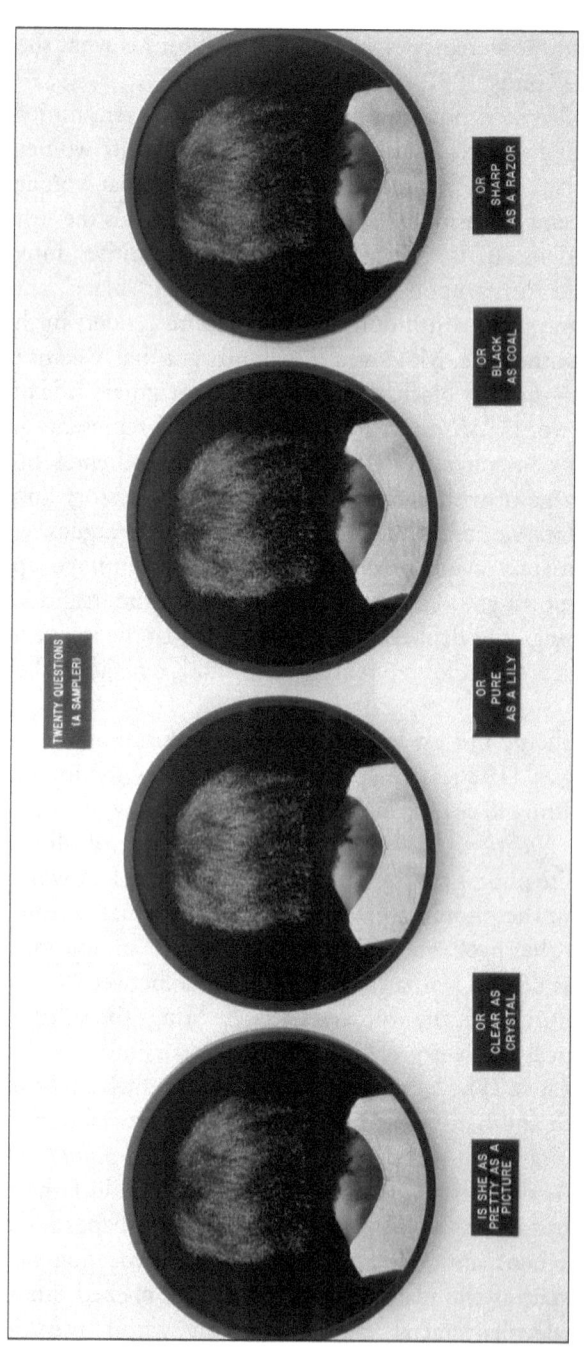

FIGURE 5.2. Lorna Simpson, "Twenty Questions (A Sampler)" (1986)

assumed "innocence" and "transparency" of whiteness; the last two evoke a racist logic that associates blackness with "soot" and "danger." These similes are not presented in a straightforward way, but exactly how Simpson critiques them is difficult to pinpoint. Her critique can be located in the suggestions that emerge from the work's composition. For example, Simpson places the question "Is she pure as a lily," which harkens back to nineteenth-century ideas about white ladyship, near the work's center, directly below the title. This question highlights the moralizing and policing of sexuality at work in perceptions of beauty, and the placement suggests the question produces and separates the same image of a black woman without the expressive qualities of a particular face. Moreover, since each question is set in relation to an image repeated four times, *Twenty Questions (A Sampler)* suggests that all questions about women's prettiness are basically the same.

Through a deceptively simple compositional arrangement, *Twenty Questions (A Sampler)* asks viewers to confront the nexus of racism and sexism informing habitual perceptions of "prettiness" and "pictures" and then reflect upon the insidious damage they cause. The back of the model's head seems to be a preemptive rejection of such inquiries and makes answering the questions the plaques pose irrelevant, as it refutes the conflation of a woman, her image, and an assessment of her prettiness. Together, the defiant opacity of the model's head, the anonymity of a ready-made sampler (which the repetition of the same photograph exemplifies), and the set of clichéd, irrelevant questions that cannot be answered all suggest a sad banality.

When analyzing or responding to the decidedly contemporary work of Weems and Simpson, portraiture might not come quickly to mind, as it is often still assumed to be transparent and objective. According to art historian Benjamin Buchloch, portraiture relies upon "the instantiation of the subject within a seemingly 'natural' iconic resemblance," and therefore can reinforce rather than refute longstanding cultural perceptions about the individual's correspondence to visual typologies (1994, 54). Moreover, the idea that portraiture visually expresses interior essences is one of the genre's longstanding assumptions, which dovetailed with ideas produced by and informing nineteenth-century science. In *American Anatomies: Theorizing Race and Gender*, Robyn Wiegman outlines nineteenth-century science's "newly developed technologies for rendering the invisible visible," which made "the visible epidermal terrain" represent "the interior structure of human bodies" (1995, 31). Wiegman argues this process of making the invisible visible produced a conception of race as "an inherent and incontrovertible difference of which skin was the most visible indication" (1995, 31). The exposure of and focus on structures inside the physical body transformed easily, it seems, into ideas about character and subjectivity, spiritual depths and psychological interiors. In her study *American Archives: Gender, Race, and Class in Visual Culture*, Shawn Michelle Smith analyzes the appearance of the photographic portrait in archives thought to be distinct—photo albums of America's emerging middle-class and Alphonse Bertillon's Rogue's Gallery of criminal types, for example—to argue that American visual culture of the nineteenth century, newly suffused with photography and increasingly characterized by social mutability, "produced a model of subjectivity in which exterior appearance was imagined to reflect interior essence" (1999, 4).

Both *Mirror, Mirror* and *Twenty Questions (A Sampler)* disrupt the instantaneity of naturalized perceptions and question the process through which images express interior essences and do so by critically engaging with portraiture. Calling attention to this engagement places Weems' and Simpson's work within historical frames that exceed the contemporary. It helps us see how these artists allude to and draw from African American art and visual culture from the nineteenth and early twentieth centuries, when the portrait was a prominent tool for asserting the honor, actuality, and visibility of African Americans. As *Mirror, Mirror* and *Twenty Questions (A Sampler)* make clear, Weems and Simpson are suspicious of such assertions about the portrait but do not wholly reject them either. Instead, they analyze how the portrait sutures one's image to the visual dimensions of the cultural symbolic; they examine the portrait's production of and participation in concepts such as 'honor,' 'actuality,' and 'visibility.' *Mirror, Mirror*, for example, is not a portrait in any expected sense; it does not display the portrait's seamless qualities. It depicts a black woman's attempt to see herself in the mirror of femininity's cultural value and exposes the visual components of racism and sexism as the impediments to this attempt by restaging, halting, and narrating their synthesis. *Mirror, Mirror* re-presents the portrait to depict a paradigmatic moment or stage in the subjective life of black women as they confront the cultural imperative to embody a negation that will sustain the visual and cultural prominence of white femininity.

Weems and Simpson take portraits apart to work within their codes and connotations, to reveal their participation in the production of race and gender, and to expose their tie to cultural concepts such as beauty and reproduction. In doing so, Weems and Simpson show that portraiture is much more than the standard visual genre for representing the individual;

it is a significant, often unnoticed part of a cultural apparatus that polices the codes through which individuals become visible. Certainly portraiture is not the only genre these artists engage with, and no doubt there are as many differences as there are similarities between Weems' and Simpson's work. However, I argue Weems and Simpson allude to and grapple with portraits of the past to reimagine black women's places in the visual dimensions of the American symbolic order. This argument places Weems and Simpson's work within traditions that precede postmodernism and identity politics. It calls attention to their work's continuation of and participation in an issue African American art and visual culture of the nineteenth and early twentieth century highlighted by necessity: negotiating between refutation and recognition. That is, because it emerged within hegemonies hostile to people of color shaping and asserting their visibility, one could argue African American art and visual culture moved between rejecting the frame of recognition offered by the dominant culture and insisting upon black peoples' place within it.

In the nineteenth century, the human sciences became prominent, and race was increasingly located in and identified through the body. In short, the body became racialized in the nineteenth century, and photography, invented in 1839, helped to produce and define the body as an image. Wiegman demonstrates that nineteenth-century human sciences not only justified white men's dominant place on the racial chain of being's hierarchical scale but also made the visual features of the human body into a code for identifying race. "[T]he corporeal," Wiegman writes, became "the bearer of race's meaning" (1995, 23). Moreover, on the comparative scale informing the racial chain of being, blackness was a "feminine racial formation," and African American women were placed there indirectly, or not at all (Wiegman, 1995, 55). Photography, which became a definitive part of visual culture after its midnineteenth-century appearance, contributed to producing the body as a system of signs and then identifying the body's physical signs through the categories of race and gender. While photographers borrowed poses and conventions of portrait paintings, photography put the portrait to uses that exceeded its previous, most often honorary, purposes. When used as visual evidence for the pseudosciences of physiognomy, phrenology, and craniology, the portrait, or rather, visual depictions derived from the portrait, became a prominent site for identifying and fixing a person through the visual economies of race and gender. Despite the portrait photograph's disciplinary potential, it also offered the opportunity to place oneself within the frame of cultural recognition. Wiegman argues that in the twentieth century, the visual "function[ed] . . .

as a newly configured public sphere," and certainly the photographic reproduction of the nineteenth century inaugurated the process by which the public and the visual began to tightly intersect (1995, 3). As the nineteenth century moved into the early twentieth, sitting for a portrait became an emblem of one's participation in the public sphere, and the portrait became a site of contestation about race, gender, and its meanings.

Central to my argument is Weems' installation entitled *From Here I Saw What Happened and I Cried* (1995–96). In this work, Weems reprints and reframes photographs of African Americans in the J. Paul Getty Museum's photography collection, many of which are nineteenth-century daguerreotypes, tintypes, and ambrotypes. In her re-presentation of these images, Weems made simple but suggestive choices. She enlarged the photographs, printed them in a bright but dark red, and placed them within circular black mats. Relatively subtle, these mediations suggest the images were, and still are, framed by cultural perception and do not objectively portray the facts of race, gender, sex, or flesh. They also suggest the signs highlighting the constructedness of images are not always easy to identify. On the glass placed over the images, Weems has meticulously inscribed words and phrases in Roman capitals; the letters cast thin shadows over the photographs. These words and phrases are the artist's response to the images and name the exploitation the photographs bear witness to visually. The photographs and Weems's inscriptions simultaneously compose a story of lives determined by slavery and subsequent forms of racial oppression in the United States. More specifically, *From Here I Saw What Happened and I Cried* attests to the denigrating images African Americans were forced to embody and the insidious work of justifying disenfranchisement these images performed.

At the opening of the installation, Weems re-presents four of Louis Agassiz's daguerreotypes of African American slaves from Columbia, South Carolina. Agassiz was an anthropologist who became influenced by Dr. Samuel Morton's theory of polygenesis (which proposed that the different races were "born" separately) and his vast collection of skulls. He traveled to the plantations of South Carolina and commissioned Joseph T. Zealy, a local daguerreotypist, to take these photographs in the hopes of proving the theory that various races were separate species (Wallis 1996, 102). In *Reading American Photographs*, Alan Trachtenberg notes the disjunction between the signs of portraiture in these photographs and the images themselves, which are "not 'representative' . . . of an imagined and desired America, but examples or specimens of a 'type'—a type, moreover, of complete otherness" (1989, 54). To render their adherence to anthropological types, the subjects have all been photographed naked, which contributes to the frank abjection of these images and their production of "complete otherness." In the profile photograph of a young woman, which was given the title *Delia, Country Born of African Parents, Daughter of Renty, Congo* (1850), the hint of clothing near the bottom of the image suggests that she has been told to take off her clothes for the purpose of this photograph. Analyzing these images, photography historian Deborah Willis writes, "The taking of the photograph reinforces the act of physically 'stripping' them of their clothes" (2002, 23). Though these photographs focused on the bare facts of flesh, they drew from a repertoire of compositional codes. The profile pose used in *Delia* is an instance of "the facial angle," which was the invention of eighteenth-century Dutch scientist Peter Camper. "The facial angle" facilitated measuring the tip of the forehead to the outermost point of the lips and was a crucial tool for comparative physiognomic studies (Wallis 1996, 105). This daguerreotype shows how the profile view creates visual alignments between the side of the breast and the side of the face, therefore underscoring arguments that concepts of sex subtend the concepts of race and therefore inform physiognomy's determinative mapping of the body.

Weems re-presents three other Agassiz photographs: two images of men and one of a woman. Photographed head on, these subjects look straight into the camera. In all four images, we see the presence of flesh and the subjects' lack of control over the visual presentation of that flesh. Because they have been reduced to their bodies, the stoic sorrow of their stares detaches them from the flesh they bear. Willis claims these images "convey" a "pornography of [the portrayed subjects'] forced labor and of their inability to determine whether or how their bodies would be displayed" (2002, 23). The frontal and profile views, the absence of expression, and the nakedness were unquestioned conventions in the classificatory projects of anthropology as well as comparative physiognomic studies. These conventions fostered the purpose of recording, and then comparing, the shapes and proportions of the specimens' bodies. Together these conventions signify the "objective" presentation of flesh and a clear understanding of its meanings. From the vantage point of the present—"from here"—it is clear these conventions, combined with the assumption that daguerreotypes reproduced reality with exactitude, naturalized racist perceptions, proved the superiority of the white race, and therefore justified slavery. Moreover, these images reveal the powerful rhetorical and political purposes to which the photograph's assumed neutrality can be put.

Weems strikes a delicate balance between questioning the codes of photographic objectivity and allowing the images to testify to actual occurrences with abiding consequences. In her inscriptions, Weems addresses the people in the photographs with a clear and sympathetic accuracy. Across the Agassiz daguerreotypes, she writes: "YOU BECAME A SCIENTIFIC PROFILE"/"A NEGROID TYPE"/"AN ANTHROPOLOGICAL DEBATE"/"& A PHOTOGRAPHIC SUBJECT." Weems has placed these phrases at the center of the images, slightly beneath the subjects' collarbones. She wants viewers to read the images through these words and the categories, institutions, and practices they identify, and thereby see them as inscriptions with real historical and material effects. Moreover, the phrases are not distinct but link the images together into the syntax of a statement as well as a historical narrative. A key aspect of *From Here I Saw What Happened and I Cried* is the recreation of a collective subjectivity, and the text's emergence into historical narrative is a crucial part of the work's argument for recognizing the collective dimension of racial oppression. At the same time, Weems' address to each image evokes the impact of racial oppression on distinct individuals. That is, Weems' inscriptions ask viewers to speculate about the subjectivities that did not conform to the reductions and denigrations of racial typologies. In contradistinction to the unfolding of this historical narrative, which weaves in the impact of racism on individual lives, we can see that the separate photographs and their focus on individual bodies as types violently exclude the economic and historic terrain from the frame and therefore do not reveal how the institution of slavery and its derivatives produced images of the black body for its own purposes. In other words, in *From Here I Saw What Happened*, Weems brings historical contexts back to these images. In his discussion of Weems's installation *Sea Island Series* (1991–92), in which she placed "reproductions of Agassiz's slave daguerreotypes" beside "pictures of remnants of African culture the Gullah brought to America," Brian Wallis claims, "She saw these men and women not as representatives of some typology but as living, breathing ancestors. She made them portraits" (1996, 106). No doubt Weems's work placing the Agassiz daguerreotypes within geographical and historical contexts gave the images depth and actuality, but portraiture cannot be easily distinguished from images that represent denigrating typologies.

Two images Weems links together in *From Here I Saw What Happened and I Cried*—a nude, and a portrait of a young black woman holding up a white baby—make a compelling statement about the relationships among images of black women's bodies, assumptions about black women's sexuality, and the history of their reproductive labor (1995–96, figures 5.3 and 5.4).

FIGURE 5.3. Carrie Mae Weems, "You Became Playmate to the Patriarch" from *From Here I Saw What Happened and I Cried* (1995–1996)

FIGURE 5.4. Carrie Mae Weems, "And Their Daughter" from *From Here I Saw What Happened and I Cried* (1995–1996)

Moreover, these two images highlight how other visual genres such as the nude implicitly inform the connotations of the portrait and its depiction of black women. The nude Weems includes in this series is a vertical daguerreotype from 1850 titled *Study of a Nude Black Woman* and portrays a young black woman lying on a couch covered with lace. Contextualizing this image in her study *The Black Female Body: A Photographic History*, Willis explains that nineteenth-century viewers assumed a black woman in an erotic photograph must be a prostitute (2002, 51). She also makes a connection between the work producing the lace and the work the model was assumed to perform: "Though this is a machine-made fabric, lace making was lower-class women's work, and thus has a symbolic significance as the backdrop on which [the model] rests. In spite of traditional iconographic meaning, this lace does not connote innocence, gentility, beauty, or finery" (2002, 51). Everything in the image suggests sexual availability: the model raises her left arm up so her hand touches her head wrap and her breasts are fully exposed. She places her right hand near her vagina as though masturbating and looks into the distance with a dreamy and satisfied expression. Most important, the model opens her legs for the camera. Willis writes that "the viewer is almost between her legs" (2002, 51). Weems has placed her inscription— "YOU BECAME PLAYMATE TO THE PATRIARCH"—in the space between the woman's legs, such that the words impede immediate visual access to the woman's genitalia.

The next image in *From Here I Saw What Happened and I Cried* represents another kind of access to the black woman's body. It is a portrait of a young black woman holding a white baby up to the camera. Across the image, Weems writes, "AND THEIR DAUGHTER," therefore continuing and completing the statement etched on the glass covering the nude. The pairing of these images suggests that the sexual availability displayed in the nude helps to make the subservience and reproductive labor the second image attests to possible. Known as *Portrait of a Nurse and Young Child* (1850), this image is just one in a series of nineteenth-century portraits depicting white families or babies with their black caretakers. These images graphically demonstrate the black woman's necessary but denigrated place in the American family's construction of whiteness. It seems clear that this daguerreotype was not meant to be a portrait of the nurse but of the baby she holds. Most likely, the baby's family has decided to have her portrait taken in order to memorialize her infancy and place her image within an actual or imaginary portrait gallery that documents and asserts the continuation of the family's lineage, and therefore their race. The young black woman is there as a prop or, as Weems' inscription suggests, a beloved playmate. When discussing this image as an example of photographic representations of mammies, Willis writes, "Sometimes she was included with the child like a favored doll or pet, as a record of a treasured possession who held a crucial, albeit limited and sentimental role in the household" (2002, 129). The caretaker holds the baby so closely and so high their heads and faces align, which stresses the young woman's subservience to the white baby. Furthermore, for most nineteenth-century viewers, the sharp contrast between the subjects' skin colors would naturalize and justify this depiction of subservience.

It is images such as those Weems re-presents in *From Here I Saw What Happened and I Cried* that Frederick Douglass probably had in mind when writing "A Tribute to the Negro" in 1849. In this essay, published in *The North Star*, Douglass addresses racism's shaping of visual perception and therefore its manifestation in photographic images. His statements also suggest that what one person considers a portrait, another might see as a denigrating image. Douglass asserts, "Negroes can never have impartial portraits at the hands of white artists. It seems to us next to impossible for white men to take likenesses of black men, without most grossly exaggerating their distinctive features. And the reason is obvious. Artists like all other white persons, have adopted a theory dissecting the distinctive features of Negro physiognomy" (in Willis 1994, 17).

Written just ten years after the invention of the daguerreotype, Douglass' statement reveals a shrewd and prescient understanding of photography's rhetorical power. Indeed, the portrait photographs accompanying Douglass' autobiographies put this knowledge to work, as they argue his work is authentic and his humanity is actual and honorable. As Colin Westerbeck points out in his essay "Frederick Douglass Chooses His Moment," there are important parallels among the rise of photography, Douglass' escape from slavery in 1838, and his subsequent career as an abolitionist writer and spokesman: "His rise to prominence ran parallel with the rise to popularity of the daguerreotype as a medium for portraiture" (1998, 145). In the statement above, Douglass not only argues against white artists' portrayals of black people, but argues *for* the political importance of black photographers to create and assert images of black people's participation in rather than their distinction from the national body.

Douglass' attention to portraiture reveals it was a crucial site for claiming and shaping representations, perceptions, and theories of the racialized body. And Deborah Willis's scholarship continues to show that as photography became increasingly available, the portrait photograph became a tool for composing images of honorable identities, capable of contesting the racist images that saturated the visual dimension of late nineteenth-century culture. In the Harlem Renaissance, artists and intellectuals composed portraits of themselves and each other in order to re-imagine African Americans' place and stature in American culture, which reflected ordinary African Americans' (indeed, every American's) increased presence in front of the camera. The portrait photograph announced a visible presence, a worthy actuality. It attested not only to the self's inauguration into the visibility of the symbolic order but also to the possibility of shaping that symbolic order.

It is not often noted that in 1923, when the Harlem Renaissance was emerging, W. E. B. Du Bois urged young African Americans to take up photography. In his "Opinion" column in *Crisis*, Du Bois asked: "Why do not more young colored men and women take up photography as a career? The average white photographer does not know how to deal with colored skins and having neither sense of the delicate beauty or tone nor will to learn, he makes a horrible botch of portraying them" (in Willis 2003, 51). Traditionally, studies of the Harlem Renaissance have focused on its painters, sculptors, and writers, but a few scholars such as Willis have begun to emphasize photography's role in the rich cultural production of this period and its contribution to the development of the New Negro. Willis writes, "Black photographers created a new visual language for 'reading' black subjects, an image of self-empowerment—a 'New Negro'" (2003, 52). In this context, notions that the portrait photograph attest to or verify the honorable truth about the person depicted cannot be disregarded as simply naive.

However, as visual and cultural theorists argue, positive images of honor are produced by exclusions and repressions. In "'Black Is, Black Ain't': Notes on De-Essentializing Black Identities," filmmaker and writer Isaac Julien addresses the issue of "positive images" in postmodern identity politics, but I think his ideas are also pertinent to photographic assertions in the nineteenth and early twentieth centuries: "Identity politics in its positive-images variant," Julien writes, "is always purchased in the field of representation at the price of the repression of the other" (1983, 261). In other words, the production of a positive image is also the reproduction of a negative image. Positive images repress and insidiously emphasize the claims of the negative. Because photography has such an influence on visual economies, it contributes to this logic. In "The Body and the Archive," Allen Sekula argues that from its inception, the photograph operated within the dialectics of honor and repression. With photography, and particularly with the photographic portrait, Sekula writes that "[w]e are confronting, then, a double system: a system of representation capable of functioning both *honorifically* and *repressively*" (1986, 6). While the portrait photograph reproduced the signs of privilege and stature the painted portrait announced, it also "came to establish and delimit the terrain of the *other*, to define both the *generalized look*—the typology—and the *contingent instance* of deviance and social pathology" (1986, 7). Calling attention to this dialectic reminds us that the reconstruction of African Americans' images through portrait photography implicitly invites surveillance. As Sekula writes, "Photography served to introduce the panopticon principle into daily life. Every portrait implicitly took its place within a social and moral hierarchy" (1986, 11). Comparative physiognomic studies, wanted posters, mug shots, documents of hysteria, and daguerreotypes like those commissioned by Agassiz—the image repertoire that works to signify the deviant, the criminal, and the racial other—are the honorable portrait's continually lurking relatives.

As *Twenty Questions (A Sampler)* reveals, an important part of Simpson's work from the 1980s involves exposing the portrait as a tool of repressive investigation. In *Three Seated Figures* (1989, figure 5.5), Simpson examines its conventions of display and the disciplinary work it performs. More specifically, *Three Seated Figures* shows how portrait photography is used to produce bodies of knowledge about the raced and gendered subject. It also suggests the production of this knowledge has been a failure: the black woman is not fully visible, and why would we assume she should be? Whereas Simpson photographed the back of the model's head in *Twenty Questions (A Sampler)*, in *Three Seated Figures* she crops three photographs of a woman so her face is cut away from the frame. Both choices defy the quest for knowledge the work stages and underscore its subtle argument against the objectifying investigations of the black woman's body. Over three color polaroids, where the faces should be, Simpson has placed three plaques upon which Simpson has written: "Prints," "Signs of Entry," and "Marks." These texts evoke scenarios of incarceration and photography ("prints"), victimization ("signs of entry," "marks"), as well as the investigative gaze of anthropology. The seated pose heightens the evocation of scrutiny. On plaques to the left and right of the photographs, Weems has placed the phrases "her story" and "each time they looked for proof." It is hard to tell if we are meant to think of "her story" in conjunction with or in opposition to "each time they looked for proof." "[H]er story" evokes the portrait's associations with biography. "[E]ach time they looked for proof" seems linked to scientific projects that attempt to prove assumptions about race and gender

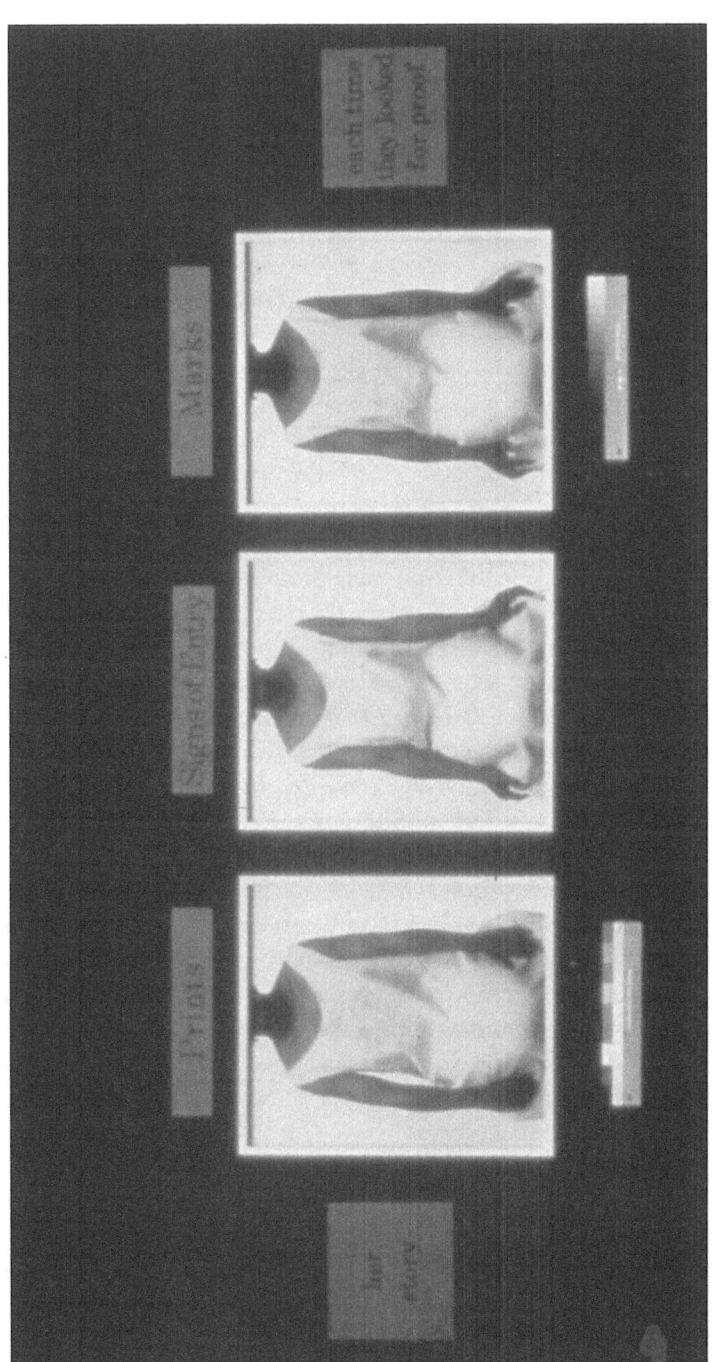

FIGURE 5.5. Lorna Simpson, "Three Seated Figures" (1989)

by examining the black women's body. Clearly, the work associates both "her story" and "proof" with a depersonalized image of the body. The title of the work, and the three slightly different ways the model has posed her hands, suggest each photograph is distinct. But the same model is in each photograph, which leads viewers to think that an investigative quest for "her story," whatever the form or motivation, produces the same depersonalized image of the black woman's body. After examining the photographs Weems re-presents in *From Here I Saw What Happened and I Cried*, it is easy to think of Simpson's *Three Seated Figures* as an allusion to nineteenth-century daguerreotypes that served as visual evidence for scientific assumptions about race and gender, but the piece works against pinning it definitively to a specific time period. Therefore, *Three Seated Figures* might also allude to second- and first-wave American feminism, its use of black women's stories as proof of its impact and relevance.

Scholars and art historians are right to claim that Simpson's pieces are not portraits, but they have not pursued how her work critically engages with this visual genre. Analyzing Simpson's work from the eighties, Kellie Jones writes: "Simpson often provided detailed visual accounts of the body in her work but denied the strategies of the portrait and the particulars of biography thought to reside in the countenance" (2002, 28). Writing about pieces such as *Twenty Questions (A Sampler)*, Marta Gili concurs: "Instead of the eloquence of a portrait, [Simpson] opts for the enigmatic silence of a character presented from behind" (2002, 12). Indeed, a characteristic feature of Simpson's work is a model posed with her back to the viewer or her face cropped from the photograph. However, I would modulate Jones' and Gili's statements and claim many of Simpson's images can be described as antiportraits. Simpson's pieces work within and against the codes and conventions of portraiture; they remain within its frame to question concepts such as 'eloquence' and their implicit roles in the economies of race and gender.

*Portrait* (1988, figure 5.6), a rectangular, vertically oriented black and white photograph depicting one side of a black woman's face, attests to the importance of portraiture in Simpson's work and defies our expectations of the genre. Cropped at each side, we only see the woman's hair, cheek, neck, jaw line, and ear. We cannot see her eyes and only a small part of a mask that covers them. The fragmented image of the mask is a telling detail. It suggests Simpson has reproduced, but from another angle, a partial and incomplete vision of this young woman that does not see or consider her eyes. Instead of the eye, the focus of this portrait is the woman's ear; it is the only physical feature we are allowed to see completely and connects to the

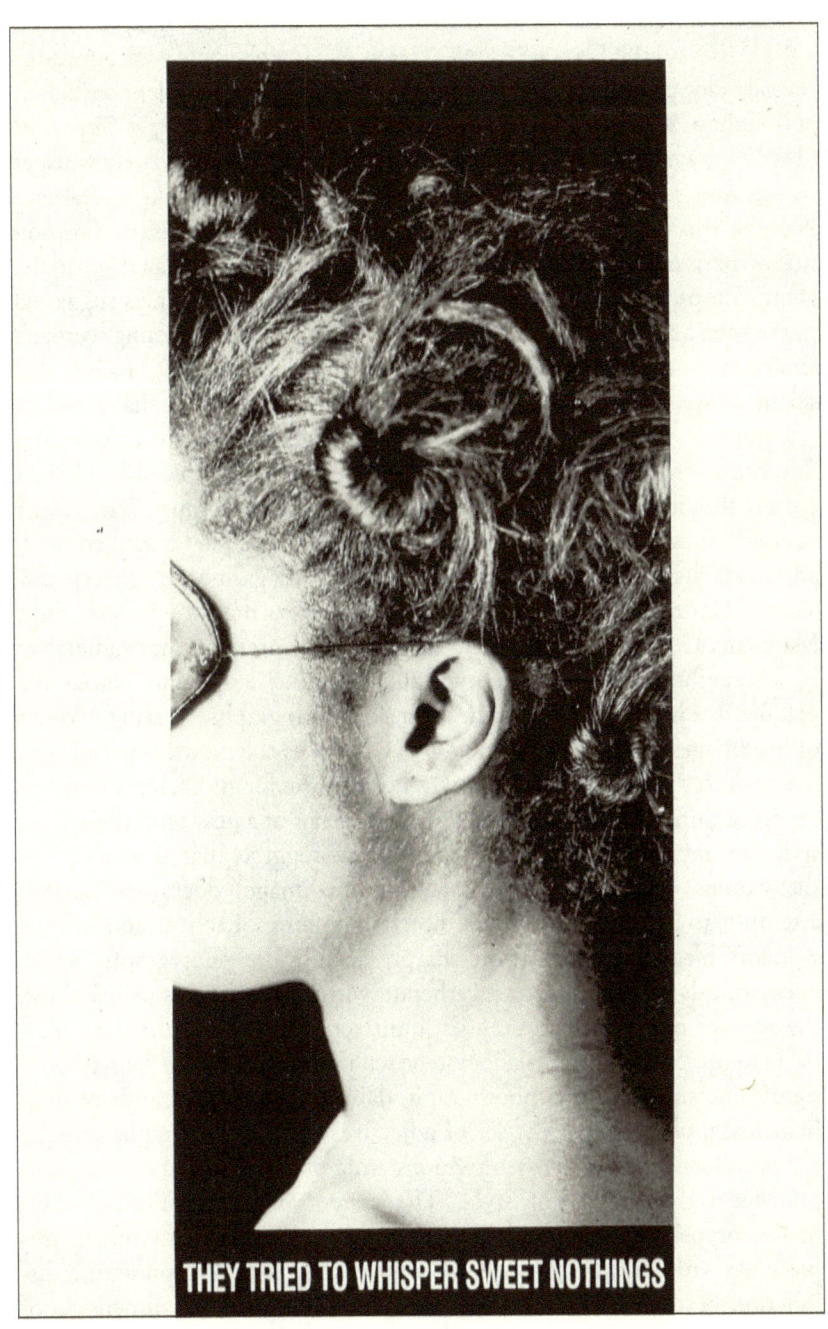

FIGURE 5.6. Lorna Simpson, "Portrait" (1988)

statement Simpson has included at the bottom of the photograph: "THEY TRIED TO WHISPER SWEET NOTHINGS." In the context of Simpson's severely cropped image, this line suggests a pernicious or violent seduction and perhaps alludes to Harriet Jacobs' *Incidents in the Life of a Slave Girl* (1861), in which a slave master and his jealous mistress alternately whisper threats and seductions to a young black girl while she works and sleeps. Naming this piece *Portrait* is ironic, as all of the formal choices Simpson makes refuse the fullness and completion normally associated with the genre. Simpson aligns portraiture with the insidious invasiveness suggested in the text, and her compositional choices seem to reflect a young woman's strategies for defending herself against the proprietary gaze of racism and sexism as well as mimic the dissecting, fragmentary effects of that gaze.

*Stereo Styles* (1988, figure 5.7), a set of antiportraits, continues Simpson's scrutiny of beauty by revealing the portrait's repressive role in a culture that implicitly links whiteness, femininity, and beauty. *Stereo Styles* consists of ten polaroid prints and ten plastic plaques inscribed with adjectives that seem to be gleaned from fashion magazines or hairstyle catalogs: "Daring, Sensible, Severe, Long & Silky, Boyish, Ageless, Silly, Magnetic, Country Fresh, Sweet." Simpson has inscribed these adjectives in a hyperbolically and stereotypically feminine script and placed the plaques in a horizontal line set between the photographs, creating two sets of five images. Like *Twenty Questions (A Sampler)* the model is posed with her back to the camera, which makes her hair the focus. Each photograph depicts a different hairstyle. Except for a portrait of a neat bun, these hairstyles are messy and haphazard. *Stereo Styles* suggests that at some point the woman straightened her hair, and the images document various attempts to manage the effect of straightening. Each strand of the woman's black hair stands out sharply against the photographs' white backgrounds, which in turn reverberate with the whiteness of her dress, the ribbons in her hair, and the feminine script inscribed into black plastic plaques. Simpson has deliberately sculpted some of the hairstyles to signify messiness. In one photograph, daisies hang from strands of limp hair. Juxtaposed against the set of adjectives, these photographs critique the prevalence and ubiquity of white standards of beauty; their insidious presence in the language of "style." The "stereo" of the title of course refers to stereotypes but also alludes to the splits and doubles at work in this piece. As with *Twenty Questions (A Sampler)*, *Stereo Styles* represents a disjunction between the images and texts, and the gendered dimension of racial categories—the implicit whiteness of femininity—produces this disjunction.

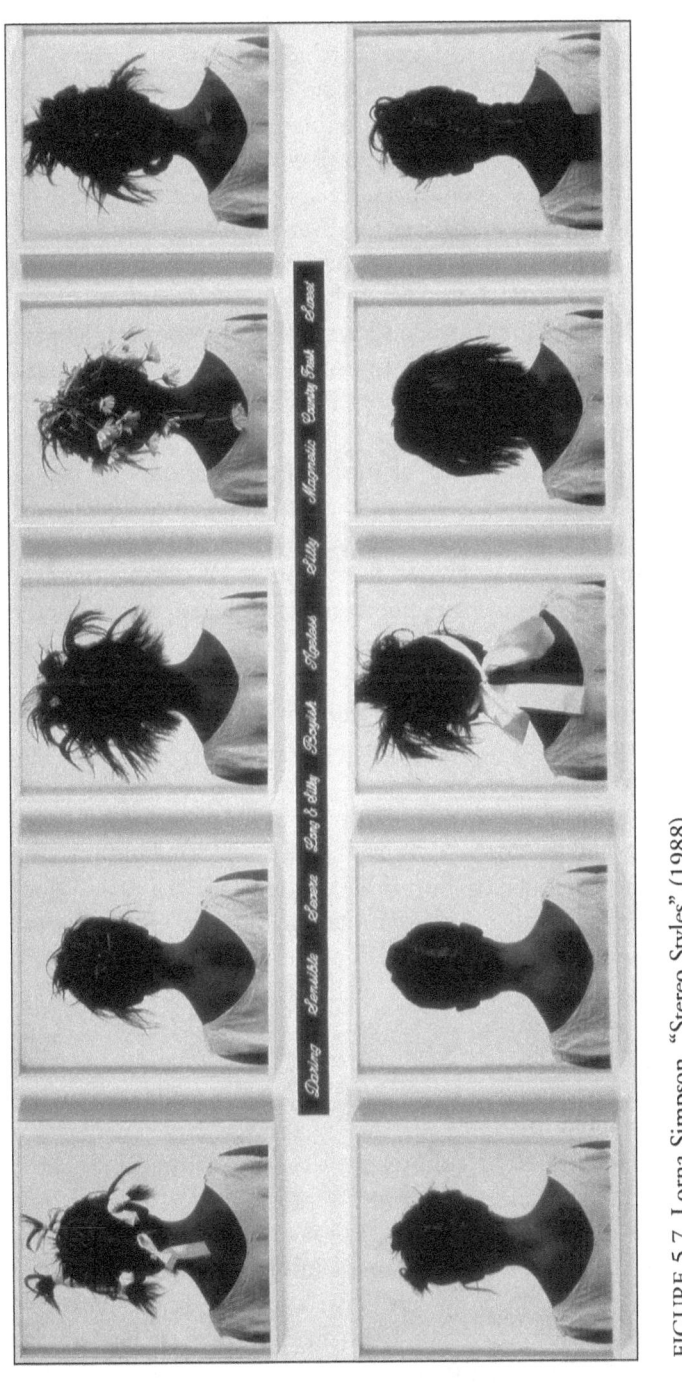

FIGURE 5.7. Lorna Simpson, "Stereo Styles" (1988)

The time, effort, and expense of straightening black women's hair makes it an issue that intersects race and class, and an analysis of Simpson's antiportraits would be incomplete without attention to those highlighting the economic dimensions of black women's cultural visibility. In this context, *Stereo Styles* suggests black women's efforts to conform to the standards of a neat, presentable appearance required for getting and keeping a decent paying job. In *Five Day Forecast* (1988, figure 5.8), Simpson places the words for each day of the work week in stark capital letters where a woman's face should be. Below the photographs of the woman's torso and her strong, defined, and defiantly crossed arms is a linked chain of "misses": "misdesription, misinformation, misidentify, misdiagnose, misfunction, mistranscribe, misremember, misgauge, misconstrue, mistranslate." Her pose communicates strength, but the image seems circumscribed by both the list of mistakes and the days representing the workweek. Is she linked to a series of mistakes because of economic necessities? Does *Five Day Forecast* ask us to think of the anger and disappointment that must be excised from a black woman's countenance during the week? Or does it reflect back mistaken perceptions of that countenance? What time and place do the image and its connotations of work allude to? Though the shift she wears is not necessarily time specific, it may refer to simple garments women wore during slavery, therefore provoking viewers to reflect on images of the past in their perceptions of the present.

The work of literary critic Hortense Spillers illuminates how the history of race and gender in America shapes the present and therefore helps us map the complicated historical and ideological terrain Weems and Simpson engage with to refute. In her well-known essay, "Mama's Baby, Papa's Maybe: An American Grammar Book," Spillers reluctantly but strategically identifies herself through a series of names that encircle the body and identity of the black woman: "Peaches," "Brown Sugar," "Sapphire," "Earth Mother," "Granny," and "Black Woman at the Podium," among others (Spillers 2003, 203). Using the first-person pronoun metonymically to mark the presence of a diverse collectivity negated and simplified by American culture, Spillers writes from both outside and inside the narrow space these names afford to remark on their concatenation of meanings: "I describe a locus of confounded identities, a meeting ground of investments and privations in the national treasury of rhetorical wealth" (2003, 203). Spillers draws attention to the thick ideological bulk of these ready-made identities, the quickness of their transmission, and the immediacy of their recognition. These names, which "isolate

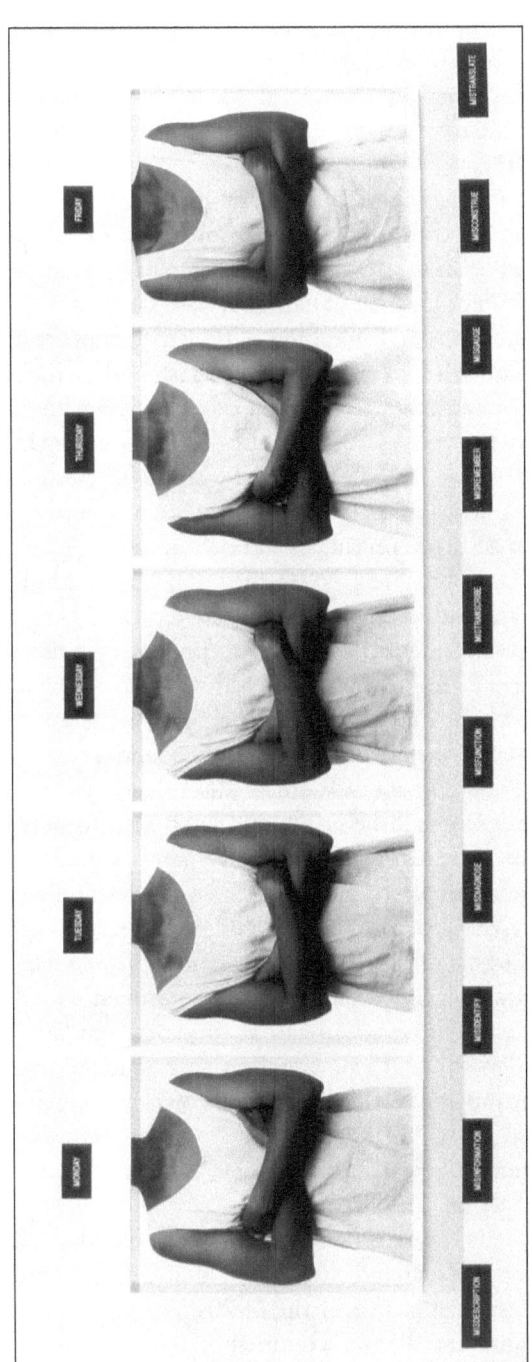

FIGURE 5.8. Lorna Simpson, "Five Day Forecast" (1988)

overdetermined nominative qualities," are, according to Spillers, "[e]mbedded in bizarre axiological ground, they demonstrate a sort of telegraphic coding; they are markers so loaded with mythical prepossession that there is no easy way for the agents buried beneath them to come clean" (2003, 203).

Spillers' claim that black women are "embedded in bizarre axiological ground" offers a compelling place from which to read Weems' and Simpson's work. For an inveterate image repertoire dense and empty from overuse accompanies the chain of names Spillers cites; these images accelerate the instantaneous "telegraphing" of these names, compound the density of their "mythical prepossession," and strengthen their capacity to "bury." Coming clean from the burden of embodying the underside of cultural hierarchies is not easy but is also not impossible. It requires an investigative excavation into the fossilized histories of cultural perception and what Spillers describes as "marvels of my own inventiveness" (2003, 203). Marvels of aesthetic invention and cultural investigation, the work of Weems and Simpson reveal how words and images bind together to create, disseminate, and solidify overdetermined meanings that define and deplete the bodies and identities of African American women. Their work inhabits and rearticulates the various ways in which black women embody what Spillers names "the paradox of non-being," a being interpellated and produced to mirror the subjectivity, validity, and actuality of others ("Interstices: A Small Drama of Words," 2003, 154).

This "paradox of non-being" is intimately tied to pervasive myths about black women's sexuality. The black woman is Western culture's sexual emblem but has all too often been denied the possibility of negotiating or inventing the terms of her sexual agency. In the chapter "Interstices: A Small Drama of Words," Spillers renders a spectacle of enforced passivity and drained potentiality: "[B]lack women are the beached whales of the sexual universe, unvoiced, misseen, not doing, awaiting *their* verb" (Spillers 2003, 153). Unreflective strains of American feminism have contributed to this history of invisibility, repression, and exhausted arrest. As Spillers writes, "Across the terrain of feminist thought, the drama of sexuality is a dialectic with at least one missing configuration of terms" (2003, 153).

Judy Chicago's *Dinner Party* (1974–79) revealed the sexuality of black women is the visual and discursive "interstice" in American feminism and feminist art practice of the 1970s. A monumental project of recovery, Chicago's installation commemorated women's reproductive labor and collectivity by creating place settings for thirty-nine women of historical stature or mythological resonance. At a large triangulated table made of glimmering tiles inscribed with women's names, Chicago and her collaborators set places for women with ceremonial placemats adorned with elaborate needlework; each woman was represented at her designed place with a brightly colored plate sculpted into an idiosyncratically rendered vulva—except for Sojourner Truth. The former slave who famously inquired "Ain't I a Woman?" at an 1851 women's convention in Akron, Ohio, and therefore placed the implicit identity of the American women's movement—"white ladyship"—into question, was represented with three portraits of her face, not her vulva. At a table validating women's collective ambitions and individual appetites, this portrait not only denies Truth's sexuality and sexual agency, it also brackets off blackness within a paradigmatic construction of woman. *Dinner Party's* visual and physical substitution quite explicitly demonstrates Spillers' claim that the myth of black women's sexuality is the inverse mirror of her traumatic desexualization, her "symbolic castration" (2003, 157). Vividly and cogently, Spillers explains: "The black-female-as-whore forms an iconographic equation with black-female-vagina-less, but in different clothes, we might say. . . . Thus, the unsexed black female and the supersexed black female embody the very same vice, cast the very same shadow" (2003, 164).

Chicago's desexualized image of Truth unwittingly reproduced but also exposed the racism and sexism of feminism's first wave. In the preceding paragraph, I noted Sojourner Truth is famous for her 1851 speech at a woman's convention in Akron, Ohio. She is also known for bearing her breast in 1858 in Indiana. These two events are often conflated into one emblematic scene. Historian Nell Irving Painter explains: "In the post-1960s, post-Black power era of the late twentieth century, a fictive, hybrid cameo of these two actions presents an angry Sojourner Truth, who snarls, 'And ain't I a woman?' then defiantly exhibits her breast" (1994, 464). Moreover, that famous line does not exist in the historical records. In her essay "Representing Truth: Sojourner Truth's Knowing and Becoming Known," Painter argues this emblem of Truth, which "works metonymically as *the* black woman in American history," is a "figurative construction" satisfying the need to imagine a "straight talking, authentic, unsentimental" black woman (1994, 464). The appropriations of white abolitionists such as Francis Dana Gage and Harriet Beecher Stowe as well as Truth's own skilled self-promotion as a preacher fostered this construction. Painter writes that Gage and Stowe "sought to capture [Truth] in writing," and Truth's illiteracy made her vulnerable to their attempts (1994, 471). In the context of Gage's transcription of Truth's 1851 speech, Painter writes, "The disjuncture between self-representation and representation at the hands of others creates unexpected complications" (1994, 470). While Truth couldn't read or write, she became not only literate but proficient in the language of portrait photography. Painter reads the "writing" in Truth's own portrait photographs, which she sold to support herself, as evidence of Truth's skilled use of the informational systems of her time, a statement of "literal embodiment," and her entrance into history (1994, 488). "[F]or she used photography," Painter writes, "to embody and empower herself, to present the images of herself that *she* wanted remembered" (1994, 462). Truth's portraits vividly support Willis' claim that even in the nineteenth century, portrait photography gave African Americans the opportunity to fashion images of themselves for themselves. Weems and Simpson draw from but also complicate the portrait as a site of self-fashioning.

Isolated and immediately recognizable images "telegraphing" assumptions about black women's sexuality (or lack thereof) marshal against the possibility that black women can possess sexual agency. In *Untitled (Kitchen Table Series)* (1990), Weems disputes this telegraphing process by placing representations of a black woman's sexuality within a visual and literary narrative. *Untitled (Kitchen Table Series)* is a photo essay that tells the story of a black woman's life from the vantage point of one solid place, the kitchen table. In this series, the kitchen table is a stage for representing the story of a strong, politicized black woman approaching midlife and moving through a resonant but difficult relationship. In the texts, Weems draws from different discourses and styles to highlight the various ways in which the central protagonist expresses her desires, represents herself, and lives her life. Often, these discursive layers do not seem to synthesize into completion, and that is part of Weems' point. The black and white photographs, spare but dramatically lit, do not illustrate the narrative but contribute another layer to this multivalent portrayal. After a poetic description of their meeting—"They met in the glistening twinkling crystal light of August/September sky"—the piece articulates the protagonist's view of monogamy: "She felt monogamy had a place but invested it with little value. It was a system based on private property, an order defying human nature." Between these texts is a black-and-white photograph of a black woman and man at a kitchen table entitled *Untitled (Man Smoking)* (1990). The couple plays cards and look at each other intensely. The man smokes; the woman's hand curls over her mouth, a gesture accentuating the sexually alive expression in her eyes. On the wall behind this couple, through the smoke, is a poster of Malcolm X, fist raised and finger pointed, which brings a political dimension to this subtle representation of a black woman's sexuality.

*Untitled (Kitchen Table Series)* tells the story of this relationship through a series of deliberately staged photographs that draw from a variety of visual genres. Plate 34, *Untitled (Woman standing alone)*, is a portrait: the protagonist leans across the table with her arms outstretched and looks straight into the camera; her gaze is strong but friendly. In the next photograph, *Untitled (Woman feeding bird)*, the woman stands in a nightgown with laced seams and edges, feeding a bird. She faces the left wall of the kitchen, and the photograph depicts the profile of her body. *Untitled (Nude)*, which appears after *Untitled (Woman standing alone)* and *Untitled (Woman feeding bird)*, is not a typical nude, as it works against the visual genre's objectifying displays and its signature concessions to voyeurism. The bright overhead lamp highlights her skin and the shapes of her features. She is nude, as the title tells us, but since she sits between the table and the chair, we see only parts of her body: her face and its closed eyes, the upraised arm bent at the elbow and holding her head, her collarbones and the tops of her breasts. Her back is arched, and below the table's edge we can see just a part of her open thighs. Her body is not fully exposed, but it is not veiled either. Focused, alone, and satisfied, everything suggests the woman is masturbating. Weems' choice to leave the room bare, without the birdcage, playing cards, quilts, newspapers, posters, drinking glasses, and mirrors that serve as narrative props in the other photographs, makes the woman's sexuality the undeniable focus of the image. While formal choices contribute to the honest self-assurance of *Untitled (Nude)*, the images preceding it—*Untitled (Woman standing alone)* and *Untitled (Woman feeding bird)*—inform and support its connotations of strength. Part of a multivalent portrait that develops in narrative time and through a shifting set of discursive registers, Weems utilizes many formal and thematic factors that work against reading *Untitled (Nude)* as a discrete image that reduces an image of a black woman to a sexual emblem. One of these strategies is to consciously place the nude's evocation of sexuality in relation to, rather than repressively distinct from, the portrait's assertion of presence, honor, and strength.

Simultaneously oversexing or desexing the bodies of African American women makes their participation in biological reproduction a site for political debate, scrutiny, and surveillance. In her 1989 piece *Untitled (Prefer, Refuse, Decide)* (1989, figure 5.9), Simpson quietly alludes to assumptions about and connotations of African American women's reproduction, evoking but not explicitly referring to racist and sexist practices

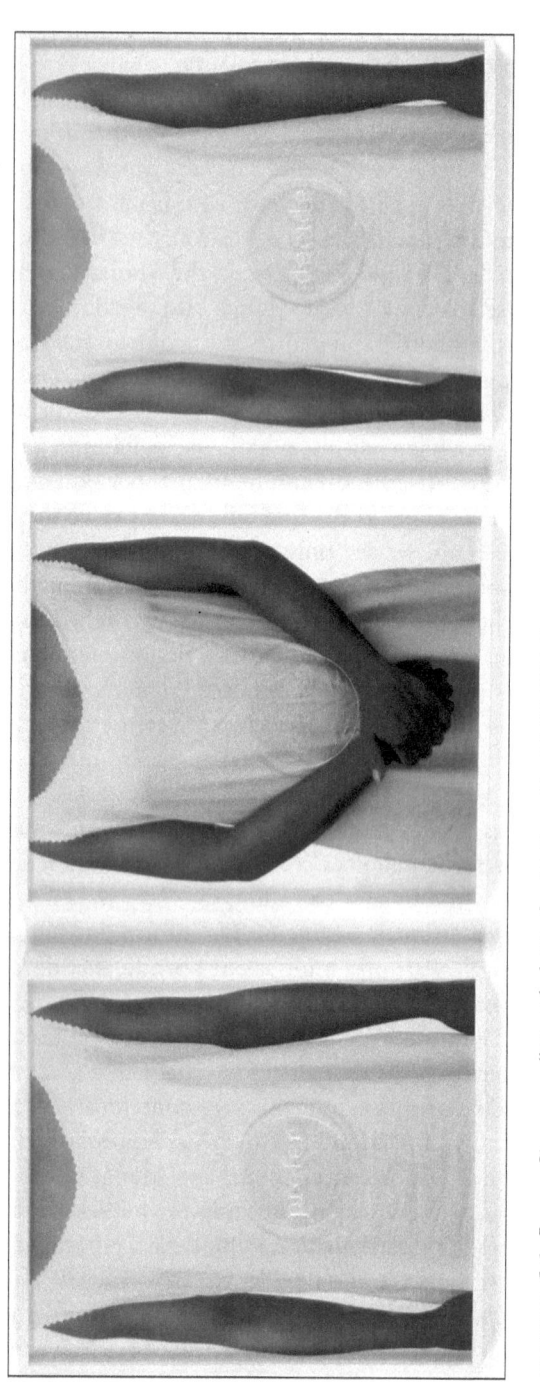

FIGURE 5.9. Lorna Simpson, "Untitled (Prefer, Refuse, Decide)" (1989)

marking its history: forced sterilization, the forced reproduction underpinning the U.S. slave economy, and the spectacle of the welfare mother. *Untitled (Prefer, Refuse, Decide)* consists of three color polaroids, cropped at the shoulders and just below the pubic area, which depict the middle area of a woman's body. We do not see the portrayed woman's face, only her arms, the uppermost part of her chest, and the unassuming white shift she wears. Three plastic circular plaques, inscribed with the verbs "prefer," "refuse," and "decide," have been placed at the woman's abdomen. Together these verbs and their placement suggest reproductive agency and choice, yet the plaques, placed against the white dress, are difficult to read. This subtle element, combined with the depersonalizing cropping of the photographs, makes the verbs' connection to agency weak, barely present, not fully actual. But *Untitled (Prefer, Refuse, Decide)* does more than argue that black women's agency is not considered when women's reproduction is at issue. In the central photograph, the plaque inscribed with "refuse" has been placed above the woman's ceremoniously crossed hands. "Refuse" is the most defiant of the three verbs, but the pose is almost demure, as if to suggest African American women's strategies of refusal have been subtle by necessity. What does the woman refuse? Since "choice" is absent from the set of words, perhaps the piece refuses more than the most explicit marks of victimization I have alluded to above, but the words and ideas through which women's reproductive rights have been imagined. Perhaps *Untitled (Prefer, Refuse, Decide)* argues the bodies of black women have been fantasmatically constructed as one depersonalized, easily reproducible body that represents the limits of women's reproductive choices.

The plaque placed in the central photograph of *Untitled (Prefer, Refuse, Decide)* announces a primary strategy of Simpson's work: refusal. In the previous paragraph I read the work's complicated engagement with ideas and assumptions about black women's reproduction, but this reading relies upon an analysis of what *Untitled (Prefer, Refuse, Decide)* refuses most explicitly—the portrait photograph, its expression of interiority, and its assumed objectivity. Cropping these images to exclude the face is an act of refusal that contributes to the eerie anonymity of these images; placing the clear plastic plaques inscribed with words in the photographs comments on the assumed transparency of photography (and perhaps language as well). Art historian John Tagg argues that the photograph's rhetoric can be located in its transparency, and reading this rhetoric requires detachment. Many visual theorists and historians of photography have made similar arguments, but the following statement from Tagg's study *The Burden of Representation* reveals how closely photography and portraiture intertwine. Tagg writes that "the transparency of the photograph is its most powerful rhetorical device. But this rhetoric also has a history, and we must distance ourselves from it, question the naturalness of portraiture and probe the obviousness of each image" (1993, 35). By simultaneously questioning portrait photography and addressing assumptions about black women's reproduction, Simpson reveals the complicated connections among portraiture, bloodlines, and genealogies.

Weems' *Family Pictures and Stories* (1978–84) also refutes denigrating perceptions of black women's reproduction but with less defamiliarizing strategies. In *Family Pictures and Stories*, Weems assembles family snapshots and stories to offer evidence of the normalcy, resonance, and complexity of African American familial and cultural life. Weems produced this photo essay in response to the infamous Moynihan report entitled *The Negro Family*, which attempted to document the "crisis" in the African American family and blamed this supposed crisis on its matriarchal history. In Weems' construction of a family album, viewers see men, women, and children participating in the scenarios of their lives, which are not thoroughly determined by racial politics or crisis. Resisting a cleanly composed aesthetic, Weems' 35 mm photographs honor the women in this family but do not commemorate them, so the women are not abstracted away from the everyday textures of material conditions. In other words, *Family Pictures and Stories* resists heroicizing African American women and placing their images in isolated frames. Plate 7, entitled *Van and Vera with Kids in the Kitchen* (1978–84, figure 5.10) portrays two women, the narrator's sisters, conversing in a kitchen. In the space between them are three bustling, animated girls, an open refrigerator, and a window with small flowerpots on the windowsill. The woman on the left holds a baby with a bottle in her arms; her hand, gesturing while she talks, creates a blur in the photograph. *Van and Vera with Kids in the Kitchen* captures a typical moment of crowded kitchen chaos. In the text, the narrator reflects upon the ease of her sisters' intimacy and the agility with which they balance their identities as mothers and autonomous adults: "It amazes me that even in the midst of a bunch of crazy kids, my sisters still manage to carry on a half-way decent conversation. I'm really impressed."

Similar to *Untitled (Kitchen Table Series)*, *Family Pictures and Stories* uses the narrative elements of the photo essay to bring depth and complexity to visual depictions of African Americans. *Family Pictures and Stories* is an insider's view of African American family life, not the objectifying

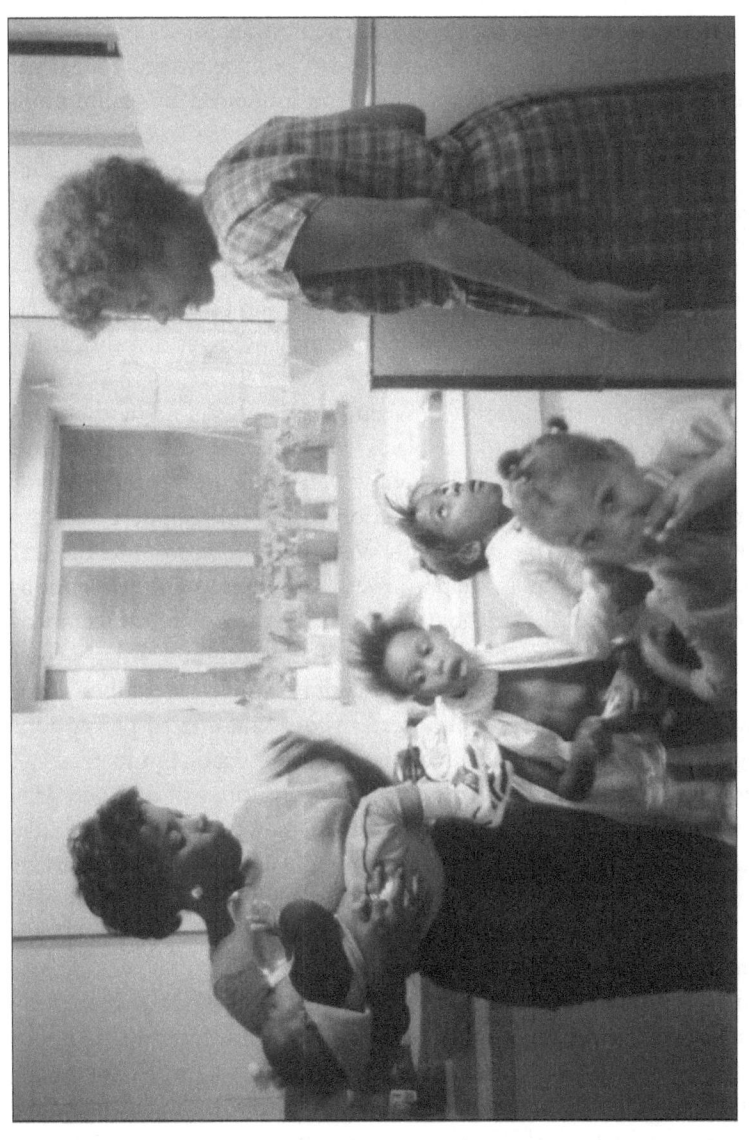

FIGURE 5.10. Carrie Mae Weems, "Van and Vera with Kids in the Kitchen" from *Family Pictures and Stories* (1978–1984)

inscription of sociology that reads images through its own assumptions, narratives, and conclusions. Yet the photographs are not staged as redemptive celebrations that portray African American culture in a "positive" light. They are not what Julien describes as positive images that are "purchased in the field of representation at the price of the repression of the other" (1983, 261). However, they do not foreclose the issues "positive images" raise, their continual appeal when one lives in a culture subtended by assumptions about the superiority of whiteness. About *Family Pictures and Stories,* critic and curator Thelma Golden writes, "Weems delved head-on into the slippery territory of positive and negative images, making clear the passion and dexterity necessary to avoid the facile aspect of this paradigm" (1998, 31). Though they work within "the slippery territory of positive and negative images" quite differently, neither Weems' nor Simpson's work can be reduced to the well-intentioned but ultimately flawed act of substituting positive for negative images.

By engaging with portraiture, Weems and Simpson reveal that contesting negative perceptions of the black woman is one of their concerns. They approach this work cautiously, however, and the layering of words and images is part of this work's negotiation within this "slippery territory of positive and negative images." Both Weems and Simpson include text within the portrait's frame to shape viewers' responses to and perceptions of images. Distinct but inextricable within the textures of cultural embeddedness, Weems and Simpson separate the words and images that together form the wires of "telegraphic coding" Spillers describes. Text, their work shows, has the potential to transform automated perceptions into interpretive readings. These readings are not didactic but instead call attention to the stubborn and complicated imbrications of race and gender in cultural perception. Phrases, words, names, and narratives interrupt, in Wiegman's words, "the security of the visual as an obvious or unacculturated phenomenon," which therefore undermines the security of race and gender as visible, knowable, and identifiable categories (1995, 24). In turn, images call attention to the imaginaries that accompany particular words, phrases, and narratives. These strategies of juxtaposition unsettle the conflation of image, sex, race, and skin and therefore work against the black woman's body "reduc[tion] to mere spectacle" (hooks 1992, 62). Using language to call attention to the construction of spectacles, which in this case are one dimensional, easily recognizable, and culturally pervasive images, Weems' and Simpson's work reveal the mechanisms for creating and repressing the constitutive underside of positive images. Since "positive" images of womanhood and femininity are often still implicitly white, this is crucial to the work of reconfiguring how black women are perceived.

In visual art, the inclusion of text is a sign of the contemporary. Barbara Kruger composes designs mimicking the interpellating shouts of advertising. Mary Kelley creates installations in which text enacts the construction of the psychoanalytic subject. Adrian Piper's text-based work provocatively challenges viewers' assumptions about skin color, race, and violence. Kruger, Kelley, and Piper are just three of many contemporary visual artists, who, like Weems and Simpson, utilize text to reveal layers of ideological meanings. Martha Jane Nadell's study *Enter the New Negroes: Images of Race in American Culture* (2004) shows that the intertwining of text and image is not exclusive to contemporary art practices. Following W. J. T. Mitchell's argument that questions of power and concepts of difference "surfac[e] within the word/image problem," Nadell analyzes what she describes as "interartistic" work from the Harlem Renaissance (2004, 7–8). "Word and image," Nadell writes, "tell part of the story of how images of race shifted during the first half of the twentieth century in response to earlier images and cultural shifts" (2004, 9). "[O]ther images" include mammies, Uncle Toms, and Sambos: stereotypes that proliferated during the late nineteenth and early twentieth centuries. In response, Harlem Renaissance writers, artists, and intellectuals took it upon themselves to bust open these stubborn distortions and assert new truths about African Americans. They were keenly aware of how images of blacks in visual culture "were paramount in codifying ideas of race" (Nadell 2004, 17). Examining works such as Alain Locke's *The New Negro: An Interpretation* (1925), the magazines *Survey Graphic* (1925), *Fire!!!* (1926), and *Harlem* (1928), Nadell shows how Harlem Renaissance writers, artists, and intellectuals "attempt[ed] to formulate—through word and image—new ways of imagining African American identity" (2004, 36). Directing perceptions of and reactions to images through text, these works reveal a sensitive attentiveness to the fact that in illustrated versions of novels such as *Uncle Tom's Cabin* (1852), "[t]he text and illustrations buttress each other" and therefore help to "claim authenticity and authority for the depictions of African Americans" (Nadell 2004, 28).

Because photographic portraits were thought to depict the physical appearance of a person as she appeared to the naked, physical eye, it was a tool for re-claiming "authority," "authenticity," and the moral connotations of both. An advertisement for the photogravures of C. M. Battey, which appeared in the December 1915 issue of *The Crisis* magazine, foreshadows portrait's place in the Harlem Renaissance's construction of personal, cultural, and political pride. It also reveals the work text performs framing, shaping, and emphasizing visual arguments. In this particular advertisement, Battey sells a set of photogravures entitled *Our Heroes of Destiny*, which features portrait images of Frederick Douglass, John M. Langston, Blanche K. Bruce, Paul Lawrence Dunbar, and Booker T. Washington. Below these images the advertisement cites the words of cultural and civic leaders who stress the importance of Our Heroes of Destiny. The words of Rev. Dr. Reverdy C. Ransom reveal a lot about the values assumed to be inherent in the portrait images of leading African American men: "Your splendid production of 'Our Heroes of Destiny' marks the era of perpetuating characteristic and faithful likeness of the famous men and women of our own race, to be handed down to younger generations, inspiring them with ideals which if carefully nurtured in their young lives will in their mature ages prove excellent examples of pure and dignified manhood and womanhood" (Willis-Thomas 1985, n.p.).

Though the photogravures (lithographs modeled on photographs) of these leaders connote honor, dignity, and vision, the text adds another layer of rhetorical emphasis. It tells readers how to see and identify with the images. Certainly using text and image in tandem for the purposes of reinforcing messages is a strategy of advertising and emerged out of changes in printing technology that allowed for the easy reproduction of images in printed texts (Nadell 2004, 17). However, this advertisement also reveals the recuperative roles text and image played reconfiguring perceptions of African Americans. Ransom's statement clearly suggests *Our Heroes of Destiny* was made to help produce a genealogy of race strong enough to shape perceptions of the African American past, present, and future. Less clear, however, is the advertisement's implicit reliance on ideas about reproduction and the insidious conceptual presence of racial purity. The portrait photographs W. E. B. Du Bois commissioned for the Paris Exposition of 1900, to which I now turn, also offer insights into how ideas about reproduction and racial purity shaped images and perceptions of African American women.

There are many aspects of the portrait photographs W. E. B. Du Bois included in the American Negro exhibit at the 1900 exposition that suggest they meant to inspire the ideas in the advertisement for C. M. Battey's photogravures. These portraits are intended to feature "excellent examples of pure and dignified womanhood," but the standard of purity was more complicated for black women. They argue the women within their frames are ladies, worthy of the honor bestowed upon white women and therefore capable of reproducing a "pure" and "dignified" race. Elegant, nuanced, and ladylike, the portraits of women Du Bois included in the exhibition refute myths of the African American woman's supposed sexual availability and provide the visual component of the New Negro Woman's explicitly gendered identity. The clothing, lighting, looks, and poses in these portrait photographs announce the African American woman's rightful place in femininity's imaginary space. Dressed in Victorian attire complete with chin-high collars, lace, and cameos, the expressions on their faces are not exaggerated but serene and dignified. The pearl grays, and soft, diaphanous whites of these black-and-white photographs underscore the argument that these women are ladies. Many of the portraits veer toward profiles or silhouettes, the least confrontational of poses, and subtly invite the viewer to see the dignified innocence of the women's acts of looking, reflecting, and thinking while also arguing against denigrating physiognomic readings of the black face.

The portrait photographs of women Du Bois included in the Paris Exposition were intended to announce and create the New Negro Woman. A recognizable and discernible gender identity made this announcement of newness possible. In *American Anatomies*, Wiegman explains that for the African American slave, as well as those who might be retroactively identified through that category, possessing a clearly discernible gender identity provided "possibilities of escaping the category of the inhuman" (1995, 11). Not only do these photographs suggest that placing oneself within the portrait's frame of visibility often entailed embodying a discernible gender identity, but they may implicitly strengthen the punitive image repertoires and accompanying assumptions against which they argue. Some might claim that instead of pointing out how very little in American history gave black women the opportunity to become ladies, these portraits sanction the assumption that the "Old" Negro Woman was not worthy of respect.

In "The Trope of a New Negro and the Reconstruction of the Image of the Black," Henry Louis Gates expresses ambivalence about the New Negro and the reconstruction of the African American's image. For Gates, the New Negro is a call for a repressive insistence upon success, an amnesia founded upon self-negation and blame. The trope of the New Negro, according to Gates, suggests it was the burden of African Americans to refute the names and images that were not of their own making. Reflecting on Booker T. Washington's anthology *A New Negro for a New Century* (1900) and its rhetoric of uplift, Gates writes that the slavery of the not-too-distant past "is buried beneath all of the faintly smiling bourgeois countenances of the New Negroes awaiting only the new century to escape the recollection of enslavement" (1988, 139). While Gates wants to stress that the New Negro was only a slight and repressive step away from the Old Negro, he is forced to acknowledge the astonishing preponderance of racial stereotypes in turn-of-the-century visual culture. "By 1900," Gates writes, "it would have been possible for a middle-class white American to see Sambo images from toaster and teapot covers on his breakfast tables to advertisements in magazines, to popular postcards in drugstores" (1988, 150). Therefore, Gates recognizes the necessity of the New Negro: it was a trope and strategy of survival. But acknowledging political and psychological necessities does not foreclose the possibility of questioning their ultimate effectiveness. The visual art of Weems and Simpson revisits the portrait photograph to reveal and contest the assumptions informing its history. However, their work does far more than expose complicities or faulty efforts. It acknowledges the necessity of cultural recognition while reconfiguring its terms; it also points to the difficulty of excavating, reshaping, and reimagining the racist and sexist formulations within cultural perceptions.

Weems' and Simpson's work achieves this balance by showing that the past shapes the present through small, often overlooked details. Both bodies of work show that details build and synthesize into automated perceptions and composite images of the raced and gendered subject. Moreover, it is in the details where assumptions confront the materiality of visual images and therefore are places where perceptions might be reconfigured. Therefore, Weems and Simpson compose their images with a careful, shrewd attention to detail. Weems works against the portrait's emphasis on singularity, its excision of context and history, and places images within narratives that signify collectivity. Whereas Weems brings more detail to portraiture, Simpson reduces portraits to their fundamental components. By deconstructing portrait images, Simpson shows how the details of the genre contribute to arguments about the subject within its frame. Simpson's *Details* (1996, figure 5.11), re-presents a gallery of late nineteenth- and early twentieth-century portraits perhaps similar to the one displayed in Paris under the auspices of Du Bois' approving eye. Instead of representing faces, Simpson isolates and focuses upon the hands of the portrait subjects. In *Details*, we see the hands of African Americans crossed, resting at their sides, placed on books, tables, and musical instruments, holding a telephone and a child's ball. These hands, separated from images of bodies and faces, call attention to the composed arrangements of the photographs. We associate hands with making and

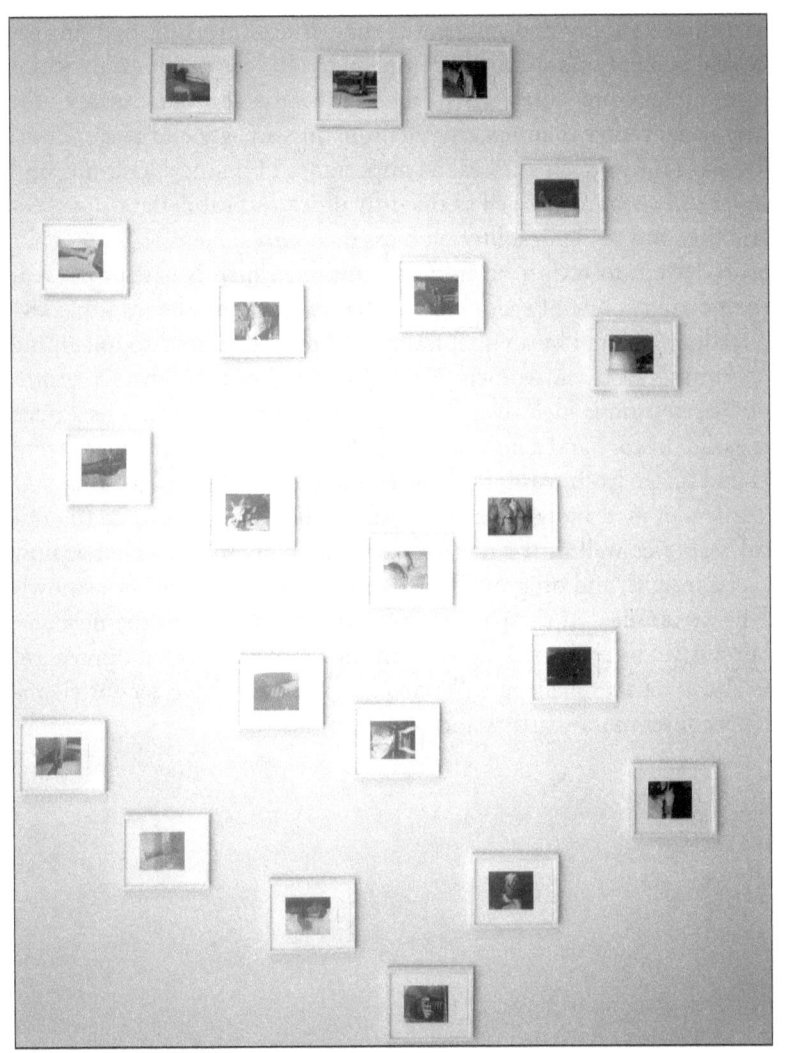

FIGURE 5.11. Lorna Simpson, "Details" (1996)

constructing, and *Details* seems to stress African Americans' acts of self-making on the photographer's stage.

This chapter's brief foray into the African American visual culture of the nineteenth and early twentieth centuries is meant to place Weems' and Simpson's work within historical arguments about African Americans' cultural visibility and political agency. Indeed, this history emphasizes visual perception's stubborn complicity with racist and sexist ideologies and therefore highlights the "inventiveness" necessary for reconfiguring, rather than reactively reinforcing, images and perceptions. My focus on the portrait stresses the importance of political, cultural, and psychological visibility, as well as the difficulties and subtleties of possessing visibility and recognizability on one's own terms. Neither Weems nor Simpson delve into realms beyond recognition, which is part of the reason the portrait is one of their work's subjects. Text and the multiple levels of reading inspired by a visual framing of text are crucial to imagining new portrayals of black women. Kellie Jones writes that "the act of linguistic intercession is inclusive; it sets up a rereading that contains a trace of the earlier history and a new reality" (2002, 91). Untangling word from image and image from word, both Weems and Simpson unsettle the symbolic orders of race and gender into visible relief, revealing its configuration of reality as well as the ideological blind spots that marshal against discovery, insight, and progress. To refute without repressing, to acknowledge the presentness of the past, to see and write a space of the new and less oppressive, to resist making women the emblem of racial oppression or salvation are the challenges Weems and Simpson have set for themselves, as contemporary artists and black feminists.

# 6

## The Coloniality of Embodiment

### Coco Fusco's Postcolonial Genealogies and Semiotic Agonistics

EDUARDO MENDIETA

---

> My name is Coco Fusco, and actually, I was born in the U.S. and am genetically composed of Yoruba, Taino, Catalan, Sephardic, and Neopolitan blood. In 1990, that makes me Hispanic. If this were the '50s, I might be considered black.
> —Fusco and Gómez-Peña, "Norte: Sur"

> Well, I would say that my identity has always been a problem for most people. They are constantly trying to change it. When I was born, the nuns in the hospital thought they were doing my parents a favor by classifying me as white. Then my mother got deported just after I was born and took me to Cuba with her, where everyone saw me as *mulatica clarita*.
> —Fusco and Gómez-Peña, "Norte: Sur"

The work of Coco Fusco eerily epitomizes the situation of postethnic racial subjects in a post–civil rights, post–cold war, and what Fusco herself has termed the "pan-American postnationalism" era (1995, 21–24). Loathe as we may be to admit it, there are times when it becomes inevitable to think of an artist's works as being representative of a historical juncture. Coco Fusco's *oeuvre*, which includes performances, writings, criticism, reviews, photographs, videos, installations, journals, and letters, has over the last two decades registered the shifts exacerbated and catalyzed by the end of the cold war. Fusco's work, however, cannot be simply consigned to the dramas and comedies of *fin-de-siecle* imperial America. Each historical moment contains within it the marks of earlier historical moments. Her work, therefore, cannot but also register the imperial *history* of the United States of America. This is what makes her work particularly significant and illustrative. If it is chronotopologically indexicalized, marking the now and here of geopolitical time, it is also a temporal map that guides us through the contradictions, forces, and above all, *dispositifs*, on which the present imperial *pax Americana* is predicated and that conditions the coming future. Coco Fusco, a racially mixed postcolonial subject, is also a child of the sixties civil rights movements of racialized subjects in the United States. She is doubly racialized and doubly ethnicized. On the island, she is a *mulata*, descendent of slaves who bought their freedom. On the mainland, she is a Cuban Latina, who is visually racially mixed. There, she is marked by the privilege of dollars and an American passport. Here, she is a Latina/Hispanic, Cuban American citizen. As the child of Cuban immigrants, she has matured on the troubled waters between the mainland and the island. In the case of Coco Fusco, a quasiexilic experience gave rise to an outlook that positions itself beyond both the nostalgia of the return to a mythic homeland, and the untroubled acceptance of any identity whatsoever. For this reason, she is also postsocialist and post–Latin American, if by the former we mean the way in which Cuba stood for the promise of a socialism with a Latin American face, and by the latter, we understand the way in which Latin America was invented in the nineteenth century to invidiously juxtapose Anglo-Saxon crass materialism against communitarian, humanistic Latinity. Her work is blunt, lucid, sobering, albeit infused by a profound sense of humanity and care, but without being moralistic, nostalgic, or derogating.

By now it should be evident that Coco Fusco's work invites many lines of analysis. Since it is so layered, and so deliberatively self-conscious, it begs a prismatic hermeneutics, which would use each register to analyze not just the conditions of artistic production in a post–cold war and postethnic situation but also the very meaning and possible valances of race and gender and the reinscription of the exotic, forbidden, and liminal. In this chapter I will focus on only two aspects of Coco Fusco's work, advancing two theses, which are closely connected if not mutually implicating: (1) her work offers elements of a postcolonial genealogy, thereby giving her audiences a new set of connections and relationships; (2) she instigates what I would like to call a "semiotic agonistics," thereby challenging and contesting both specific meanings (such as what it means to be "American," as mentioned earlier) and how those meanings are produced (such as the ways in which identity is determined according to birthplace or ethnic kinship as defined in relation to the ethnic majority, as in the case of the nuns where Fusco was born). In Fusco's work we are able to discern a critical, creative, and confrontational type of work that enacts new forms of agency by reinscribing social space through bold interventions in the racial imaginary of Euro-Atlantic society. The first thesis, then, argues that in Coco Fusco's performances we are able to discern the artistic-conceptual elaboration of what I would like to call a "postcolonial genealogy." Genealogies scan and map three elements of the matrix of agency: discourses, truths, and institutions. A postcolonial genealogy is a type of analysis that focuses on the *dispositifs* that subject and subjectivize, that subalternize by othering while also auguring the very conditions of the contestation of that subjectivization and subjecting. My claim is that Fusco's work has doggedly focused on the institutional spaces, their respective discourses, and the truths that they produced and peddled, and that in tandem have produced postcolonial agents. The postcolonial, it will become clear, registers the triple "post" of postsocialist, post–Latin American, and postpax Americana, in the geopolitical historical calendar. In Fusco's performances we encounter unmasking, reinscription, and interpellation of the institutional spaces (for example, the museum, or the mall), the discourses (for example, art criticism, or humanitarian-moralizing feminism that knows best what "dark" women need), and the truths (of art, sex/gender, race) that betray our place on the pyramid of imperial/colonial power.

The second thesis has to do with the irreverent, insurgent, generative, and contestational character of her work. If the colonial condition has to do with the asymmetry of a master gaze that refuses and disallows the subaltern to look back, Coco Fusco's work is about destabilizing that asymmetry by daring to look back, to gaze back, to answer back, insolently, eloquently, assuredly, without shame or vacillation. This act of looking back is enacted through semiotic agonistics. By "semiotic" I make reference to how Fusco's work is about destabilizing the signified and the signifier, by appropriating the former while ridiculing and parodying the latter. By "agonistic," I make reference to how Fusco's work is an avowed intervention into the public sphere. In fact, it is more than that; it is a struggle for the public sphere that begins with the creation of alternative public spheres (see Fusco 2000, 1–20). Semiotics, or the semiological, makes reference to a dynamic process of signifying, rendering legible and discernable meanings within worlds, that uses images, words, and gestures synergistically synthesizing the semantic, the syntactic, and the pragmatic aspects of signs (on this use of "semiotics," see Hodge and Kress 1988). The semiotics I have in mind here is that of Charles S. Peirce rather than that of Fernand Saussure. Whereas Peirce's semiotics focuses on the primacy and synthesizing role of the triadic relation of sign (thirdness always presupposes firstness and secondness, and for this reason he called his semiotics "pragmaticism"), Saussure's focuses primarily on the syntactical and semantic relations among signs. With Peirce's semiotics we are closer to the realization that when we say semiotics we mean *worlds of meaning*—or the meanings/significations that disclose worlds as worlds, as contexts of significance (for a discussion of Peirce's semiotics see Apel 1995).

Signs are, however, speech acts, or "communicative acts," which are above all possible because of the public spaces in which they are enacted and performed. Semiotics and agonistics are two sides of the same public event. In Fusco's work, semiotic agonistics is both insurgent and creative; it is against and for. The "post" in the postcolonial *denounces* as much as it *announces*. It signals a temporal juncture: what comes is prefigured as the obsolete is rendered past.

## THE MEDIUM IS THE MESSAGE

> Whether its goal has been to escape the strictures of the art market, to break with the tradition of contemplating objects, to explore extreme behavior, or to draw the aesthetic experience back into the sphere of communal ritual, performance art is almost invariably centered on the artist's body.
> —Fusco, *The Bodies That Were Not Ours and Other Writings*

There is an almost oxymoronic aspect to a text that seeks to discuss properly, and with hermeneutical capaciousness, a body of work whose heart and gravitational center is the performance *of* body and the body *in* performance. Unlike commenting on a text, by way of another text, where the phenomenology of communication remains on the same plane, approaching Fusco's work by way of a written text betrays and elides the phenomenological aperture, what Martin Heidegger called *"prima philosophia,"* namely, phenomenological disclosedness, of her performances. Worlds are disclosed, or rather *worlds are worlded*, that is to say, worlds are not found in the sense of encountering something preexisting, but rather they are produced and created by meanings, language games, traditions, and semiologies (ways of representing the world). Worlds are worlded, more specifically, by way of weaving a somatic semiology, that is, the body as a sign and the signs that transmit and transit culture as bodies. Worlded worlds create the historical and material stages in which and through which social agents can, and sometimes must, assume certain places, locus, of action or agonistics. *Thus, beware of this text.* It is a twice-, perhaps thrice-, removed approximation. I have read most of Fusco's writings, descriptions of performances, and her web page, and I have seen pictures of her performances. But I have not heard her voice, nor have I seen her in performance. Yet I have been mesmerized by her writing, her clarity, and her "passionate irreverence" (Fusco 1995, 25–26). Neither *corpus delicti*, nor guilty by association, but I have been to several of Guillermo Gómez-Peñas' performances and readings in San Francisco, which is how I discovered Coco Fusco. Again, the point is not that I know, and experienced the work of, someone who knows and worked with Coco Fusco. The point is that this is a text that is just a text about texts, when the point is to have been phenomenologically challenged and deranged by her performances. Indeed, a text about a text, read quietly and privately, neutralizes the effect of Fusco's performances, which are meant to uproot us from our quotidian ways.

As always, we must abjure mere hermeneutical humility, if I *ain't got it right*, it *ain't* because of Coco Fusco or her work but because of me and my own fetishism of the written word. The preceding was an antecoda.

The other antecoda is that I am neither an art critic nor an artist. I approach her work not as someone who wants to assess her work as a contribution to the art world nor how it stands as an artistic event as seen by another artist. Her work challenges me as a *philosophical* event, as an event that merits geopolitical philosophical mediation. Like the artist, the philosopher is a creature of her time, her geopolitical tick-tack, here and now, on the world-historical map-clock, which is Adrienne Rich's chronotope, that is, a place on the map is a time in history.

The following is a truth, which is not a non sequitur—the very philosopher who claimed that phenomenological truth is pure disclosedness, the kind of event that is both historical and existential, could not recognize how his own proclivities were historically and existentially conditioned. And today, most continue to indulge him in this act of self-delusion. This philosopher was Martin Heidegger. In one of his most memorable and influential pieces of reflection, "The Origin of the Work of Art," from the mid-1930s, Heidegger described a painting by Van Gogh, which he thought represented worn out peasant shoes. Heidegger's discussion of Van Gogh's painting is strategically placed in a subsection of the essay entitled "thing and work." The aim of Heidegger's phenomenological analysis is to demonstrate how the shoes, as things represented, already evoke an entire world. A thing *is* by virtue of the world in which it exists, and it exists by virtue of *how it is disclosed* through and for humans. Still, the shoes are worn, torn, almost already useless as shoes, but in their destitute status as no longer shoes, or no longer useful as shoes, these very shoes point to the soil, the earth, the sun, the sky, the rain, the weather—a world that is beyond human subjectivity, a world that is the stage of human subjectivity. The shoes are witness and testimony. They attest to, and give evidence of, something that supersedes human willfulness, deliberateness, instrumental rationality, in a word, *das Ge-stell*, *en*-framement, the positing of something *as* something, though not as the truth of being, but as the concealment of such being due precisely to Dasein's own form of disclosedness. The work of art is fundamentally a disclosing that discloses the concealing of human disclosedness. As a work of art reveals, it renders us forlorn and dejected, for we have been found out in our acts of untruth, or more precisely, *inauthenticity*.

It is all so wonderful. In this beautiful essay from 1935, less than a year away from his administrative debacle, less than a decade following the momentous *Being and Time* of 1927, Heidegger approaches a truth that he could never fully grasp: a work of art *worlds* because it is, in the first place, already an act of *worlding* (*welten*). For him the work of art is about the event of disclosure of being, not about the disclosure of social relations. But already in 1935, Heidegger should have known better. This is the year of the great Nuremberg rallies of the National Socialist Party, so diabolically engineered and staged by Albert Speer, filmed by Lenny Reifenstahl's *In the Triumph of the Will*, and masterfully exploited and peddled by the minister of propaganda, Joseph Goebbels. In 1935, Heidegger should have known that the object of the work of art had been dematerialized by mass production and mass consumption. Heidegger should have realized, like Walter Benjamin did, that art could also be turned into a tool of political aesthetics at the service of political fetishization and idolatry. After Auschwitz, the Gulags, Hiroshima, and the many, many pictures of white cops fire hosing and letting loose their dogs on African Americans, art can no longer be naively about "the thing." The cubists, impressionists, pointillists, and futurists of the early part of the twentieth century had already begun to dismantle the alleged objectivity of the thing. Representational art was at an end. Its heyday may have been during the height of Cartesianism: when a subject stood in opposition to an object, but this heyday is surely a mythology, as the institution of art and what it produces does not always run parallel to the meanderings of philosophy. If we follow Hegel, philosophy conceptualizes what was first being disclosed in the aesthetic realm. Thus, Cartesianism may be said to register the already dawning crisis of the opposition between an autarkic-epistemological subject and a preexisting, ontologically stable, object.

This is a truth, in the sense that truth is always phenomenological disclosedness, beauty is no longer approachable by way of the object, or the representation of things, or what Arthur Danto has called "representational equivalences." Beauty is no longer that for which art quests. The *promesse de bonheur*, the utopian promise that motivates art, that calls art forth, is no longer in the beauty that can be representationally mimicked. Beauty is beyond the visible; beauty is no longer physical. Beauty has turned conceptual. Beauty is insight qua sight that sees through the fetish, the mere appearance, of the mass-produced object. And this is why Coco Fusco is so interesting. She is an artist that performs beauty by *arting* (if we understand art as *worlding*, or in other words, as a verb and not a noun) the body. This performed body and body as performance is a way of representing that immediately mocks representation, for it is a way of approaching the materiality of embodiment with the awareness that all representation is fetishistic. Which brings me to the penultimate antecoda.

Performance is about the ephemeral, the act as an event, chrono-topologically indexed—here and now are indices of geopolitical time (see Adrienne Rich reference above). If art must and can survive beyond the demise of the object and its representation, if art is to mean anything beyond the crisis of Cartesian subjectivity—read Cortes's *ego conquiro*, as Enrique Dussel has so eloquently argued—if art is to at all be truth as phenomenological disclosedness, although now translated/betrayed beyond Germano-, Greco-, Eurocentrism, then art has to turn us to the *world that worlds*, the worlding of worlds—the way in which agents constitute lifeworlds and lifeworlds constitute subjects—in which objects are commodities raised to the -nth power. If art is to mean anything today, then it can only be on the grounds of its turning into a major performance of an exorcism of the material world and commodified subjectivities. And this is why, again, Coco Fusco is so fascinating to me, a pan-American postnational agent, who, not unlike Heidegger, is trying to figure out what philosophy and art can say to each other after the death of the Cartesian subject, and the failure to find the Newtonian object, in an age of growing economic disparities and complacent bureaucratic multiculturalisms.

The final, truly, antecoda has to do with the title of this chapter. What do I mean by "coloniality of embodiment"? The term *coloniality* was coined as an adjective by Latin American social theorist Anibal Quijano, who used it to describe relations between the former colonial powers and recently decolonized societies (Quijano 2001, 117–31; see also Gorsfoguel 2003, 1–40). Relations between a metropolitan, colonial center and a peripheral, recently decolonized outpost remain asymmetrical, unbalanced, and differentiated precisely because of the colonial past that determined their historical relationships. Quijano uses 'coloniality' to modify and conjugate power. Power never exists pure and isolated. It only exists historically and is institutionally inflected and transmitted. Just as economic, political, and social relations remain clearly determined by the colonial character of the former relations between the colonial center and the subaltern periphery, Quijano suggests further, epistemological power continues to be refracted by coloniality. In other words, forms of knowing, cognizing, theorizing, and representing the world are rendered asymmetrical by the coloniality of the power that authorizes, or deauthorizes, legitimates, or delegitimates, certain epistemic frameworks and assertions.

Coco Fusco's work exemplifies how embodiment is also determined by the coloniality of power relations. The body does not exist as a prehistorical *prius*, a *tabula rasa* on which then society grafts or inscribes its particular grammar of vices and virtues, passions and disgusts, desires and psychosis. Rather, the body is the detritus, the very specific product of forms of embodiment. The coloniality of embodiment merely directs our attention to the fact that since the sixteenth century, very specific regimes, modalities, technologies of embodiment have been determined by coloniality. To the coloniality of power corresponds the coloniality of embodiment. To the flesh that is the trace of social desire corresponds the flesh as the register of social control. The coloniality of embodiment is one way in which we can understand how it is that social agents such as Coco Fusco can be so differentially and inconsistently racialized as they transgress and irrupt across a cartography written by slavery, Jim Crow, civil rights, an unfinished cold war, and bureaucratic multiculturalism. These inconsistent, risible, and thus also patently cruel and arbitrary logics of racialization do not obey the rationality of a formal principle but rather the fiat of power. *But where there is power, there is also resistance.*

## THE HUMAN ZOO, OR THE DIORAMAS OF IMPERIAL PAGEANTRY

The cage became a blank screen onto which audiences projected their fantasies of who and what we are. As we assumed the stereotypical role of the domesticated savage, many audience members felt entitled to assume the role of the colonizer, only to find themselves uncomfortable with the implications of the game. Unpleasant but important associations have emerged between the displays of old and the multicultural festivals and ethnographic dioramas of the present. The central position of the white spectator, the objective of these events as a confirmation of their position as global consumers of exotic cultures, and the stress on authenticity as an aesthetic value, all remain fundamental to the spectacle of Otherness many continue to enjoy.

—Fusco, *English Is Broken Here*

One of the most consistent themes in Coco Fusco's performances is the body in exhibition, or more precisely, the idea that for some embodiment is intricately entwined with the very practice of being exhibited, of being under the panoptic gaze of others, who cannot be looked at in return. In a series of performances during the early 1990s, prompted by the quincentenary of the so-called discovery of the New World, Coco Fusco, in cooperation with Guillermo Gómez-Peña, looked straight at the pornoscopic imagination of the colonial West. In Madrid, London, New York, Sydney, and Buenos Aires, Fusco and Gómez-Peña were exhibited in a cage as "Two Undiscovered Amerindians." These two Indians hailed from the island of Guatinau, located somewhere in the Gulf of Mexico, and which had been mysteriously overlooked and bypassed by European colonialism. They lived in the cage and performed pseudoauthentic acts, such as weaving voodoo dolls, grooming and petting each other, speaking in fictitious indigenous languages. They also allowed themselves to be touched and fed by museum visitors. For an additional fee museum and exhibition visitors could get a peek at an "authentic Guatinaui male genitalia." The central idea of this mocking act was to enact a practice that had been so central to the very performance of European and Western colonial power. The performance "Two Undiscovered Amerindians" made reference to many of the traditional practices of exhibiting peoples—pillaged, cannibalized, and carnivalized—from colonized lands. Fusco in fact gathered a catalog of these exhibitions of what we can call "imperial pageantry," which began in 1493, when Columbus brought back to Spain an Arawak and left him on display at the Spanish court, continued through the early nineteenth century, when "The Hottenton Venus" (Saartje Benjamin) was exhibited throughout Europe because of her unique female anatomy (it is not to be forgotten that after she died her genitals were dissected and put in a

FIGURE 6.1. Coco Fusco and Guillermmo Gómez-Pena, "Two Undiscovered Amerindians"

jar for exhibition; her labia apparently were extremely unusual [Sharpley-Whiting 1999, 16–31]), and concludes in 1992, when a "black woman midget is exhibited at the Minnesota State Fair, billed as 'Tiny Teesha, the island Princess'" (Fusco 1995, 43).

The performance's success, however, was measured by the diversity of responses it evoked in the many viewers. These responses, however, betrayed how the colonial subjectivity of colonial masters lives on in post–cold war Western societies. One particular response is indicative. A disturbed and offended visitor to the Washington, D.C., version of the exhibition called the "Humane Society" to complain and denounce what one must imagine was in this caller's worldview an outrage. The caller was told that "humans" were outside the jurisdiction of the Humane Society. The irony, but also profound misrecognition revealed in this humanistic gesture, is deeply telling of how humans in cages are not even human, even as one may consider them worthy of some measure of humane respect and even sympathy. Another very telling response was that articulated by some sailors, who thought that the cage was a good idea because the putatively undiscovered Amerindians might become frightened and attack visitors. Others thought that because they were different they *did* belong in cages. Others felt that they did not belong in cages because they were not visibly deformed and thus were not freakish enough. Many also complained to the museum administrators because they had been deceived and misinformed—had they seen through the artifice and theatricality of it, just as they yearned that the true thing, the authentic undiscovered savage, had been presented to them? This is the question. Even if we were to encounter not yet discovered and colonialized peoples, would we, could we, exhibit them as fascinating creatures in cages? Indeed, what is the nature of the fascination in this act of pornoscopia? Is it scientific curiosity, or is it a display of imperial power for the sake of the pedagogy of the colonial subject, who is educated into the privileges of such pornographic gaze?

During the mid 1990s, Coco Fusco collaborated with Nao Bustamente in developing the performance entitled *Stuff* (figure 6.2). As Fusco put it, "*Stuff* is our look at the cultural myths that link Latina women and food to the erotic in the Western popular imagination. We weave our way through multilingual sex guides, fast-food menus, bawdy border humor, and much more. In the course of the performance, we mingle with audience members, treating them to a meal, host of rituals and exotic legends, and occasional rumba and at least one Spanish lesson as part of our satirical look at the relations between North and South" (Fusco 2001, 111.) If

FIGURE 6.2. Coco Fusco, "Stuff"

*Stuff* had been a written text, one could say that it was a palimpsest, a texture on which layers upon layers of text had been written, effaced, written, to be effaced again. *Stuff*, however, was a performance, in which parts of a script were added or withdrawn, in which dialogue may and must have been improvised, and into which all kinds of participants were drawn.

There are two particularly interesting sections of the performance that I would like to highlight. One has to do with the consumption of the exotic, the other with the cheap and duplicitous moralism of patriarchial society. I turn to some lengthy though wonderful quotes. In scene 1, Coco Fusco and Nao Bustamente sit at a table, writing postcards. Fusco picks up one and reads it:

> May 10th, Hamburg: Hello my sweet Suzy, I just can't seem to get away from sex! I'm staying in St. Paul, the bizarre sex district of this city. The working girls here dress like aerobics instructors. I guess it's more practical than the usual puta-wear. Well, the locals and the tourists are eating it up. They are really crazy about the Brazilian girls. Ooh la la, the brazilenias are beautiful and I guess it's cheaper for the men to have them here than to go to Brazil. Dark-skinned women drive the Germans wild! Everywhere I go there is a lingerie ad staring me in the face that features a gorgeous black girl with huge breasts. I see the ad all over the place, but I can't seem to remember which company I'm supposed to buy from. The girl is oh oh so-distracting. (Fusco 2001, 112–13)

Women, in particular women of color, are indeed stuff. They can be circulated like commodities, displaced and relocated in accordance with the imperatives of colonial desire. If it is cheaper and more advantageous to have the exotic and hypersexualized Latinas brought over to Europe, then a whole industry of sexual tourism that traffics in women develops. If the market cannot come to Europe, then the customer will come to where the exotic beauty may be found. The note here is on the commodification of women by way of their exoticization. Yet another note is also marked here, and that is the gratuitous and exorbitant exhibition of female and colored bodies. Such surplus of visibility is not proportional to economic profit; something else drives it. It is the libidinal economy that foments and celebrates the consumption of the black and raced flesh that alone explains the saturation of the visual field by the desired, although depoliticized and neutralized, flesh of the black and subaltern women.

In another act of the performance, Coco Fusco, now assuming the persona of Judy, who is wearing a "black mini dress and wild wig," addresses the audience in Spanish:

You can call me Judy. Depressed? Sure I get depressed. But it's a job, honey. What can I do? Nobody chooses to be born in a mess like this one. I try not to think about things too much. When I feel down, I start thinking about a new way to fix my hair. The Italians like wild hair, so I permed mine to look more morena, what do you think? We have to eat, right?

My family? Oh, they're used to it. When I bring a Gallego home, my family doesn't see him, they see a chicken, rice, beans and platanos—a full fridge. When I tell the guys that I'm doing it to buy a pound of ground beef, they feel better about giving me money, and they leave me more. I don't say I like to be in a nice room with air conditioning for a change. I could sit in an office all day—I did that when I was working in a bank. What did I get then? Oh darling absolutely nothing. (Fusco 2001, 120)

This is not Amsterdam or Madrid for that matter. It is Cuba. Judy is a *jinetera*. Sexual tourism comes to the last cold war outpost by way of pax Americana. Who are these sexual tourists: Italians, Germans, Gallegos (Spaniards), and of course Americans, who come by way of Mexico. The *jinetera*, however, tends to be a *mulata*, a mix between black and mestizo. She is the exotic mix of Mediterranean and Caribbean genotypes: dark, sultry, Afro, hazel eyes, and voracious sexual appetite. The *mulata*, however, has historically been related to the production of food. As the house slave, she fed the master, who was invariably her illegitimate father. She clothed, watched, and pampered the master's children, who when old enough would in turn assert their right of property by way of sexual terrorism. The *mulata* is a quintessential figure of food, food producer and provider, server, and preparer. Today, the *mulata*'s role is rewritten, in the palimpsest of colonial racial embodiment, when as the sexual object of choice of the tourist dollars, she becomes the main, and sometimes only, breadwinner. In the Caribbean, the metonymic groin of the West, sugar, coffee, and sex have coalesced in the body of the *mulata*, who today is a *jinetera*.

In an essay written in 1996, entitled "Hustling for Dollars: *Jineteras* in Cuba," Fusco explores fully the historical vectors and contradictions that converge in the phenomenon of the *jinetera*. On the one hand, there is a whole history of the hypersexualization of the *mulata* that harkens back to the slavery time in Cuban history. On the other hand, there is a more recent history, such as the history of the revolutionary Puritanism that sought to cathex the libidinal forces of the revolution into higher production outputs. In a society where consumer goods were few because they were indicative of bourgeois decadence, and because they were also luxuries that were not available due to U.S. blockade, sex became a cheap and often easy alternative source of pleasure. In Cuba, however, sexual libertinage (a form of erotic resistance to the state, à la hippie culture of the 1960s) due to a revolutionary history converges tragically with the instigated sexual gluttony and affluence of societies integrated into the circuits of a global economy that grants unimpeded travel and access to almost any commodity. As Fusco put it: "What Cuba's current situation brings into relief is the connection between sexual freedom and affluence. That a tropical socialist utopia that became famous as a site of sexual liberation in the 1980s would be transformed by necessity into a scenario ripe for its sexual *exploitation* in the 1990s is just one of the more painful indicators of what it means for Cuba to be reentering a global post-industrial economy" (2001, 114).

The *jineteras* have of course become major targets of government control, surveillance, and abuse. They are celebrated by many as heroes, reviled by others for their loose morals. The government, however, as Fusco points out, is not particularly interested in the well-being of the *jineteras*. They are a source of concern because they stand for a "black market" that it cannot monitor, tax, and exploit. Fusco says that "who profits is they key issue. What one's position is on adult women's resorting to prostitution in Cuba hinges on the degree to which one can entertain the idea that sex work, even for a woman in a poor third world country, involves an exchange of benefits, and that it could be a viable option by comparison to other choices available for survival" (2001, 147). This horizon of options—which, due to the racially differentiated valances of bodies in Cuban society, per force must include sex work for some—also becomes the region of a reassertion of white privilege and psychotic purity. As the Cuban state seeks to control the work of *jineteras* due to political-economic interests, society is invested in monitoring the *jineteras* because they have become once again symbol of a threat to sexual purity. Fusco writes: "The current obsession with controlling the *jineteras*, I believe, is linked to deeply rooted cultural attitudes about sex between black women and white men" (150). There is only one way in which *mulatas* can be with white men, and that is at the scene of an asymmetrical commercial exchange soiled by the blood of sexual terror initiated with slavery. This scene and horizon of overdetermined options is what we have here called "coloniality of embodiment," by which I mean that all forms, technologies, and what Foucault called "*dispositifs*" of embodiment are indexed and suffused by the power traces of and overdetermination by colonialism. It is not the same to be born white in South Africa and white in Tennessee or Alabama or to be born Mulatto in Cuba or Mulatto in Massachusetts. These differentials represent coloniality of embodiment.

In Fusco's work we have one of the most lucid and deliberate meditations on and analysis of the way in which bodies, or rather and more precisely, *practices of embodiment* are conditioned by the colonial histories of the Americas. There are the histories of the sundering of will and intention from body and action that the reduction of the slave to property entailed. There is also the chromatic indexing of slavery with blackness, naturalized through legal institutions and practice that emphasize and biologically trace matrilineal descent (see Martino 2002, esp. chapter 1).

The demotion of the black human to property also granted the license to a boundless sexual violence, a sexual violence that moves simultaneously on two registers. On one side, there is the violence that *can* be performed with utter impunity against the black flesh qua property. On the other side, there is the violence that *must* be performed when blacks have dared, or are suspected of having dared, to transgress the sacred boundary that guards white privilege and sovereignty. Rape as the *performance of the putative right* of the master is mirrored in the bloody ritual of lynching black males for their alleged sexual transgressions (see Dray 2002; cf. Mendieta 2004 on the role of lynching as a racial violence to force a reinscription of the plantation order). As Angela Davis put it, "Lynching . . . complemented by the systematic rape of black women, became an essential ingredient of a strategy of terror that guaranteed the over-exploitation of black labor and, after the dismantling of gains made during the reconstruction, the political domination of black people as a whole" (Davis 1998a, 133; cf. Davis 2003). What Davis calls here "a strategy of terror" we can call the "syntax of a racial imaginary," the way in which certain subjects are rendered omnipotent and supremely sovereign and others wholly available, even dispensable. The syntax of racial imaginaries localizes some as subjects while rendering others mere inert material to be acted upon. For this reason, to this syntax also belongs the way in which blackness must be both utterly visible and completely absent. This is what Fusco so adroitly captures in her performances that attend to the body of the colonial subject that is both the scene of a crime and the scene of the performance of a desire (see Fusco 2000, 2–3).

This imaginary that instigates certain passions and fears is profoundly determined by the visual or rather by the dialectic of *seeing* and *being seen*. As Homi Bhabha notes, "in order to conceive of the colonial subject as the effect of power that is productive—disciplinary and 'pleasurable'—one has to see the *surveillance* of colonial power as functioning

FIGURE 6.3. Coco Fusco, Video Still, "The Incredible Disappearing Woman" (2003)

in relation to the regime of *scopic drive*. That is, the drive represents the pleasure of 'seeing,' which has the look as its object of desire, is related both to the myth of origins, the primal scene, and to the problematic of fetishism and locates the surveyed object within the 'imaginary' relation" (Bhabha 1994, 76). Society is regimented by making each white subject a peeping tom: they must want to look, and their look is lascivious. Their look asserts a power to see without being seen. Meanwhile, the seen, who is seen, who has to be seen, can only be seen, without looking back, without being allowed to register the look as a look addressed to another subject. Black beauty saturates the streets of Amsterdam—the place of one of Fusco's performances—and the television screens of American mass culture, but only as the beauty of a *scopic drive* that fetishicizes. But as Bhabha notes in the essay from which I just quoted, the scopic drive is haunted and threatened by the returned look of the other. It is this look of the other that challenges the asymmetry of the grammar of this racial imaginary. Coco Fusco's look is that look that dares to look back and laugh, ridicule, and defetishicize that imagined and imputed identity. Hortense J. Spillers' words can be used here to give expression to the innovative and radical character of Fusco's work: "[T]he project of liberation for African-Americans [postnational Pan-American postcolonial subjects in Fusco's grammar] has found urgency in two passionate motivations that are twinned—1) to break apart, to rupture violently the laws of American behavior that make such syntax possible [the syntax that reduced humans to things]; 2) to introduce a new semantic field/fold more appropriate to his/her historic movement" (Spillers 1987, 79).

In her performances Coco Fusco trades in identities, not in order to claim that one is more authentic than the other but in order to destabilize all imposed identities. She is also the sexual and racial other, exotic and mesmerizing, who ridicules and contests the pornoscopic gaze of an allegedly immutable subject. That she glides across the racial matrix of the Americas through her work, makes her performances lessons in historical imagination. Fusco's work, however, does not stop with denunciation. She also toils on the region of the *novum*. Her performances are semiological agonistics that seek to introduce a new semantic field. Once we understand the failed syntax of a racial order, a new semantic field may be accessible. There was a time when bodies *were* not ours. To insist on the *post* is necessary. Something must come after. Postnational, post-Latin American, postcolonial, post-ethnic, postsocialism, post-pax Americana: a window into what comes after these posts is opened in Coco Fusco's performances.

# Part III
Changing the Subject

# 7

## Pueblo Sculptor Roxanne Swentzell

*Forming a Wise, Generous, and Beautiful "I Am"*

RUTH PORRITT

> I think that women who have been hurt, or anybody who has been hurt, tends to need to be reassured that things are OK, like there's a warmth around them. [. . .] And I think that women and motherhood can give that kind of warmth. In the traditional Pueblo thinking, the mother is a real central figure for caring. I want to relay that kind of message so that people who have been hurt can feel a sense that there's a mother taking care of us. I think the Pueblo view of life can help the rest of the world, but I don't make my work just for Indian people; I want to reach all kinds of people.
> —Roxanne Swentzell in Abbott, "Sculptor Roxanne Swentzell: Expressions in Clay"

> People who nurture—mothers—tend to be much more humble, but in that humbleness there is a wisdom, a generosity, and when not crushed, there is a beautiful *I am*, just plain and simple.
> —Swentzell, "Artist's Statement"

As a contemporary Pueblo sculptor, Roxanne Swentzell is working within the challenges of two different cultural ideas about women, portraying both Pueblo women's creative capacity and their unique gender position. While choosing to maintain some values she has lived as a Native American, Roxanne makes sculptures for a global community she also recognizes as her own. Her representations of Pueblo women's embodied emotional experiences leap the *impasse* of either/or—either gender essentialism or social constructivism—in order to create new sites for women's feelings, thoughts, and actions. Ultimately Roxanne offers a revisionary approach to our attempts to understand *woman*: she is not defining a category that needs to be universally described, nor is she addressing a constituency that needs to be politically organized, but rather she is representing individual instances of embodied, expressive actions that deserve to be recognized for their sustaining emotional power, a humble power that tends to work in harmony with the generative resources of the natural world. Although this respectful emotional power has been more frequently chosen by women and so modeled by them, it is a power that men can also learn to chose and model.

For Roxanne, careful attention to our emotional lives increases our capacity for self-understanding even as it develops our ability to empathically learn from others. "I am a sculptor of human emotions. I want to show people a different part of themselves than they usually show. I always hope the piece is strong enough to reach someone in their heart in an emotional way that will make them feel like they had a spiritual experience of some sort. I keep believing that if I can keep reaching those depths in myself, it's going to help others reach that, too" (Pardue 1997, 2). "I think of [my sculptures] as emotional things and they all come to me in a state of emotion. A lot of the time it will be right before I go to sleep. I just feel them in my body. I know what I want to make" (Pardue and Coe 1998, 43).

Roxanne's creative making is distinguished by what I will call her "standpoint emotional integrity," a characteristic I identified after considering the writings of Kay Walkingstick, Oscar Howe, and Nancy Hartsock. Walkingstick's standard of integrity applies to Roxanne: "My criterion for all serious art is that it have the voice of integrity. . . . This art has been developed by individuals educated in the traditions of twentieth-century modernism, but also in touch with their Indian heritage, their cultural differences, and their spiritual concerns. . . . They do not share an aesthetic sensibility, but rather a strong self-identity as Indian people and as artists" (1992, 16). Although artists with integrity do not ascribe to any one school of thought, their own integrated sense of self-identity provides the impetus for their work. In a letter to one of his friends, the Sioux painter Oscar Howe addresses this sense of self-identity to underscore the emotional and intellectual quality of the artist's work; for him the most meaningful art manifests "individualism [emotional and intellectual insight]" (Strickland and Archuleta 1993, 10). Howe's concept of 'individualism' is not a narcissistic egoism, but rather the self-reflective development of a personal vision that integrates the emotional with the intellectual. Such an individual stands ready to make a singular contribution—through insight—to others. Some Native American artists may have an individuated perspective that is also illuminated, in part, by what Nancy Hartsock calls "standpoint epistemology": "'standpoint epistemology' is an account of the world as seen from the margins, an account that can expose the falseness of the view from the top and can transform the margins as well as the center . . . an account of the world which treats our perspectives not as subjected or disruptive knowledges, but as primary and constitutive of a different world" (Hartsock 1990, 171).

A *standpoint* position assumes the individual's awareness of at least two comparative frames of reference. When I write of *standpoint emotional integrity*, I am discussing a sensitive individual's perceptive consciousness of intercultural and intracultural differences, particularly as discrepancies in values or beliefs are carried by emotional recognitions. The person's clarifying apprehension is not intentionally divisive, for the individual is not motivated by aggression but by an aspiration to understand more fully, an aspiration often inflected by a strong sense of wonder and hope. Through her thoughtful reflections and creative making, the individual manifests a talent for forming an undivided—if emotionally complex—whole. By appreciating the process of increased emotional/intellectual understanding, as challenging or painfully sad as that process may be, the individual is enlivened by transforming insights that can result in feelings of humble awe.

Not only is standpoint emotional integrity located on the margins of mainstream culture, but also it is specifically embodied; the sensations that signal our emotions arise out of our bodies as physical responses to our experiences with other people and our environment. For Roxanne, our fullest kinds of knowing are initiated by our honest emotional recognitions:

> Right now I think a lot of people are realizing that we can't keep going the way we have been. There's so much pain in this realization that it takes us inside ourselves. Hopefully, the next phase is to go completely inside where we can find ourselves again. That may be painful, but we have to go through to the other side. It's a process. You have to go through the steps to the other side, to come out of the suffering of not being ourselves. I do not mean yourself with an image attached to it such as *Indian, white, banker, artist*, etc. I'm talking about yourself as an individual with the ability to be part of this whole universe as *you* without a title attached, without a name or culture to hide behind. When you take all of these off, what is left? That is who I want to reach. In that place there are a lot of feelings

that are not moving and so are not allowing us to grow. You have to understand that things are dying, including yourself—perishing inside. And that's painful. You have to know by feeling and experiencing that, or else it doesn't change. When you understand why, then it changes. You've gone through the door. I've thought a lot about all this because I've had to. I have a strong need to know why things are the way they are. My parents definitely encouraged me to think about *why*" (1997, 219). [. . .] As a contemporary artist I see my work as not just preserving my culture but continuing it. I draw on the tradition and then innovate and experiment. It's a living thing. (Pardue 1997, 2)

In 1962 Roxanne was born into a Tewa-speaking family famous for its pottery. Her mother, Rina Naranjo Swentzell, gave Roxanne access to the culture of the Santa Clara Pueblo. Her father, Ralph Swentzell, a German-descent faculty member at St. John's College, gave her access to an academic world influenced by European American culture:

> When I think of it, I can still hear Gregorian chants playing in my memories, and see Rubens' paintings and Michelangelo sculptures. Then my mother, grandmother, cousins, uncles, aunts—Pueblo dancers, drumbeats, Indian clowns, and feast days when we would run through the crowds catching the things they would throw. Then sitting on the ground watching the feet of the dancers, not realizing for a long time that the sound of the drumbeats were from a drum and not from their feet hitting the earth. These two worlds danced through my childhood. Maybe because I am from both worlds I can see what I see. (Swentzell 1997, 219)

As a young child Roxanne accompanied her mother as she made her pots: "My mom potted so the clay was right there where I saw it all the time. I had a speech impediment so I had to communicate in other ways, and I started making figures that would depict what I meant. I hated going to school so I made a clay figure of a little girl crying to explain how I felt. I made hundreds of these figures" (Peterson 1997, 195). Roxanne had discovered that she could make the clay express, in figurative form, what she hoped to articulate. Her mother, Rina, was particularly aware of Roxanne's artistic development. According to Rina,

> [Roxanne] was born with an energy that assumed connection with the earth. As a crawling baby, she wanted to be outdoors on the ground where she could put dirt in her mouth and smear it all over herself. Later, before school age, she loved to work with me in the pottery shop. Even then, she made clay figures of people and animals in her world. These figures were what she saw and felt around her. There was her dog, Flower, in a posture

that was not to be confused with any other dog. There was her dejected self sitting at a desk in school with the feeling that no one was ever more unhappy. (Fauntleroy 2002, 11)

In addition to working alongside her mother, Roxanne also visited her uncle, Michael Naranjo, and stayed with him while he made clay sculpture. Michael was blinded in Vietnam. Although he gave Roxanne her own clay to shape, he was unaware of when it became too dark for Roxanne to see what she was doing. She continued to follow his lead, sculpting "by feel" in the darkness. "He didn't have light bulbs in his studio because he didn't need them, so I would sit there in the dark. I was always impressed by his being able to sculpt that way," says Roxanne (Abbott 1997, 23). Her ability to express herself directly through her hands' touch upon the clay, the sense of the clay as felt form and not just a visual form, is a distinctive trait she credits to her experiences with her Uncle Mike.

By the time Roxanne was in junior high school, she began constructing her clay figures as if they were pots, preferring the ancient coil-and-scrape technique used by the Pueblo. Although she had been making pots for her own functional use, as her interest in sculpting continued to develop, she adapted her clay techniques to her figures. "I make [my sculptures] in a traditional manner, meaning that they're coiled like pots. I sometimes call them fancy pots because I coil them up just like a pot and form them as I go along" (Abbott 1997, 24). Her parents recognized Roxanne's aptitude for sculpting, so she was sent to the Institute of American Indian Art in Santa Fe for high school. Roxanne entered that educational experience not only with her sculpting talent, but also with skills for thinking about *why* she was doing her work. "Both my parents were very encouraging when they saw that I had a talent for working with clay. They were people who wanted me to think about what I did, to have a reason for why I did what I did, and not just do things haphazardly. My mother was known for her Pueblo philosophy and she writes quite a bit. They encouraged me to have a whole philosophy" (Abbott 1997, 23). Roxanne's tendency to reflect upon her own work gave her an independent perspective that helped her critically engage her educational experiences. She decided for herself how she would approach her own work.

> Many of the teachers at the Institute of American Indian Arts were white people who were trying to get Indian artists to make what the white people thought was Indian art. This caused a lot of conflict for me. I thought *If I am an Indian then I'll automatically be making Indian art because that's what I am.* If we see through *our* eyes then whatever we are will come out.

> And that means whether I am an Indian or not. It doesn't really matter. What matters is that whatever appears from within us is true. I learned to listen to myself and not be so influenced by what other people wanted me to make. I am going to represent the world through my eyes—and not as somebody told me I was suppose to. (Roxanne Swentzell 1997, 216)

Her clarity about her own values enhanced her ability to make work that was esteemed by her instructors. The school gave Roxanne her first show in their museum. The following year she moved to Portland, Oregon, to attend the Portland Museum Art School.

> People in art school looked at art very differently than I did. I got really depressed when I was in Portland because I felt that the people there had separated art from their lives and from everything around them. It became a dead world to me. I couldn't understand why people would do art just for art's sake. To me, art always had to come from a life experience—or what was happening around me. It seemed so strange to be walking a city street or through a parking lot and see the homeless on the side of the road, or see people crying. The focus of the art school seemed to be disconnected from these realities. I could not pretend I never saw that, then try to make this piece of artwork that had nothing to do with what I had just witnessed. Making a piece of art, to me, had to be as full an experience of myself as I could possibly relay. If I was going through a lot of pain in my life, I couldn't possibly make a sculpture of a jolly guy, because my tears would ruin his smile. I've tried to say something I really didn't feel in my art, but it just looks and feels like a lie to me. (Roxanne Swentzell 1997, 216)

Roxanne's response to her art school experience indicates a radical difference between the Tewa approach to art and modernist European American conceptions of art. Modernist conceptions of art as creative making often assume distinctions among art, craft, and daily tasks. The Tewa approach to art as creative making does not hold these distinctions, but rather overcomes them through a broader recognition of the value of all constructive human agency working in cooperation with the environment. According to Roxanne's aunt, Nora Naranjo-Morse, "In the Tewa language, there is no word for art. There is, however, the concept for an artful life, filled with inspiration and fueled by labor and thoughtful approach" (1992, 15). For the Tewa, the artful life encompasses both the individual and cultural processes of rejuvenation or revitalization, spanning all actions that seek, find, regain and renew life (Sweet 1985, 12). Rina affirms the connection between people's artful life and their relationship with the environment:

> Much has been written about native language not including *art* as a word because the individual creative act in the traditional [Tewa] world was about doing things in a way to feel oneness with other humans as well as with the earth, clouds and wind. Achieving an understanding of the flow of life within which one participated was the goal [. . . S]ensitivity was expected not only of special people, or people called *artists*. Every person was expected to be sensitive to his or her physical, emotional and spiritual context. Therefore, every person was a creator, a reshaper, who had the capability to bring unassociated elements into some definable whole or form. (Rina Swentzell 1998, 14, 9–10)

Creative making is an alert practice where ethics and aesthetics become interanimating, a practice that includes an attentive, respectful love for others as well as for oneself. "With my sculptures I try to reach people's emotions so they can remember themselves. . . . Using gestures and expressions, I try to bring these little people to life—to communicate in a way other than with words. It's good practice to use the other senses besides just the mouth. I'm trying to do that with everything I do. Everything we do has to be sacred. It doesn't matter if you're baking bread or making a sculpture—or walking, it's got to be done in the same manner. It's got to be done with love for yourself" (Roxanne Swentzell 1997, 221). This kind of self-respect is not self-centered but rather motivates each person's respectful awareness of the entire surrounding environment and the balance between males and females.

> What I try to get across to people is a way of seeing the world. That is the Pueblo philosophy I was taught—the way of seeing the connectedness we have with everything around us and being in touch with ourselves on both the spiritual level and in the physical sense. More and more, I see people out of touch with the physical environment around them. I think that's a key thing to what I try to express. A lot of my stuff, too, has to do with the female. The female and male in Pueblo societies were much more balanced that in the Western view. Because the Western view is so male-oriented, I tend to push a lot of the female aspects to try to balance that out. The female has many strengths that are ignored in Western society but which are recognized in the Pueblo world. (Abbott 1997, 23–24)

Karen Kilcup agrees with Roxanne's assessment that, on the whole, women were more respected in Native American cultures than in European-influenced cultures. Although there was a diversity among tribal groups that makes generalization difficult, Kilcup concedes that "we can say that Indian women were often more valued than their European counterparts, perhaps because they lived within communal organizations where every member of the group contributed to its well-being.... Many Indian cultures affirmed women's power" (2000, 2). Rayna Green reminds us that Native American social forms that involve men and women in complementary, mutual roles—roles wherein both genders interact equally with natural resources—cannot be productively analyzed in terms of many European American feminist theories of female oppression (1980, 264). If Native American women in the past experienced a balance of power as liberating, then they will tend to seek that balance rather than fight for a perceived freedom from constraint. For Roxanne, part of reestablishing that balance of power is making visible women's experiences. "Women's lives are incredible but have been largely unseen, and because of this I do a lot of women's issues. I mean my heart goes out to women so much. It seems like the older I get the more this topic interests me. If I do ten pieces, nine of them are women and one is a man. And without consciously thinking that way. It just comes out that way because that's what ends up coming through me" (Roxanne Swentzell 1999, 16).

After living for a year in Portland, Roxanne returned home to marry, work in clay, and raise two children, her son, Porter, and her daughter, Rose. She exhibited and sold her work, winning a total of eight awards at the annual Santa Fe Indian Market in 1986. After taking a five-year break from Indian Market, she returned in 1994, to win the Wheelwright Museum and Joseph Block Sculpture Award. When her sculptures were included in the 1994–95 "Sisters of the Earth" traveling exhibition, Roxanne wrote a statement for the accompanying catalog that described how her focus on the human figure is her personal way of posing several related questions: "How do we, as human beings, fit into the world around us? Why have we made ourselves so separate from nature? Could this be the reason we feel so lost and empty and alone at times? Could our remembering where we come from and how we are connected to all the earth's species bring us back home? Could finding our *true selves* bring us closer to all other beings? And, could this be the thing we are most afraid of, or could this be the very thing we all yearn for so deeply in our hearts?" (Roxanne Swentzell 1994a). During her second marriage Roxanne and her partner founded a nonprofit organization, Flowering Tree Permaculture Institute, to study environmental living. After a 1995 visit to Roxanne's home on the reservation of Santa Clara Pueblo to meet with the young Rose, Bruce Hucko describes his impressions: "Rose leads an independent life. She and her older brother are home-taught and live in an adobe building designed and constructed by their mother and friends without a blueprint. Organic, self-sustaining farming is practiced outside the house. Inside, hand-made tools and furniture accentuate the simple, spacious living space. Anywhere else the Swentzell's style of living would be considered alternative, but here, on a sunny June day, it just seems to make common sense" (Hucko 1996, 64). Rose offers her own observations: "I think my life is a lot different than a lot of other kids' lives. My cousin Devonna has computer games and all kinds of things like that. I don't. We don't even have electricity! Most kids have the TV constantly playing. They don't ever get to take care of plants and chickens, turkeys and sheep. . . . I learn by watching Mama, just watching. I like forming things with my fingers. It's easier to get three dimensions in clay than with drawing. And it tastes good!" (Hucko 1996, 64).

The Pueblo people's relationship with clay provides a direct link between themselves and their environment. Clay is considered "a gift from Mother Earth, and like all of her gifts, it is sacred" (Timble 1987, 10). The landscape of the Southwest is an expanse of desert, mesa, and mountain, which is so formidable and austere that it resists being mastered. The land, Mother Earth, cannot be easily exploited. There is nothing diminutive or feminine about this landscape, given the European American understanding of those terms; yet the land is the basis for Pueblo life. For the Pueblo people who live, understandably, in reverence for this landscape, there is no disdain for Mother Earth, for mud and clay, for women or for vessels—or the relationships between them. Roxanne explains the Pueblo beliefs:"We're from this earth, we are creatures of this earth, she is our mother. Remember where you come from. She is the one who gives you life, and if you destroy her, you destroy yourself. When you work clay, you understand your interdependence, your connections . . . I am a mud person" (Rosenberg 1995, 82–83). The dynamic correlation between clay and the human body is also lived by Nora Naranjo Morse: "For hundreds of years Pueblo people have treasured their powerful relationship with clay. Veins of colored earth run along the hillsides of New Mexico, covering remote trails with golden flecks of mica. Channels of brown and scarlet mud wash across the valleys, dipping and climbing the sprawling landscape. Intricately woven patterns of clay fan out under the topsoil, carrying the life of pottery to the Pueblo people" (Naranjo-Morse 1992, 9). "I am an open vessel. I never know what life's experiences will give me, what opportunity will inspire my creativity" (Peterson 1994, 184).

Like Nora, Roxanne retains confidence in her culture's own way of informing the metaphors of woman-as-earth and woman-as-vessel, despite the disfavor these metaphors may now have in European American feminist circles. Assuming the European American male construction of feminine earth and vessels as passive and submissive, some mainstream feminists have critiqued these metaphors as exploitative of women in their own culture. Surely we should dispense with the concept of the land as virgin and subject to man's power to rule, tame, and reform *her*. Surely we should dispense with the concept of the woman as a passive vessel awaiting man's seed or goal or purpose, an idea as old as Aristotle. These metaphors reinforce the devaluation of women and their subordination. However, the Pueblo people's experience of the southwestern landscape and their deep appreciation for clay vessels endows their own metaphors of woman-as-earth and woman-as-vessel with completely different values that affirm women.

Roxanne's 1998 clay sculpture *Mixing Clay* makes the equation between the woman's body and clay explicit, for with her feet the standing Pueblo woman, nude, is mixing the "clay," which both composes the figure and is its subject. The clay woman tests the clay in her fingers to feel if it has the correct level of bond. In *Making Herself, 2000* (figure 7.1) Roxanne shows a nearly complete figure who uses a continuous clay coil originating from her pelvis to form her one remaining leg: "She's concentrating hard because she doesn't want to mess up," says Roxanne (Fauntleroy 2002, 62), noting that she considers this piece a self-portrait. Pueblo women are affirmed by their relationship with the materials of the earth and their association with the power of Mother Earth. For Pueblo people, creativity with clay is a female prerogative.

*Made in Her Own Image, 1999*, represents a delighted clay woman who has formed a clay man by holding herself as the standard, a humorous reversal of the male-centered Judeo-Christian creation myth. Speaking of any woman's assured ability to produce through clay, Ernest Tapia of Santa Clara says, "A woman can make anything, any kind of shape with her own hands" (Timble, 1987, 13). The ability to shape and reshape is not a form of creativity particular to a male godhead. Women's creative and procreative power is highly regarded in Pueblo culture, and women do establish an esteemed standard. Pueblo men are complemented by other people's recognition of what some European Americans would consider an essentially female characteristic. "If you are a man and you are called Gia— a nurturer—then you are being told something very good about yourself, for you have a way of being which is like a mother," Roxanne says (Rosenberg 1995, 83). For the Tewa, the ability to nurture is valued by both women and men; it is not considered an essential characteristic of females. Women's choices to express emotional warmth and tender concern are not denigrated to a second-rate status, for women are valued in Pueblo culture.

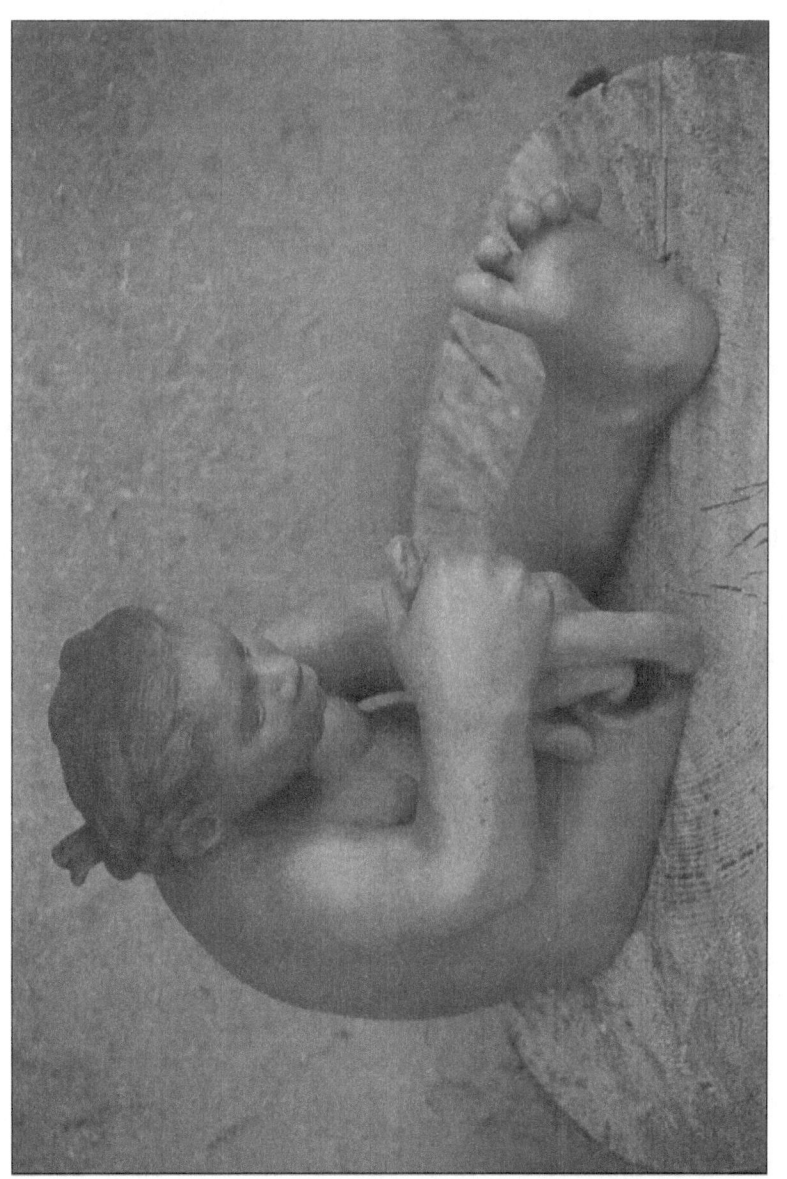

FIGURE 7.1. Roxanne Swentzell, *Making Herself*, 2000, Clay 8"W x 12"D x 10"H

The Tewa myth of origins provides some suggestions for how traditional Pueblo groups have valued women. Rather than offering a chronicle of how a male god creates something out of nothing and then fashions a male as the first human, the Pueblo myth begins with a populated Mother Earth as a given. However, the Tewa people and animals were living underground, beneath Sandy Place Lake, in a realm that was dark but where there was no death; they resided there with the two supernaturals who were the first mothers of all the Tewa, "Blue Corn Woman, near to summer" and "White Corn Maiden, near to ice" (Ortiz 1969, 14). Eventually these two mothers initiate the extended process of investigation that will lead to the migration of the Tewa to the world above them, which until that time had been "unripe," its clay surface too soft.

The Tewa myth of origin is remarkable for its heterogeneity, its depiction of a persistently good-willed sense of trial and error, and the cooperative efforts of all beings to assist with the migration to the earth's surface, resulting in their successful emergence. Although the entire myth is too elaborate to recount here, one of its most unusual features is that four times the migration effort is halted and the group returns to the underground realm because the beings realize they "are not yet complete and that something else was needed" (Ortiz 1969, 15). During the second return, the sacred clowns, the Kossa, were created to entertain the people when they would grow tired and unhappy. The clowns were marked with alternating stripes of dark and light—much like rock strata—to show that they embody alleged contrasts such as male/female, summer/winter, night/day. To resolve conflict and reestablish harmony, the clowns prompt an affectionate humor based on wisdom or well-intentioned foible, not a derisive humor based on foolishness or mockery. Upon the final return, the Women's Society was formed. Now all beings agree that everything is complete, and the migration prepares to proceed once again. Throughout the Tewa myth of origin, women are portrayed as generative yet humble, as taking initiative yet not regarding themselves as superior to others, as attentively watching over the entire community, and as providing necessary perspectives that are required to form a completeness that makes the whole. These same caring features of strength are complimented in men when Tewa people call them "Gia."

Women's relationship with Mother Earth is restorative as well as generative. When Roxanne portrays Pueblo women's disappointment in love, she often implies that the woman's relationship with Mother Earth will soothe the emotional pain. In pieces such as *Broken Hearts, Broken Bowls, Now What? 1996* Roxanne presents the woman's loving body as a potentially damaged vessel. The saddened figure sits holding two halves of a fractured bowl in each of her hands. The same circular design embracing both the rim of the broken bowl and the woman's torso not only indicates the correlation between the woman's body and the vessel but also recapitulates, from Pueblo tradition, "the continuous movement which represents the connective breath of the universe" (Naranjo 1994, 47). Roxanne implies that the woman's ability to work constructively with a broken vessel will inform how she decides to work constructively with her own broken heart. If you look closely at the Pueblo landscape, you find that it is the resting place for thousands of ancient pottery shards, which are valued as signs of previous human making. Pottery shards are also ground to use as temper for new clay. In the end, nothing is truly lost in the Pueblo cycle of clay. Likewise, sadness acknowledges the distressing experience of loss or anticipated privation, a poignant sorrow, which means that, ultimately, an honest emotional life has been retained. Roxanne speaks about the significance of sadness and how it helps us gain insight into our human condition, ultimately contributing to peace:

> I hope we can all realize that we are very sad, blind people right now and that all of us are searching for what we long for—a place, a sense of importance, and love. And we deserve that *something*, no matter who we are. I would like us to be able to communicate with each other in a way that we never could before. It's just like talking to you. You are searching for love and I am searching for it, too. Because we are hearing with our hearts instead of our preconceived notions, we have just filled ourselves up. I think it will get so we can do that with anybody. We will be able to say *When I cry I know she will understand why I am crying. When I laugh I know she will know that I am not laughing at her. She will know I am laughing because I feel good.* And I can scream because I am hurt and you know why. Then when you cry in front of me I can say *Go ahead, cry.* At that time we will have peace. (Roxanne Swentzell 1997, 222)

Peace requires people's mutual ability to protect each other's vulnerability in sadness: we should recognize the tender human aspirations for a good life that are intrinsic to heart-felt loss. Sadness is not feared as debilitating but respected as granting capacity, for in our loss we know clearly what we valued, what we aspired to do or be. The seated figure of *A Moment in Time, 1998* closes her eyes and tips her head sideways as if to yield to a resolute sadness. Although her inward focus is solemn, her sense of resignation seems to strengthen her rather than weaken her. In *Oh, My, 2000*, the woman clasps her strong hands to her stricken face, suddenly aware of loss. The urgent sadness of loneliness is presented in

*Someone to Talk To, 2001*; the woman's face shows that "in that state of real self-reflection, we are utterly alone," says Roxanne (2002, 56).

However, it is exactly through the sadness of self-reflection that we can grow in self-awareness. Even the *Despairing Clown, 1992*, who is usually wise and humorous, peels off the Kossa-striped skin to look beneath the veneer of his role and sadly wonder what he should do next. The dark clay woman of *Hidden Feelings, 1997* is removing a white porcelain mask with its fixed smile of pleasant cheer. Her own face manifests her frightened sadness, for she recognizes that, try as she might, she cannot adopt the dominant culture's disapproving attitude toward sadness. If she feels a foreboding sadness, then that is what she should express to others. Although sadness is frequently classified by psychologists as one of the basic emotions expressed beginning with infancy, it is remarkable that as of 2000 no major synthetic work on sadness had been written in the English language (Barr-Zisowitz 2000, 607). This may reflect a censorious or repressive attitude toward sadness within the European American culture. Since sadness is a signal that we have emotionally recognized a distressing problem, often a problem that has been ignored by other people, sadness has a potentially subversive quality. Sadness precedes the plaintive request for change and can be apprehended as a humble form of honest emotional power that deserves respect. Lacking a culturally developed awareness of sadness, European Americans may not be as able to move into forms of constructive change that are initiated by states of sadness and grief. To affirm the value of sadness and grief for Native Americans, Renya Ramirez observes how emotional vitality and genuine insight for constructive reform require that we express real loss rather than pretend that it has not happened (Ramirez 1998, 323).

Several of Roxanne's sculptures include sadness as an aid for reclaiming the self from destructive social conventions. The dejected woman in *Pinup, 2000* (figure 7.2) holds a poster of a curvaceous female torso over her body. Her brown clay face has been covered with white foundation, her artificially pale skin is highlighted with pink blush on her cheeks, and she sports red lipstick to match the red fingernails in the poster. She has lost her individuality in order to attain the "perfect" body, face, and skin dictated by European American culture's social standards for females. Her pensive and apprehensive expression shows that she has begun to recognize the dismal outcome of her loss of self. "There seems to be the need to tell this story—about images versus reality—over and over in my work," Roxanne comments (Fauntleroy 2002, 30). In *Framed, 2001* the rueful woman holds a gilded frame in front of her face, showing how separating

FIGURE 7.2. Roxanne Swentzell, *Pinup, 2000*, Clay 13"W x 14"D x 18"H

out any one part of a person for scrutiny is dehumanizing. The mortified woman of *In Crisis, 1999* is stunned by how clawlike and threatening her long, red-painted fingernails seem to her. "She recognizes that these images of what she's supposed to be, especially from television, are an attack on her," Roxanne explains (Fauntleroy 2002, 32). The alternative image of the self-defined woman who overcomes damaging social dictates about her body-self appears in *Kneeling, 2003*. Her serene face and closed eyes indicate her peaceful withdrawal from external influences. She lovingly embraces herself with her crossed arms. In her artist's statement for this figure, Roxanne says, "She gently holds herself, unaware of anything but the feel of her own body. In a way she is kneeling to herself." The same appreciation for embodiment is recorded joyfully in *Soaking in the Sun, 1990* (figure 7.3). As the woman feels the warmth caress her, she clasps her hands with gratitude and pleasure. "Our simple desires, like sitting in the warm sun, are sometimes our deepest reminders that we are truly fruit of this planet," says Roxanne (Fauntleroy 2002, 74).

Experiencing our embodied consciousness in sympathetic relationship with the natural world gives us a sense of wondrous awe and humility. Although many of Roxanne's sculptures address this theme, *Window to the Past, 2000* (figure 7.4) is based on Roxanne's vivid memory of a particular childhood event. To respect Mother Earth, Roxanne's mother taught her not to dig into the earth to willfully find ancient shards or artifacts. If something came to the surface through a natural process, such as the wash of rainwater, then she could accept it as a gift from the earth. One day Roxanne studied an anthill and discovered a tiny stone bead among the loosened grains of dirt. As she held the bead between her fingers, Roxanne wondered who had made it, worn it, or given it to another. She imagined the possible incidents involving the history of the piece of stone as it left the earth for human community only to return to the earth so that, eventually, an ant would bring it on another migration out of the earth. "You're tunneling through that little hole in the bead, getting a peek into the past. You're tunneling through time. Through the smallest of things, you have a connection with the past," says Roxanne (Fauntleroy 2002, 16). The clay woman holds the stone bead in her hand, knowing that, in order to be made, it was once held in another person's hand. Her soft, transfixed gaze implies her thoughtful reflections on the implications of her find. The seemingly fragile bead has endured. She feels humble awe at how the bead and herself are both tiny yet significant parts of the generous systems of natural processes that will continue through time. Her humility and the wisdom that results from her emotional insight prompts

FIGURE 7.3. Roxanne Swentzell, *Soaking in the Sun, 1990*, Clay 11"W x 12"D x 16"H

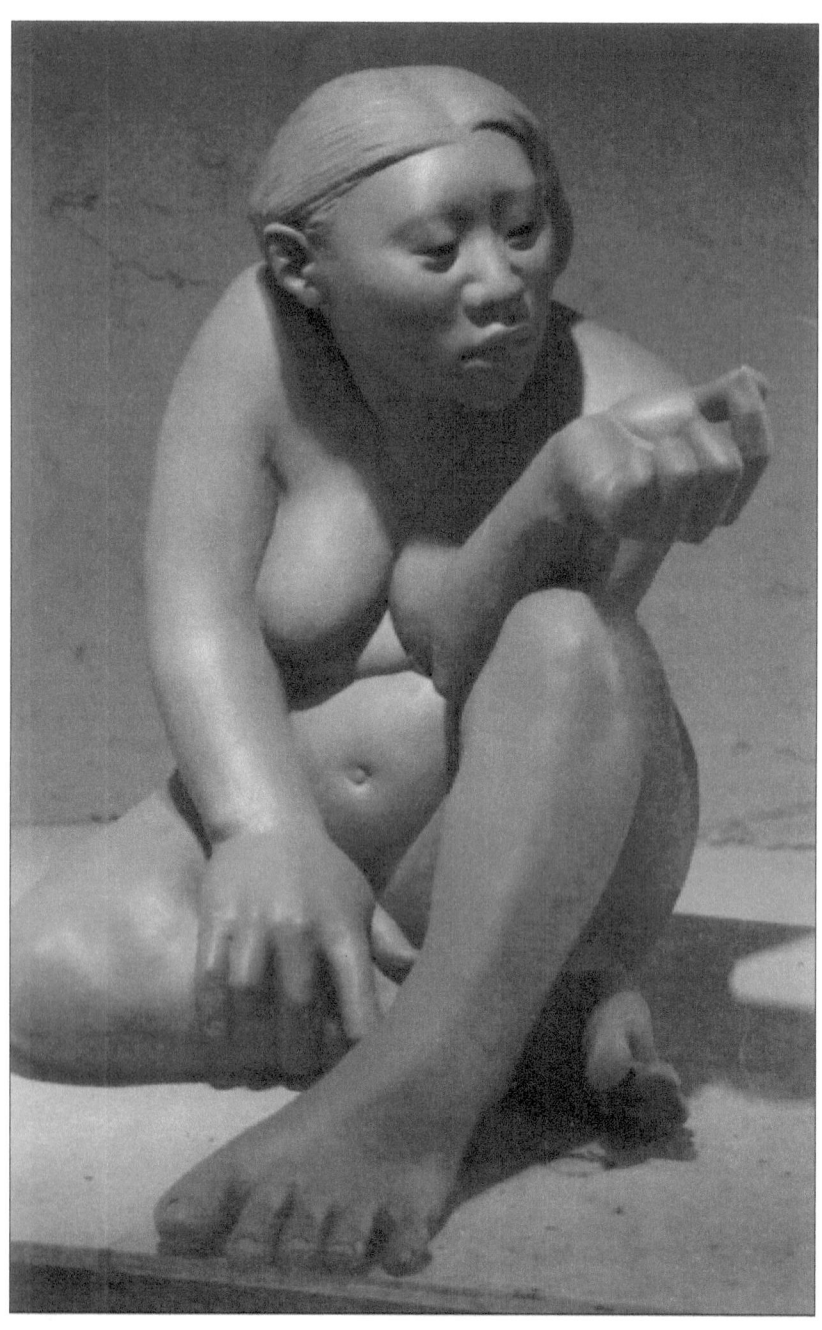

FIGURE 7.4. Roxanne Swentzell, *Window to the Past, 2000*, Clay 3'W x 3.5'D x 3'H

her beautiful sense of "I am" just plain and simple—she has no need for any role or social construction to give her a sense of identity.

Roxanne's sculptures represent individual instances of embodied, expressive actions that deserve to be recognized for their sustaining emotional power, a power that tends to work in cooperation with the generative resources of the natural world. Although this humble emotional power has been more frequently chosen by women and so modeled by them, it is a power that men can also learn to choose and model, for it is a potential capacity within any human being. Some men may have been acculturated to devalue or dismiss emotional power because it seems humbling to them, reminding them of their mortal bodies and how their competitive participation in realms of social power can never prevent the final loss of their physical life. As Susan Bordo has observed, both the modernist "view from nowhere" and the postmodernist "dream of everywhere" share the same misguided desire to escape from a material world where people are situated in physical bodies that produce knowledge (Bordo 1990, 145). People influenced by modernism or postmodernism can consider learning from the standpoint of Pueblo women and men who have worked with clay and felt their bodies' generative power as it joined with the generative power of the earth: "Each person is capable of thoughtful and creative action. . . . [T]o feel the creative power of the universe and to express this power as a way of participating in it gives [people] the feeling of being special and ordinary at once," claims Rina Swentzell (1997, 355). Personal significance need not be lost in the confusion of dualities promoted by European American culture, where the dichotomies of mind/body, male/female, white/Indian establish divisions that prevent more comprehensive understandings (Allen 1986, 134). When Roxanne was commissioned by the National Museum of the American Indian in Washington, D.C., to make a sculpture that would encompass the hemisphere's hundreds of indigenous cultures, she produced *For Life in All Directions, 2004*, a wall installation of six people who dance together and reach out to include other people. Visitors to the museum spontaneously smooth their hands along the figures' hands, as if accepting their implied invitation to join them (Ault 2004, 50). Roxanne's standpoint emotional integrity has drawn upon her experiences of at least two different cultures to make sculptures that expressively communicate to members of the global community. She says, "I want to symbolize women, and my culture, and humanity. I am trying to say things to the world, and the response has been amazing! My pieces are crossing cultural and all kinds of boundaries. People from all over the world see things in my pieces. It has been very, very exciting to me, the ultimate communication" (Peterson 1997, 195).

> I Sculpt
> To reach out to you
> Hoping to go past
> the words and thoughts
> that bind us
> to a shallow world
> Hoping
> to catch a moment
> of direct connection
> between your soul
> and mine
> then for that second
> we will remember
> what is important
> and in remembering
> there is hope.
> —Roxanne Swentzell

# 8

## The Syncretism of Native American, Latin American, and African American Women's Art

*Visual Expressions of Feminism, the Environment, Spirituality, and Identity*

PHOEBE FARRIS

---

### INTRODUCTION

This chapter discusses aspects of traditional Native American religion/spirituality and traditional African religion/spirituality that are evident in the art of Latin American, African American, and Native American women artists. Artists that fuse both African and Native American religious symbols in a syncretic manner as well as those who are inspired by only one of these cultural sources will be highlighted. Emphasis will be on twentieth- and twenty-first-century artists, particularly those whose art work coincided with social movements of the 1960s through the 1990s that referenced black nationalism, pan-Indian identity in the United States, *indigenismo* in Latin America and the United States Southwest, women's liberation, and identity politics in general.

In Native American cultures the arts, beauty, spirituality, and activism are intertwined as symbols of the spiritual and physical worlds that enrich daily lives and ceremonies. As protectors and reminders of the living universe, symbols bridge the gap between the spiritual and physical realms. Public life brings together dancing, poetry, and the visual arts, uniting them in a single function; ritual serves as the all-embracing expression of life. Contemporary Native American women artists explore ancient art traditions, styles developed during colonialism and reservation confinement, and newer, experimental art concepts. Their art often functions as social criticism by using content that expresses alienation from the dominant American culture. Whether the work is abstract in form or more representational, it usually has a social context.

In looking at the art of African American women from the 1960s and continuing today, it is evident that many have been inspired by symbols from ancient Egyptian culture such as pyramids, ankhs, and hieroglyphs, west African cosmology from Benin/Nigeria and Asante/Ghana, and Islamic cultural influences from North Africa. African traditions are often expressed visually through the syncretism of Christianity, Native American beliefs, Judaism, and Muslim traditions in a shamanistic approach to art that stresses the sacredness of nature, the healing power of art, and racial/ethnic identity restoration. Women artists from mixed cultural/racial backgrounds often incorporate religious/spiritual motifs from the array of Native American beliefs still prevalent in the Americas despite conversions to Christianity.

For women artists in the United States such as Yolanda Lopez, Amalia Mesa-Bains, Adrienne Hoard, and Betye Saar, the eagle, the Egyptian pyramid and ankh (cross), and the Virgin of Guadalupe have meanings that signify "solidarity by suturing the heroic and the ordinary, the real and the spiritual, the local and the spiritual, the local and the global, the past and the present, man and woman, Mexican and Chicano or Chicana, African American and African, and all Third World peoples" (High 1997, 127).

## LATIN AMERICAN WOMEN ARTISTS

Beginning in the nineteenth century and continuing into the twentieth century the Latin American aesthetic was "revolutionized and conditioned by political unrest, social circumstances, avant-garde groups, the search for a national identity, tenuous cultural boundaries, struggles of independence, the colonization of pre-Hispanic peoples, the influx of blacks from Africa, the infiltration of European traditions, crossbreeding, and racial integration" (Sánchez 1999, 126). The only European tradition that had a significant impact was surrealism, and in Latin America surrealism fused with indigenous spiritual, mythological, and cultural traditions.

The paintings of Tarsila do Amaral and Tilsa Tsuchiya acknowledge the aesthetics and spirituality of their indigenous roots in Brazil and Peru respectively, incorporating modern surrealism with native beliefs. In Mexico Frida Kahlo's influences were pre-Columbian imagery, syncretic folk Catholicism, and surrealism.

A contemporary artist who is especially proficient in fusing both African and Native American religious symbols in a syncretic manner is Regina Vater. Working in both the United States and her native Brazil, Vater's installations and videos embrace the hybridization of European, African, and American Indian beliefs with an emphasis on nature's sacred forces. Vater references the metaphysical and shamanistic rituals of indigenous and African traditions as they connect to the sacredness of nature—making art that is both modern and organic/natural, art that is created not just for aesthetic purposes but also for its energy fields (Sánchez 1999, 126).

Examples of Vater's work that highlight her use of syncretism are *Verve* (1997), an installation influenced by African ground paintings and Navajo sand paintings that uses corn, rice, and beans to create a spiral Jaguar's eye symbolic of Afro-Brazilian healing and *Magi (O)cean* (1970), an installation on a beach in Rio de Janeiro that used syncretic representations of the rainbow snake, Oturmaré, goddess of hope, which in Catholicism is called "Nossa Senhora de Aparecida" (the black Madonna).

In her writings and her multimedia visual art expressions, Regina Vater emphasizes that the African spirit is everywhere in Brazil—in the food, the words, the sensorial spirituality, the endurance under adverse conditions, the music, the freedom of bodily movements, and so on. Vater herself describes this: "For the African culture, the body acts as a stage for our emotions, or connection to the life energy . . . our creativity and the primordial tool of our spirituality. Through the African tradition (which survived in Brazil through the strategy of syncretism) . . . the Africans blended their ancient gods with symbols taken from Catholicism, Judaism, and the Native American and Muslim traditions" (Vater 1997, 72).

In the United States, Mexico, and her homeland, Cuba, Ana Mendieta incorporated the symbols of Afro-Cuban Santería with feminist beliefs of "the personal is political" in earthworks and performance art that utilized dirt, vegetation, fire, water, blood, gunpowder, and her own body. Mendieta's *Silueta* series that began in the seventies consisted of archetypal female figures cut, drawn, and impressed into the earth. Other series involved Mendieta lying nude in an Aztec grave, covered in flowers and white grave clothes to symbolize indigenous burial bundles. During visits to Cuba in the eighties, Mendieta carved female deities on the walls of the Jaruco caves, an ancient indigenous Taino spiritual site. In her art "the female outline remained its focus, burned, drawn, and carved on leaves, bark paper, and logs, or molded from mud, which then parched and cracked. In 1985 Mendieta met her death, and the earth, falling from a high window in an eerie echo of her art" (Lippard 1990, 86).

Chicana artist Yolanda López uses the Virgin of Guadeloupe as a major figure in her art, deconstructing the Virgin's passivity as a suffering Indian/mestiza Christian and transforming her into a contemporary active indigenous image. In 1978 López created a triptych of portraits showing herself, her mother, and her Indian grandmother as the Virgin of Guadeloupe with the cape or mantle of stars and the sun-ray body halo that are the Virgin of Guadeloupe's traditional attributes. However, López also added a snake to each image and featured herself running with her face gazing straight ahead. The Virgin of Guadeloupe, a syncretic figure, became an icon of motherhood and *mestizaje*, "a traditional figure who emerged only fifteen years after the Conquest as the Christianized incarnation of the Aztec earth and fertility goddess Tonantzin and heiress to Coatlicue, the Lady of the 'Snaky Skirt,' in her role as blender of dualities. López perceives the Guadeloupe as an instrument of social control and oppression of women and Indians. She points out that the Church tried to suppress the 'Indian Virgin' and only accepted her when her effectiveness as a Christianizing agent became clear" (Lippard 1990, 42). Influenced by the Chicano and civil rights movements, Yolanda López feels that creating art is a means for her to practice good citizenship—a method for challenging stereotypes about Mexicans and raising public consciousness. Also a writer, López coauthored (with Moira Roth) the chapter "Social Protest . . . Racism and Sexism" (Broude and Garrard 1995).

## AFRICAN AMERICAN WOMEN ARTISTS

There is no one monolithic African American art, but within the work of individual African American artists one finds the embodiment of what it means to be black or African American, in all its complexities. For the purposes of this chapter, *black* or *African American* refers to people of African descent whose lives have been impacted by some or all of the following factors: the transatlantic slave trade, European colonialism, Western imperialism, racism, and global dispersion.

Although at times indistinguishable from the cultural forms of other American ethnic/racial groups, African American styles of worship, performance, music, the visual arts, and literary expression usually stand out among American cultural products, representing a common vision that resonates in the black Diaspora. This common cultural vision is evident in a *black aesthetic*—"the name for a collection of philosophical theories about the arts of the African Diaspora: an aesthetic grounded in the idea of a new, that is, a post-Emancipation and postcolonial black identity which, from Jazz Age Harlem . . . to the sound system of south central Los Angeles, thrives in black communities where artistic creativity and performance are the basic cultural currencies" (Farris 1999). The black aesthetic can also be characterized not only as alternative to its mainstream counterparts but also as proactive and aggressive in its desire to articulate, testify, and bear witness to that cultural difference (Farris 1999).

The following are some of the twentieth-century African American women artists who have incorporated African spirituality into their aesthetic expression: Lois Mailou Jones (1905–1998), who studied masks from non-Western countries, visited eleven African countries to conduct research on the continent's art and artists, and following her marriage to a Haitian incorporated Afro-Haitian Voodoo symbols and other aspects of Haitian culture into her art; Betye Saar, whose interests in astrology, palmistry, Tarot, voodoo, and shamanism influence her mixed-media assemblages that deal with the similarities of religions in Africa, Asia, and Latin America; her daughter Alison Saar, who worked as an art conservator repairing icons and pre-Columbian and African objects, which led to a career as a sculptor creating imagery influenced by vodun, Santería, Mexican altars, and Native American totem poles; and Lorraine O'Grady, an African American whose parents emigrated to the United States from Jamaica. O'Grady's performance piece, *Nefer titi/Devonia Evangeline* (1980) included a ritual reenacted from the Egyptian Book of the Dead and also critiqued inauthentic African religious practices in the United States.

Artist Adrienne Hoard is known for her shaped canvases, which have progressed from hard-edged geometric perimeters to free-form organic shapes of brilliant saturated color with sources from African and Native American histories of abstraction and universal spiritual cosmologies. Also an educator and scholar, Hoard's research into the psychology of visual perception of color and shape and linkages between visual abstraction and various indigenous aesthetics has had a profound impact on her development as a painter and her career in photography and design.

Hoard's intuitive feel for color can be traced to early family experiences in homes where abundant color, ceramic figures, artifacts, and music dominated the atmosphere. Her paternal grandfather, who imigrated to the United States from the Caribbean in the 1890s, and his wife, her paternal grandmother who was Blackfoot/Siksika, shared an oral storytelling tradition in which inanimate objects become animate, and animals could speak. Their spirituality included her grandfather's Christianity and her grandmother's memories of pre-Christian Siksika religion based on solar ceremonies and colorfully patterned religious paraphernalia—influences that later impacted Hoard's cosmological paintings (Farris 1999).

During the 1980s, research travel to Korea, Italy, Brazil, and Peru greatly influenced Hoard's painting themes, culminating in the series *Tribal Birds, Cosmic Movements,* and *Etruscan Voyage.* In 1989, she presented a paper on black aesthetics at the Third International Symposium on Art Teaching and Its History in São Paulo, Brazil. During the late nineties Hoard again traveled to Brazil and also to South Africa. While in Brazil she gave a paper at the Afro-Latin American Research Association and met Bahian (Brazilian priestesses), and in Pretoria she interacted with Ndebele women artists. Both groups of women create abstract, colorful altar forms that represent visual and spiritual traditions relevant to female deitites and guardian spirits.

Hoard's photo-documentation and watercolor studies of these Afro-Brazilian and South African altar forms were the inspiration for her *Gate Mothers* series: *Bahia IV: Birdwoman, Trumphet Dancer, Dark Lady Dance, The Dance of Innocence,* and *The Dance Weavers.* Spiritually Adrienne Hoard describes the *Gate Mothers* as a tribute to divine guardian spirits, an offering to black women healers and artists in Brazil, South Africa, and the Diaspora.

Martha Jackson-Jarvis is noted for mixed-media installations that explore aspects of African, African American, and Native American spirituality, environmental issues, and the roles of women in preserving indigenous cultures. Her use of broken pottery shards and other objects strewn on the floor in site-specific installations is inspired by her grandmother's practice of placing crockery and pottery shards on family graves. This southern burial tradition is based on African concepts of preparing souls for the afterworld. Other southern traditions that influenced Jackson-Jarvis' later art development were associations with the use of clay by Native Americans and the belief that Native American spirits are always present in land that is now known as the United States (Wasserman 1999, 357).

Jackson-Jarvis describes her clay pieces as "power objects." Pieces that resemble skeletons of underwater life are arranged in environments of sand, wood, and other natural substances, covering the ground in a circular formation and then extending to the walls. Works from this phase of her career are *The Time Gathers, The Gathering and Arc of the Southern Sun*, and the 1988 *Gathering*—an installation forty feet in diameter consisting of fired and glazed clay forms, broken dishes, and architectural tiles—links to African-derived funeral rituals.

In the 1990s Jackson-Jarvis shifted away from installations and began constructing free-standing sculptural forms and wall relief sculptures. The 1993 series *Last Rites Sarcophagi II* included seven coffin-shaped tables titled *Plants, Earth, Air, Water, Healing, Blood*, and *Ancestor Spirits*. Created with clay, slate, glass, copper, cement, and wood, this environmental series deals with earth's potential destruction, life cycles, and the interconnectedness of humans, animals, and nature.

Jackson-Jarvis eschews the dichotomies between "high art" versus crafts and utilitarian art versus "art for art's sake." Her respect for pottery, an earth-based art form usually created by women in tribal societies is taken out of its usual practical application and applied to so-called intellectual formats such as conceptual art or installations. However, the spiritual aspect of her art links it back to traditional African and Native American cultures that do not separate art and religion, art and healing. Also, the theoretical basis of installation art that demands a temporary location and eventual destruction or recycling has parallels with Native American healing practices such as Navajo sandpainting. It is interesting to note some of the commonalities between traditional African and Native American art and contemporary commonalities expressed by artists such as Jackson-Jarvis (Powell 1997, 15).

Compared to Hoard's and Jackson-Jarvis's synthesis of African, Native American, and Latin American visual expressions of spirituality, Renée Stout is more grounded in a specifically African spiritual/art/healing context—that of the Kongo Minkisi. In the 1980s Stout started making medicine bundles or charms similar to objects used in Kongo and voodoo rituals. In contrast with many of the fetishes, which are small, *Fetish no. 2* (1988) is life sized and functions as a psychic self-portrait and as a power figure. "The figure is a female nude with medicine pouches resting around her shoulders and other medicines encased in her belly. Stout becomes a Nkisi as an expression of self-empowerment and a link between her present, past, and future. Minkisi represent the connection between the material world and the spiritual world of the ancestors" (Powell 1997, 15).

Interested in exploring the past and reconstructing a cultural identity, Stout blends the past with the present and reality with fiction; incorporating objects from the lives of friends and relatives she creates assemblages and installations that are influenced by voodoo and Kongo religious beliefs. *She Kept Her Conjuring Table Very Neat* (1990) is a table covered with roots, herbs, bones, and a photograph of a real person that is reconstructed into a fictional narrative. In addition to her interests in African art, culture, and religion, Stout researches African American root stores, spiritualists, palm readers, and folk medicine to better understand African spiritual retentions in African American culture.

## NATIVE AMERICAN WOMEN ARTISTS

Five hundred years after the arrival of Columbus in the "New World," the cultural influences acting on Native American art remain varied and complex. Many aesthetic changes have taken place in the twentieth and twenty-first centuries as native peoples have participated more fully in the dominant culture and incorporated artistic traditions from the United States, Europe, and other parts of the globe into their own traditions. Native American artists are in the process of developing new definitions of Indian art. Any insistence that Indian art remain "traditional" as a way of preserving culture is a form of cultural discrimination because cultures are dynamic, not static. Although contemporary Native American culture has lost some of its symbolism and rituals because of assimilation, its essence remains. Native American thinking has never separated art from life, what is beautiful from what is functional. The Native American aesthetic has survived colonialism, servitude, racial discrimination, and rapid technological change.

Today many people are familiar with the so-called traditional Indian school of painting associated with the Santa Fe, New Mexico school of Dorothy Dunn—a flat shaded treatment of historic native imagery often identified in the public's mind as "real Indian art." The 1960s may be considered the turning point, when Native American artists began to break away from this so-called white-influenced "traditional" painting style and began to develop and define their own visual, literary, and performing arts. Like all other aspects of Indian culture, women were in the forefront of this transition, with Helen Hardin, Pablita Velarde's daughter, being a pioneer in the 1970s. The Institute of the American Indian Arts (IAIA), founded in 1962, nurtured many of today's significant women visual artists such as Linda Lomahaftewa (Hopi/Choctaw), Roxanne Swentzell (Santa Clara Pueblo), and poet/musician Joy Harjo (Muskogee Creek).

I am not able in the space of one chapter to discuss all of the contemporary Native American women artists who have impacted the twentieth and twenty-first centuries, only a small percentage. Contemporary Native American women artists with varying visions such as Emmi Whitehorse (Navajo), Kay Walking Stick (Cherokee), Jane Ash Poitras (Cree), Nora Naranjo-Morse (Santa Clara Pueblo), Gail Tremblay (Onandaga/Micmac), Hulleah Tsinhahjinnie (Navajo, Seminole, and Creek), Jean LaMarr (Pauite/Pit River), Shelley Niro (Mohawk), Rose Powhatan (Pamunkey), Sara Bates (Cherokee), Jaune Quick-to-See Smith (Enrolled Flathead Salish, member of the Confederated Salish and Kootenai Nation), and yours truly, Phoebe Farris (Powhatan), just to mention a few, are dealing with issues such as the environment, genocide, native spirituality, racism, and feminism.

Nadema Agard (Lakota/Powhatan/Cherokee) is a visual artist as well as a repatriation consultant, museum educator, and performance artist. She uses all of these roles to enhance and proliferate multicultural Native American art, adapting to new challenges and new worldviews while still maintaining an indigenous perspective. As a syncretist with a pan-Indian view of native art/religion/culture, Agard incorporates symbolism from a variety of native cosmologies—the Southwest, the Plains, the Southeast, the Northeast, the Great Lakes Woodlands, and Mesoamerica. In the early 1990s much of Agard's paintings, transformational boxes, and installations honored the belief systems of Mesoamerica, that is, the syncretism of the Aztec and Catholic religions now practiced by Mexican Indians, Mexican mestizos, and U.S. Chicanos. Her *Virgin of Guadeloupe Is the Corn Mother* (42" x 60" acrylic/canvas mixed media) addressed the image of the Virgin of Guadeloupe as also Tonatzin (Aztec mother of God). The Aztec adaptation to Catholicism ensured the hidden survival of Aztec beliefs. Nadema describes this piece as demonstrating the power of tribal art as a "vehicle for cultural and political resistance and a spiritual grounding for a world that has become unbalanced."

Agard's newer series produced in the late 1990s, *Starblanket Heaven*, is dedicated to her paternal family on the Standing Rock reservation. The star motif of the art works is based on star blankets or morning star quilts. The star, an ancient Lakota symbol, is also sacred to Christians as the star that guided the Wise Men to the infant Jesus. When converting to Catholoism, the Lakota adapted the star quilts of the missionaries as a way to continue their own religious ceremonies. Agard's traveling exhibit consists of soft sculpture pieces, mixed media, and pastels. The colors used throughout the show relate to the four directions and the four races of humanity; north is white/Caucasian, south is yellow/Asian, east is red/Native American, and west is blue or black/African, as believed by the Lakota peoples. An artist/scholar with what she calls a "multivision," Agard hopes that her work will promote balance and respect for all religions, all races, all cultures, male and female.

Helen Hardin (Santa Clara Pueblo) successfully combined the imagery, composition, and color common among traditional Indian painters with a geometric abstraction of shapes, colors, and composition. Geometry gave her linear structure and a method of investigating light, space, and color. Hardin was also influenced by the sense of detail and cultural heritage displayed in the work of her mother, the renowned artist Pablita Velarde. In 1975 Hardin was the only woman artist in a Public Broadcasting System (PBS) film series about Native American artists. By 1976 her role as a leader in contemporary Native American art was being recognized as her work grew in depth and complexity. Hardin worked on a Kachina series through the 1970s and into the 1980s. Considering kachinas (intermediaries responsible for rain, corn, and fecundity) to be her spiritual forebears, Hardin painted them as cloud people. During the early 1980s Hardin embarked on a series of paintings and etchings with themes relating to women. These include *Bountiful Mother, Medicine Woman, Listening Woman, Winter Woman*, and *Creative Woman. Changing Woman* (1981), executed as both a painting and an etching, is considered one of her most ambitious works—a self-portrait of the artist as a young woman and ageless kachina. With Hardin's women series, the connection between kachinas, humanity, and herself is clarified. In 1984 Hardin died from breast cancer, leaving uncompleted her final work, *Last Dance of the Mimbres*.

Strongly interested in women's rights in marriage and reproduction, Carm Little Turtle (Apache/Tarahumara) uses photography to visually explore relationships between men and women, feeling that the way people relate to the opposite sex on a personal level carries over into politics. The *Earthman* series is her most popular and widely shown theme on that topic. In these hand-painted sepia-toned photographs, Little Turtle, her husband, Ed Singer, and other relatives are actors/characters in a variety of staged scenes. In *Earthman Thinking about Dancing with Woman from Another Tribe* (1991), Earthman, symbolic of any man, is seated with his back turned away from the woman, his face cupped in his hand, elbow resting on his knee. He is looking downward, deep in thought and ignoring the sexy, voluptuous woman next to him. The woman's body is cropped to the waist. The viewer sees a red parasol covering her stomach and a pair of legs covered in skin-tight, leopard-spotted dance leotards. She stands precariously in spike-heeled shoes on the edge of a cliff. The artist seems to be saying that regardless of how attractive women try to make themselves, men often think of other women instead of appreciating their own partners. In *She Was Used to Abiding by Her Own Decisions* (1989), the woman's profile is partially hidden by a parasol, and the man's face is completely obscured by a hat. While the woman is looking away, her partner ties the laces of her shoes together, thus attempting to hinder the woman's mobility and independence.

In addition to visually exploring indigenous perspectives on spirituality, feminism, and identity, another major concern for many Native American artists is the environmental destruction of Turtle Island, the Native American name for North America. As an artist, curator, and political activist, Jaune Quick-to-See Smith (Enrolled Flathead Salish, member of the Confederated Salish and Kootenai Nation) is a role model for many Native American artists and for all artists with a consciousness. Her multimedia paintings, which incorporate sign language, glyphs, pictograms, and collage, are concerned with issues such as the environment, sovereignty, racism, and sexism. Her public art commissions in which she collaborates with other artists address the same issues, focusing on regionally specific concerns. Design, color, line, and other elements are used by Quick-to-See Smith to portray present-day realities as well as what is spiritual and beyond the material world conceived by Western culture. Abstract and narrative, the symbols found in her art such as teepees, horses, headdresses, sweet grass, indigenous plants, the human figure, and petroglyphs, tell stories about Native American life in general as well as her own personal stories. Her inhabited landscapes show powerful movement within a geometric space, combining styles as diverse as nineteenth-century Plains Indian art ledger books, abstract expressionism, and cubism from the geometry found in native cultures.

A former member of Greenpeace, the environmental group, Jaune's work focuses strongly on environmental issues because she feels that the earth's destruction is one of the—if not *the*—most pressing global concerns. She has taken a stand against using art materials that pollute the environment, take excessive storage space, and are costly to ship. One of her environmental series is based on the Salish/Flathead history of making parfleches (a rawhide suitcase folded like an envelope to carry food, clothing, etc.). Called *The Nomad Manifesto*, it consists of 15" x 15" folded squares that carry messages about the environment and Indian life. They are made from rag paper (no trees) and biodegradable materials such as Sumi Japanese watercolors, charcoal, rice paper, and rice glue. Challenging misconceptions about indigenous culture, Jaune uses her art, lectures, and writing to educate the dominant culture and to reeducate native peoples.

Kay WalkingStick (Cherokee) has achieved national and international success through her art as well as her thought-provoking writings and lectures on contemporary Native American art. A prolific painter since the mid-1970s, WalkingStick's notoriety emerged in the 1980s when she began painting abstract, surreal landscapes on a diptych format. Her use of diptych panels for her paintings is connected to the way she perceives life and art. For her, it is important that the two portions are connected yet still have some mystery surrounding their relationship. These two portions are often portrayed as opposite concepts in which one panel becomes a continuation of the other. In addition to paint, Kay's surfaces contain dirt, metal shavings, pottery shards, small rocks, and wax that is cut and gouged to reveal the layers below the surface. In the nineties WalkingStick introduced copper in her work to represent the economic urges underlying the rape of the earth. In most of the landscapes, one side is more realistic, with recognizable mountains, water, and terrain, whereas the other is more abstract or geometric. The diptychs also represent WalkingStick's biraciality, unifying the two sides of living in an Indian and non-Indian world.

WalkingStick's *Where Are the Generations?* (1991, copper, acrylic, wax, oil on canvas, 28" x 50") is a haunting landscape that has many layers and is both concrete and specific and metaphysical. The right side of the canvas is a rugged, mountainous, desert landscape. On the left panel a small receding circle is centered on the canvas. The circle is a landscape with cloud formations on the horizon and murky waters. Within the cloud formations and almost hidden is printed: "In 1492 we were 30 million. Now we are 2 million. Where are the children? Where are the generations? Never born." Having both modern, formal qualities and an indigenous political message, this painting, like many of WalkingStick's works, reflects both her Western-trained art background and her native sensibility.

Rose Powhatan is an enrolled member of the Pamunkey tribe. The Pamunkey was once the leading tribe in the Powhatan Confederacy, which covered Virginia, Washington, D.C., and parts of Maryland and North Carolina. Thematically there is a constant thread that runs throughout

Powhatan's work; respect for indigenous culture and a commitment to presenting the Pamunkey tribe and the Powhatan Confederacy in a positive, reverent, uplifting mode of visual art expression. As a visual artist and storyteller Rose uses a narrative approach to her subject because she feels that Eastern Algonquin tribes have not been given full respect in regard to being included as part of the picture in *Indian country.*

Powhatan makes use of traditional Eastern Woodlands indigenous design concepts in her work. The authenticity of her work demands involvement in research to document the legitimacy of cultural retentions. There is a decided sense of place inherent in Powhatan's work—a self-explanatory art that establishes who she is, where she is from, and what she is about. A work that is definitely about a sense of place is *Totems to Powhatan,* a 1988 installation that Powhatan and her husband, artist Michael Auld, created as a METROART commission. The work, consisting of a series of wood totem figures standing in a circle, was exhibited for one year at the Vienna, Virginia, Metro station. The carved heads on the totem poles represent various Powhatan Confederacy chiefs, and the black and red engraved designs portray significant symbols such as Powhatan's mantle, deer, Pamunkey-Powhatan picture writing, and circles representing the original tribes of the Confederacy.

Powhatan is also engaged in research focusing on the retention of indigenous culture in the Americas, the Caribbean, and the Pacific. She has found a commonality of cultural expression among Australian Aborigines, New Zealand Maoris, Dominican Caribs, and North American indigenous peoples that transcends national boundaries. For Powhatan, respect for traditional cultural values is the tie that she sees binding all indigenous peoples together in their art.

Since the late 1980s most of my art exhibits and slide presentations deal with my documentation of contemporary Native American culture east of the Mississippi River and the Caribbean. I have traveled to powwows and other cultural events, interacting with relatives, friends, and the public at the Rankokus Powhatan-Renape Reservation in New Jersey, the Pamunkey and Mattaponi Reservations in Virginia, the Chickahominy Tribal Cultural Center in Virginia, the Haliwa-Saponi Cultural Center in North Carolina, Pembroke State University in North Carolina (founded and operated by the Lumbee tribe until taken over by the state), the Shinnecock Reservation in Long Island, New York, and the Piscataway campground in Maryland.

My photographs at these events of people dressed in both powwow regalia and everyday clothing reveal the diversity prevalent among eastern tribes, with some contemporary Native Americans resembling their early ancestors, others showing the results of intermixture with other races. The regalia that the photographs show is a blend of the Plains Indian pan-Indian styles and more tribal specific clothing such as the turkey feather headdresses worn by Powhatan chiefs that stand straight up rather than fan out like Plains Indian eagle headdresses.

Also, as part of this series, is photo documentation of reconstructed colonial Native American villages on the Pamunkey Reservation in Virginia and the Rankokus Powhatan-Renape Reservation in New Jersey. The photographs show the various stages of building traditional homes with willow branches, tree bark, and shrubbery. *Rankokus Powhatan-Renape Nation, New Jersey* (1995–2000), a series of photographs of the largest grouping in a wooded setting, has a timeless quality, with only the color photography to remind the viewer that they are contemporary images.

I have also photographed people of native ancestry in Puerto Rico, Cuba, and Mexico. Not recognizing externally imposed national boundaries, I refer to all of the Americas as "Indian Country." I have been inspired in my research by fellow Powhatan intellectual Jack D. Forbes, professor emeritus of Native American Studies at the University of California, Davis, and my approximately twenty-eight or more relatives who have careers in the arts and mass media, including Pamunkey painter Georgia Mills Jessup, who is represented in the permanent collection of the National Museum of Women in the Arts. Our family's artistic expression is influenced by our own Powhatan-Pamunkey heritage, intermarriages with other racial/ethnic groups (African American, Caribbean, and Asian), and our collections of Pamunkey pottery, Japanese Raku pottery, and Oriental rugs. I am fond of saying that we were multicultural before it became a commodified fad and politically correct.

## CONCLUSION

Native American and other women of color have expanded the scope of politically significant art through a syncretism that embraces visual expressions of feminism, the environment, spirituality, and identity through linkages with Turtle Island (North America), Latin America, the Caribbean, and Africa. Working in a myriad of media and styles, they are researching the fusion of past and current history, of gender and race, deconstructing stereotypical mainstream representations of their identities as women and persons of color.

In looking back to pre-Columbian heritages, Latin Americans, United States Chicanos, and some African American artists embraced and reclaimed ancestral Toltec, Aztec, Mayan, Taino, and indigenous North American pyramids, mound cultures, sculptures, murals, myths, and healing practices. Latin American and Chicano artists in particular sought spiritual and cultural links to civilizations and identities that existed prior to their mestizo transformations. For women artists the Virgin of Guadeloupe's pre-Christian Indian identities became sources for artistic expression.

In looking back to an African heritage, African American artists from the United States and Latin American artists from Brazil and Cuba discovered Egyptian pyramids and religious death rituals, western and central African masks and healing ceremonies, and South African altar art forms. And in their discoveries artists found cultures that did not separate art from healing, art from spirituality—art from life in general. In looking at their current cultures artists found memories of Africa in southern United States burial traditions and folk customs and Latin American/Caribbean Santería, Candomble, and vodun. African spiritual traditions from the past and contemporary syncretic manifestations have been the inspiration for much of the art produced by African Americans and peoples of African descent or mixed heritage in Latin America and the Caribbean.

Where does the art of Native American women belong in a pluralistic, postmodern, poststructuralist world that allegedly allows for cultural/ethnic/racial fluidity and hybridity? In the various *postism* worlds, the concept of 'identity' is undergoing profound changes, as is the concept of 'high/fine art' versus 'low/popular art.' Native American women artists and intellectuals, along with Native American men, are in the process of developing new definitions of Native American art and redefining Native American ethnic heritages. Native American women have always been an integral part of the creative vision and continue to contribute to Indian aesthetics independently, in collaboration with other women, and in tandem with Native American men.

The ways in which women artists of color from a variety of backgrounds attempt to maintain and creatively express their oppositional stances to racism, sexism, environmental destruction, religious intolerance, and other socio-political problems vary. Many of them bravely refuse to compromise the quality or content of their work for prestige or financial rewards. Whether working for grassroots arts organizations, creating public murals, or working within the establishment as art educators, museum professionals, etc., the artists profiled in this paper and the numerous others highlighed in my book (1999), have maintained their specific community ties and in some cases involved themselves in national/international coalitions with other people of color. Regardless of their divergent paths, a commonality shared by all is healing power of art.

# 9

## Dalit Women's Literature

*A Sense of the Struggle*

NANDITA GUPTA

### DALIT WOMEN'S WRITINGS: A SENSE OF THE STRUGGLE

At a very broad level the Indian caste system refers to the hierarchical division of society based on ritual purity derived from lifestyles and hereditary occupations traditionally monopolized by the members of various caste groups. This hierarchy was sanctioned by religious texts. *Dalit* refers to the social groups defined as outcastes by the dominant caste groups. The dalit were also called "untouchables" because they are considered too polluted to even touch and represented the lowest orders of the caste system in India. These "outcastes" performed tasks considered most degrading and impure (such as sweeping, washing, scavenging, leatherwork, etc.) and were denied the most basic human rights. The position of dalits is comparable to the blacks in apartheid-ridden South Africa and the United States in the early nineteenth century.

Dalit mobilization in the twentieth century has been one of the most significant social efforts for greater democratization of society, and literature is one arena where dalit assertion has made its explosive presence felt. However, underlying the ideology of protest and change in dalit (or any other) literature are more complex codes that signify gendered spaces within society. It is my claim that in their writings dalit women "talk differently" (Guru 1995, 2549) from their male counterparts and that, consequently, issues of gender need to be specially highlighted in the study of their works. I use dalit women's writings as a text from which to extract, explore, and map out elements of their consciousness. I have attempted to place them firmly within the literary discourse in which, hitherto, they were invisible. In touching upon several themes that arise from the available literature, I draw parallels with writings by dalit men and hope to show areas of convergence and divergence, which help in gleaning (in certain broad respects) some preliminary ideas of how their consciousness is structured and informed by their sociological experience. I also expose the *absences of certain issues*, which reveals numerous sociological considerations.

At the outset, I must indicate several limitations of my study. This chapter deals exclusively with twentieth-century dalit literature from Maharashtra, a region in southwestern India, since this literature is the most easily available in English translations. Furthermore, when I speak of male or female writings, I deal with selected works of selected writers. For male writings I have relied exclusively on Arjun Dangle's edited collection *Poisoned Bread* (Dangle 1992), which provides a compilation of poetry, short stories, autobiographical extracts, and essays. *Poisoned Bread* presents only one work (poem/story) of each writer. When I speak of male writers, I refer to the collective analysis of works in *Poisoned Bread* exclusively as a male voice, not the entire corpus of writings by Marathi dalit men, which would be too vast to undertake here. Since the representation of female writings in the anthology is too meager (itself an indication of the limited space given to dalit writings by women), I have relied on a few articles that deal with women's writings exclusively. These were specially written to highlight works of women writers that differed significantly from those of male writers. These articles do not represent the complete oeuvre of any woman writer. Therefore, the idea that women's writings within dalit literature are radically different from male writings should be approached with some caution. I have highlighted the aspects of difference. I do not claim to present an "authentic" voice of dalit women. An exciting find was an article on writings by Telegu women (Rani 1998). (*Telegu* is the name for people from Andhra Pradesh, a region in South India.) Since this offered only a few lines of poetry by some writers, initially I thought of excluding it from my research. Yet the works were so strikingly different in language and treatment of the same issues as those explored by Marathi women that I decided to include them as a point of comparison. Though they write about similar issues, the extremely harsh language and the stronger sense of self of Telegu women point to a different, perhaps more brutal qualitative experience of oppression.

## DALIT BACKGROUND

Dalit writers and intellectuals hold Bhimrao Ambedkar (1891–1956), the unchallenged social, political, and intellectual leader of dalits in the first half of the twentieth century, to be the founder of the militant dalit consciousness, which forged the dalit literary and political movement. Ambedkar's mandate of "Educate! Organize! Agitate!" rallied numerous people. In 1950, the first batch of dalit graduates from Siddartha College set up the Siddhartha Sahitya Sangh, a literary society, out of which the Maharashtra Dalit Sahitya Sangh (literally—"literary society of Maharashtrian dalits") was later formed. The first conference of dalit writers was organized in 1958 in Bombay. A period of literary outburst followed in the forms of poetry, short stories, magazine movements, and so on. Another decisive step, inspired by the black movement in the United States, was the formation of the Dalit Panthers in Bombay on July 9, 1972, by youths Namdeo Dhasal, Arjun Dangle, and J. V. Pawar.

## LITERATURE AS A GENDERED SPHERE: GYNOCRITICS AND THIRD WORLD CRITICISM

The principal tenet of feminist criticism is that a literary work cannot be understood apart from the social, historical, and cultural context within which it is written. Feminist literary criticism sees literature as an important arena of political struggle, a "crucial component of the project of interrogating the world in order to change it" (Schweickhart 1989, 24). In the wake of this development, gender has been recognized as a "crucial determinant in the production, circulation and consumption of literary discourse" (Showalter 1989, 1). The introduction of gender into the field of literary studies marked a new phase in feminist criticism—an investigation into the way that all reading and writing by both men and women is marked by gender.

The emphasis on women as writers arose with "Gynocritics" or the feminist study of women's writings. Gynocritics assumes that all writings by women (a) necessarily articulate a gendered experience, and (b) necessarily take place within a dominant male discourse through acts of "reason, appropriation and subversion" (Showalter 1989, 5). Elaine Showalter has used Myra Jehlen's argument that feminist criticism has demonstrated the patriarchal myth of the universality of the literary "cannon" and shown that what is called literature was actually "men's writing"

(1989, 5). Jehlen argued that in light of this discovery the agenda for feminist criticism was a "radical comparitivism" in which texts by male and female authors working within the same historical condition and genres are juxtaposed to reveal the "contingency of the dominant male tradition" (cited in Showalter 1989, 5).

The notion of an undifferentiated gynocritics was critiqued by third world and black feminist theorists, who posited that women's consciousness and therefore writings were structured by ideologies of class, race, and imperialism. They have highlighted the western bias of gynocritics as a feminist ideology—"As [gynocritics] enumerates the themes and sets up the agenda for women's writing the world over the present day concerns of western feminists are writ large to encompass the world, and the world collapses into the west" (Tharu and Lalita 1995 v. 2, 26–27).

There was a recognition of the need for the interrogation of gynocritics from a third world perspective, which would analyze "patriarchies reconstituted in the interest of Orientalism, Imperialism, the Enlightenment, Nationalism" (Tharu and Lalita 1995 v. 2, 15). There was also recognition that women writers are complicit in and reproduce the ideologies of their world in their works. However, they do so from "complexly constituted and decentered positions" (Tharu and Lalita 1995 v. 2, 38). Women do not merely receive and reproduce ideologies, they experience and contest them as well. Women's writings are to be read as a sign for women's agency in a world in which they exist on the margins.

If we are to recognize women's agency, their writings should be read not for their alliances with dominant ideologies but for the "gestures of defiance or subversion implicit in them" (Tharu and Lalita 1995 v. 2, 39). Kumkum Sangari has pointed out (Sangari in Pawar 1996) that patriarchies function simultaneously through coercion and through making a wide social consensus along with obtaining differing degrees of consent from women and are resilient because of the "consensual element in them . . . which is open to constant and consistent reformulation" (Sangari 1996, 17). Narratives are in a dynamic relationship between the dominant tradition and female agency. She cautions that the "feminist project of retrieving the agency of women . . . has often suffered from a degree of simplification produced through the anxiety to recover a roster of independent or rebellious women and enter them into liberatory schemes" (1996, 25). This has resulted in an oversimplified view not only of social structure but also of women's agency. Sangari indicates that the feminist purpose will be better served by "retrieving the nature of existing potentials and constraints, in other words, 'a sense of the struggle, which will ultimately yield a far richer notion of women's agency than has hitherto become available'"(1996, 25).

## DALIT WOMEN IN SOCIETY: MOTHER/VICTIM DICHOTOMY VERSUS PROUD DIGNIFIED AGENTS OF CHANGE

One of the most frequently represented themes in dalit writings is that of women as the worst victims of an exploitative system based on caste and gender inequality. By and large, women are depicted exclusively as "victims" of either upper-caste males or more abstractly the "system." The roles that dalit women play within the family and society and their agency in resistance are not depicted. This is evident in the eighteen poems selected from *Poisoned Bread* for their portrayal of women. For example Baban Chahhande's "Labor Pains" (in Dangle 1992, 47) deals with the economic exploitation of dalit women as laborers trapped in an endless cycle of work unbroken even by childbirth—"When labor begins, her head holds a load/and her eyes, a shadow of anxiety for food . . . thus she delivers and her hands/set fiercely to work again." A parallel theme is that of sexual exploitation, which underscores the extreme sexual vulnerability of the dalit female. Sudharkar Gaikwad's The "Unfed Begging Bowl" is an example—"Do not beg with the heart of your femininity; anyhow you will have to prepare yourself for copulation" (1992, 25).

Intrinsic to this theme is the representation of the female body. In men's writings, the female body is foregrounded more often, generally in a graphic or crude manner and constantly brought into the public gaze. This is done for the purpose of illustrating the condition of the dalit community, of which the brutally exploited female body becomes a symbol. For instance, Jadhav's "Under Dadar Bridge"—"She would bray, that she donkey of Bhadrapad/. . . brutally exposing both her nakedness/and mine" (1992, 57).

Most of the women in poems by men that speak of the condition of women or have a female persona are given the role of mother—a figure that evokes pity or sympathy. Rarely is the mother given agency and individuality. In Nimbalker's "Mother" the male poet is given the space for self-confirmation—"Even now my eyes search for mother . . . when I see a thin woman with firewood on her head/I go and buy all her firewood" (1992, 36). Occasionally, the mother figure is an instrument for a savage condemnation of a brutal society, where she becomes wild, uncontrolled, animallike—"She was engrossed in pulling out hunks/from the catflesh . . . [and] her eyes were sharp like the razor edge/that scalps the world/. She would take the scab off the green wound/and show me the ancient leprosy/coursing through her blood" (1992, 57).

This context makes Jyoti Lanjewar's mother figure in her poem "Mother" all the more remarkable (in Zelliot 1996). The poem consists of snapshot images of the life of a woman laborer—hard at work building skyscrapers, roads, and dams and bringing up children alone. Lanjewar depicts her burdened character as having *pride*—"rejecting the scraps of food offered to you/with pride"; *agency*—"chasing anyone who nudged you deliberately/with your sandal in your hand" (1996, 82); a proud sense of being *responsible* for future generations—"taking the little bundle from the cradle to your breast/saying, "study, become an Ambedkar.""

In Telegu dalit women's writing, the mother figure is universalized and politicized on a vast scale, not personalized as it is by Mahrashtrian writers. Swaroopa Rani highlights the fact that the labor of women provides the foundations on which the structure of society is built. Women are the sustainers of the nation. Rani quotes her own poetry—"Mother without your touch/there is neither air nor light/on this earth/unless your hands delve into the/slush to catch jewel bright fish/the country's hunger/will remain unfed" (1998, 23).

## WOMEN AND DALIT POLITICAL ASSERTION

It is significant that none of the male writers depicts dalit women as acutely politically conscious or inspired by political leaders of their community and large participants in historic political movements that forged the militant dalit consciousness of its times. Yet such images are an integral part of the self-identity of dalit women themselves. They proudly claim the history of struggle of the dalit community, and there is a very strong sense of having been important participants in it.

Jyoti Lanjewar's "Mother" gives a glimpse of the life of a laborer woman, who is also seen as an inextricable part of three historic events in Maharashtra—"I have seen you/at the front of the long march . . . shouting 'change the name'/taking the blow of the police sticks on your upraised hands/going to jail" (Zelliot 1996, 82–83). "The long march" refers to a protest march that took place in March 1979, after the reversal of a government decision to rename Marathwada University in honor of Ambedkar. The poet too had joined the march. Marathwada is also referred to in Mina Gajbhiyes' "Weeping Wound of Centuries" where it becomes a trope of revolt—"I had sutured with difficulty/the weeping wound of centuries/these stitches are all ripped out/ripped out by Marathwada/. . . let the village become a burning ground/along with me/I will not live like a pariah dog, nowhere" (Zelliot 1996, 70). Lanjewar's "Mother" depicts two other important events—"I have seen you/saying when your only son/fell martyr to police bullets/you died for Bhim, [an affectionate name for Ambedkar] your death means something/saying boldly to the police/if I had two or three sons, I would be fortunate/they would fight on." This is a reference to a death caused by police firing at a dalit youth in the Worli riots of April 1974. There is a further reference to Diksha Bhumi—the site of mass conversion of Mahars to Buddhism as a final rejection of the Hindu social order in 1956 in Nagpur (a city in Maharashtra).

Hira Bansode in her poem of praise to Ambedkar entitled "O Great Man" refers to the first and crucial movements led by Ambedkar in the history of struggle for basic human rights, such as access to common places of worship and sources of water. "Kala Ram and Chawdar Tank/the history of pain/is carved on each of our hearts" (Zelliot 1996, 80). In 1927, Ambedkar led a procession to a public pond, Chawdar Tank, in an attempt to drink water from a public source as a symbolic exercise of rights. This resulted in caste riots and ritual cleansing of the tank by the so-called upper castes. From 1930 through 1935, there was a fruitless and violent movement in Nasik (a city in Maharashtra) for entry into a famous temple, Kala Ram. Both these historic movements included large-scale participation by women. It is extremely significant that dalit men never depict women as part of political moments, indicating how their political activism is negated in the male consciousness as women are represented nearly exclusively as domesticated beings.

While women write about political leaders, there is a dearth of female figures of inspiration. This points toward an absence of women beyond mobilization, an absence from decision-making bodies and leadership roles. The saviors of the dalit community are held to be Ambedkar and Jotiba Phule (1827–1890). Jotiba Phule was a (so-called) low-caste leader and social reformer in nineteenth-century Maharashtra. Phule, alongwith his wife, Savitribai, started the first school for women in Maharashtra in 1848. Savitribai was the first woman teacher in modern Maharashtra. Though she made equal efforts for the education of dalits, especially the women, she is not remembered with similar reverence. To a certain extent women have internalized the notion of the role of women as ancillary to that of men.

## GENDER INEQUALITY IN DALIT SOCIETY: CRITICISM AS WELL AS COMPLICITY OF DALIT WOMEN

It is only women's writings that evidence a criticism of the patriarchal practices within the dalit community. This is not a continuously overt theme, but there are definite indications that can be gleaned from the works of women writers. Dalit women face patriarchal control of sexuality and also violence within the family. This has been illustrated by both men and women writers. The poet Pratibha Pore deals with marital rape—a theme never touched upon in men's writings. Telegu women's writings express in much stronger terms the rage of women against patriarchy. Chellapalli Swaroopa Rani indicts patriarchal and caste oppression—"[W]hen has my life been truly mine/in the home male arrogance/sets my cheek stinging/while in the street caste arrogance/splits the other cheek open" (1998, 22). Vijay Kumari condemns not just upper-caste male atrocities but also the gross insensitivity of the men of one's own caste—"[W]hen Kotti Reddy pulled your/sari in the corn field/the humiliation/when your husband seeing your/torn sari said you were/overfed/the shrinking of your heart" (Rani 1998, 23).

The women's writings also touch upon an important issue that never occurs in men's writings, patriarchal community practices of dalits, chiefly the practice of dedicating girl children to various goddesses, a tradition that invariably turns them into *devdasis* (temple prostitutes). Anuradha Gurav condemns this in very strong language in her poem "Request"—"We give our children to the god Khandoba/... of our own free will/we make our daughters lie beneath men/we mother fuckers like dumb beasts/hock our lives" (Zelliot 1996, 87). Strikingly, this is as vehement as the Telegu women writers, though Swaroopa Rani links it with entire patriarchal historiography—"[M]y fame is that/I was recognized as a whore/even as a new born babe/my story that should bring/the head of this civilization/low into the depths of hell/in which chapter of the volumes/of famous history of your country/do you intend to write it?" (1998, 22). Here we see the emergence of a nascent dalit women's alliance that transcends regional boundaries, a consciousness shared with similar intensity against an exploitation they alone face.

Conversion to Buddhism by Ambedkar in 1956 signaled a complete rejection of the Hindu social order and of the notion of reform of the orthodox Hindus as means to end the caste system. Buddhism therefore held the hope for ultimate emancipation of dalits. Hira Bansode's "Yashodhara," however, deals with Buddhism as no other work has done by focusing on Buddha's forgotten wife—"O Yashodhara . . . we were brightened by Buddha's light/but you absorbed the dark/. . . He went, he conquered, he shone/while you listened to the songs of his triumph/. . . but history doesn't talk about/the great story of your sacrifice/a great epic would have been written about you!/. . . I am ashamed of the injustice/you are not found/in a single Buddhist vihara [temple]" (Zelliot 1996, 71–73). Yashodhara is seen, not just as tragic figure but also as a woman who played a role in Buddha's final accomplishment. Since, as Zelliot indicates, "almost all the literature written by Buddhists in the conversion movement is by men, and the vast majority of leaders in local Buddhist groups are men" (1992, 102), the poem is a harbinger of the feminist consciousness, which has, in its first stirrings, begun to interrogate the most sacrosanct institutions.

In the representation of the male and female child, I find the norms that marginalize females starkly depicted, and in this the women are implicated as well. There is a marginalization of the dalit girl child in the literary consciousness of dalit writers, male or female. Education is extremely important to the dalit community as a tool for empowerment. However, in women's writing, I found only one abstract reference to the importance of educating daughters, in Sugandha Shende's "Ovi Panchak": "a vow that I shall send my daughters to school" (Bhaware 1980, 12). There is a sense, as Zelliot points out, of being "educators of their sons" (Zelliot 1996, 91). Shende's "Mourning Comes to an End" celebrates the end of ignorance through a male child—"And clasping the hand of your son/take him to the village school" (Bhaware 1980, 12). This is replicated in male writings: Waman Kardak's poem "Send My Boy to School," and Prahlad Chendwankar's "My Father" represent zeal to get male children educated. The girl child is absent from representation and, consequently, consciousness.

The absence of the girl child in the role of receivers of education is striking because dalit women in general are very conscious of the importance of education. Savitribai's letter (Tharu and Lalita 1995 v. 1, 213–14) reveals an acute consciousness of the significance of knowledge for untouchables and women. Muktabai, a student in Phule's school, in an essay (Tharu and Lalita 1995 v. 1, 215–16) had drawn attention to the specificities of the experience of lower-caste women, displaying a consciousness revolutionary for its time. Two autobiographical extracts in *Poisoned Bread* (the only two by women: Shantabai Kamble's "Naja goes to school—and Doesn't" and Kumud Pawde's "Story of My Sanskri") describe the obstacles faced by dalit women in acquiring an education, both within and without the family. Pawde links up her struggle with that of Savitribai Phule—"I had begun to have some idea of what Savitribai Phule must have endured on account of her husband Mahatma Jotiba Phule's zeal for women's education" (Dangle 1992, 103).

The male child is always used as an instrument for action or resistance, as for example in Lanjewar's "Astitva"—"[O]ut of this ravenous humanity/a sprout came forth/. . . to demolish the edifice of the rich/closing fast his little hand/My son has just opened his eyes" (Bhaware 1980, 14). This is similar to Daya Pawar's "Blood Wave," a man's address to his pregnant wife—"Fists tight . . . clenched for a blow/. . . let's burn, scorch, fire-harden him/in leaping flames, this phoenix/feeding on live coals/will brave the powerful skies/and all that this nation never offered/to you or me—the joy, the glory—/he will pull down to his feet" (Dangle 1992, 62–63). This has fuller expression in Trayambak Sapkale's "That Single Arm"—"[H]e sliced off/the attacker's arm from the shoulder/Then looked at me triumphantly" (Dangle 1992, 3). Ironically, while women's writings show a strong sense of political participation as a crucial component of self-identity, pride of contribution by the next generation comes through sons, as Lanjewar's "Mother" shows—"If I had two or three sons, I would be fortunate/they would fight on" (Zelliot 1996, 83).

## SELF-IDENTITY OF DALIT WOMEN

Does dalit women's self-identity focus on caste or gender; that is, do they see themselves as dalits or as women first? The issue is complex, and there are no clear-cut answers. Dalit women identify themselves (as do the men) as a part of the community, but, unlike the men, *not exclusively*. This is significant because dalits in general have a high level of identification with the community. Male writers speak of oppression as dalits, but, of course, not specifically as males. There is no consciousness of a male identity beyond the community. For the men, self-identity stops at the boundaries of caste consciousness. In women's writings, self-identity strains not just at the boundaries of society and nation but also those of the caste and family. Hira Bansode's famous poem "Petition" illustrates the consciousness of an individual gendered identity—"[M]y father, my brother, my husband . . ./under the weight of these well fleshed relations/my hollow existence gives way/. . . I have lost my identity/my independence, my rights, my opinions/see how everything falls on me. In my home, in my society, in my country/who am I if I am nobody" (Novetzke 1995, 293).

In Telegu dalit women's writing there is an even stronger condemnation of patriarchy (upper caste and Dalit), which denies women's individuality. Darisi Sasi Nirmala writes, "I am dragged/here and there/under someone's buttocks/a seating plank/someone or other/drags me along/by a nose rope/to make me dance" (Rani 1998, 22). Swaroopa Rani links up the caste system with patriarchy: "For generations I have/borne this leprous caste ridden *male* world/. . . on my head" (italics mine). This is an idea that has been presented in works of several theorists who have analyzed the caste system from a gendered perspective.

The women definitely see spaces for alliances among all dalit women as a route of emancipation. Sugandha Shende's *Priya Bhagini* ("Dear sister") celebrates a dalit sisterhood: "Priya Bhagini, awake quick/cast your glance outside the home/you are no longer a woman helpless and weak/you have grown strong enough to support the world/know thyself, know thy power, and/Drive the fear out from your hearts/. . . let the wings of ambition spread/And go on soaring high to heaven" (Bhaware 1980, 12). Do the dalit women conceive of the possibility of an overarching alliance with all women? This is a very complex issue—the answer would be both yes and no. The relationship with upper-caste women is highly complicated, as it is enmeshed within the matrix of caste and gender with all its ideological, political, and social reverberations. They are aware of both the specific nature of their oppression in which upper-caste/class women also participate, and are simultaneously aware of the emancipatory potential of a cross-caste/class alliance with women. This is evident in the use of the figure of upper-caste women in their writings. The figure of the upper-caste woman is presented in Marathi dalit women's writing in two forms—predominantly mythological figures but also as real women with whom they live their everyday lives. The use of mythological figures indicates two facts—there is a sense of solidarity with all women who have been victims of Brahmanical (upper-caste) patriarchal oppression and also the invisibility of dalit women figures in dominant historiography and mythology from which such figures are drawn.

In Marathi dalit women's writings the only mythological non-Brahmanic reference is to Shabri in Hira Bansode's "To Shabri" (a tribal woman in the Indian epic *Ramayan* who fed the hero Lord Ram berries she had already tasted to give him the sweetest ones—generally, a figure of naive love and devotion). Significantly, the poet inverts the figure from that of silent love and devotion to a speaking agent—speaking not only for dalit men but also for upper-caste women: "[W]hy didn't you ask omniscient Ram/About the heart rending sacrifice of Eklavya's thumb [a tribal archer in the epic *Mahabharat* who was asked to cut off his thumb when he threatened to surpass the hero Arjun's skill in archery. He is seen as a figure of unjust emasculation of dalits].... About blameless Sita's exile ... [symbol of the silent, suffering yet dutiful wife who followed her husband Ram into exile,was kidnapped by Ravan, and asked to prove her "purity" through a trial by fire].... If you had revealed the curse of your caste I would have found fulfillment/Shabri, here you went wrong?" (Novetzke 1995, 288).

On one level the figures of Kunti (mother of the Pandava brothers, heroes in the *Mahabharat*, who abandoned her illegitimate child, Karna) is used to express a sense of betrayal, a sense that upper-caste women are participants in dalit women's oppression. Therefore, at times the caste consciousness is too strong to visualize an overarching alliance with women. Hira Bansode's "Sanskriti" equates Indian culture with a betraying mother, Kunti—"[Y]ou denied us your motherhood./Beneath caste dominance/You smothered our bravery" (Novetzke 1995, 284). Yet at other times there is a complete identification with upper-caste women as victims of a male dominant culture. Bansode's "Petition" illustrates this— "As thousands of Draupadi's are stripped/Brothers don't just sit/Bowing your heads" (Novetzke 1995, 293–94). (Draupadi, wife of the Pandav brothers, was set as a wager in a gambling game by her own husband and later sought to be disrobed in public by the Pandav's cousins and rivals. Out of a misplaced sense of obligation to an oath given, no one attempted to save her.) Her poem "Yashodhara" equates Yashodhara with the sacrificing, silent wives of Hindu mythology—"You would have become famous in purana and palm leaf like Sita and Savitri" (Savitri is the symbol of the ideal devoted wife. She pursued the God of death and compelled him to return her husband's soul; Zelliot 1996, 72). "Slave" is a scathing indictment of the treatment of all women in India: "When Sita entered the fire to prove her fidelity/where Ahilya was turned to stone because of Indira's lust [Ahilya was tricked into cohabiting with Lord Indra and cursed by her husband to become a stone. She was redeemed from the curse when the footsteps of Ram fell on her]/... where Draupadi was fractured to serve five husbands [Draupadi was forced to be the wife of the five Pandava brothers because of a chance remark by their mother that all of them should share equally in everything]/... where a woman's identity fades like nature's blossoms/... she remains in the shadow of someone else's light/... In that country a woman is still a slave/... To be born a woman is unjust" (Zelliot 1996, 74–75). Dalit women become spokespersons for women only when they focus on oppression of gender not of caste.

Again this theme finds a much stronger expression in Telegu women's poetry, which demonstrates a much stronger caste and gender consciousness among the Telegu dalit women. They see upper-caste women as partnering with upper-caste men not only in economic but also *sexual* exploitation by their silence. Swaroopa Rani says that "dalit women have questioned and rejected caste in terms which even upper-caste women are even today unable to do. Even women who suffer patriarchy humiliate dalit women because they belong to a lower caste" (1998, 23), in support of which she quotes two sections of Sasi Nirmala's "Dalit Uralu"—"Why speak of the other?/Another woman wants to buy me/she wants me as the gold lace/to her upper-caste new sari/"(23)—or, more harshly—"Do you remember/your words when/your husband plucked me/like a chicken? Do you know how often/I was cheapened at your hands?" (24).

There is also a critique of other anti-establishment movements in India as "upper caste" because they enjoy a visibility not available in dalit women struggles. There is a sarcastic reference to the Narmada Bachao Andolan, a famous, on-going movement led by Medha Patkar (a woman) against the Hydel project in Narmada valley that will displace thousands of tribals in Madhya Pradesh, a region in Central India. "You peacocks of high caste/preening your plumes/in the Narmada valley/your call echoes and rouses/each corner of the world/but my sisters struggle/to dam the swollen stream of arrack/choking them/their hoarse voices/will be buried/in the Telugu earth." The "swollen streams of arrack" refers to the anti-arrack (country liquor) movement in Andhra, which was a fallout of the women's literary campaign among the poor and lower-caste women. While the strong identification with their own liberatory movements is laudable, the hostility toward emancipatory movements elsewhere involving ecological issues is disturbing. It points toward a regional and caste consciousness that is too strong to join one's struggles with those of a different caste.

However, Swaroopa Rani in general does condemn patriarchy in all forms. She disagrees with dalit men who "in the course of their condemnation of caste have also humiliated upper-caste women" (1998, 24). She also calls for an alliance of all women and dalits, saying that "women and dalits have been sacrificed at the altar of Manudharma [an ancient code of laws given by the sage Manu, which legitimized caste and gender hierarchy and discrimination]. Women and dalits need to collectively struggle against a common enemy . . . that would replace Manudharma with Manavdharma [literally—"humanity"] (1998, 24). While there is an extremely strong caste consciousness at the level of ground reality among women, there is, on a more theoretical plane, a recognition of the need for an alliance between all victims of "Brahmanism" (upper-caste ideology), irrespective of caste or gender.

## CONCLUSION

Dalit women write differently from dalit men because of their different sociological experience. They do not represent themselves, as the male writers do, as mere symbols for the debasement of the dalit community. They see themselves as speaking and acting agents for the community, though, ironically, the focus remains on the male child as a symbol of hope for the community. They are also conscious of an individual gendered identity beyond the family and community, though this is not rigorously pursued. The category of "dalit" and the category of "woman" are in constant engagement with each other, opening up spaces of both convergence and divergence. As dalits, women are conscious of being victims of caste oppression in which men and women of the upper class or caste participate. They call for an end to this system. As women they face patriarchal violence and control from men both of the upper caste and of their own community. They also recognize that all women face patriarchal controls, albeit in different forms. They are not conscious of any specific way to end this, especially violence within the family and patriarchal community practices. For this they do see spaces for alliances among women of all castes and classes. They see themselves as exploited economically and sexually, and to this they add the dimension of exploitation by their own community members. Their ultimate aim, however, remains liberation of humankind.

# Part IV
Home Is Where the Art Is:
Shaping Space and Place

# 10

## The Role of "Place" in New Zealand Māori Songs of Lament

AILSA L. SMITH

### INTRODUCTION

The Māori people of New Zealand have a word for "their place" in the landscape. They call it "tūrangawaewae" (a standing place for the feet). Being an oral people by inclination they have a way with words, as when orators exercise the right to which their *tūrangawaewae* entitles them, to stand on the *marae* (the ceremonial center of Māori cultural life) and speak of matters pertaining to that place. Similarly, women and men expressed themselves in telling imagery in the past when they sang to ease the intolerable burden imposed by death or other tragic loss.

The songs they sang were *waiata tangi* (crying songs or songs of lament), a form of oral literature that was heavily influenced by the places in which its composers and subjects were situated in the course of their everyday lives. These songs were recorded in large numbers in the nineteenth century, when the multitudinous references they contained to people and places in the tribal territory were topical and relevant. The meanings of many "place" references have since been lost, because the overlay of settler place names has obliterated the indigenous history those earlier names were intended to preserve.

Today, we as Māori sing *waiata tangi* as a mark of respect for earlier generations. Or, rather, we sing those songs whose air or *rangi* has been retained by the descendants of their composers or of the dead whose passing sparked their composition; or by the tribes who preserved them as *taonga tuku iho*, treasures handed down from the past. We do not, however, speak of the past and present as if they are rigidly demarcated, for our ancestors live on in us and in the landscape, and we are constantly aware of their presence. This sense of the conflation of past and present as a single, comprehensible "space" is inherent in the way Māori people regard time, for we walk backward into the future with our thoughts directed toward the coming generations but with our eyes on the past, because that is the "seen" and "known" part of our collective experience. Perhaps this is why we have such long memories and do not easily forget the wrongs done to our forebears that have resulted in the mental, emotional, and spiritual turmoil of recent times.

## THE TREATY OF WAITANGI

In 1840 the British Crown signed a treaty with the Māori tribes of New Zealand. The English text of the Treaty of Waitangi, as it became known, was translated into the Māori language using missionary Māori, which failed to address nuances in meaning between the two languages. Although considerable numbers of Māori were literate in their own language by this time, the Māori text of the treaty was explained orally by government treaty negotiators, who added their own interpretations where necessary to maximize Māori acceptance of its terms. Compared to the more than five hundred leaders (including some women) who signed the Māori text of the Treaty, only thirty-nine signed the English version because a copy of the Māori text was not available at the time. Were it not for these thirty-nine signatures, the Māori text of the treaty would have unquestioned authority in the eyes of the Crown, instead of exerting a moral and persuasive force only.

The wording of the English version of the treaty differs little from treaties that Britain had drawn up with indigenous peoples in other parts of the world and then observed with less apparent concern for its national integrity than for the success of its mercantile and colonizing endeavors (Williams 1989). The difference between those treaties and the Treaty of Waitangi is that the latter was drawn up in Māori and English, the two texts differing substantially in certain key areas. Thus, in the first article of the English text, the Māori chiefs ceded sovereignty to the Crown; in the second, they were guaranteed full and undisturbed possession of their lands and other domains for as long as they wished to retain them; and, in the third, they were extended the rights and privileges of British subjects. Māori believed they had given the Crown *kāwanatanga* (governance) over its British subjects in New Zealand (Orange 1987), that they had been confirmed in the unqualified exercise of their *rangatiratanga* (chieftainship) over their lands and other *taonga* (treasures), and that they had taken on the rights and duties of British citizenship.

Māori have since personalized the guarantees contained in the treaty: the Queen's regard toward the signatory chiefs as her equals; the wording of the treaty as a sacred covenant; and the respect, amounting to reverence, with which the document itself has been invested, with its ancestral signatures or marks and often the *moko* (the representation of a chief's facial tattoo) attached. Nevertheless, inconsistencies between the Māori and English texts have left the Māori people with a legacy of promises quite at variance with those understood by the settlers, the immediate beneficiaries of the treaty.

The settlers, who gave the treaty little thought after its signing in 1840, were convinced that they had a right to settle in New Zealand by virtue of their status as members of a self-designated "superior" race. As such, they felt they had a duty to improve the lot of the Māori people by setting them an example of industriousness and contributing to their material prosperity by placing an economic value upon their land and making it a tradable commodity rather than, as it had been, a seemingly inalienable source of tribal prestige and sustenance.

The original intention of the British Crown, in considering whether to annex New Zealand, may have been to establish enclaves of British influence surrounded by territories where Māori customs and practices would prevail (Ward 1973). If so, this intention was not adequately revised when the political climate changed due to colonizing initiatives such as those of the New Zealand Company, which overcame the more humanitarian considerations of the time by prompting a resurgence of Britain's competitive, imperialistic spirit. The New Zealand Company was responsible for a largely unregulated flood of British migrants who arrived in New Zealand after 1840, to join those British citizens who were already there and whose turbulent ways had obliged Britain to formalize a treaty with Māori leaders in the first place. Contrary to the expectations of those leaders, who wished to encourage manageable trade relations with other countries, migration led to an insatiable demand for Māori land and to increasingly bitter relations between Māori and Pākehā (the Māori name for settlers of Anglo-European origin).

In Taranaki, on the West Coast of the North Island, the situation was particularly tense because much of the land appeared to be unoccupied when the settlers arrived in 1841. Intertribal warfare had caused an emptying out of the region in the preceding decades, although the land could be reoccupied at any time under Māori tribal tenure. The Taranaki tribes began moving back to their homelands in earnest in the late 1840s, after settlers had taken up residence on ancestral lands to the north of the newly established town of New Plymouth, competition for those lands requiring that settler land entitlements be renegotiated with the tribes. The decade that followed was marked by dissension within tribes between those who wished to sell to the settlers and those who did not and a hardening of attitudes on the part of the settlers toward a native race whom they felt needed be taught its place in relation to the sovereign might of the British.

The cause of the war that ensued in Taranaki in 1860 and spread to other parts of the North Island has been variously ascribed to the demand for land, to the assertion of British sovereignty, and to the inevitable conflict that resulted wherever Britain went in its colonizing endeavors. The war between Māori and the British (and later colonial) forces is generally referred to as the "land wars," although British determination to exert sovereign power was an ever-present factor in deciding how the Crown would act toward its treaty partner. Illegal land confiscations and the individualization of land titles to facilitate the Europeanization of Māori land were part of an ongoing drive to enforce the lessons that should have been learned from the land wars; although the reality today is that Māori are as determined as ever to regain "their place" in the landscape, in terms of their prior occupation of the soil and their status as *tangata whenua* (literally, "people of the land").

Inspired in part by the black power movement in the United States, Māori took to the streets in the 1970s, forcing the government to reexamine its Māori policies. As a result, a commission of inquiry known as the Waitangi Tribunal was set up to look into Māori grievances over land confiscations and unjust dealings by past governments. Following the tribunal's recommendations, millions of dollars in settlements have been paid to various tribes. These payments by the government, in return for the extinguishing of Māori rights to claim in the future, are directed at the settlement of grievances against the Crown for postcolonial land loss and cultural deprivation.

Like other European countries imbued in the past with a colonizing spirit, or established under colonial imperatives, New Zealand is now under an obligation to answer to the international community concerning the welfare and status of its indigenous people (Kingsbury, 1989). Many New Zealanders, especially non-Māori, do not appreciate this fact nor the deleterious effect that the lack of an adequate resource base has had on Māori progress over the past century and a half. Particularly vocal are those who uphold the notion that "we are all New Zealanders, and this is a democratic country" and who remain unswayed by arguments concerning the common justice of the course taken by (and indeed the moral responsibility of) recent governments in attempting to redress the legislative wrongs of the past.

In a climate of increasingly vocal though largely uninformed criticism of the tribunal process, and of the scale and settlement of Māori claims, the need is clear for a greater understanding by non-Māori of the relationship between Māori and the land. This relationship does not depend upon Māori "ownership" as such, for it is inconceivable according to traditional thinking that Māori should own Papa-tū-ā-nuku, their earth mother. Rather, it is she who owns them, through having nurtured them from their East Polynesian origins to their later "becoming" as Māori, in tribal regions with landmarks and foods characteristic of that place and its geographic and climatic conditions. Ownership, or more appropriately land tenure was confirmed by a process of settlement and cultivation, in which the concept of '*ahi kaa*,' the "lit fires" of continuous occupation, sent an unmistakable message to others that prior occupation rights would be strenuously protected.

In the early stages of European occupation of New Zealand, land transactions that were perceived as sales by would-be purchasers were more in the nature of usage rights, such as Māori themselves practiced. Land was communally held, and while tracts of land might be made available to outsiders for specific purposes, the expectation was that this land would revert to the tribal group once it was no longer needed for that purpose. Initially at least, then, alienation of land was inconceivable. It was only later that permanent loss became a reality that had to be coped with by mental and emotional adjustments, in the ongoing process of adapting to colonial ways.

Today, ancestral Māori land is most simply defined as land that belonged to Māori ancestors. That is, this land—held at one time in communal, native, or aboriginal title—refers to all the land in New Zealand, whether Māori themselves hold individual title at the present time. Such an association of Māori and the land could be seen as a stereotype, but it is also a statement of a perceived significant difference between Māori and Pākehā, in which the former seek to establish a moral connection to places that the latter now hold through Crown processes.

The task of determining whether Māori assertions of links to the land are sincere and genuine, or whether they are ideologically driven, was a challenge I felt motivated to act upon; although, in all fairness, my concern was also prompted by an apparently opportunistic trend in some Māori claims that lent a heavy emphasis to spiritual links to the land. To the outward appearance this type of claim gave the impression of a politicization of views held by largely urbanized Māori, many of whom are now divorced from their tribal roots.

How could I, then, as an indigenous woman, reconcile these differing perceptions with my awareness of the colonial process and the despoliation of Māori *taonga* (treasures) over the generations? My challenge thus became one of identifying a credible source of data—from Māori sources—that would demonstrate conclusively how Māori regarded the land in former times, in order to appeal persuasively to the reason that lies beneath an often unprepossessing exterior of cultural intolerance in this country.

The data source I chose to work with was a collection of some eighty Māori *waiata tangi* (laments) in manuscript form, recorded in the late nineteenth century by my *tupuna* (great-grandfather), Te Kahui Kararehe of Taranaki. The appropriateness of using these songs as my source documents lay in their recognized value as carriers of tribal information, since their formal structure and slight rhythm provided mnemonic aid in recalling knowledge and transmitting it unchanged over many generations. I therefore felt they could be probed for information on Māori feelings for place that was as authentic, if not more so, than any other source available today.

I had worked with these songs previously, but more as an exercise in individual interpretation than in an effort to understand their overall nature and content. Using them as working texts for my doctoral thesis (Smith 2001), I had to search for them throughout my *tupuna*'s writings and then transcribe, edit, translate, and interpret them. So began a personal journey of discovery into the minds of my Taranaki people as I sought for genuine insights into the role of "place" in their lives, by analyzing the particular genre of oral literature they had left behind.

## STUDY BACKGROUND

The songs I researched were replete with personal and place names: of tribal boundaries; genealogical lines of descent and ancestors both female and male; cultivations and *mahinga kai* (food gathering areas); *wāhi tapu* (sacred sites) such as ancient battlegrounds and burial places; and more. Many place names were descriptive because Māori meant them to be informative: of food supplies and other resources, the physical terrain, environmental sounds, and ancestral exploits. In particular, place names give an insight into the history of the tribal group, since that history is called to mind in the recital of those names. One aspect of the significance of place, therefore, is its connectedness with ancestral events that occurred at definite locations within the tribal territory so that an awareness of the geographic location of a place is not complete without an accompanying awareness of the emotional significance of that place to the tribal group through ancestral associations over time. A word that refers to this interconnectedness of time and place is *wā*, the circumstance of an event, which binds people and place together in a space that is both relative and ongoing.

Particularly noticeable in the song texts I studied was an all-pervading sense of place, an aspect I felt should appeal to western minds because of its emphasis upon the "seen" components of the landscape. Although I could have focused upon more esoteric elements in the *waiata*, an emphasis upon descriptive aspects would, I felt, encourage readers to think imaginatively, while at the same time it recognizes the preference of Māori, like other oral peoples, to communicate in words and phrases with visual and perceptual appeal.

The approach I decided upon was to isolate threads of imagery from the *waiata* and group them for analysis, my aim being to highlight a preoccupation with the environment of individuals and groups who were facing a crisis associated with death or other adversity. At such times one might expect that only those aspects of enduring significance would find a place in the compositions that resulted from such engagements with reality. Since the landscape element is a recurring theme in many *waiata tangi*, it can be readily seen that the landscape (or "place") occupied a prominent position in the minds of the composers and their audiences.

In this chapter I use the terms *place*, *land*, and *landscape* interchangeably. From a Māori perspective, places were discrete pieces of land that held special significance by virtue of an ancestral event that happened there: the birthplace of a chief, a *taumata* or high point where a traveler might rest and survey the surrounding countryside, the site of an ancient *pā* or stronghold. Where a number of such places occurred in close proximity, as might be expected over an extended period of occupation in a particular area, those places effectively combined to become—or were the building blocks that made up—land.

Land as a recognized tribal area served a utilitarian purpose as the place from which the community drew its sustenance. The word for land (*whenua*) refers also to the afterbirth of a newborn child, since the land was personified as Papa-tū-ā-nuku the earth mother, the source of all life.

In this sense land, as the natural provider of the community's needs, was more than just a portion of the earth's surface but possessed an emotional significance that transcended geographic boundaries.

Landscape was the land viewed self-consciously because of the altered emphasis placed upon it in the new, settler-dominated society. In the climate of heightened cultural awareness that Māori experienced during the nineteenth century, land came to be viewed more as an object than a subject of regard, with an increasing emphasis upon its economic value and less upon its former roles as the provider of food and, through place names, an oral record of tribal histories. Nevertheless, Māori writers today use the term *landscape* to refer to everything associated with the land in its ancestral, cultural, and natural aspects; the key to understanding such references is an awareness of the role of *whakapapa* or genealogical lines of descent as a crucial component of individual and group identity. Thus what an outsider might regard as an empty recital of landscape features and names masks a deeper and more elemental awareness of the connectedness of people to "this" landscape through time, which stretches back beyond mortal and godlike ancestors to the earliest ages of the world.

Today, Māori introduce themselves to each other on formal occasions by giving their connections to their *iwi* (tribe) and *hapū* (subtribe), to significant ancestors, and to outstanding landmarks in the tribal territory, such as a mountain, river, or lake. These group-specific ancestral and territorial markers establish a referential framework to which others can relate and tie the people of that group to a particular geographic area in a tapestry of indissoluble family and community linkages.

The settings in which those formal occasions take place can be a tribal or urban *marae*, a *kura* or *whare wānanga* (secondary or tertiary learning institution), or a *kōhanga reo* (infants' "language nest"), where instruction in cultural values is given in the Māori language, an official language of New Zealand since 1987. Whatever the setting, the outcome is the inculcation of pride in "being Māori," a significant component of which is an awareness of and association with one's ancestral homelands. The catalyst for such an awareness today derives most significantly from a mood of growing Māori assertiveness in the 1980s, when the Waitangi Tribunal's powers were extended retrospectively to 1840 to allow the Crown to address breaches of the Treaty of Waitangi from that date forward.

I turn now to a discussion of *waiata tangi* and the way in which they capture the essence of Māori feelings for "their place" in the landscape, which they once occupied with confidence in their right to belong in such settings.

## THE NATURE OF *WAIATA TANGI*

*Waiata tangi* contain a wealth of classical, local, and historical references, expressed in some of the most beautiful examples of the language. Consisting of sometimes as many as sixty lines, these songs of lamentation are complex, with their often densely packed imagery drawn from mythology, legend and folklore, ancestral and archetypal precedents, kinship relationships, and personalities. The range of landscape imagery covered in the texts I studied included references to lightning; mountains and other high points of land; the stars and moon; forests and trees; the ocean and tides; land and sea birds; winds and clouds; rivers and lakes, paths and beaches; the sun, seasons, smoke and mists; the built environment; vegetation (medicinal and scented herbs, famine foods); fish and fishing; and metaphysical references to the pantheon of Māori gods. Although neither prescriptive nor exhaustive, this list gives an indication of the all-encompassing nature of Māori perceptions of their world and of their situatedness within it.

As might be expected from the name, *waiata tangi* were inspired by misfortune or disaster and performed a necessary function in helping the bereaved or bereft adjust to circumstances beyond their control. Further, in providing a means of publicly expressing feelings of distress and grief, *waiata tangi* drew the tribal group together in an affirmation of mutuality and support.

Many laments refer in their opening lines to some aspect of the natural world, to which the composer's attention was drawn in a creative moment. This could be a configuration of stars, the sun's rays lighting up the morning sky, fog drifting down over the horizon, or the long hours of darkness during which the composer lay awake and reflective. Settings such as these invoked the mood of introspection needed for the *waiata* to be presented appropriately and for the audience to appreciate it. That such settings relate to the natural landscape is indicative of the importance of the environment in the lives and consciousness of the Māori people.

A question that might be asked, nevertheless, is whether Māori saw the land in terms of its picturesque or scenic qualities, as well as its more complex cultural connections. From a study of trends in *waiata* composition it becomes apparent that older *waiata* contained many metaphysical and archaic references, which could only be understood by the application of specialist knowledge gained in traditional schools of learning. Following colonization and the loss of tribal lands, naming became more overt, deliberate, and conscious, with an increasing incorporation of descriptive elements into the wording of song texts so that those who lacked that earlier specialized knowledge could share in the mood of the occasion.

Two examples, referring to the movement of birds in the landscape, illustrate the descriptive aspect of *waiata tangi*. The first uses the term *ripeka* (cross), to refer to the way in which long-legged wading birds run "cross-legged" over the sand. The second employs the word *kopa* (folded, like a wallet or satchel with a flap lid), to describe a young bird gaining height with downwardly thrusting wings so that it appears to "fold" and "unfold" in flight. Examples like these illustrate the profound sense that Māori had of their environment, which they encapsulated in words with the power to impart that sense to others. Today, such novel and distinctively different ways of looking at the environment convey a sense of delight and appreciation of the minds that could conceive of such aptness and vividness in the crafting of this mode of expression.

*Waiata* were in fact composed by borrowing formulaic phrases from existing *waiata* and reassembling them to fit new or changed circumstances; giving rise to new songs in their own right. Although this process suggests a mechanistic approach to composition (and was regarded eurocentrically as plagiarism), *waiata* were as finely crafted as the skill of their composers could make them, with originality and creativity as ultimate goals. Any suggestion, therefore, that a composer's "way with words" was compromised by reusing elements from other *waiata* is readily countered by considering reasons for *waiata* composition: to sway audiences by their persuasive power, to impress with their ability to evoke images that were apt and telling, to draw communities together in times of crisis, and to perpetuate the deeds of ancestral figures whose successes had secured the land and its resources for their descendants.

Another question that might be asked is whether a gendered approach is evident in the subject matter and tone of *waiata tangi*—whether heroic or homely, vengeful or reflective, or some other mood that fits the overall purpose of these songs. Although the identity of the composers could not be ascertained in some twenty percent of the songs I studied, male composers appeared to outnumber their female counterparts by three to one. This is not to say that the composition of *waiata tangi* was predominantly a male province, for women could express themselves as forcefully or plaintively in this type of *waiata* as in other kinds with which they were more traditionally associated, such as *waiata aroha*, *waiata whakautu*, *kaioraora*, and *apakura*.

*Waiata aroha* or love laments were mostly composed by women but could be modified by men to express deep emotions other than the more commonly encountered themes of unsatisfied or unrequited love. Associated too with the theme of love, *waiata whakautu* or songs of reply were composed by women who had become the subject of ill-natured gossip. In Māori society words were often the only medium through which a woman could assert herself, and a skillfully worded composition did much to restore her reputation in the eyes of the community (Orbell, 1978, 12). These songs often named places in the tribal territory, but more to emphasize the composer's own standing than, as in *waiata tangi*, to recount themes of relevance to the deceased.

A virulent form of *waiata*, *kaioraora* (cursing songs) could be resorted to by a woman whose husband had been killed in battle (although, atypically, the few I studied from Taranaki were written by men). *Kaioraora* were not, properly speaking, laments but were closely associated with such songs because of their common focus on death. *Apakura* served a similar function to *kaioraora* but took the form of an exaggerated lament intended to arouse the composer's community to avenge the death of a close male relative. The weeping of the archetypal figure Apakura, who gave her name to this kind of composition, was likened to—or could be heard in—the sound of the waves (White 1887, 149), a connection of particular significance in Taranaki because of its geographic location in a predominantly coastal setting.

Although *waiata* were characteristically built up from formulaic phrases and the dismantling of other *waiata*, women were equally capable of innovation in composition. Different again from the focus of the song types discussed above, a lament by a woman for her dead son retains the structure and poetic conventions of a *waiata tangi*, while including themes drawn from missionary teachings. A consideration of certain lines illustrates the effortless way in which she blends traditional and transitional elements in a poignant appeal to the Christian God, whose name in some cosmologies is that of the supreme being of the Māori pantheon. Those lines read, in translation: "God in Heaven, look down then on my greenstone treasure/Hiding below here in your shelter."

To Māori, greenstone or jade was as precious as is gold to western minds, and this honorific reference is highly symbolic. Nevertheless, the further reference to "hiding . . . in your shelter" is a Christian image, not a Māori one, and places this *waiata* at the cusp of those that could be investigated for traditional feelings for place.

A transitional element with more calculated intent is found in a *waiata* composed by the woman poet Hurungarangi, in which she urges her people to "stand for New Zealand, and gain the victory." Here, the reference to New Zealand is an unusual one but can be understood if it is realized that Māori were referred to as "New Zealanders," throughout most of the nineteenth century, by the predominantly European-born settler population. In applying this concept to her people and legitimating them as the rightful occupiers of the soil, Hurungarangi robs their tribal foes of this distinction. More important, and by implication, she denies it to the settlers as well.

Another unusual feature suggested by Hurungarangi's choice of phrase is that, although such concepts might be borrowed from the colonial presence, that presence was rarely if ever acknowledged in songs that resulted from confrontations with Imperial (and later colonial) forces during the land wars. The ultimate enemy was death and separation from the land and the living. Thus the significance of those themes the *waiata do* mention, as well as those they do not, becomes all the more compelling.

An example comes from a lament composed after the battle of Te Morere (Sentry Hill) in 1864, when the followers of the religious leader Te Ua Haumene were defeated by British troops. The *waiata* begins with a reference to the play of lightning out at sea and around the peak of the tribal mountain and to the configuration of stars that denoted death and disaster. Those who died in the fighting, among them the sons of the southern Taranaki composer, Tamati Hone Oraukawa, were addressed in honorific terms and associated with distinctive landmarks in the tribal territory. No mention was made of the troops whose bullets had brought them down to lie, as another phrase puts it, like canoes that had been whirled about by eddying currents.

After the engagement at Te Morere, women came onto the battlefield to search for their kin, to help the wounded, and to weep over the dead. Women are the classic mourners in any society, but men, too, could contemplate the loss of a child or a staunch friend in terms that were, for the characteristically warlike Māori race, uncharacteristically tender and reflective. So the aged Makere of northern Taranaki, who had lost a grandson, could call for assistance "to take me to the headland at Okawa/To feel for and grasp the heart of the land." (But how do I, removed in space and time and "othered" by gender and changes in cultural upbringing, explain "the heart of the land" and the unutterable sense of loss that calls forth a phrase such as this?)

So, too, my *tupuna* Te Kahui could say of his two sons who had died in childhood: "Maku e tangi kau nga wai e rere/He wai tukunga kiri no te ipo ma ra e" (I weep beside the flowing waters/The place where my loved ones jumped and swam).

The phrase *tukunga kiri* refers to the way in which Māori children jumped feet first into the water, an image that is profoundly reminiscent of carefree childhood. So too are these lines that he composed for his daughter, who also died in childhood: "Then perhaps you are in your river, little one/Dipping in and out of the water." Here, though, the phrase "your river" is no fond irrelevance. Rather, its significance lies in the Māori practice of naming places to assert ownership, in just such a fashion as Māori today, by virtue of their *tūrangawaewae* status, stand on the *marae* and deliver a *whakataukī* or *whaikōrero* that names tribal boundaries and other significant landmarks. This "right to name" was implicit in the composition of *waiata tangi* for, as a female member of Te Kahui's family wrote in one of his manuscripts, "no Maori would compose a song or lament for any place unless they had a full right to it. This is a custom of the Maori people."

I give the term *heroic* to songs of this nature, to *waiata tangi* and the allied song types referred to above, since in composing and performing these songs the composers were placed in larger than life situations, which were played out in front of immediate and discerning audiences. Although many songs begin on a somber note, in keeping with their prevailing theme, they finish strongly and assertively. They therefore deserve the title of heroic since they exemplify the unquenchability of the human spirit.

So a woman might express resignation in the face of loss by concluding with these words:

> Sitting here in the days of summer,
> A host of cicadas throbs about me,
> And birdsong resounds,
> And people pass away into nothingness.

(But, again, how am I to understand and then interpret, across the boundaries of space and time, the desolation of resignation arising out of a contemplation of "nothingness"? More, how can I articulate the sense of what is meant, so that others may grasp it?)

In the closing lines of another *waiata*, composed by Te Kahui for Te Whetu, the "fighting general" of Taranaki during the land wars, a succession of word pictures evokes the similarly philosophical nature of his conclusions:

> Now Tamanui-te-ra shines his rays upon the land;
> The land dries up, the sea dries up,
> The lizard stretches out and basks in the heat.
> Come then, my friend. Your older brothers

> Will heap up clouds after you . . .
> What is life's essence, that it can be withdrawn?
> What is life's essence, that it can be overcome?
> It cannot be overcome, it is a post of Tangaroa that stands!

In this *waiata* the setting is the heat of summer, while the cumulus clouds are rising to great heights and, in this context, giving the best possible conditions for the soul's onward flight. The "post of Tangaroa," which can only be understood with reference to the cosmology of the Taranaki region, is an enduring symbol of the Māori will to survive.

In summarizing this discussion of gendered approaches in *waiata tangi* it becomes evident that content and tone range from softer themes enunciating a sense of loss, such as a woman might articulate—memories of children or a beloved spouse, and the intimacies of family life—to grander, more epic themes of death and survival and those that eulogize a figure of tribal importance.

I turn now to a consideration of Māori cosmologies, the most widely known being that given to Governor Sir George Grey in the nineteenth century by Te Rangikaheke, a Te Arawa (central North Island) leader. I also discuss a little-known version from Taranaki, in order to demonstrate the spirituality that links Taranaki Māori with their environment and their past.

## MĀORI COSMOLOGIES

Māori feelings for their place in the landscape are premised upon an awareness of the sky above them and the ground beneath their feet as two personalized beings, Ranginui-e-tū-nei (Rangi) and Papa-tū-ā-nuku (Papa), the sky father and earth mother. Between these primal parents as they lay together in space, as yet unseparated, dwelt a number of sons whose function was to oversee the welfare of various spheres of natural activity upon the earth. Deprived of light and space in which to grow, the sons of Rangi and Papa debated how, and indeed whether, they should thrust their parents apart. In the Te Arawa version given to Sir George Grey, the initiative was taken and the action performed by Tāne, presiding deity of forests and trees.

If one considers the prevailing vegetation of the Te Arawa region, with its forest cover of tall trees, it is obvious that Tāne's trees do, indeed, hold Rangi aloft in his present position. And yet, in another part of the country with a different set of geographic features, what might the result of the debate have been?

In Taranaki, I found an isolated account in manuscript form of the story of Rangi and Papa, which names Tangaroa, presiding deity of seas and fish, as the son who separated the primal parents. The significance of this version is that it is entirely consistent with the local landscape for, if one stands to the west of Mount Taranaki and faces seaward, it becomes evident that the sea, Tangaroa, effects the separation of his parents by pushing the sky out to the horizon. This emphasis on the sea is a prevailing theme in Taranaki *waiata tangi* since that region, surrounding the soaring volcanic cone from which both region and tribes take their name, is bounded on three sides by the sea.

Standing with one's back to the mountain one also faces toward Hawaiki, the mythical homeland of the Māori people, to which the spirits of the dead returned on the outgoing tide. Such a tide off the Taranaki coast is referred to in *waiata tangi* as "*he tai mihinga tangata*" (a people-greeting tide), while a tide devoid of spiritual freight is "*he tai tangata kore*" (a tide without people). A third aspect of gazing out to sea from the slopes of the mountain is that one looks out over the most fertile acres of this region, where a concentration of sacred sites (carved rocks, former *pā* sites, named cultivations), as well as access to the rich food resources of the coast, is locked up in land confiscated by the Crown in the 1860s and largely given over to Pākehā settlement.

As a result of the separation of Rangi and Papa a number of oppositions came into play. These legitimated the use by humans of their environmental kin as food and explained the conflicting forces of nature: the tempestuous battering of trees by the wind, the assertive nature of humans in their fight against the elements, and the ceaseless interplay of sea and land along the coastlines. This latter aspect is particularly noticeable along the southern Taranaki coast, where crumbling cliffs testify to Tangaroa's preeminence. A phrase in a *waiata tangi* emphasizes this preeminence by telling the dead person not to "stay in the forest of Tāne/But listen to the tides crying beyond Heiawe" (a place in a coastal setting associated with the deceased).

The "post of Tangaroa" referred to earlier almost certainly comes from the perception that anything associated with Tangaroa—a post signifies steadfastness or immovability—cannot be overcome by external forces but endures forever. This phrase therefore represents the unwavering determination of the Māori people to withstand moves by the colonial government to deprive them of their ancestral lands, and hence their history, their livelihood, and their identity.

The Taranaki account is silent regarding a further stage in the cosmological saga, in which Tāne sought for the female principle in order to establish human life upon the earth. According to the Te Arawa version he finally achieved this after bringing into being all other created forms, such as rocks, water, trees, birds, insects, and reptiles. He thus became the common parent of all and the being through whom Māori claim a spiritually enhanced relationship with the environment in all its manifestations.

## SUMMARY

An indigenous people who place great store upon intergenerational links with ancestral lands, the Māori people of Aotearoa/New Zealand traditionally expressed those links in mythopoetic imagery in *whakataukī* (proverbs), *whaikōrero* (oratory) and *waiata* (songs). In particular, the classical song type known as *waiata tangi* exhibits a strong sense of place component, based on an intimate acquaintance with tribal lands over centuries of occupation in specific areas.

The overwhelming evidence from an examination of Māori feelings for place, as exemplified in Taranaki *waiata tangi*, is that the relationship between people and the land has its roots in the enduring nature and distinctiveness of Māori worldviews. Bonds forged over generations of interaction in the tribal territory resulted in *iwi*-specific ways of accounting for the landforms of that territory, according to its particular characteristics. This led to the formulation of cosmological beliefs that were framed in the light of a holistic conceptualization of kinship bonds. These beliefs were transmitted intergenerationally through the evocative power of the spoken word and through the visualization it necessarily engendered. Interwoven with the substance of those beliefs were the value systems of the Māori people, which interpenetrated every aspect of their relationship with the natural environment. At all times there was a reinforcing of the fundamental concepts that underpinned Māori society and led to its enduring nature in tribal form. Thus meanings that adhere to the land may not lightly be changed without threatening the identity of the individual and the existence of the tribal group that forms part of that identity. An awareness of this fact will go a long way toward explaining why Taranaki Māori fought to retain their *tūrangawaewae* or foothold in the nineteenth century and why unaddressed Māori land claims remain today as a burden upon the conscience of the nation.

## CONCLUSION

What then is my sense, as an indigenous woman, of the sense of place of my ancestors in the tribal landscape? Having concluded this study, I am convinced of the existence of a deeply spiritual link between Māori and the land, based as much upon the latter as the natural provider of our needs in former times as upon the creation accounts that give a graphically compelling account of the interrelatedness of life in its myriad forms. Through primary socialization within the family or tribal community, and secondary socialization in centers of learning where Māori cultural values are imparted and instilled, these accounts serve to remind us of our identity in relation to the places that granted us, through our ancestors, existence. There can be no stronger link to the land than this.

# 11

## Theater Near Us

### Librarians, Culture, and Space in the Harlem Renaissance

KATHERINE WILSON

In the later years of the Harlem Renaissance, two successive theater groups rehearsed and produced their shows in the basement of a branch of the New York Public Library on 135th Street. Both groups were deliberately modeled on the Little Theater (or Art Theater) movement, originally a white, early twentieth-century project, defined as distinct from the commercial theater forms much more prevalent at the time. Regina M. Anderson Andrews (1901–1993), a Harlem librarian who was also involved in this new kind of theater, lightly satirized the typical entertainments in her play, *The Man Who Passed*. In this work, the character Kid boasts of his plans to hop from social club, to light theater spectacle (the Lafayette), a dance, and a party: "dere's de Gran' Ball given by the 'Inspired Cousins of Georgia,' at de Manhattan—a midnight show Tuesday at de Lafayette, to be followed by a breakfas' dance at Susie's to say nothing of a little private affair some of de boys is pullin' off for some high yaller visitin' ladies" (Andrews 1996, 46). In contrast to this flurry of light fun, Little Theater in African American communities was a deliberate, theorized experiment to bring serious entertainment into their own neighborhoods; it was cultivated by the educated and professional elite, integrated in schools (especially Howard University in Washington, D.C.), and promoted by the major newspapers, *Crisis* and *Opportunity*, which sponsored play-writing contests, published winning plays, and printed essays that argued over the aesthetic controversies of what Negro drama should be. The influential voices in these debates were those of the "New Negro" movement's powerful visionaries, who were men—W. E. B. Du Bois, who promoted the "propaganda" play, and Alain Locke, who argued for "folk" entertainment—*and* women who played a central role in their activities as producers of these theater projects. Yet the women's works and writings have been overshadowed by the well-publicized discourses of their male counterparts.

In an era when serious high-brow theater was only white and staged only downtown, when Negro roles were restricted to minstrel stereotypes (as even black performers corked their faces), Du Bois articulated the mission to produce artistic, uplifting theater that was "(1) a theater about us, (2) a theater by us, (3) a theater for us, and (4) a theater *near* us," a vision that linked *what* the play was about, *who* wrote it, who *saw* it, and—what is more rare to twentieth-century art manifestos—*where* it happened (Du Bois paraphrased in Andrews 1975, 70). Regina Anderson later recalled that even when there were downtown revues featuring blacks, "few were presented in Harlem where the black playwright's audience lived" (1975, 69). Thus, this concern for artistic self-representation was entwined with the issue of geography—that is, of *space*.

The first theater group to establish a home in the local library was affiliated with Du Bois' periodical *The Crisis*. It was organized by him with others, including women, notably playwright Eulalie Spence (who did not wholly subscribe to Du Bois' aesthetic policy) and Regina Andrews. Called the "Krigwa Players" (an acronym adapted from "*Crisis* Guild of Writers and Artists"), it lasted only a year from 1926 to 1927. From Krigwa's ashes arose the Negro Experimental Theater, later the Harlem Experimental Theater, or HET (c. 1928–1935), the second theater to occupy the library basement; this incarnation arose without Du Bois but nonetheless was still largely consistent with his aesthetic credo.

While Krigwa and HET did stage plays by white playwrights both new and old, the groups were determined to stage humble productions of new, serious one-acts by black playwrights, plays that promoted positive and presumably realistic reflections of Negro experience. The project aimed to develop theater talents among African Americans, particularly playwrights, to bring serious drama to the neighborhood, and to stage characterizations that were more accurate and positive. Usually they grouped three short plays a night, charging a modest price in order to pay the writers, who had often placed in the playwriting contest at the *Crisis*. To work where they lived, a noncommercial black theater project had to contend with the squeezed overcrowding and inflated rents of Harlem—where landlords were by and large not black—while operating on a shoestring budget (on conditions in Harlem, see Drake and Cayton 1993, Kusmer 1986, and Ottley and Weatherby 1967). It was the library space that allowed the theater to happen *without* compromising its principles—the library let the theater happen "near us."

As a sociopolitical-cultural movement, the Harlem Renaissance grew from deliberate cultivation, arrangement, and negotiation—not from spontaneous combustion or a natural coincidence of genius. As with all social transformation, the Harlem Renaissance involved the transformation not only of ideas but also of space—I do not use the word in its metaphorical senses (as in "spaces of the imagination") but in its literal sense: streets, homes, stores, churches, and basements were literally changed in the course of this revival. This modification of municipal space for cultural production by African Americans is the subject of this chapter, which was based on archival research in the papers of librarian and theater artist Regina Andrews, whose files are housed in the collection she herself helped to build—the New York Public Library Schomburg Center. Recent theories about the social shaping of space inform this reading of the past, as they bring space up from the taken-for-granted background and outline categories with which to consider how space is used in each particular social configuration (social practice), how it is represented in cultural images (blueprints, or in this case, drama), how people shape space for cultural and social events, and how gender affects all those dimensions (see Sharp 1999, 257–59). An attention to space helps in consideration of a question that springs from the story of Krigwa and HET: how is it that Negro theater came to occupy the basement of the public library, an extension of a practically (if not legally) segregated and white-dominated city? The convergence of marginal black art and municipal space was contingent on multiple developments, each of which will be elaborated in turn: (1) the transformation of Harlem's demography (by 1920 it had flipped from a mainly Jewish suburb to a black-populated urban concentration, black populated but almost nowhere black owned); (2) the ethos of the public library, an institution and ideology, which then was a fairly recent development; and (3) the conscientious agency, or praxis, of key figures among Harlem's privileged class, most prominently men, but importantly also a sizable proportion of women (on the latter, see Brown-Guillory 1988, Perkins and Stephens 1998).

## REGINA ANDREWS

At the intersection of these dimensions (Harlem, the library, and theater) was the librarian Regina M. Anderson Andrews (1901–1992). A mixed-race, well-educated Chicago native, Andrews ensconced herself as one of the so-called Talented Tenth, the more privileged and influential stratum of Negro New Yorkers who maneuvered the circulation of African American culture in—and for—Harlem. Though not yet the subject of a full-length biography, Andrews' life and works are mentioned briefly across numerous studies and reference texts related to African Americans generally or the Harlem Renaissance in particular (see for example Brown 1992, Jefferson 1993, Mitchell 1975, Roses and Randolph 1990). At successive phases of her career, Andrews, in different ways, acted *on* culture *through* space. Before her marriage, with her women roommates, twenty-something Regina Anderson hosted what we may call a "salon" in their home on Sugar Hill. The gatherings became known in shorthand by the house number, "580." This salon, like Georgia Douglass' equally famous "S-Street" salon in Washington, D.C., functioned as an informal cultural center, facilitating the circulation of ideas and strengthening social networks. In salons hostesses transformed a private, domestic, feminine sphere into a cultural forum; they changed the shape of the social space in a way that made them central agents in the circulation of a culture otherwise largely public and masculine; they also invented a black cultural venue when established cultural venues were elsewhere and white.

This maneuvering of space continued as Andrews, while a clerk in the 135th Street library, helped broker the use of its basement for theater—a process explained below—as well as arranged exhibits for young visual artists she met at the "580" soirees. After World War II, with more authority as head librarian of another branch located just south of Harlem, she welcomed the next generation of theater artists to that library basement, as theater artist Lofton Mitchell recalled fondly in his narrative of the era (Mitchell 1975, 71). Within the library system, Andrews also orchestrated other *non*theatrical cultural events—youth discussions and "family nights" centered on topics—varied projects that served compatible and similar purposes, as elaborated below.

Besides arranging the theater's use of the space, Andrews herself belonged to the earlier theater groups, Krigwa and HET: she served on their boards, performed in productions, and wrote three plays, at least two of which were staged by HET (though outside the 135th Street library). Her plays—spare, moral, and realist one-act dramas—are not set in the domestic feminine sphere, which was common, or almost mandatory, for women writers of any race at the time. Andrews set each of her plays in a quasipublic interior—an underground railway station (*Underground*), a Southern Baptist church (*Climbing Jacob's Ladder*), and a black-

FIGURE 11.1. "Party for Langston Hughes on roof of 580 St. Nicholas Avenue, Harlem" (1924). Back row, left to right: Ethel Ray (Nance), Langston Hughes, Helen Lanning, Pearl Fisher, Rudolf Fisher, Luella Tucker, Clarissa Scott, and Hubert Delany. Front row, left to right: Regina Anderson (Andrews), Esther Popel, Jessie Fauset, Marie Johnson, and E. Franklin Frazier.

owned Harlem barbershop (*The Man Who Passed*). Together, the plays touch on key tropes in African American experience and imagination—oppression by white society, Christianity, lynching, Harlem, hair, and passing. *Underground* (the script occasionally misidentified as *Mathilde* and written under the pseudonym Ursala Trelling) is set in a "station" of the underground railroad; it is less a place to congregate than one to pass through, a refuge en route to freedom in the North. Though the opening pages are missing, the remainder of the manuscript makes clear the crux of the plot: a slave family eludes the bounty hunters when the daughter disguises herself as a white belle, one whom the goons chivalrously admired. The heroine Mathilde's maneuver highlights the double entwined sense of "passing," as a racial disguise, on the one hand, that allows freer movement across restrictive social boundaries; on the other, passing as white, the young woman can pass from slave-holding South into the North. *Climbing Jacob's Ladder: A Tragedy of Negro Life* can be categorized as a "lynch play," a subgenre label used to group the dramas, usually by women, in which lynching was key to the plot (see Perkins and Stephens 1998). While most lynch plays are set in a home, Andrews set hers in a Southern Baptist church. At an interchurch meeting, the congregation, distracted by their mistrust over money, fails to rescue their member who has been arrested and then lynched; when they start to act, they are petrified by fear of lightening. In this plot, in contrast to Andrews' usual civic ideal, the gathering in one place actually fails to improve social circumstances; just having a room to meet in, the play suggests, is not enough without participants' willingness to cooperate and unify.

*The Man Who Passed* was Andrews' only play based in Harlem. She wrote it under a male pseudonym, adopted from her Jewish maternal grandfather, Henry Simmons, though some male chroniclers attribute her election of pen names to feminine modesty (e.g., Brown 1992, 20). As in *Underground*, the main character, Fred, also passes in both racial and spatial senses, though Andrews constructs his choice to cause his own alienation, not freedom. Fred has forsaken the Negro world to live as white among whites downtown but must return to Harlem to the one barber who can set his hair the right way—to look white. Ironically it is precisely a place within the despised neighborhood, the barbershop, that enables him to "pass" the boundaries of segregation into the downtown white districts. Andrews' 1920s barbershop functions as a kind of masculine community center, where men circulate and banter among one another, as the character Kid comes for the haircut fashionable enough for the busy social life he boasts about in the quotation above. When a client in the shop

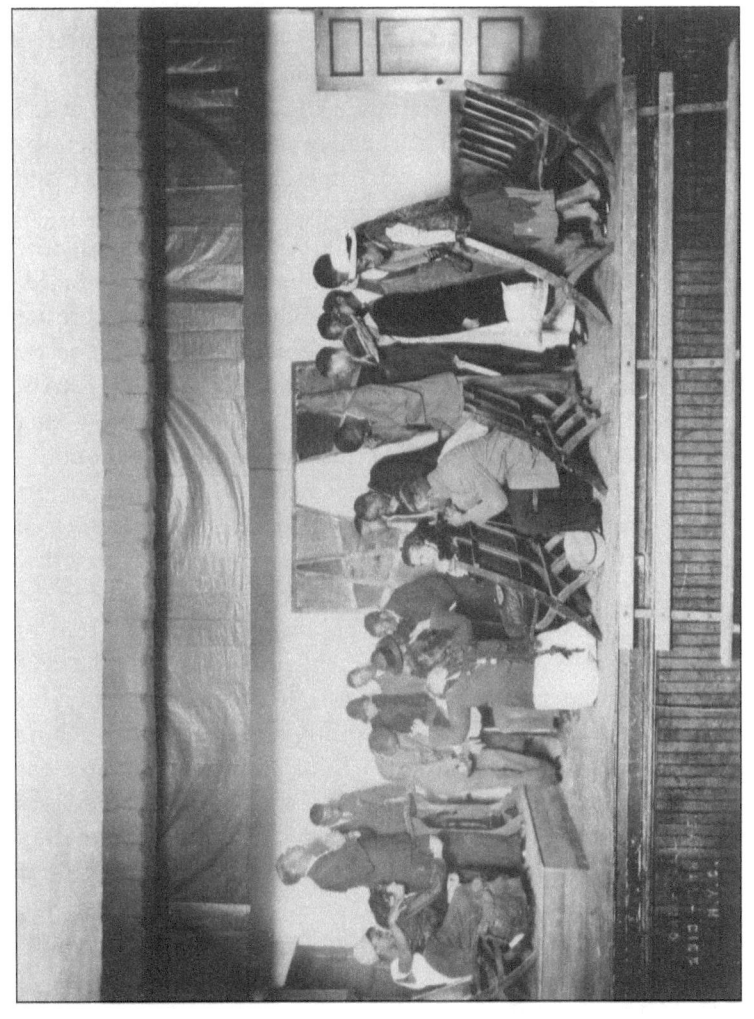

FIGURE 11.2. "Scene from Harlem Experimental Theater production of Climbing Jacob's Ladder by Regina Anderson Andrews" (1924)

entertains the men by reading a newspaper aloud, Fred learns that his parents have died. The tragic *mulatto* figure of the play, a male version of the more typical *mulatta*, has abandoned the black spaces, and in so doing, severed his ties with community and family—the social dimension of his experience, in other words, is embedded in space.

Andrews' representations of space favored public venues—church, underground railway, and barbershop—a preference indicative of her civic values. Beyond her representation of space, she seems to have worked to affect actual cultural space and did so in ways that can be considered in terms of gender. A recurrent theme made evident by Andrews' collected papers, read through the lens of recent space and gender theory in social sciences (as articulated by Doreen Massey and Shirley Ardner, among others), is that Andrews extended the identity of a certain feminized space in order to facilitate what can be considered secular congregations—gatherings for exchange that would foster community as she saw it. During the Harlem Experimental Theater years, that community was African Americans in Harlem. Ultimately, though, Andrews seemed to strive for integration and to express what might be called "transnationalist" values insofar as she sought community not only for African Americans, or American minorities, or the African diaspora, but across cultures and races. What informed Andrews' concerns for specific African American "uplift," in other words, was a pluralist ethos of democratic citizenship and a trust in the promise of what might be called "the public sphere"—a stratum of social experience between official government and private life (the concept is modified from German philosopher Jürgen Habermas). This vision of equal civic participation, promoting dialogue, and enriching social networks requires space in which to gather—a requirement Andrews clearly recognized. Presenting the inauguration of a library auditorium, Andrews wrote in her speech, "I know of no community more in need of a room such as this, a room which offers space for neighborhood clubs, plays, lectures and classes" (1938, 1). By her own estimation, under Andrews' leadership after the late 1940s, the Washington Heights branch "became a meeting place for people from all continents" (Andrews 1961, 1).

Andrews' strategy of congregating used theater as just *one* means for the same community-building goal. Though she did act and coordinate and write for theater, what endured across her career was less the artistic ambition and more the cultural gathering that fostered and uplifted a community, harnessing the space of public libraries or churches to do so. This will to congregate, as elaborated below, both converged and collided with the public-service ethos of the library, the system in which she worked.

## THE 135th STREET BRANCH OF THE NEW YORK PUBLIC LIBRARY

The New York Public Library system had fused only a generation earlier in the beginning of the twentieth century. Before, the "Harlem Free Library," as it was called, had been a subscription service for Harlem's then-Jewish community. By 1903 the burgeoning city system swallowed the Harlem Free Library, turning what had operated as an autonomous institution for middle-class patrons into one branch within a large, city-run network that served a poor neighborhood (Dain 1972, 275).

The building, the institution, and the collection each developed along slightly separate trajectories. The library *building* was completed two years after the merger in 1905, funded in the surge of Andrew Carnegie philanthropy. The architect trio responsible for the branch also designed the private Morgan Library, the main hall of Columbia University, and the 125th Street branch, constructions that share with the 135th Street library the turn-of-the-century grand and stately style. Whatever the architects' intent, though, such styles have no fixed connotations; the impression made by the physical design is obviously produced in conjunction with other cultural associations circulating within a given community. The building's appearance might have reinforced the suggestion that the library was linked to import and power—but none of the clients' myriad, glowing recollections of the 135th Street branch makes even passing mention of its grandiose design. What this suggests is that how it looked to them registered less than how it was *used* by them. (The 135th Street branch building still exists but has been reconfigured into the annex of the newer building, combining with the Countee Cullen branch, which sits in the shadow of the larger, more modern Schomburg Center.)

The New York Public Library as *institution*, distinct from its building, coalesced in accord with a model of quantifiable uniformity characteristic of industrialism, operating from its center (Forty-second Street) to the periphery (branches), as headquarters mandated a uniform catalog system, inscribed policy, and assigned head librarians to branches (Carpenter 2001, 376). This was a hierarchy that Andrews would resist several times in her career. The motivations behind libraries, like other social outreach enterprises, involved multiple and perhaps contradictory aspects: to conserve significant texts, to educate the public, but also to control the masses, especially as the social body grew increasingly foreign and dark with the influx of people from Europe and the U.S. South (Bogardus 1993, 2484). Carnegie, the principle funder of this proliferation of educational institutions, assured skeptics that libraries, by bringing reading to the working class, would thereby avert revolution (Carpenter 2001, 376). The urge for social control, though, was paradoxically accompanied by liberal, democratizing tendencies, tendencies librarians such as Andrews and her boss extended to almost radical lengths. One of the leading library apostles, Melvin Dewey (of decimal system fame), inculcated what proponents called a "library faith"—an admixture of efficiency and civic zeal—its mission to serve as many people as possible, and to offer them what they want, without censorship (Roseberry 1970, 67). Dewey propagated his ethos through the graduate programs he founded in "library Economy" (later called "library science"). His schools trained Andrews' white boss, Ernestine Rose, and Andrews.

Middle-class white women quickly filled the library schools and the lower ranks of the libraries. By 1920, the majority (ninety percent) of librarians were women, a proportion larger than even social workers and teachers (Garrison 1979, 173); in 1920 the NYPL hired the first black librarian in the 135th Street branch, Catherine Allen Latimer, who later became the reference librarian of its Negro Division. Women librarians are now so common that it is easy to overlook the historical specificity of this formation. Some feminist historians of space have traced a patriarchal strategy of separating women from sources of knowledge, whether in locked chests or in rooms of Victorian houses (Daphne Spain, summarized in Sharp 1999, 259). In the case of the library, though, the space of knowledge—which easily *might* have become a prohibitively masculine citadel—came to be considered a feminine sphere. Why would a public center of information and knowledge come to be operated by women? First, it sits within a particular sphere of society: the branch library was associated with *culture*, distinct from the sex-segregated arenas of economics or politics. Second, it seemed an extension of the (bourgeois) home: early public library discourse identified librarians literally as "hostesses" (Garrison 1979, 179). The link of library with home further solidified when branches opened special sections dedicated to children.

At the practical level, from the library's point of view, middle-class women were valued not only because they came with broad education and multiple languages but also because they brought those advanced skills at rates much cheaper than those of educated men. Administrative discourse was rife with explanations of why women were suited to libraries: women "like literary work" and, as a conference speaker put it in 1877, "they soften our atmosphere, they lighten our labor, they are equal to our work, and for the money they cost . . ." (quoted in Garrison 1979, 175). From the working women's point of view, libraries were welcoming, at a time when most other professional careers were still formidably hostile or closed. As one historian noted, then, in filling the library posts women "merely left the home, not the women's sphere" (Garrison 1979, 184). If that sphere had a feminine shape, though, librarians such as Andrews and her white boss could maneuver its contours and boundaries into a more unequivocally public form.

Despite the welcome to women generally, Andrews' own professional trajectory suggests a limited position within the library for women who were African American: though Andrews arrived with experience in library work, according to a note on her curriculum vitae draft, the officials affixed her to the black neighborhood. In her draft of the resume, Andrews added a note explaining that after she had lobbied for a merited raise, it took a letter from W. E. B. Du Bois to influence the director "to adjust Miss Anderson's (later Mrs. Andrews) salary to the comparable level of white professional librarians" (Andrews, c. 1961, 1). It was only when she relocated to the 115th Street branch in the mid-1940s that she was able to rise to the position of head librarian—the first African American in New York to reach that level.

## THE THEATER IN THE LIBRARY BASEMENT

It is not clear from the piecemeal references to the Harlem Experimental Theater by what means members arranged to occupy the basement of the 135th Street branch. Andrews, as younger, newer, and black did not wield direct authority. Rather, she probably negotiated with the white, senior librarians to open the basement to rehearsals and evening shows for HET. Library histories laud the white head librarian, Ernestine Rose, for having integrated the branch with the community. This treatment is understandable, given the achievements of the period: the library instituted adult education programs, established the city's first "Negro Division" (which would become absorbed in the Schomburg collection), hosted annual art exhibits, and hired a mixed-race staff. The praise of Rose, however, makes no mention of the theater (which may not have been her focus), and it obscures the contribution of her African American staff. Regina Andrews, meanwhile, remembered that her boss allowed basement theater: "Ernestine Rose . . . welcomed the first theater group. I have always been very glad that I was on Miss Rose's staff because she gave me a great deal of latitude in planning cooperation with community organizations" (Andrews in Mitchell 1975, 72). Andrews' public recollection positions Andrews herself as the hinge between the community and the library, even as it acknowledges the white supervisor who made room for that positioning.

From black history narratives, the brief accounts found in definitive encyclopedias and archive fragments are contradictory and blurred, some treating Du Bois as prime mover (even when he was not involved), some crediting other African American women, and most generally gliding over the phenomenon as if theaters *naturally* arise in public library basements (see Brown 1992, 21; Jefferson 1993, 365). What seems as significant as *who* formed the theater group was *where* it was formed. In her recollections written for Loften Mitchell's anthology about black theater, Andrews stresses that groups were mobilized in (or born out of) the library: "[S]omewhere along the line a few of us sat in the basement of the 135th Street Library one night, and we began to talk about wanting to write and produce our own dramas. . . . [W]e began to have our meetings concerned with the theater at the 135th Street Library. . . . And so the Harlem Experimental Theater was born" (Andrews in Mitchell 1975, 73). Andrews stressed the physical space as the ground for these projects; she invoked the prestige of an official city institution. By stressing the library where she was librarian, she also marked her central role in this part of black theater's history.

So Andrews and some small unidentified group founded the Harlem Experimental Theater as an incarnation of Krigwa in 1929 and, with Ernestine Rose's approval, annexed the library basement for the group's projects until Andrews was transferred to a downtown branch two years later, and the Harlem Experimental Theater relocated to St. Philip's Parish nearby, where her plays where staged. Andrews in some cooperation with the white head librarian extended the utilitarian public service ethos of the library, turning the public space into a temporary house for this progressive theater.

Later, her own theater work behind her, as head librarian of the 115th Street branch, Andrews welcomed the post–World War II generation of black theater artists into her branch's basement. This time around, however, such unorthodox, off-hours use of library space vexed the library authorities. Loften Mitchell recalled admiringly that, when the officials from the Forty-second Street headquarters confronted Andrews at her branch, "she told the downtown bosses to go to hell" (Mitchell 1975, 65). In the end, though, headquarters prevailed, as they evicted theater from the library basement, restoring the "proper" parameters of the library, at which point Andrews moved on to other, less provocative projects of public culture in the library.

Why focus on a library basement, on *where* the Harlem theater happened, and happened so briefly? Recent studies of space emphasize that space is not fixed, external, politically neutral, or irrelevant. These theories, sparked by interdisciplinary work in geography and social sciences, remind those who think about culture that human bodies and social processes do not occur *outside* space but are mutually of space. Doreen Massey formulates space and place as "constructed out of social relations," as "social relations 'stretched out'"—that is, extended (1994, 3). Rather than one abstract expanse—the space learned in geometry lessons—and rather than accepted space as a given, or "unproblematic in its identity," this conception envisions multiple, simultaneous spaces, "cross-cutting, intersecting, aligning with one another, or existing in relations of paradox or antagonism"—so it promotes analysis of how the identities of space and place are "unfixed, contested, and multiple" (Massey 1994, 3). Shirley Ardner, approaching her theme of "social maps for women," articulates how human engagement acts reciprocally with the physical three-dimensions in a complex dialectic, as society constructs its spaces—"space reflects social organization"—but then, in turn, "once space has been bounded and shaped it is no longer merely a neutral background: it extends its own influence" (1981, 13). This basic sense of its importance has proliferated into various emphases and approaches. Some scholars move on to examine the socially-constructed division of private from public space; others, following 1970s French theory (of Henri LeFebvre in particular), work from a three-part taxonomy of spatial practice, official representation of space (as depicted in plans and reports), and the more underground, "representational spaces," from which people can resist dominant forms of space (see Sharp 1999, 258). This chapter offers a modest gesture of foregrounding space within historical cultural studies, by highlighting a case in which place is paramount. Without redesigning the façade, or relocating a wall of the edifice, Andrews, in cooperation with leading Harlem cultural figures and library officials, helped to transform a municipal institutional space into a cultural venue, turning a basement into a respectable theater where African Americans could produce culture, representing what they understood as their own lives and concerns (including the spaces that mattered to their lives).

As the history of the library suggests, concepts of space are entwined with concepts of race, a conflation Andrews illustrated in her play *A Man Who Passed*. They are also enmeshed with concepts of gender. One strand of feminist analyses (misleadingly labeled the "cultural" approach) argues that women's cultural work navigates a different space and chronology from that of men, a difference that adjusts the timeline of the Harlem Renaissance (since several key women's writings came in the late stretch), while it also alters the model of space, preferring a vision of multiple centers, more fluid, multigenerational, and built on mutual support, rather than a centralized space defined by a single generation of achieving individuals. Such gendered historical interpretations help to reconceptualize the larger circulations of cultural production and women's roles within them, a view different from, though complementary to this study's focus on Regina Andrews' cultural maneuverings through space.

Historically speaking, from the perspective of Andrews and her Harlem Renaissance contemporaries, space—or the *where*—clearly mattered. Her plays show that Negro communities were shaped not only by who was in them but also where they were. In *The Man Who Passed*, this racial geography is expressed in an exchange between the character Fred and his Harlem barber, as Fred imagines how his racist white boss would react were he to see how Harlem had been transformed in the era of the black migrations:

> FRED (*as if he is thinking aloud*): Gosh! Fitzgerald would have apoplexy if he came uptown and saw 125th Street black with darkies. (*Chuckles to himself.*)
>
> VAN: Yes? Well he'd have to get over that first spell so he could go up to Sugar Hill and see them up as far as 155th and Edgecombe Ave. (Andrews 1996, 48)

Andrews' play braids a didactic cautionary tale about abandoning one's community with documentary realism that accurately illustrates the drastic transformation in Harlem's demographics. African Americans and West Indians migrated to one neighborhood, a condensed cluster, where they installed a few service businesses, like the barbershop, and patronized public services, such as the 135th Street library. The theater enacted in the library basement arose from a demand for theater *near* us (as well as by, for, and about), during a cultural moment we have come to identify not in terms of time, but of place, "the *Harlem* Renaissance." The epithet underscores this primacy of place and space, even as it misleadingly obscures the vitality of other sites, such as Washington, D.C., and also of the circulations across the Atlantic and around the national network of TOBA (Theater Owner's Booking Association, a group run by white managers that scheduled performances of most traveling African American artists).

As a scholarly approach, this concept of space allows the study to oscillate between the individual agent, Regina Andrews, and the surrounding "structures," the library building as a node in a city institution, and the social network of the Harlem Renaissance. In cultural theories of our early twenty-first century era it is often suspect to emphasize an individual, an approach that harkens to the "Great White Men" heroics of long-standard history and literary studies. Still, for black feminisms and other feminisms, I do see reason to highlight a particular woman, to recycle concepts of 'strategy,' 'praxis,' and 'agency'—remembering bodies, desires, and black women's bright ideas even when at the same time we are questioning categories of agency, gender, and race. The story of how Andrews and others used this space, the 135th Street library, shifting between city property and public service and drama studio, illustrates the larger idea that social and cultural transformations also transform space and are transformed by space.

# 12

## Into the Sacred Circle, Out of the Melting Pot

*Re/Locations and Homecomings in Native Women's Theater*

JAYE T. DARBY

---

> America was once called the Melting Pot, but we are taking out of the pot what didn't melt: our voices, culture, styles, and ways of storytelling.
> —Diane Glancy, "Native American Theater and the Theater That Will Come"

While reflective of rich diversity among communities, home has always held a unique meaning among the over five hundred First Nations in North America. Far more than a just a geographic location, home, according to Paula Gunn Allen (1992), Inés Hernández-Ávila (1995), Winona LaDuke (2005), and Jace Weaver (1997), is the centuries-old source of spirituality, the site of intergenerational continuity and community, and the continuance of traditions and sacred responsibilities. Yet, for the most part, as Vine DeLoria Jr. observes throughout the recent history of indigenous peoples in the Americas since European encounter, "the major thrust has been one of dispossession of the natives by those colonizing the continent" (1985, 4). In the nineteenth century, Cherokee men, women, and children pushed out of their homes at gunpoint onto the Trail of Tears; Chief Joseph and the Ni Mii Puu (Nez Perce) forced from their homelands; and the Lakota driven from Paha Sapa, the sacred Black Hills, are notable examples.

Perhaps lesser known but also devastating were twentieth-century federal policies terminating rights to Native Americans on reservations.

Beginning in the 1950s, governmental termination and relocation policies again displaced large numbers of Native Americans from their lands, homes, and traditions, relocating them to large urban areas, where today over 60 percent of Native Americans live (Cornell 1988; Fixico 1986). Rather than promised jobs and opportunities as many Natives hoped for, too often poverty, isolation, and displacement from their homelands and powerful cultures became the measure of urban life.

Thus, while relocation as a legal term generally refers to the 1950s federal policy, relocation in contemporary Native literature has broader connotations. As Inés Hernández-Ávila discusses in her insightful essay, "Relocations upon Relocations," her use of the "term 'relocation' deliberately recalls the historical fact of relocation of Native peoples," and "the policies which created the urban Native populations we have today, and the policies which forced Native children to be sent away from their homes to boarding schools" (Hernández-Ávila 1995, 495). Relocation in this sense includes both physical and cultural dispossession from homelands, tribal cultures, and spiritual traditions.

While recent developments in Native theater share these concerns with relocation as geographic dislocation, imposed poverty, cultural disruption, forced colonization, and religious oppression, a growing body of Native women's theater, as suggested by the opening quotation by Diane Glancy, Cherokee, further contest the devastating consequences of forced removals and federal relocation policies and perform an alternative, a creative process of re/location and homecoming—Native resistance, reclamation, recovery, and renewal on stage. As Inés Hernández-Ávila (1995), Beth Brant (1997), and Joy Harjo and Gloria Bird (1997) have discussed, Native women's writing often provides homecoming on a number of levels—spiritual, cultural, artistic, and political. According to Hernández-Ávila, "For many activist Native women of this hemisphere, the concern with 'home' involves concern with 'home*land*.' Even when Native women activists no longer reside on their ancestral land bases (though many still do) they continue to defend the tribal sovereignty of their own communities as well as communities of other indigenous peoples" (1995, 492). In the case of contemporary Native performing arts, in this chapter, I suggest that through the integration of Native aesthetics, grounded in traditional ceremonial values, with contemporary issues, performance itself is integral to homecoming and centers the work. As I wrote in a 2002 essay, "While reflective of the great diversity among Indian Nations and the multiplicity of cultural expressions, re-imagined Native theater shifts location to a Native stage world and reconceptualizes the theatrical experience by placing Native values, aesthetics, traditions, and issues at the core of each performance and employing theatrical vocabularies and narrative forms intrinsic to these values" (Darby 2002, 76).

As an illustration of this transformative new direction in Native theater, this chapter offers a dramaturgical analysis of three major works: *SongCatcher: A Native Interpretation of the Story of Frances Densmore* by Marcie Rendon (2003), White Earth Anishinabe, *The Woman Who Was a Red Deer Dressed for the Deer Dance* by Diane Glancy (2002), Cherokee, and *No Home but the Heart (An Assembly of Memories)* by Daystar/Rosalie Jones (2003), Pembina Chippewa. These three works, differing in tribal traditions, dramatic form, and length, showcase the diversity and innovation of expression in contemporary Native American women's theater. In this analysis, I consider how each theater piece, based on specific tribal traditions and histories, contests the devastating consequences of relocation and decenters colonization by performing an alternative—a creative homecoming that honors Native perspectives, values, and aesthetics. Drawing on the critical work of Paula Gunn Allen (1983, 1992, 1998), Laguna Pueblo/Sioux scholar and writer, I further suggest that central to staging these homecomings in Native women's theater is the integration of Native performing arts grounded in specific tribal spiritual traditions. As Gunn Allen (1992) explains in her seminal book, *The Sacred Hoop: Recovering the Feminine in American Indian Traditions*, Native American spiritual practices, while highly nuanced and reflective of the multiplicity of communities, traditions, and practices, are millenniums old and connected to specific creation stories tied to geographic locations with unique spiritual relationships and responsibilities to sacred homelands and members of the community—past, present, and future. According to Gunn Allen, Native traditional arts play an integral role: "The tribes seek— through song, ceremony, legend, sacred stories (myths), and tales—to embody, articulate, and share reality, to bring the isolated, private self into harmony with this reality, to verbalize the sense of the majesty and reverent mystery of all things, and to actualize, in language, those truths that give humanity its greatest significance and dignity" (1992, 55).

## SONGCATCHER: A NATIVE INTERPRETATION OF THE STORY OF FRANCES DENSMORE

In her artist's statement to *SongCatcher: A Native Interpretation of the Story of Frances Densmore*, a three-act play, Marcie Rendon explains that her goal as a writer "involves the interweaving of Native people's spiritual reality coexisting alongside present-time physical reality" (2002, 2). Rendon, an award-winning writer and an internationally known activist, continues that as a playwright she is "interested in combining Native oral tradition with Western playwriting" and "strive[s] as creator and writer for the same integration my ancestors had of dialogue, music, and movement by using the modern stage and tools of the playwright," an integration evident in *SongCatcher* (Rendon 2003, 2).

*SongCatcher*, which debuted in 1998 in Minneapolis at the Great American History Theater, integrates Ojibwe sacred song traditions into an urban context. Probing issues of cultural and spiritual dislocation, the play focuses on the lives of a young Ojibwe couple, Chris and Jack, who live in an inner-city apartment in the 1990s. Like many urban Natives, the couple struggles financially as Chris works as a sanitation worker and Jack is often unemployed. Yet, the greater struggle is spiritual between Chris, grounded in traditional Ojibwe knowledge, and Jack, emblematic of many relocated urban Indians, alienated by his urban upbringing and desperately trying to reclaim his past and Native identity. However, rather than setting up a binary opposition between urban and traditional Ojibwe people, by interweaving dream sequences and making manifest Ojibwe spirituality on stage, Marcie Rendon artfully constructs contemporary Native urban life as a liminal space in which to heal the past and recover Ojibwe spirituality for a new generation. Here *SongCatcher* complements Rendon's earlier children's play, *Bring the Children Home*, which, according Ann Haugo, Rendon viewed as a "healing journey of finding your center/your base/your home" for urban Native youth (2000 247).

*SongCatcher* opens in an Ojibwe encampment in the 1880s with Spirit Woman singing Ojibwe songs to those sleeping (Rendon 2003). The stage presence of Spirit Woman enacting this tradition of giving a personal song through dreams connects the performance to sacred homelands and the ancestral past. The next scene offers a stark contrast. Physically relocated and culturally distanced from this traditional home, Jack, struggling to find his own personal Ojibwe song, is sitting in his run-down apartment and playing a tape-recorded Ojibwe song for Bill, an elder. As it becomes clear to Bill that this is a tape recording of a very old Red Lake song, he becomes uneasy. At the end of the tape, the voice of anthropologist Frances Densmore intrudes, and again Bill questions Jack's plans to use the tape for his song. Culturally compromised, Jack defends Densmore's actions of recording Ojibwe songs by insisting that she was just trying to save the songs—the mainstream anthropological justification. Behind the men, Midé images appear, connecting the taped songs to sacred songs and the "Midewiwin, or the Great Medicine Society," whose members "believe," according to Gerald Vizenor, "that music and the knowledge and use of herbal medicine extend human life" (1984, 26). These Ojibwe images visually contradict the legitimacy of Densmore's actions in taking the songs, undermining Jack's position in using her work. As Rendon explains, "For Native peoples of this continent, stories of social, familial, and historical consequence were passed generation to generation, either through the practice of oral storytelling; the creation of songs, sometimes with accompanying dance movement; or, as in the case of the Ojibwe Midé religious society, pictographs inscribed on birchbark scrolls" (2003, 4).

However, cultural and spiritual loss becomes increasingly apparent in Jack's response. Raised on country western music and Christian hymns and unaware of the larger spiritual dangers of learning a sacred song recorded by a white anthropologist, Jack remains insistent on learning the song for the upcoming powwow at Leech Lake. Gently Bill as an Ojibwe elder encourages Jack to listen for his own song from the spirits and reminds him that in the old days people received their songs through fasts, dreams, or as gifts. In the Ojibwe tradition, according to Gerald Vizenor, "The spirit teacher told the first people on the earth that they 'must fast and find out things by dreams and that if they paid attention to these dreams they would learn how to heal the sick. The people listened and fasted and found in dreams how to teach their children and do everything'" (1984, 3). So important are dreams in the Ojibwe tradition that Vizenor continues that "woodland identities turned on dreams and visions" (1984, 24).

Thus for Jack, according to Bill and Chris, the path back to his Ojibwe identity is based on traditional Ojibwe spiritual practice. Yet, as the performance begins, Jack, a victim of assimilationist educational policies, privileges Western ways of knowing over Native ones, thereby perpetuating a cycle of dispossession, evident in the lives of many urban Natives. Overcoming his current estrangement can only be achieved through conversations with elders, fasts, dreams, and ceremonies, not by reading a book written by an anthropologist. However, disconnected from his tribal past and traditional spirituality, Jack instead seeks a short cut to find his song through Frances Densmore's book, a decision that triggers an epistemological and spiritual struggle between Western and traditional Ojibwe knowledge throughout the rest of the play—key dramaturgical issues.

The next scene—the construction of a dream sequence—reveals two contrasting stage worlds—one of the traditional Dakota community first with returning hunters and then with Chris and Jack as a traditional couple falling in love and the other with Frances and Margaret (Maggie) Densmore in their parlor. As she hears songs from the Dakota encampment, Frances tries them on her piano, a jarring counterpoint to songs heard in the encampment. In the next scene, a continuation of Chris's dream finds Maggie Densmore sneaking into the Dakota encampment. Chris wakes with a start as Jack comes in, and a fight ensues as Chris discovers that Jack has also copied sacred pictographs from the Densmore book to put on his drum and continues to study her book, rather than learn from an elder. In response to Jack's view that "they're just drawings," she explains, "They're sacred. Our people went to prison or mental institutions for practicing our religion" (21).

Revealing his frustrations over having parents with mainstream aspirations and having been the only Native in an all-white school, Jack again insists that he only wants to learn about being an Ojibwe. Challenging Jack's Western conception of "learning" from books, and fearing his lack of respect for the departed, Chris again articulates a traditional view of learning that is based on spirituality and warns Jack that his actions may be an invitation to spirits to enter their apartment. By honoring the spiritual beliefs of her people, Chris displays what Paula Gunn Allen describes as "a sense of propriety" appropriate to the situation (1998, 41). However, Jack reveals the extent of Western colonization in his life by perceiving the singers as dead and gone, rather than as living spirits. As Jace Weaver, Cherokee scholar, writes, "Colonialism succeeds by subverting traditional notions of culture and identity and by imposing social structures and constructs incompatible with traditional society" (1987, 20)

In scene 6 of the first act, Jack's next dream sequence reveals the competing voices in his life—the traditional voice of Spirit Woman singing him his song and the colonized voices of his parents urging him to do his homework and do well in football. When he finally hears Spirit Woman in the dream, he asks his mother about her. Both his parents, caught in the colonizers' mindset, encourage him to forget the past, his father reminding him of the beatings his grandparents endured in boarding school whenever they tried to remember the old ways—further manifestations of the devastating effects of federal educational policies. Jack's dream fades, and lights softly frame Old Man Spirit and Spirit Woman. Having tried in vain to give Jack his song through his dreams, Spirit Woman despairs over the cultural dispossession of the Anishinabe young people—loss of language, inability to interpret dreams, and lack of knowledge of ceremonies, and Jack's current fascination with Frances Densmore. Reminding her of the power of the Creator, Old Man Spirit reassures her that although centuries of European colonization have silenced the people and denied them their traditions, the Anishinabe children will prevail and "come home": "They took our teachings and locked them up. They took our people away from the natural world. Boarding schools, prisons, adoptive families. They try to lock up the souls of our people. But the children are strong, Spirit Woman, their spirits are strong. They will come home. There is a natural order to all creation. The eagle still flies" (25–26).

Throughout the second act, a spiritual imbalance in the couple's relationship and apartment ensues on stage as the tensions between Chris and Jack escalate as Jack's entanglement with the spirit of Frances Densmore deepens. Chris, who views Densmore as "some woman who ripped us off in the first place," argues with Jack, who seems coopted by both Densmore and Western accounts of her accomplishments (27). Again, she reminds him that if he wants to learn his Ojibwe traditions, he needs to go to an elder and recommends that he see Bill. Jack remains convinced that study of the book is sufficient, still unaware of the spiritual consequences about which Chris warns him.

The staging further makes manifest Ojibwe spiritual beliefs about the living presence of ancestors. Spirit Woman and Old Man Spirit, along with the spirits of Frances, Maggie, and Lizzie enter the apartment, occupy the stage, and participate in the play's action. As Jack gets further and further drawn to Frances's work, objects move, knocks mysteriously sound, and cigarette smoke fills the apartment. Scenes flash of Frances's growing obsession and arrogance in the past as she collected songs and her growing complicity in Native oppression. Jack's dream of himself as Geronimo confronting Frances at the Chicago World's Fair reveals the grave peril of relying on Frances's work, rather than following the traditional spiritual path to learn his song—losing one's soul. After the dream, still in the thrall of Frances, Jack becomes more and more listless, missing work and practicing on the drum, the same drum Frances as a spirit now uses. He even buys a keyboard, so he can practice the musical notation in Frances's book.

On stage, equally persistent in her pursuit of Jack, is Spirit Woman, who appears in the apartment, at the convenience store, and at the local casino. A spiritual tug of war physically ensues between Spirit Woman and Frances as her presence begins to reach Jack, pulling him away from Frances. Jack repeatedly awakens after hearing her song in the distance but is still unable to remember it. Coming home tired one night and angered by Jack's withdrawal and growing spiritual malaise, Chris becomes fully aware of the spiritual imbalance caused by the spirits of Frances and Maggie and ceremonially smudges the apartment to cleanse it. The staging of this ceremonial smudging signals a major shift in the couple's deteriorating relationship and the play. For Spirit Woman and Old Man Spirit also present in the apartment suggest gentleness, rather than anger and tell Chris to pray. Purified by the smoke and grounded in prayer, Chris calls Jack back into the room, shows him feathers she received from a Maori man and from her grandma, comforts him about the song he keeps trying to remember from his dreams, and gives him a stone from an Australian Aboriginal woman who said the stone had sacred power to help hear the spirits. The sage smoke provides a barrier among the spirits of Frances and Maggie and Jack, asserting control over their personal intrusion and the larger intrusion of mainstream culture.

Act 3 culminates in the spiritual homecoming Old Man Spirit foresaw earlier and presents a vision of spiritual healing for urban Natives. Transforming the apartment into a ceremonial ground, the staging connects urban existence to the mythic ceremonial tradition, in which according to Paula Gunn Allen, the "tribal concept of time is of timelessness, as the concept of space is of multidimensionality" (1992, 147). The ceremony, lead by Bill, first reveals the betrayal and tragedy of Main'gans who sang sacred Midé songs out of vanity for Frances Densmore. Then offering healing and asserting the enduring power of the sacred in Native life, Spirit Woman's voice fills the stage:

> I sing the songs of ages past
> Nothing sacred is ever lost
> No matter what they take
> Our spirits still live on (73)

As she moves on stage, she is joined by Jack, who sings with her, finally in possession of his song. After the ceremony ends, once again Jack and Chris are in their apartment with the spirits of Frances and Maggie now gone. Jack, now spiritually grounded, is ready to go back to work and build a life with Chris. By interweaving the Frances Densmore narrative of spiritual ruin with Jack's story of spiritual recovery, *SongCatcher* reclaims spiritual autonomy within the Ojibwe tradition and affirms the living power of Native spirituality in contemporary urban life.

## THE WOMAN WHO WAS A RED DEER DRESSED FOR THE DEER DANCE

*The Woman Who Was a Red Deer Dressed for the Deer Dance* by Diane Glancy, an award-winning playwright, poet, and novelist, deals with the long-term psychological, cultural, and spiritual repercussions of Cherokee Removal in the 1830s and the current struggles of a young woman, alienated from her Cherokee past. The one-act play was first performed on December 7, 1995, at the American Indian Community House in New York, directed by Siouxsan Monson, and later published in 1998 (Glancy 2002, 205). Since then it has been reprinted three times, most recently in Diane Glancy's anthology, *American Gypsy: Six Native American Plays* (2002), to which I refer.

Identifying the work as a "dramatic/poetic piece" in her introduction to the play, Glancy locates the piece within both Cherokee spiritual traditions and contemporary experiences: "The story of Ahw'uste was taken from 'Doi on Ahu'usti' and 'Asudi on Ahw'usti,' *Friends of Thunder, Tales of the Oklahoma Cherokees*, edited by Frank and Anna Kilpatrick, pieces of the old language (Cherokee), and contemporary materials (the granddaughter's life in the soup kitchen and dance bars)" (2002, 3). Pivotal to the spirituality of the piece is this integration of the stories of Ahw'uste, the Cherokee spirit deer, from Cherokee elders. Like most of Glancy's work, the piece also has autobiographical overtones. In "Two Dresses," Glancy openly writes about personal cultural dislocation and forced assimilation in her own life, growing up with a Cherokee father and an English-German mother, explaining that "it was my mother who presented her white part of my heritage as whole" (1987, 169). Yet, according to Glancy, the memory of her quiet Cherokee grandmother continues to inspire her writing.

Through the construction of a series of "scenelets" that integrates dialogue, memory, poetry, and story, Glancy at once introduces a highly contemporary style of Native theater grounded in traditional concerns with spirituality and intergenerational continuity as Grandmother and Girl, her granddaughter, two archetypal figures, struggle with issues of tradition and continuance. The first scene opens with an intertextual connection to Cherokee sacred stories as the Girl asks her grandmother, "Have you heard of Ahw'uste?" (5). In response to her granddaughter's question, Grandmother, in the role of elder and keeper of Cherokee traditions, recalls seeing her at Deer Creek and that the deer "made the songs happen" (6).

As the piece continues, the girl, assimilated and alienated from her grandmother, contests her grandmother's belief system. Thus, on stage Grandmother and Girl engage in an epistemological and a spiritual struggle between Western and Native views. According to Paula Gunn Allen, the "dualistic division . . . between what is material and what is spiritual," characteristic of much Western thought does not exist in traditional Native views of spirituality, which "regards the two as different expressions of the same reality" (1992, 60). In a recent interview, Glancy discussed how in her work, she seeks to integrate "the seen and unseen world" and explained, "In the past, the ancestors can show up at anytime; it's a living, fluid narrative" (quoted in Cheng 2002, 38). Pushing the classic generation clash further thorough intensified dialogue, the performance raises the stakes by focusing on cultural dislocation and spiritual continuance. On the one hand, the grandmother, embracing Cherokee spirituality, objects to living in a "world," where one is "reduced to what can be seen" (8) and tries lead her granddaughter into the "unseen" world of spirits and sacred power. On the other, the girl, echoing a positivist position reflective of much of modern American life, wants her grandmother to focus on "the seen"—money for truck payments and gas, her yearning for a steady man, and the demands of a low paying job in a soup kitchen. She vehemently objects to her grandmother's refusal to recognize that these contemporary pressures force her to "go into the *seeable*—live away from your world" (8). Girl's view is aligned with what Marilou Awiakta describes as the conquerors' "hardness—the hardness of mind split from spirit" (1984, 126). Simultaneously drawn and repelled by Grandmother's stories about the spirits, Girl yearns to be part of this tradition while she rejects the impossibility of its demands in her current life, where assimilation seems to be a requirement for survival. This perspective is consistent with Gunn Allen's observation that colonization "affects a people's understanding of their universe, their place within that universe, the kinds of values they must embrace and actions they must make to remain safe and whole within that universe" (1992, 90).

Glancy poetically illustrates this chasm between the mythic and the positivistic through the girl's uneasy imagery of her grandmother becoming more like a deer: "You stuff twigs in your shoes to make them fit your hooves. But I know hooves are there" (10). In a humorous, yet poignant monologue, the girl focuses on the physical world, not the spiritual, and becomes concerned about what to do with the four feet, the tail, and how to find a job as a deer, concluding that her grandmother's instruction is only making her life more difficult. Cut off from her past, she poignantly voices her sense of alienation: "I already know I don't fit anywhere—I don't need to be reminded—" (10). She then accepts her own rootlessness as an existential condition: "I have to pass through this world not having a place but I'll go anyway" (11). The granddaughter's acceptance of her alienation foregrounds her displacement from her Cherokee heritage. According to Paula Gunn Allen, "Belonging is a basic assumption for traditional Indians, and estrangement is seen as so abnormal that narratives and rituals that restore the estranged to his or her place within the cultural matrix abound" (1992, 127).

As the performance evolves, Grandmother endeavors to provide her granddaughter a lasting spiritual legacy that will break the constrictions of her colonized mind and provide her communal bonds. Gently she explains to the girl that only through a connection to the past will she be able to live a fuller life. Grandmother intensifies her efforts with a story of seeing Ahw'uste. A breakthrough occurs when the girl momentarily moved by the power of the story asks, "Your deer dress is the way you felt when you saw the deer?" (14). Grandmother responds, "When I saw Ahw'uste, yes. My deer dress is the way I felt, transformed by the power of ceremony. The idea of it in the forest of my head" (14). Yet, the girl trapped in her estrangement resists this leap from her material worldview to a spiritual one. Increasingly angered by her grandmother's reliance on stories, she demands, "Speak without your stories. Just once. What are you without your deer dress? What are you without your story of Ahw'uste?" (14). Articulating the living continuity of sacred stories, Grandmother responds, "We're carriers of our stories and histories. We're nothing without them" (14). Grandmother's insistence on stories for continuance reflects a deeply held traditional orientation, one in which, according to LeAnne Howe, "Native stories are power. They create people. They author tribes" (1999, 118). Jace Weaver shares a similar view, "Indeed, it may be that the People cannot have life outside of stories, their existence contingent upon the telling and hearing of communal stories" (1997, 40). In the play, the tension increases as the girl counters in the colonized voice of individualism, "We carry ourselves" (14).

*The Woman Who Was a Red Deer Dressed for the Deer Dance* culminates as Grandmother begins to pray, "*Gu'-s-di i-da-da-dv-hni* My relatives—" (17). In a response to her prayers, at the end of the performance, Girl in a lyrically constructed monologue finally accepts Grandmother's teachings as she understands the story of Ahw'uste, embraces her Cherokee spirituality, and symbolically designs her own deer dress. She thereby redefines herself in contemporary terms: "I'm sewing my own red-deer dress. It's different from my grandma's. Mine is a dress of words. I see Ahw'uste also" (18). Here her "red-deer dress" circles back to her grandmother's story of Ahw'uste at the beginning of the play and celebrates the oral tradition in which "words" have power and "carry meaning," according to Glancy (1987, 170). This circularity, characteristic of older tribal narratives, guides this highly contemporary piece, provides a homecoming for the girl, and affirms the living power of story on stage.

## NO HOME BUT THE HEART
## (AN ASSEMBLY OF MEMORIES)

Rosalie Jones, whose professional name is Daystar, is an internationally recognized dancer and choreographer (Magill 1998). In 1980, she founded DAYSTAR: Contemporary Dance-Drama of Indian America, whose work Hanay Geiogamah described as "some of the most experimental, bracing, and compelling Native-theme dance works imaginable for the times" (1995, 130). In *No Home but the Heart (An Assembly of Memories)*, which opened in Santa Fe in 1999 at the Maria Benitez Cabaret, Daystar furthers the dance-drama, a new Native performing arts aesthetic, which she developed, based on the fusion of ceremonial traditions of dance, song, and story with modern dance. In her keynote address, "Inventing Native Modern Dance: A Tough Trip through Paradise," at the Twenty-third Annual American Indian Workshop at Trinity College in Dublin, Ireland, in 2002, she emphasized the underlying spiritual underpinnings of modern Native dance: "In the native world view, dance and song are intimately fused to the ceremonials and the ceremonials are tied to the cosmologies, and the cosmologies are tied to the life and being of the Creator. It is because of the Creator that we are able to sing and dance and therefore, to give thanks for his many gifts to us" (Jones 2002).

In *No Home but the Heart*, Daystar explores the physical displacement and spiritual return of her mother's French-Cree family, who were forced out of Canada in the late 1800s to drift throughout the Northern Plains in the United States (Jones 2003). Integral to the staging throughout the piece is the Panel of Ancestors with Daystar's great-grandmother, Susan Bigknife, in the center, framed by her grandmother and mother, which serves to honor the ancestors and connect the story to the past. Through twelve scenes interweaving story, dance, and music, the work chronicles four generations of Native women, their grueling struggles against oppression, and their fierce determination to maintain their family and tribal ties, beginning with Great-Grandmother in the nineteenth century, and ending with Daughter in current times.

The Panel of Ancestors alone on stage opens the piece. Then lights dim, and in the darkness, a voiceover by Great-Grandmother as a young woman in 1880 begins the family's long story of dispossession:

> I don't remember where I was born.
> Maybe out of a wooden-cart or on a buffalo hunt,
> I don't remember and nobody wrote it down.
> I do know that my sister and me were taken from our
>     parents and raised by the nuns—you know. (83)

Bitterly she recalls that the nuns' education must not have been very helpful because her sister threw her off a steamer and deserted her on the prairies. Through the Traveling Dance, Great-Grandmother as a young woman portrays her fear and confusion at being left behind, abandoned and friendless in a strange place.

Scene 2 shifts to a voiceover of Great-Grandmother in 1880 as she reminisces about the brutality of her three husbands—the first one who abandoned her, the second one who shot and tried to kill her and later sickened and died, and the third one "who put out my eye" (85). In the face of this adversity, the spirits comfort, strengthen, teach, and guide her:

> That's when the spirits spoke to me.
> That's when I learned the secrets of wind and water
> and roots and leaves.
> That's when I learned how to doctor. (85)

During the Medicine Dance, Great-Grandmother ceremonially purifies a sacred space on stage and gives thanks to the Four Directions. Even though she is physically displaced, through this dance, she enters a ceremonial space connected to the spirits. This spiritual connection resonates throughout the rest of the piece. As Daystar writes, "While the achievement of survival can be manifest in a people's material culture, it is in their songs, dances, and oratories that the testament of their enduring spirit is truly found" (1992, 169).

Scene 3, entitled "The French Connection," flashes back to 1783, providing an expositional bridge from the two opening scenes to the next six scenes. The Narrator, alone on stage, sardonically provides a history lesson in the Canadian government's complicity in dispossessing

Great-Grandmother's community, the Métis. Describing the emergence of Métis culture as "a wonderful blend of the Indian and the French," which developed through intermarriage between the French traders and the Cree and Chippewa, Narrator then parodies the Canadian governmental policies, which required one to be French or Indian, not "both," resulting in a rebellion led by Louis Reil in 1885, who was subsequently hanged (87). Crushing this rebellion forced a "native exodus to the U.S." of Métis, Cree, and Chippewa (Yates 2003, C4).

The next six scenes graphically thrust the audience into the devastating physical realities of this forced migration and the cultural consequences to Great-Grandmother, Grandmother, and Mother. In scene 4, entitled "The Specter of Death," set in 1836–1837, the stage convulses with The Smallpox Dance. The dancer, wearing a smallpox mask, a red winding-sheet, and pale shirt and leggings covered with smallpox, graphically embodies the agonies of the smallpox epidemic that decimated Northern Plains peoples in 1837. In scene 5, Daystar deftly interweaves her family history while contesting destructive U.S. Indian policies. Punctuated by the refrain, "the Indians were in the way" (89), Narrator's monologue exposes the ideology of the westward movement, the imposition of reservations, the "ROTTEN POLITICS" over who was allowed to become an enrolled Chippewa tribal member, and the treachery of the "Ten Cent Treaty," in which the U.S. government paid "93,000 dollars for one million acres of land" (90).

Set in the early 1900s, scenes 6 and 7 introduce Grandmother to the stage as she enacts her struggles to survive on the margins of both mainstream American life and her native community. In scene 6, the Clog Dance fills the stage with the charm and vitality of the Métis culture. In sharp juxtaposition, Narrator's monologue relates the ensuing homelessness and subsequent poverty of thousands, including Grandmother and the Little Shell Chippewa Band as they were no longer recognized as federally enrolled members of a tribe (92). As they "moved farther west, trying to find a home, any kind of home," Narrator continues that they faced the destruction of the buffalo "and scavenged for buffalo bones—left over from the carcasses of thousands of dead buffalo," slaughtered as part of annihilative federal policies against the Plains people (92).

Scene 7 heightens the intensity of this suffering and poverty. In a voiceover as an old woman, Grandmother ruthlessly deconstructs the U.S. government's promise that they "could live in new way," based on farming (93):

> Living the 'new' way was a trade-off of sorts.
> We traded elder wisdom—for no wisdom.
> There were no doctors, not even aspirin
> for childbirth and gunshot wounds and TB
> and alcoholism. (93)

In the compelling Chair Dance, Grandmother dances from youth to age, physicalizing her escalating pain as she gave birth to seven children with no medical care and the resultant agony of her fallen womb. The high-backed chair she uses sits center stage, a stark symbol of European domination. Scene 8, set in 1940, ushers in Mother as a maid, working two jobs to survive and striving to realize the American dream "to join those ladies at the top of the hill" (96).

The final four scenes, through both story and choreography, enact a major shift from displacement to self-determination and return Mother and Daughter home to their Chippewa traditions. In scene 9, set in 1950, Mother in a voiceover laments the psychological price of assimilation and owning "a house next to those nice ladies on the hill": "I knew who I was, on the inside. But on the outside, I became the 'invisible' Indian" (97). Her dance, the Balancing Dance, begins with Mother in a ball gown, white full-length gloves, and a mask with feathers and enacts her seeming acceptance of mainstream culture as she waltzes around the stage. Narrator attacks her mixed heritage with full-blood taunts. Silencing these anxieties raised by her mixed heritage, as a Native chant replaces the waltz music, the dancer playing Mother strips off her mask and gloves, takes a rattle from Narrator, and ceremonially honors her ancestors. Then, according to the stage directions, "*she begins a round dance step, in a small circle*" (99). The song and dance intensify, and Mother concludes "*with four vigorous shakes of the rattle and a triumphant woman's call,*" echoing Great-Grandmother in scene 2 (99).

Throughout scenes 10 and 11, Daughter embraces her ancestors through moving voiceovers and choreography. In scene 10, set in present day, Daughter, in the Mistaken Identity Dance, rejects misperceptions about her identity with a "*karate blow*" (101). Then in scene 11, Daughter embodies her heritage as she does the Remembering Dance, part 2, reenacting the earlier choreography of her grandmother. In a voiceover, as she stands in front of the Panel of Ancestors, she claims her rightful place:

> I am not 'half' anything.
> I am the sum total of my ancestors.

> I am my mother. I am my father. I am my
>   Grandmother. I am my Great-Grandmother.
> I am the living legacy of the woman who survived
>   the Red Death of 1837. (102)

Only then does she reveal the official letter from the Bureau of Indian Affairs she received four days after her mother's death, designating her "A DESCENDENT OF THE PEMBINA CHIPPEWA PURSUANT TO THE PROVISIONS OF THE ACT OF DECEMBER 31, 1982, PUBLIC LAW 97–462" (103).

Through the artistic choice of Jingle Dress dancing, Daystar masterfully fills the stage with Chippewa spirituality in scene 12, "No Home but the Heart," set in "The Timeless Present," which opens with the jingling sound of the cones of the dress and continues with the dance (104). The tradition of the Jingle Dress Dance, according to Tara Browner, originated in "Whitefish Bay, a reserve village located on the shores of Lake of the Woods in southwestern Ontario" and draws on the belief "that what the Creator or guardian spirit gives to an individual through a vision is a complete understanding of what they have experienced" (2002, 53–54). As scene 12 unfolds, by retelling the story of Maggie White's illness, her father's vision, and the healing power of the Jingle Dress Dance, Narrator recalls the spiritual origins of the dance for the audience. Thus, Daystar's final dance sequence, the Spirits Dance, brings the play full circle to Great-Grandmother's earlier Medicine Dance (104). As Browner explains: "One of the most profound elements of Jingle Dress dancing is its spiritual power, which originates as an energy generated from the sound of the cones that sing out to the spirits when dancers lift their feet in time with the drum. The very act of dancing in this dress constitutes a prayer for healing" (2002, 53). The performance of the Jingle Dress Dance transforms the stage as those on stage dance a homecoming that resonates with their homelands and honors their sacred ties. Describing the underlying spiritual nature of her work and that of many others engaged in Native modern dance in her 2002 keynote address, Daystar avowed: "We are climbing the *ladder to the Creator's House*. We are crying and singing and dancing for the visions of our future" (Jones 2002). *No Home but the Heart* is a moving vision of recovery and hope.

## CLOSING REFLECTIONS

According to Paula Gunn Allen, "There is surely cause to weep, to grieve; but greater than ugliness, the endurance of tribal beauty is our reason to sing, to greet the coming day and the restored life and hope it brings" (1992, xi). *SongCatcher: A Native Interpretation of the Story of Frances Densmore* by Marcie Rendon integrates Ojibwe song traditions into urban life. *The Woman Who Was a Red Deer Dressed for the Deer Dance* by Diane Glancy celebrates the power of story to transform. *No Home but the Heart (An Assembly of Memories)* by Daystar/Rosalie Jones integrates story and dance to honor the continuity of family and community. As carriers of "tribal beauty," each uniquely performs homecoming and affirms the sacred.

# Works Cited

Abbott, Larry. 1997. "Sculptor Roxanne Swentzell: Expressions in Clay." *Indian Artist: The Magazine of Contemporary Native American Art*, Fall: 22–25.
Acampora, Christa Davis. 2006. "Unlikely Illuminations: Nietzsche and Frederick Douglass on Power, Struggle, and the *Aisthesis* of Freedom." In *Critical Affinities: Nietzsche and Africana Thought*. Ed. Jacqueline Scott and Todd Hamilton. Albany: State University of New York Press.
Alarcón, Norma. 1989. "The Sardonic Powers of the Erotic in the Work of Ana Castillo." In *Breaking Boundaries: Latina Writing and Critical Readings*. Ed. Asunción Horno-Delgado. Amherst: University of Massachusetts Press. 94–107.
Allan, Jita Tuzyline. 1995. *Womanist and Feminist Aesthetics: A Comparative Review*. Athens: Ohio University Press.
Allen, Paula Gunn. 1998. *Off the Reservation: Reflections on Boundary-Busting, Border-Crossing Loose Canons*. Boston: Beacon.
———. 1992 (revised edition) and 1986. *The Sacred Hoop: Recovering the Feminine in American Indian Traditions*. Boston: Beacon.
———. 1991. *Grandmothers of the Light: A Medicine Woman's Sourcebook*. Boston: Beacon.
———. 1983. Ed. *Studies in American Indian Literature*. New York: Modern Language Association of America.
Allende, Isabel. 1985. *The House of the Spirits*. New York: Knopf.
Álvarez, Enid. 1995. "La increíble historia de la Santa Loca y sus martirizadas hermanas." In *Las formas de nuestras voces: Chicana and Mexicana Writers in Mexico*. Ed. Claire Joysmith. México: Universidad Nacional Autónoma de México, 141–51.
Álvarez, Julia. 1994. *In the Time of the Butterflies*. New York: Plume Books.
———. 1991. *How the Garcia Girls Lost Their Accents*. New York: Plume Books.
———. 2000. *In the Name of Salomé*. Chapel Hill, NC: Algonquin Books.
Andrews, Regina M. *The Man Who Passed*. N/D. Typescript. Regina Andrews Papers. New York Public Library: Schomburg Center for Research in Black Culture: Manuscript, Archives, and Rare Books Division. In *Harlem's Glory: Black Women Writing 1900–1950*. Ed. Lorraine E. Roses and Ruth E. Randolph. Cambridge: Harvard University Press, 1996. 45–55.
———. 1975. "A Voice: Regina M. Andrews." In *Voices of the Black Theater*. Ed. Loften Mitchell. Clifton, NJ: White.

———. 1961. "Curricula Vitae." Typescript and pencil manuscript. Regina Andrews Papers. New York Public Library: Schomburg Center for Research in Black Culture: Manuscript, Archives, and Rare Books Division.

———. 1938. "Opening of the Little Theater Auditorium Nov. 1938." Speech. Typescript. Regina Andrews Papers. New York Public Library: Schomburg Center for Research in Black Culture: Manuscript, Archives, and Rare Books Division.

———. (Ursala Trelling). 1932. *Underground.* Typescript. Regina Andrews Papers. New York Public Library: Schomburg Center for Research in Black Culture: Manuscript, Archives, and Rare Books Division.

———. 1925. *Climbing Jacob's Ladder.* Manuscript. Regina Andrews Papers. New York Public Library: Schomburg Center for Research in Black Culture: Manuscript, Archives, and Rare Books Division. In *Strange Fruit: Plays on Lynching by American Women.* Ed. Kathy Perkins and Judith Stephens. Bloomington: Indiana University Press. 1998.

Anzaldúa, Gloria. 1990. *Making Face, Making Soul = Haciendo caras: Creative and Critical Perspectives by Women of Color.* San Francisco: Aunt Lute Foundation Books.

———. 1987. *Borderlands/La Frontera: The New Mestiza.* Spinsters Ink/Aunt Lute Books.

Apel, Karl-Otto. 1995. *Charles S. Peirce: From Pragmatism to Pragmaticism.* Atlantic Highlands, NJ: Humanities Press International.

Ardener, Shirley. 1981. "Ground Rules and Social Maps for Women: An Introduction." In *Women and Space: Ground Rules and Social Maps.* Ed. Shirley Ardener. New York: St. Martin's. 1–34.

Ault, Alicia. 2004. "Artistic Touch." *Smithsonian* [December]: 50.

Awiakta, Marilou. "Amazons in Appalachia." In *A Gathering of Spirit: Writing and Art by North American Indian Women.* Ed. Beth Brant (Degonwadonti). Rockland, ME: Sinister Wisdom Books. 1984. 125–30.

Bandele, Asha. 2002. "Meshell Ndegeocello: Excavating True Artistry on Her New Album." *Essence,* March.

Baraka, Imamu Amiri. 1966. *Black Art.* Newark: Jihad.

Barr-Zisowitz, C. 2000. "Sadness." In *The Handbook of Emotions.* Ed. Michael Lewis and Jeannette Haviland-Jones. New York: Guilford.

Beauvoir, Simone de. 1948 (reprint 1992). *The Ethics of Ambiguity.* Trans. Bernard Frechtman. New York: Philosophical Library.

Bennett, Tanya Long. 1996. "No Country to Call Home: A Study of Castillo's *Mixquiahuala Letters.*" *Style* 30, no. 3: 462–78.

Bhabha, Homi. 1994. *The Location of Culture.* New York: Routledge.

Bhaware, N. G. 1980. "The Anguished Cry: Poetry by Dalit Women." *Eve's Weekly,* May 24–10.

Bobo, Jacqueline, ed. 2001. *Black Feminist Cultural Criticism.* Malden, MA: Blackwell.

Bogardus, Ralph F. 1993. "Urban Cultural Institutions." In *Encyclopedia of American Social History*. Ed. Mary K. Cayton, Elliot J. Gorn, and Peter W. Williams. New York: Charles Scribner's Sons. 3: 2484–88.

Bordo, Susan R. 1990. "Feminism, Postmodernism, and Gender-Scepticism." In *Feminism/Postmodernism*. Ed. Linda Nicholson. New York: Routledge.

Brand, Peg, and Mary Devereaux, eds. 2003. *Women, Art, and Aesthetics*. Special Issue of *Hypatia* 18, no. 4.

Brand, Peggy Zeglan, and Carolyn Korsmeyer, eds. 1995. *Feminism and Tradition in Aesthetics*. University Park: Pennsylvania State University Press.

Brant, Beth. 1997. "The Good Red Road: Journeys of Homecoming in Native Women's Writing." *American Indian Culture and Research Journal* 21, no. 1: 193–206.

Brody, J. J. 1991. *Anasazi and Pueblo Painting*. Albuquerque: University of New Mexico Press.

Broude, Norma, and Mary D. Garrard, eds. 1995. *The Power of Feminist Art: The American Movement of the 1970s, History and Impact*. New York: Abrams.

Brown, Anne E., and Marjanne E. Gooze, eds. 1995. *International Women's Writings: New Landscapes of Identity*. Westport, CT: Greenwood.

Brown, Barnsley. 1992. "Regina M. Anderson." In *Notable Black American Women*. Ed. Jessie Carney Smith. Detroit: Gale Research. 20–22.

Brown, Wendy. 1995. *States of Injury: Power and Freedom in Late Modernity*. Princeton, NJ: Princeton University Press.

Brown-Guillory, Elizabeth. 1988. *Their Place on the Stage: Black Women Playwrights in America*. Westport CT: Greenwood.

Browner, Tara. 2002. *Heartbeat of the People: Music and Dance of the Northern Pow-wow*. Urbana: University of Illinois Press.

Buchloch, Benjamin H. D. 1994. "Residual Resemblance: Three Notes on the Ends of Portraiture." In *Face-Off: The Portrait in Recent Art*. Melissa E. Feldman. Philadelphia: Institute of Contemporary Art. 53–69.

Burns, Lori, and Mélisse LaFrance. 2002. "Me'Shell Ndegéocello: 'Mary Magdalene'" (1996). In *Disruptive Divas: Feminism, Identity, and Popular Music*. New York: Routledge. 133–67.

Carby, Hazel V. 1987. "Introduction." In *Iola Leroy or Shadows Uplifted*. France W. Harper. 1892. Boston: Beacon. ix–xxvi.

Carpenter, Kenneth E. 2001. "Libraries." In *Encyclopedia of American Cultural and Intellectual History*. Vol. 3. Ed. M. K. Cayton and P. W. Williams. New York: Charles Scribner's Sons. 376–80.

Casselberry, Judith. 1999. "Womanist Spirituality in Popular American Music: Black Feminism, the African World View, and Songwriting." M.A. thesis, Wesleyan University.

Castillo, Ana. 1999. *Peel My Love Like an Onion*. New York: Doubleday.

———. 1997. "Yes, Dear Critic, There Really Is an Alicia." In *Máscaras*. Ed. Lucha Corpi. Berkeley, CA: Third Woman. 153–60.

———. 1996a. *Loverboys: Stories.* New York: Norton.
———, ed. 1996b. *Goddess of the Americas/La diosa de las Américas: Writings on the Virgin of Guadalupe.* New York: Riverhead Books.
———. 1995a. *Massacre of the Dreamers: Essays on Xicanisma.* New York: Plume.
———. 1995b. *My Father Was a Toltec and Selected Poems.* New York: Norton.
———. 1994. *So Far from God.* New York: Plume.
———. 1993. "The Distortion of Desire." In *The Sexuality of Latinas.* Ed. Norma Alarcón, Ana Castillo, and Cherríe Moraga. Berkeley: Third Woman. 147–50.
———. 1990. *Sapogonia: An Anti-Romance in 3/8 Meter.* Tempe, AZ: Bilingual Press/Editorial Bilingüe.
———. 1986. *The Mixquiahuala Letters.* New York: Anchor Books.
Charles, Nick. 1996. "Me'Shell Takes Risks with 'Risqué' Song." *New York Daily News,* June 25.
Cheng, Scarlet. 2002. "Album of a Native American Past." *Los Angeles Times,* June 2, Calendar, 37–38.
Chicago, Judy. 1979. *The Dinner Party: A Symbol of Our Heritage.* New York: Doubleday.
Chonin, Neva. 2002. "Finding Her Own Groove: Ndegeocello Is Feeling as Free as Her Name." *San Francisco Chronicle,* June 23, Sunday Datebook.
Christian, Karen. 1997. *Show and Tell: Identity as Performance in U.S. Latina/o Fiction.* Albuquerque: University of New Mexico Press.
Cinander, Martha, and Matthew Finch. 2000. "Ana Castillo Interview." <wysiwyg://31/http://216.71.173.167/AuthorInterviews/anacastillo.html> 5 May.
Clarke, Cheryl. 1986. *Living as a Lesbian.* Ithaca: Firebrand.
Cline, Lynn. 2002. "Meshell Ndegeocello's Funky Baseline." *Santa Fe New Mexican,* October 25.
Collins, Patricia Hill. 2000. *Black Feminist Thought: Knowledge, Consciousness, and the Politics of Empowerment.* New York: Routledge. 2nd edition.
Cone, James. 1972. *The Spirituals and the Blues: An Interpretation.* New York: Seabury.
Cornell, Drucilla. 2000. *Just Cause.* New York: Rowman and Littlefield.
———. 1998. *At the Heart of Freedom: Feminism, Sex and Equality.* Princeton, NJ: Princeton University Press.
———. 1995. *The Imaginary Domain: Abortion, Pornography, and Sexual Harassment.* New York: Routledge.
Cornell, Stephen. 1988. *The Return of the Native: American Indian Political Resurgence.* New York: Oxford University Press.
Dain, Phyllis. 1972. *The New York Public Library.* New York Public Library Astor, Lenox, and Tilden Foundations.
Dangle, Arjun, ed. 1992. *Poisoned Bread: Translations from Modern Marathi Dalit Literature.* Bombay: Orient Longman.

Darby, Jaye T. 2002. "Re-Imagining the Stage: Tradition and Transformation in Native Theater." In *The Color of Theater: Race, Ethnicity and Performance*. Ed. Roberta Uno with Lucy Mae San Pablo Burns. New York: Continuum. 60–81.

Darling, Cary. 1994. "Controversial Singer/Songwriter Doesn't Care What People Think about Her." *Orange County Register*, September 1.

Davies, Carol Boyce. 1994. *Black Women, Writing and the Identity: Migrations of the Subject*. New York: Routledge.

Davis, Angela Y. 2003. *Are Prisons Obsolete?* New York: Seven Stories.

———. 1999. *The Prison Industrial Complex*. San Francisco: AK Press Audio.

———. 1998a. "Rape, Racism, and the Capitalist Setting." In *The Angela Y. Davis Reader*. Ed. Joy James. Malden, MA: Blackwell.

———. 1998b. *Blues Legacies and Black Feminism: Gertrude Ma Rainey, Bessie Smith, and Billie Holiday*. New York: Vintage.

———. 1995. "I Used to Be Your Sweet Mama: Ideology, Sexuality and Domesticity in the Blues of Gertrude 'Ma' Rainey and Bessie Smith." In *Sexy Bodies: The Strange Carnalities of Feminism*. Ed. Elizabeth Grosz and Elspeth Probyn. New York: Routledge. 231–65.

———. 1990. "Black Women and Music: A Historical Legacy of Struggle." In *Wild Women in the Whirlwind: Afra-American Culture and the Contemporary Literary Renaissance*. Ed. Joanne M. Braxton and Andrée Nicola McLaughlin. New Brunswick, NJ: Rutgers University Press. 3–21.

———. 1984. "Art on the Frontline: Mandate for a People's Culture." In *Women, Culture, and Politics*. New York: Vintage Books. 198–218.

Daystar. (See Jones, Rosalie.)

Delgadillo, Theresa. 1998. "Forms of Chicana Feminist Resistance: Hybrid Spirituality in Ana Castillo's *So Far from God*." *Modern Fiction Studies* 44, no. 4 (Winter): 888–916.

Deloria Jr., Vine. 1985. Introduction to *American Indian Policy in the Twentieth Century*. Ed. Vine DeLoria Jr. Norman: University of Oklahoma Press. 3–14.

Dewey, John. 1987. *Art as Experience*, From *John Dewey: The Later Works, 1925–1953*. Vol. 10. Ed. Jo Ann Boydston. Carbondale and Edwardsville: Southern Illinois University Press (Originally published 1934).

Drake, St. Clair, and Horace R. Cayton. 1993; 1945. *Black Metropolis: A Study of Negro Life in a Northern City*. Chicago: University of Chicago Press.

Dray, Philip. *At the Hands of Persons Unknown: The Lynching of Black America*. New York: Modern Library, 2002.

Ecker, Gisela. 1985. *Feminist Aesthetics*. Boston: Beacon.

Fanon, Frantz. 1967. *Black Skin, White Masks*. Trans. Charles Lam Markmann. New York: Grove.

Farris, Phoebe. 1999. *Women Artists of Color: A Bio-Critical Sourcebook to Twentieth Century Artists in the Americas*. Westport, CT, and London: Greenwood.

Fauntleroy, Gussie. 2003. "Native Sculpture Today." *Native Peoples: The Arts and Lifeways* (January/February): 26–31.

———. 2002. *Roxanne Swentzell: Extra-Ordinary People*. Santa Fe: New Mexico Magazine Artist Series.

Ferguson, Ann. 1989. *Blood at the Root: Motherhood, Sexuality, and Male Dominance*. London and Winchester, MA: Pandora.

Fixico, Donald L. 1986. *Termination and Relocation: Federal Indian Policy, 1945–1960*. Albuquerque: University of New Mexico Press.

Fuller, Charles H. 1967. "Black Writing Is Socio-Creative Art." *Liberator* 7, no. 4: 8–10.

Fullwood, Steven G. 2002. "Q&A: Me'Shell NdegéOcello." *Africana*, June 3.

Fusco, Coco. 2001. *The Bodies That Were Not Ours and Other Writings*. London and New York: Routledge.

———. 2000. *Corpus Delecti: Performance Art of the Americas*. London and New York: Routledge.

———, ed. 1995. *English Is Broken Here: Notes on Cultural Fusion in the Americas*. New York: New Press.

Fusco, Coco, and Guillermo Gómez-Peña. 1995. "Norte: Sur." In *English Is Broken Here: Notes on Cultural Fusion in the Americas*. Ed. Coco Fusco. New York: New Press.

Frye. Marilyn. 1983. *The Politics of Reality: Essays in Feminist Theory*. Trumansburg, New York: Crossing.

Galvin, Peter. 1993. "Girl Toy: Me'Shell Ndegéocello: Plantation Lullabies." *The Advocate* no. 640, October 19.

García Márquez, Gabriel. 1970. *One Hundred Years of Solitude*. New York: Avon.

Garrison, Dee. 2003; 1979. *Apostles of Culture: The Public Librarian and American Society*. Madison: University of Wisconsin Press; New York: Free Press.

Gates, Henry Louis. 1988. "The Trope of a New Negro and the Reconstruction of the Image of the Black." *Representations* no. 24. Special Issue: America Reconstructed, 1840–1940. Autumn: 129–55.

Gayle, Addison. 1971. *The Black Aesthetic*. Garden City, NY: Doubleday.

Geiogamah, Hanay. 1995. "Old Circles, New Circles: The World of Native Dance." *Indian Artist* 1, no. 2 (Fall): 130–37.

Gili, Marta. 2002. *Lorna Simpson*. Salamanca, Spain: Centro de Arte Contemporaneo.

Glancy, Diane. 2002. *The Woman Who Was a Red Deer Dressed for the Deer Dance*. In *American Gypsy: Six Native American Plays* by Diane Glancy. Norman: University of Oklahoma Press. 3–18.

———. 2000. "Native American Theater and the Theater That Will Come." In *American Indian Theater in Performance: A Reader*. Ed. Hanay Geiogamah and Jaye T. Darby. Los Angeles: UCLA American Indian Studies Center. 359–61.

———. 1987. "Two Dresses." In *I Tell You Now: Autobiographical Essays by Native American Writers.* Ed. Brian Swann and Arnold Krupat. Lincoln: University of Nebraska Press. 167–83.

Golden, Thelma. 1998. "Some Thoughts on Carrie Mae Weems." In *Carrie Mae Weems: Recent Work, 1992–1998.* New York: Braziller. 29–34.

Goldsby, Jackie. 1993. "Queen for 307 Days: Looking B(l)ack at Vanessa Williams and the Sex Wars." In *Sisters, Sexperts, Queers: Beyond the Lesbian Nation.* Ed. Arlene Stein. New York: Penguin Books. 110–28.

Gordon, Lewis R. 1997. "Existential Dynamics of Theorizing Black Invisibility." In *Existence in Black: An Anthology of Black Existential Philosophy.* Ed. Lewis R. Gordon. New York: Routledge.

Gordon, Lewis R., and Jane Anna Gordon. 2006. *Not Only the Master's Tools: African-American Studies in Theory and Practice.* Boulder, CO: Paradigm.

Gould, Janice. 1992. "The Problem of Being Indian." In *De/Colonizing the Subject.* Ed. Sidonie Smith and Julia Watson. Minneapolis: University of Minnesota Press.

Graffe, Steve. 1995. "Sisters of the Earth." *Ceramics Monthly*, September: 12–14.

Green, Rayna. 1980. "Native American Women." *Signs: Journal of Women in Culture and Society* 6, no. 2: 248–67.

Gregory, Dick. 1970, 1997. *Dick Gregory at Kent State.* Kent, OH: Poppy Records. Reissued on compact disc: Narberth, PA: Collectables Records.

Grosfoguel, Ramón. 2003. "Introduction: Geopolitics of Knowledge and Coloniality of Power: Thinking Puerto Rico and Puerto Ricans from the Colonial Difference." In *Colonial Subjects: Puerto Ricans in a Global Perspective* by Ramón Grosfoguel. Berkeley: University of California Press. 1–40.

Guru, Gopal. 1995. "Dalit Women Talk Differently." *Economic and Political Weekly*, October 14–21.

Hammonds, Evelynn M. 1997. "Toward a Genealogy of Black Female Sexuality: The Problematic of Silence." In *Feminist Genealogies, Colonial Legacies, Democratic Futures.* Ed. M. Jacqui Alexander and Chandra Talpade Mohanty. New York: Routledge. 170–81.

Hansberry, Lorraine. 1959. *A Raisin in the Sun.* New York: Signet.

Harjo, Joy, and Gloria Bird. 1997. Introduction to *Reinventing the Enemy's Language: Contemporary Native Women's Writings of North America.* Ed. Joy Harjo and Gloria Bird with Patricia Blanco, Beth Cuthand, and Valerie Martínez. New York: Norton. 19–31.

Harrington, Richard. 1994. "Wake-Up Call: Me'Shell Ndegéocello's 'Plantation Lullabies' Is Anything but Sleepy." *Washington Post*, February 13.

Hart, Patricia. 1989. *Narrative Magic in the Fiction of Isabel Allende.* Rutherford: Associated University Press.

Hartsock, Nancy C. M. 1983. "The Feminist Standpoint: Developing the Ground for a Specifically Feminist Historical Materialism." In *Discovering*

*Reality.* Sandra Harding and Merrill B. Hintikka. Dordrecht, Holland: D. Reidel. 283–310.

———. 1990. "Foucault on Power: A Theory for Women?" In *Feminism/Postmodernism.* Ed. Linda Nicholson. New York: Routledge.

Haugo, Ann. 2000. "'Circles upon Circles upon Circles': Native Women in Theater and Performance." In *American Indian Theater in Performance: A Reader.* Ed. Hanay Geiogamah and Jaye T. Darby. Los Angeles: UCLA American Indian Studies Center. 228–55.

Heidegger, Martin. 1971 [written in 1935]. "The Origin of the Work of Art." In *Poetry, Language, Thought.* Martin Heidegger. Trans. and intro. Albert Hofstadter. San Francisco: Harper and Row. 17–87.

Hein, Hilde, and Carolyn Korsmeyer 1993. *Aesthetics in Feminist Perspective.* Bloomington: Indiana University Press.

Hernández-Ávila, Inés. 1995. "Relocations upon Relocations: Home, Language, and Native Women's Writing." *The American Indian Quarterly* 19, no. 4 (Fall): 491–507.

High, Frida. 1997. "Chiasmus—Art in Politics/Politics in Art: Chicano/a and African American Image, Text, and Activism of the 1960s and 1970s." In *Voices of Color: Art and Society in the Americas.* Ed. Phoebe Farris. New York: Prometheus/Humanity Books.

Hilburn, Robert. 1996. "She Can't Hide Her Feelings." *Los Angeles Times,* August 25, Calendar.

Hodge, Robert, and Gunther Kress. 1988. *Social Semiotic.* Ithaca, NY: Cornell University Press.

hooks, bell. 1994a. *Teaching to Transgress: Education as the Practice of Freedom.* New York, Routledge.

———. 1994b. *Outlaw Culture: Resisting Representations.* New York: Routledge.

———. 1992. *Black Looks: Race and Representation.* Boston: South End.

———. 1990. *Yearning: Race, Gender, and Cultural Politics.* Boston: South End.

———. 1984. *Feminist Theory: From Margin to Center.* Boston: South End.

Howe, LeAnne. 1999. "Tribalography: The Power of Native Stories." *Journal of Dramatic Theory and Criticism* 14, no. 1 (Fall): 117–25.

Hucko, Bruce, and the Children of Santa Clara, San Ildefonso, San Juan, Pojoaque, and Nambe Pueblos. 1996. *Where There Is No Name for Art: The Art of Tewa Children.* Santa Fe, NM: School of American Research Press.

Jackson, Paul. 2002. "Meshell: The Thinker's Bass Player." *The Daily Yomiuri* [Tokyo], June 13.

Jamison, Laura. 1997. "Me'Shell Ndegéocello." *Rolling Stone,* November 13.

Jefferson, Annetta. 1993. "Andrews, Regina M. Anderson." In *Black Women in America: An Historical Encyclopedia.* Ed. Darlene Clark Hine. Vol. I. Bloomington: Indiana University Press. 365–36.

Johnson, Kevin C. 2001. "Ndegeocello Puts Her Music in the 'Trying to Create' Category." *St. Louis Post-Dispatch,* December 7, sec. E.

Jones, Kellie. 2002. "(Un)Seen & Overheard: Pictures by Lorna Simpson." In *Lorna Simpson*. London: Phaidon. 28–103.
Jones, Rosalie (Daystar). 2003. *No Home but the Heart (An Assembly of Memories)*. In *Keepers of the Morning Star: An Anthology of Native Women's Theater*. Ed. Jaye T. Darby and Stephanie Fitzgerald. Los Angeles: UCLA American Indian Studies Center. 76–106.
———. 2002. "Inventing Native Modern Dance: A Tough Trip through Paradise." Keynote Address presented at the Twenty-third Annual American Indian Workshop at Trinity College, Dublin, Ireland, 26 March.
———. 1992. "Modern Native Dance: Beyond Tribe and Tradition." In *Native American Dance: Ceremonies and Social Traditions*. Ed. Charlotte Heth. Washington, DC: National Museum of the American Indian Smithsonian Institution with Starwood. 169–83.
Julien, Isaac. 1983. "'Black Is, Black Ain't': Notes on De-Essentializing Black Identities." In *Black Popular Culture*, by Michele Wallace. Ed. Gina Dent. New York: New Press. 255–63.
Kilcup, Karen L., ed. 2000. "Writing *The Red Woman's America*." In *Native American Women's Writing c. 1800–1924*. Oxford: Blackwell.
Kilpatrick, Jack F., and Anna G. Kilpatrick. 1995. *Friends of Thunder: Folktales of the Oklahoma Cherokees*. Norman: University of Oklahoma Press. Originally published in 1964 by Southern Methodist University Press in Dallas, Texas.
Kingsbury, B. 1989. "The Treaty of Waitangi: Some International Law Aspects." In *Waitangi: Māori and Pākehā Perspectives of the Treaty of Waitangi*. Ed. I. H. Kawharu. Auckland: Oxford University Press. 121–57.
Kingston, Maxine Hong. 1977. *The Woman Warrior*. New York: Vintage Books.
Kristeva, Julia. 2001. *Feminine Genis, Volume One, Hannah Arendt*. Trans. Ross Guberman. New York: Columbia University Press.
———. 1989. *Black Sun: Depression and Melancholy*. Trans. Leon S. Roudiez. New York: Columbia University Press.
Kundera, Milan. 1984. *The Unbearable Lightness of Being*. Trans. Michael Henry Heim. New York: HarperCollins.
Kusmer, Kenneth L. 1986. "The Black Urban Experience in American History." In *The State of Afro-American History: Past, Present, and Future*. Ed. Darlene Clark Hine. Baton Rouge: Louisiana State University Press. 91–135.
Lacan, Jacques. 1977. "The Mirror Stage as Formative of the Function of the I as Revealed in Psychoanalytic Experience." 1949. In *Écrits: A Selection*. Trans. Alan Sheridan. New York and London: Norton. 1–7.
LaDuke, Winona. 2005. *Recovering the Sacred: The Power of Naming and Claiming*. Cambridge, MA: South End.
Lecaro, Lina. 2002. "Head, Heart and Soul." *Los Angeles Times*, October 24.
LeDœuff, Michéle. 1989. *The Philosophical Imaginary*. Trans. Colin Gordon. London: Althone.
Leigh, Bill. 2002. "MeShell Gets Real." *Bass Player*, March.

Lippard, Lucy R. 1990. *Mixed Blessings: New Art in a Multicultural America.* New York: Pantheon Books.
Lorde, Audre. 1984. *Sister/Outsider.* Trumansburg, NY: Crossing.
Lugones, María. 1987. "Playfulness, 'World'-Travelling, and Loving Perception." *Hypatia* 2, no. 2 (Summer): 3–19.
Magill, Gordon L. 1998. "Rosalie Jones: Guiding Light of Daystar." *Dance Magazine* 72, no. 8 (August): 64–68.
Martinez, Jacqueline. 2000. *Phenomenology of Chicana Experience and Identity: Communication and Transformation in Praxis.* Lanham, MD: Rowman and Littlefield.
Martinot, Steve. 2002. *The Rule of Racialization: Class, Identity, Governance.* Philadelphia: Temple University.
Massey, Doreen. 1994. *Space, Place and Gender.* Minneapolis: University of Minnesota Press.
McClintock, Anne. 1995. *Imperial Leather: Race, Gender, and Sexuality in the Colonial Conquest.* New York: Routledge.
McDonnell, Evelyn. 1994. "Me'Shell Ndegéocello." *Rolling Stone*, December 29.
Medicine, Beatrice. 1983. "Indian Women: Tribal Identity as *Status Quo.*" In *Woman's Nature: Rationalizations of Inequality.* Ed. Marian Lowe and Ruth Hubbard. New York: Pergamon.
Mendieta, Eduardo. 2004. "Plantations, Ghettos, Prisons: U.S. Racial Geographies." *Philosophy and Geography* 7, no. 1: 43–59.
Milligan, Bryce. 1999. "An Interview with Ana Castillo." *South Central Review* 16, no. 1 (Spring): 19–29.
Mitchell, Jacqueline, et al. 1991. "Entrevista a Ana Castillo." *Mester* 20, no. 2 (Fall): 145–56.
Mitchell, Loften. 1975. *Voices of the Black Theater.* Clifton, NJ: White.
Mohanty, Chandra, et al., eds. 1991. *Third World Women and the Politics of Feminism.* Bloomington: Indiana University Press.
Moore, Nicole. 2002. "Last Woman Standing." *One World* (February/March).
Morrison, Toni. 1987. *Beloved.* New York: Penguin.
Mullin, Amy. 2003. "Feminist Art and the Political Imagination." *Hypatia* 18, no. 4 (Fall): 189–213.
Nadell, Martha. *Enter the New Negroes: Images of Race in American Culture.* Cambridge, MA: Harvard University Press, 2004.
Naranjo, Tessie. 1994. "Pottery Making in a Changing World." *Expedition* 36, no. 1: 45–59.
Naranjo-Morse, Nora. 1992. *Mud Woman: Poems from the Clay.* Tucson: University of Arizona Press.
Neal, Mark Anthony. 2003. *Songs in the Key of Black Life: A Nation of Rhythm and Blues.* New York: Routledge. 9–21.
Ndegēocello, MeShell. 2002. *Cookie: The Anthropological Mixtape.* Beverly Hills: Maverick Recording Company.

Nestle, Joan. 1987. *A Restricted Country*. Ithaca, NY: Firebrand.
Novetzke, Christian. 1995. "Twice Dalit: The Poetry of Hira Bansode." *Journal of South Asian Literature* 28, no. 1: 279–96.
O'Grady, Lorraine. 1992. "Olympia's Maid: Reclaiming Black Female Subjectivity." In *New Feminist Criticism: Art, Identity, Action*. Ed. Joanna Freuh, Cassanda L. Langer, and Arlene Raven. New York: HarperCollins. 152–70.
Oliver, Kelly. 2004. *The Colonization of Psychic Space*. Minneapolis: University of Minnesota Press.
Omvedt, Gail. 1990. *Violence against Women: New Movements and New Theories in India*. Delhi: Kali for Women.
Orange, C. 1987. *The Treaty of Waitangi*. Wellington: Allen and Unwin, Port Nicholson.
Orbell, M. 1978. *Maori Poetry: An Introductory Anthology*. Auckland: Heinemann Educational.
Orloff, Brian. 2002. "Freedom in Music." *St. Petersburg Times* (Florida), October 15.
Ortiz, Alfonso. 1969. *The Tewa World: Space, Time, Being and Becoming in a Pueblo Society*. Chicago: University of Chicago Press.
Ottley, Roi, and William J. Weatherby. 1967. *The Negro in New York: An Informal Social History*. Dobbs Ferry, NY: Oceana with the New York Public Library.
Oyewumi, Oyeronke. 2003. *African Women and Feminism: Reflecting on the Politics of Sisterhood*. Trenton, NJ: African World.
Painter, Nell Irving. "Representing Truth: Sojouner's Truth Knowing and Becoming Known." *The Journal of American History* 81, no. 2 (September 1994): 461–92.
Pardue, Diana. 1997. "The Clay People of Roxanne Swentzell." In *Thirty-Ninth Annual Heard Museum Guild and Indian Market*. Museum Brochure. Tucson, AZ: Heard Museum.
Pardue, Diana, and Cathyrn Coe. 1998. "Earth Symbols: Nora Naranjo-Morse and Roxanne Swentzell." *Native Peoples: The Arts and Lifeways*, Winter: 42–47.
Parsons, Elsie Clews. 1994. *Tewa Tales*. Tucson: University of Arizona Press.
Perkins, Kathy, and Judith Stephens, eds. 1998. *Strange Fruit: Plays on Lynching by American Women*. Bloomington: Indiana University Press.
Peterson, Susan. 1997. *Pottery by American Indian Women: The Legacy of Generations*. Washington, DC: National Museum for Women in the Arts Publication by Abbeville.
Phoenix, Val C. 1994. "Me'Shell: Uncensored, Unfettered." *Deneuve*, March/April.
Powell, Allison. 1996. "The Sybil of Soul." *Interview*, July.
Powell, Richard J. 1997. *Black Art and Culture in the Twentieth Century*. London: Thames and Hudson.
Powers, Ann. 1996. "Black and Blue: Me'Shell Ndegéocello Fights for Your Rights on Peace beyond Passion." *Rolling Stone*, September 5.

Quijano, Anibal. 2001. "Colonialidad del Poder. Cultura y Conocimiento en América Latina." In *Capitalismo y geopolitica del conocimiento: El eurocentrismo y la filosofía de la liberación en el debate intelectual contemporáneo.* Ed. Walter Mignolo. Argentina: Ediciones del Signo. 117–31.

Quintana, Alvina E. 1991. "Ana Castillo's *The Mixquiahuala Letters*: The Novelist as Ethnographer." In *Criticism in the Borderlands: Studies in Chicano Literature, Culture, and Ideology.* Ed. Hector Calderón and José David Saldívar. Durham, NC: Duke University Press. 72–83.

Ramirez, Renya Katarine. 1998. "Healing through Grief." *American Indian Culture and Research Journal* 22, no. 4: 305–33.

Rani, Challapalli Swaroopa. 1998. "Dalit Women's Writing in Telugu." *Economic and Political Weekly*, October 31.

Rapaport, Amos. 1994. "Spatial Organization and the Built Environment." In *Companion Encyclopedia of Anthropology: Humanity, Culture, and Social Life.* Ed. Tim Ingold. London: Routledge. 460–502.

Rege, Sharmila. 1998. "Dalit Women Talk Differently: A Critique of Difference and Towards a Dalit Feminist Standpoint Position." *Economic and Political Weekly*, October 31.

Rendon, Marcie. 2003. *SongCatcher: A Native Interpretation of the Story of Frances Densmore.* In *Keepers of the Morning Star: An Anthology of Native Women's Theater.* Ed. Jaye T. Darby and Stephanie Fitzgerald. Los Angeles: UCLA American Indian Studies Center. 1–75.

Rogers, Ray. 1996. "The Passion of Me'Shell." *Out,* July.

Romero, Simon. 2000. "An Interview with Ana Castillo." *Modern American Poetry.* <http://www.english.uiuc.edu/maps/poets/a_f/castillo/interview.htm> Accessed May 5, 2000.

Rose, Cynthia. 1996. "The Voices of Ana Castillo." *The Seattle Times.* <http://www.seattletimes.com/extra/browse/html/altanac_091296.htm> Sept. 12. Accessed May 5, 2000.

Roseberry, Cecil R. 1970. *For the Government and People of This State: A History of the New York State Library.* Albany: State Education Department.

Rosenberg, Judith Pierce. 1995. "Roxanne Swentzell." In *A Question of Balance: Artists and Writers on Motherhood.* Watsonville, CA: Papier-Mache Press. Roxanne Swentzell clarified and updated her statement in 2004 via email with Ruth Porritt.

Roses, Lorraine E., and Ruth E. Randolph. 1990. "Regina M. Anderson" [Ursula Trelling]. In *Harlem Renaissance and Beyond: 100 Black Women Writers 1900–1945.* Boston: Hall.

Saeta, Elsa. 1997. "A *MELUS* Interview: Ana Castillo." *MELUS: The Journal of the Society for the Study of the Multi-Ethnic Literature of the United States* 22, no. 3 (Fall): 133–50.

———. 1994. "Ana Castillo's *Sapogonia*: Narrative Point of View as a Study in Perception." *Confluencia: Revista Hispanica de Cultura y Literatura* 10, no. 1 (Fall): 67–72.

Sánchez, Cynthia A. 1999. "Latin American Women Artists." In *Women Artists of Color: A Bio-Critical Sourcebook to Twentieth Century Artists in the Americas*. Ed. Phoebe Farris. Westport, CT, and London: Greenwood.

Sanders, Joshunda. 2001. Liner Notes for *Cookie: The Anthropological Mixtape*. www.freemyheart.com/warmth.html. Accessed October 1, 2002.

Sandoval, Chela. 2000. *Methodology of the Oppressed*. Minneapolis: University of Minnesota Press.

Sangari, Kumkum. 1996. "Consent and Agency. Aspects of Feminist Historiography." In *Women in Indian History*. Ed. Kiran Pawar. Patiala and New Delhi: Vision and Venture.

Sartre, Jean-Paul. 1948. *Orphée Noir* [Black Orpheus]. Preface to *Anthologie de la nuvelle poésie négre et malgache*. Paris: Presses Universitaires de France.

Savelson, Kim. 1997. "Space." In *Encyclopedia of Feminist Literary Theory*. Ed. Elizabeth Kowaleski-Wallace. New York: Garland.

Schulz, Jennifer Lea. 1997. "Cultural Infrastructure: The Production and Circulation of the Harlem Renaissance." PhD dissertation, University of Washington.

Schweickhart, Patrocine. 1989. "Reading Ourselves." In *Speaking of Gender*. Ed. Elaine Showalter. London and New York: Routledge.

Seigal, Buddy. 1994. "Seething Is Believing in Equality." *Los Angeles Times*, August 27, Calendar.

Sekula, Allan. 1986. "The Body and the Archive." *October* 39 (Winter): 3–64.

Sell, Mike. 2001. "The Black Arts Movement: Performance, Neo-Orality, and the Destruction of the 'White Thing.'" In *African-American Performance and Theater History: A Critical Reader*. Ed. Harry J. Elam Jr. and David Krasner. New York: Oxford University Press.

Shange, Ntozake. 1981a. *Three Pieces*. New York: St. Martin's.

———. 1981b. "Spell #7: geechee jibara quik magic trance manual for technologically stressed third world people." In *Three Pieces*. New York: St. Martin's.

———. 1981c. "A Photograph: Lovers in Motion." In *Three Pieces*. New York: St. Martin's.

Shange, Ntozake, and Neal Lester. 1990. "At the Heart of Shange's Feminism: An Interview with Neal Lester." In *Black American Literature Forum*. Indiana State University, 717–30.

Sharp, Joanne. 1999. "Space." In *A Feminist Glossary of Human Geography*. Ed. L. McDowell and Joanne Sharp. London: Arnold.

Sharpley-Whiting, Tracey, and Joy A. James, eds. 2000. *The Black Feminist Reader*. Malden, MA: Blackwell.

Sharpley-Whiting, Tracey-Denean. 1999. *Sexualized Savages, Primal Fears, and Primitive Narratives in French*. Durham, NC: Duke University Press.

Shohat, Ella, ed. 1998. *Talking Visions: Multicultural Feminism in Transnational Age*. New York: New Museum of Contemporary Art. Cambridge, MA: MIT Press.

Showalter, Elaine, ed. 1989. "Rise of Gender." In *Speaking of Gender*. Routledge: New York and London.

Smith, A. L. 2001. "Taranaki Waiata tangi and Feelings for Place." Unpublished PhD thesis, Lincoln University, Canterbury, New Zealand.
Smith, Shawn Michelle. 1999. *American Archives: Gender, Race, and Class in Visual Culture*. Princeton, NJ: Princeton University Press.
Spillers, Hortense J. 2003. *Black, White, and in Color: Essays on American Literature and Culture*. Chicago and London: University of Chicago Press.
———. 2003. "Interstices: A Small Drama of Words." In *Black, White, and in Color: Essays on American Literature*. Chicago: University of Chicago Press. 152–75.
———. 2003. "Mama's Baby, Papa's Maybe: An American Grammar Book." In *Black, White, and in Color: Essays on American Literature*. Chicago: University of Chicago Press. 203–29.
———. 1987. "Mama's Baby, Papa's Maybe: An American Grammar Book." *Diacritics* 17, no. 2 (Summer): 65–81.
Spivak. Gayatri. 1995. "Can the Subaltern Speak? Speculations on Widow Sacrifice." In *The Postcolonial Studies Reader*. Ed. Bill Ashcroft, et al. New York: Routledge.
Steele, Cynthia. 1995. "Encuentros y desencuentros culturales en *The Mixquiahuala Letters*, de Ana Castillo." In *Las forms de nuestras voces: Chicana and Mexicana Writers in Mexico*. Ed. Claire Joysmith. México: Universidad Nacional Autónoma de México. 125–40.
Stephens, Judith L. 1999. "The Harlem Renaissance and the New Negro Movement." In *The Cambridge Companion to American Women Playwrights*. Ed. Brenda Murphy. Cambridge, England: Cambridge University Press. 98–117.
Strickland, Rennard, and Margaret Archuleta. 1993. "The Way People Were Meant to Live." In *Shared Visions: Native American Painters and Sculptors in the Twentieth Century*. New York: New Press.
Suleri, S. 1992. "Woman Skin Deep: Feminism and the Postcolonial Condition." *Critical Inquiry* 18, no. 4: 756–69.
Sweet, Jill D. 1985. *Dances of the Tewa Pueblo Indians*. Santa Fe, NM: School of American Research Press.
Swentzell, Rina. 2002. "A Flower the Color of the Earth." In *Roxanne Swentzell: Extra-Ordinary People*, by Gussie Fauntleroy. Santa Fe: New Mexico Magazine Artist Series.
———. 1998. "Pueblo Cosmos." In *Pueblo Artists: Portraits*. Santa Fe: Museum of New Mexico Press.
———. 1997. Review of *Where There Is No Name for Art*. *American Indian Culture and Research Journal* 21, no. 4: 354–55.
Swentzell, Roxanne. 2002. "Artist's Statement." *Roxanne Swentzell: Extra-Ordinary People*. Santa Fe: New Mexico Magazine Artist Series.
———. 1999. "Artist's Statement." In *Clay People*. Museum Catalog. Santa Fe: Wheelwright Museum of the American Indian. Roxanne Swentzell clarified and updated her statement in 2004 via email with Ruth Porritt.

———. 1997. "Hearing with Our Hearts." In *Surviving in Two Worlds: Contemporary Native American Voices*. Ed. Lois Crozier-Hogle and Darryl Babe Wilson. Austin: University of Texas Press.

———. 1994a. "Artist's Statement." In *Sisters of the Earth: Contemporary Native American Ceramics*. Exhibition Catalog. Helena, MT: Holter Museum of Art.

———. 1994b. "Artist's Statement." In *Watchful Eyes: Native American Women Artists*. Exhibition Catalog. Phoenix: Heard Museum.

Tagg, John. 1993. *The Burden of Representation: Essays on Photographies and Histories*. Minneapolis: University of Minnesota Press.

Tharu, Susie, and K. Lalita, eds. 1995. *Women Writing in India, Vols. I and II*. Delhi: Oxford University Press.

Thomas, Devon. 2002. "Me'Shell Ndegeocello Speaks on Life and Times." *Michigan Daily* (Ann Arbor), April 10.

Tillery, Linda. 1977. *Linda Tillery*. Oakland, CA: Olivia Records.

Timble, Stephen. 1987. *Talking with the Clay: The Art of Pueblo Pottery*. Santa Fe: School of American Research Press.

Tolson, Nancy. 1998. "Making Books Available: The Role of Early Libraries, Librarians, and Booksellers in the Promotion of African American Children's Literature." *African American Review* 32 (Spring): 9–16.

Tomek, Ana. 2000. "Presentation on Ana Castillo's *So Far from God*." <http://www.uwm.edu/wcb.uwm/schools/48/350/gjay/12/files/tomekcastillo.htm> Accessed May 5, 2000.

Trachtenberg, Alan. 1989. *Reading American Photographs: Images as History, Matthew Brady to Walker Evans*. New York: Hill and Wang.

Vater, Regina. 1997. "The Continent of Ashe." In *Voices of Color: Art and Society in the Americas*. Ed. Phoebe Farris. New York: Prometheus Humanity Books.

Vizenor, Gerald. 1984. *The People Named the Chippewa: Narrative Histories*. Minneapolis: University of Minnesota Press.

Walker, Alice. 1983. *In Search of Our Mothers' Gardens*. New York: Harvest/HBJ.

———. 1976. *Meridian*. New York: Pocket Books.

Walker, Rebecca. 1997. "Have No Fear." *VIBe*, May.

Walkingstick, Kay. 1992. "Native American Art in the Postmodern Era." *Art Journal* 51, no. 3: 15–17.

Wallace, Michele. 1979. *Black Macho and the Myth of the Superwoman*. New York: Dial.

Wallis, Brian. 1996. "Black Bodies, White Science: The Slave Daguerreotypes of Louis Agassiz." *The Journal of Blacks in Higher Education* no. 12 (Summer): 102–106.

Ward, A. 1973. *A Show of Justice: Racial "Amalgamation" in Nineteenth Century New Zealand*. Auckland: Auckland University Press.

Waring, Charles. 2002. Interview with MeShell Ndegéocello. www.soulwalking.co.uk/Me'Shell%20Ndegeocello.html. Accessed July 1, 2004.

Wasserman, Nadine. 1999. "African American Women Artists." In *Women Artists of Color: A Bio-Critical Sourcebook to Twentieth Century Artists in the Americas*. Ed. Phoebe Farris. Westport, CT, and London: Greenwood.
Watts, Michael K. 2002. "The Revolutionary Soul Singer Steps up to the Mic." *Venus*, July.
Weaver, Jace. 1997. *That the People Might Live: Native American Literatures and Native American Community*. New York: Oxford University Press.
Werner, Craig Henson. 1995. "Harlem Renaissance." In *The Oxford Companion to Women's Writing in the United States*. Ed. Cathy N. Davidson and Linda Wagner-Martin. New York: Oxford University Press. 375–78.
Westerbeck, Colin L. 1998. "Frederick Douglass Chooses His Moment." *Museum Studies*. Art Institute of Chicago 24, no. 2: 145–61.
White, J. 1887. *The Ancient History of the Maori*, vol. 2. Wellington: Government Printer.
Wiegand, Wayne A. 2000. "American Library History Literature, 1947–1997: Theoretical Perspectives?" *Essays Commemorating the Fiftieth Anniversary of the Library Round Table*. Ed. Andrew B. Wertheimer and Donald G. Davis Jr. Washington DC: Library of Congress. 4–50.
Wiegman, Robyn. 1995. *American Anatomies: Theorizing Race and Gender*. Durham and London: Duke University Press.
Willett, Cynthia. 2001. *The Soul of Justice: Social Bonds and Racial Hubris*. Ithaca, NY: Cornell University Press.
Williams, D. 1989. *British Colonial Treaty Policies: A Perspective*. In *Honouring the Treaty: An Introduction for Pakeha to the Treaty of Waitangi*. Ed. H. Yensen, K. Hague, and T. McCreanor. Auckland, New Zealand: Penguin Books. 46–55.
Willis, Deborah. 2003. "The Sociologist's Eye: W. E. B. Du Bois and the Paris Exposition." In *A Small Nation of People: W. E. B. Du Bois and African American Portraits of Progress*. Library of Congress. New York: Amistad. 51–78.
———. 1994. "Introduction." In *Picturing Us: African American Identity in Photography*. Ed. Deborah Willis. New York: New Press. 3–26.
Willis, Deborah, and Carla Williams. 2002. *The Black Female Body: A Photographic History*. Philadelphia: Temple University Press.
Willis-Thomas, Deborah. 1985. *Black Photographers, 1840–1940: An Illustrated Bio-Bibliography*. New York and London: Garland.
Wintz, Cary D. 1988. *Black Culture and the Harlem Renaissance*. Houston: Rice University Press.
Wisker, Gina. 2000. *Post-Colonial and African-American Women's Writing*. Houndmills, Basingstoke, Hampshire: Macmillan; New York: St. Martin's.
Yarbro-Bejarano, Yvonne. 1996. "Chicana Literature from a Chicana Perspective." In *Chicana Creativity and Criticism: New Frontiers in American Literature*. Ed. Maria Herrera-Sobek, et al. Albuquerque: University of New Mexico Press, 213–19.

———. 1992. "The Multiple Subject in the Writing of Ana Castillo." *Americas Review: A Review of Hispanic Literature and Art of the USA* 20, no. 1 (Spring): 65–72.
Yates, Elizabeth. 2003. "Rosalie Jones Brings Dance-Drama to Life." *The Expositor*, March 20, C4.
York, Wendy Jill. 1993. "Lucky Star." *The Advocate*, October 19.
Zelliot, Eleanor. 1996. "Stri Dalit Sahitya: The New Voice of Women Poets." In *Images of Women in Maharashtrian Literature and Religion*. Ed. Anne Feldhaus. Albany: State University of New York Press.
———. 1992. "Buddhist Women of the Contemporary Maharashtrian Conversion Movement." In *Buddhism, Sexuality, and Gender*. Ed. Jose Ignacio Cabezon. Albany: State University of New York Press.

# About the Contributors

CHRISTA DAVIS ACAMPORA is an associate professor of philosophy at Hunter College and The Graduate Center of City University of New York. She is author of numerous articles and has edited several volumes, including *Cultural Sites of Critical Insight* (with Angela Cotten, SUNY Press, 2007) and *A Nietzschean Bestiary: Becoming Animal Beyond Docile and Brutal* (with Ralph Acampora, 2004). Her main interests are in moral psychology, aesthetics, contemporary political theory, and Nietzsche studies.

RITCH CALVIN is a Lecturer in Women's Studies at SUNY Stony Brook. His primary research interests are Mexicana and Chicana literature and aesthetics and feminist science fiction. His recent publications have been about works by Philip K. Dick, Isabella Ríos, and Ana Castillo.

JAYE T. DARBY is co-founder and co-director with Hanay Geiogamah of Project HOOP (Honoring Our Origins and People through Native Theater, Education, and Community Development). Project HOOP is a North American initiative to advance Native performing arts artistically, academically, and professionally, based at the University of California, Los Angeles. Dr. Darby is the co-editor of the anthology *Keepers of the Morning Star: An Anthology of Native Women's Theater* with Stephanie Fitzgerald (2003). With Hanay Geiogamah, she co-edited *Stories of Our Way: An Anthology of American Indian Plays* (1999) and *American Indian Theater in Performance: A Reader* (2000). She also teaches in the Graduate School of Education and Information Studies at UCLA.

DR. PHOEBE FARRIS (Powhatan) is a Full Professor of Art and Design/ Women's Studies at Purdue University. As an author, exhibit curator, photographer, and professor, Dr. Farris explores issues involving race, gender, indigenous sovereignty, Native American Studies, peace, and social justice from an interdisciplinary perspective. Her books, *Voices of Color: Art and*

*Society in the Americas* and *Women Artists of Color: A Bio-critical Sourcebook to 20th Century Artists in the Americas*, create a dialogue about the intersections of social activism and the arts.

MS. NANDITA GUPTA is an officer in the Indian Administrative Service. She is currently holding the post of Additional Deputy Commissioner, Dharamsala in Himachal Pradesh, India. She holds a masters degree in English Literature from St. Stephens College, Delhi and a Master of Philosophy degree in Sociology from Jawahar Lal Nehru University, Delhi. She has written a dissertation entitled "An Analysis of Gender Relations among Dalits: Literature, Education, and Politics in the 20th Century." Through this paper she hopes to combine her keen interest in literature and social issues.

JOY JAMES is the John B. and John T. McCoy Presidential Professor of Africana Studies and College Professor in Political Science. Her publications include: *Resisting State Violence: Gender, Race, and Radicalism in U.S. Culture*; *Transcending the Talented Tenth: Black Leaders and American Intellectuals*; *Shadowboxing: Representations of Black Feminist Politics*; and the forthcoming, *Memory, Shame and Rage: The Central Park Case, 1989–2002*. She is editor of *The Angela Y. Davis Reader* and several anthologies on radical politics and incarceration including *Imprisoned Intellectuals*; *The New Abolitionists*; and *Warfare in the American Homeland*.

KIMBERLY LAMM is completing her Ph.D. in English at the University of Washington and teaches in the Critical and Visual Studies program at Pratt Institute. Her dissertation examines literary and visual portraiture in late nineteenth- and early twentieth-century American culture. Recent work has appeared in *American Quarterly*, *Callaloo*, *Cultural Critique*, and *College English*.

EDUARDO MENDIETA is associate professor of Philosophy at Stony Brook University, where he is also the director of the Latin American and Caribbean Studies Center. He is the executive editor of *Radical Philosophy Review*. His most recent publications have been a collection of interviews with Angela Davis: *Abolition Democracy: Beyond Empire, Torture, and Prisons* (Seven Stories Press, 2005), and an edited volume of interviews with Richard Rorty: *Take Care of Freedom and Truth will Take Care of Itself* (Stanford University Press, 2006). He has also written on Enrique

Dussel, Jürgen Habermas, and Cornel West. His newest book is *Global Fragments: Globalizations, Latinamericanisms, and Critical Theory* (SUNY Press, 2007).

MARTHA MOCKUS holds the annual Jane Watson Irwin Chair in Women's Studies at Hamilton College. Her research and publications focus on musical performance as a form of queer and feminist critique. Her book *Sonic Feminism and the Music of Pauline Oliveros* is forthcoming from Routledge.

KELLY OLIVER is W. Alton Jones Professor of Philosophy at Vanderbilt University. She is the author of several books including *Family Values, Subjectivity Without Subjects, Witnessing: Beyond Recognition, The Colonization of Psychic Space*, and *Secret Weapons of War: Women, Sex and the Media*. She is currently writing a book entitled *Animal Pedagogy*.

RUTH PORRITT is an Associate Professor of Philosophy and Women Studies at West Chester University. Her work has appeared in *How Shall We Tell Each Other of the Poet?, The Bedford Introduction to Literature, Writing Poems*, and *Thirteen Ways of Looking for a Poem*, among others.

AILSA SMITH recently retired from her position as senior lecturer in the Centre for Māori and Indigenous Planning and Development at Lincoln University, New Zealand. She is of Taranaki Māori descent, and gained her Ph.D. on Māori sense of place as revealed by classical Māori songs from her tribal area. She has published a book of Taranaki Māori songs and stories which she translated from family manuscript records, and continues to explore the frontiers of interpretation and bicultural understandings in her preferred research field of Māori cultural geography.

KATHERINE WILSON is working toward a Ph.D. in Theater Studies at the Graduate Center, City University of New York, with a focus on scripts and print material in theater. Through the 1990s she wrote and performed alternative theater in New York.

# Index

abolitionists, white, 127
academia, xi, xiii, 8
academics, 83
Acampora, Christa, xi, 9
actuality, 108, 112
action, 5, 7, 9, 13, 145
activists, 15, 27, 42, 83, 87
aesthetics, 3–8, 16, 77, 81, 146, 167, 188, 232–233, 248–249; black, 185, 232–233; feminist, 16; indigenous, 185, 188–189, 248–249, 258–259; Latin American, 182–183
aesthetic, 14, 24–26, 76, 132; mutilated, 73, 74. See also *aisthesis*
aesthetic experience, 9, 71, 72, 76, 78
African spirituality, 185
Agard, Nadema, 189–190
Agassiz, Louis, 110–112, 118
Agency, xi–xiii, 4–9, 12, 13–17, 53, 57, 59, 60, 67, 68, 71, 73, 95, 100, 126, 128, 131, 140, 143, 166, 233, 245
*aisthesis*, 69, 71–74
alienation, 235
Allen, Paula Gunn, 16, 247, 249, 252, 254, 256–257, 262–263
Allende, Isabel, 21–23
Alvarez, Julia, 8–9, 47–57. See also *under* revolution
Amaral, Tarsilado, 182
ambrotypes, 110
Ambedkar, Bhimrao, 199, 202–204

America, 110; black, 82; history of race and gender in, 124; imperial, 141, 142
Andrews, Regina (also Regina Anderson), 15, 231–245
anthropology, 82, 83, 111, 112, 118, 250–254
Anzaldúa, Gloria, xi, xiii, 1–2, 25–28, 30, 33, 102
Apakura, 223
Arawak, 149
Ardner, Shirley, 238, 243
Arendt, Hannah, 53
Aristotle, 170
assimilation, 84, 85
astrology, 185
Auld, Michael, 193
Auschwitz, 146
authority, 47–50, 55, 59, 78
autonomy, 5, 77

bad faith, 60, 61
Bambara, Toni Cade, xiii
Bansode, Hira, 203, 206–208
Barthes, Roland, 29
Bates, Sara, 189
Battey, C.M., 135
Battle of Te Morere, 224
beauty, 10, 14–15, 74, 107, 108, 147, 153, 105, 158
Beauvoir, Simone de, 59–64, 66–67, 77–78
being, 3, 61, 67, 70, 146
Benjamin, Walter, 146

Bentley, Gladys, 101
Bhabha, Homi, 73, 156, 158
Bible, 49, 98
Bigknife, Susan, 258
Bird, Gloria, 248
blackness, 64–65, 68, 78, 85, 107, 127, 156
black nationalism, 181
black power, 216
blues, 91
body, 10–12, 76, 81, 108–112, 148, 154, 170, 172–175, 176, 179, 201; and action, 156; and mind, 43; and performance, 144, 147; as sign, 145; and spirituality, 7, 28, 29; enslaved, 73–74; female, 103, 131; in exhibition, 149; mapping of, 111, 113; racialized, 116. *See also* embodiment
Bordo, Susan, 179
Brand, Peggy, 6
Brant, Beth, 248
Bryant, Anita, 88
Buchloch, Benjamin, 107
Buddha, 205. *See also* Yashodhara
Buddhism, 204–205
burial traditions, 186, 195
Burns, Lori, 99, 100–101
Bustamente, Nao, 151, 153
Butler, Octavia, xiii
Bruce, Blanche K., 136

Calvin, Ritch, 8
Camper, Peter, 111
capitalism, 10–12, 86–87; struggles against, 82
Carnegie, Andrew, 239–240
Cartesianism, 146–147
Casselberry, Judith, 89
caste system, 197, 201, 206–209
Castillo, Ana, 8, 21–45
catharsis, 75–76
Catholicism, 27–28, 183, 189
Chahhande, Baban, 201

Chendwankar, Prahlad, 205
Chicago, Judy, 126–127
Chicanisma, 25. *See also* Xicanisma
Chicano(a)s, 21–42
Chicano Rights Movement, 184
Chopin, Kate, 40
Choreopoetry, 2, 71
Christian, Barbara, xiii
Christianity, 38, 48, 88, 184, 186, 223, 236. *See also* Catholicism
civil rights movement, 141, 142, 184
Clarke, Cheryl, 82, 98, 101
class, 2, 3, 9, 29, 53, 83, 124; in power relations, 47, 50–53
classism, 102
clowns 172, 174. *See also* Kossa
Coaticue, 184
cold war, 141–142, 148, 154
Colette, 53
Collins, Bootsy, 90
Collins, Patricia Hill, 82–83, 94
colonialism, colonization, 8, 11–15, 149, 155, 184, 188, 213–229; 247–248, 252–253, 256. *See also under* embodiment
Columbus, 149
communication, 8, 57, 180
communism, 27
community, 1, 4, 7–8, 10–15, 32, 40, 42–43, 59, 62, 69, 73–74, 75, 102, 247–262
compassion, 73
comrades, 37
consciousness, 28, 66
constructivism, 3, 162
Cornell, Drucilla, 59, 66–67
Cortázar, 29
cosmology, 12, 40, 172, 182, 185, 189, 223–228, 258
crafts, 187
craniology, 109
creativity, 7–8, 10, 15, 54–58, 81, 86, 170

*Crisis, The*, 231
criticism 25, 141; feminist, 199–200. *See also* Gynocritics
crucifixes, 48
cubists, the, 146
culture, xi–xiii, 2–3, 5, 7, 9–15, 24–27, 31, 34, 54, 88, 122, 145; African American, 134; American, 117, 124, 158; black musical, 90; hippie, 155; patriarchal, 38–40, 48, 53, 56, 57; popular, 92; visual, 108–109, 135, 138, 140; western, 81, 100, 103, 126

daguerreotypes, 110–112, 115–118, 120
Dalits, 13–14, 197–210; Dalit Panthers, 199. *See also* caste system
Dangle, Arjun, 198–199
Danto, Arthur, 14
Darby, Jaye T., 16
Dasein, 146
*Das Ge-stell*, 146
Davis, Angela, 10, 82, 86–88, 90, 94–95, 156
Daystar, 16, 249, 258–263. *See also* Rosalie Jones
Delany, Hubert, 235
Delgadillo, Theresa, 38–42
DeLoria, Jr., Vine, 247
Densmore, Frances, 249–254
democracy, 238
depression, 54–58
desire, 3, 9, 59–63, 65, 67–71, 73–78, 99–101, 148, 153, 156
Dewey decimal system, 240
Dewey, John, 72–73
Dewey, Melvin, 240
Dhasal, Namdeo, 199
dialectic, 118; of *seeing* and *being seen*, 156
diaspora, 185
dictatorship, 47–51

difference, 3–4
dignity, 10, 13
disinterestedness, 3
*dispositifs*, 142–143, 155
domination, 50, 53; resistance to, 9, 47, 52, 55
Douglass, Frederick, 116, 136
Draupadi, 208
dreams, 250–252
Du Bois, W.E.B, 117, 136–138, 231–232, 241–242
Dunbar, Paul Lawrence, 136
Dunn, Dorothy, 188–189
Dussel, Enrique, 147

economy, 60, 74, 153, 155; U.S. slave, 131
ecstasy, 14, 72, 96, 97
education, 4, 205–206
Egyptian culture, 182
Eklavya, 208
Eleggua's crossword, xiii
*El Movimiento* (the Chicano Movement), 27–28, 33–34
emancipation, 207, 210. *See also* freedom
embodiment, 42, 70, 105, 147–151, 154–158; exhibited, 149; "The Coloniality of Embodiment," 141
emotion, 162, 179, 222–223
environment, 12–15, 167–169, 176, 183, 186–187, 189, 191–192, 195, 219–220
epistemology, 9, 12, 43; black feminist, 83; standpoint, 163
*Eros*, 77–78
erotic, the, 71–72, 74, 77, 96–97, 151
eroticism, social, 60
*Essence*, 82
essence, 107–108
essentialism, 3, 161

ethnography, 25; musical, 82
ethics, 167
Eurocentrism, 147
Europe, 28, 31, 153
Existentialism, 9, 59–66, 145
exotic, the: consumption of, 153; reinscription of, 142;
Experience Unlimited, 92
exploitation: 201, 209

Faludi, Susan, 27
Fanon, Frantz, 9, 64–67, 78
Farris, Phoebe, 13–14, 185, 189, 193–194
Fauset, Jessie, 235
feminism, 3, 10, 13–14, 25–28, 42, 81, 87, 102, 120, 143, 127, 189, 191, 245; American, 120, 126
femininity, 9, 47–48, 50, 53, 55 101, 103, 105, 108, 122
fetish(es), 147, 187
Fisher, Pearl, 235
Fisher, Rudolf, 235
Forbes, Jack D., 194
Foster, Lillian, 101
Foucault, Michel, 11, 155
Frazier, E. Franklin, 235
freedom, xi–xiii, 4–5, 9, 49, 53, 58–62, 64, 66, 73–75, 77–78, 82–86, 90, 142, 155, 236
Fuentes, Carlos, 31
Funkadelic, 91
Fusco, Coco, 11, 141–158
futurists, 146

Gaikwad, Sudharkar, 201
Gage, Francis Dana, 127
Gajbhiyes, Mina, 203
García Márquez, Gabriel, 21
Gates, Henry Louis, 137–138
gaze, 2, 11–12, 14, 99, 118, 122, 129, 143, 149, 151, 158
genealogy, 11, 15, 132, 141–143, 220–221, 228

gender, 3, 8–9, 47, 50–53, 83, 108–110, 120, 134, 137, 140, 142–143, 238
genius, 8–9, 47, 53–58
genocide, 26, 189
genotypes, 153–154
geography, 232, 243–245
Gerestant, Mildred, 101
ghetto, 84
Gia, 170, 172
Gili, Marta, 120
Glancy, Diane, 16, 247–249, 255–258, 263
Goebbels, Joseph, 146
Goldsby, Jackie, 94
Golden, Thelma, 134
Gómez-Peñas, Guillermo, 11, 30, 141, 145, 149, 150
Gomez, Jewelle, 101
Gordon, Jane, 6
Gordon, Lewis, 6
Green, Rayna, 168
Gregory, Dick, 85
Grey, Sir George, 226
Guadalupe, Virgin of, 25, 33, 182, 189, 195. *See also* Tonantzin
Gulags, the, 146
Gulf of Mexico, 149
Gupta, Nandita, 14
Gurav, Anuradha, 204
Gynocritics, 199–200

Habermas, Jürgen, 238
hair, 236
Hammonds, Evelyn, 94, 100
Hampton, Mabel, 101
Hannis, Winifred, 91
Hannsberry, Jarraine, 82, 86
Hardin, Helen, 188, 190
Harjo, Joy, 189, 248
Harlem Experimental Theater (HET), 15, 232–234, 241–243
Harlem Free Library, 239

Harlem Renaissance, 15, 117, 135, 231–245
Hart, Patricia, 23
Hartsock, Nancy, 12, 162, 163
Hegel, 147
Heidegger, Martin, 11, 61, 144–147
hermeneutics, 142
Hernández-Ávila, Inés, 247–248
hierarchy, 8–9, 50–52, 126
High, Frida, 182
Hinduism, 204
hip hop, 82, 86, 91
Hiroshima, 46
history, 24, 53, 74, 132, 137–138, 140–141, 145, 154, 156, 176, 187–188, 213–214, 252, 256, 262
Hoard, Adrienne, 182, 185–187
home, xi–xiii, 4, 7, 10, 14–16, 240–241, 247–263. See also place *and* space
homophobia, 82, 88–92, 94, 102
homosexuality, 91. See also lesbianism
hooks, bell, xvii, 4, 10, 82–84, 94
Howe, LeAnne, 257
Howe, Oscar, 12, 162
Hucko, Bruce, 168–169
Hughes, Langston, 235
Humane Society, 151
Hurston, Zora Neale, 82
Hurungarangi, 223–224
hysteria, 118

idealization, 54
identity, 2–3, 5–8, 12, 15, 23, 28, 30, 31, 65, 73, 82, 83–84, 91, 124, 142, 158, 191, 195, 220, 229, 247–263
ideology, 27, 42, 84, 140
idolatry, 146
imagination, 6–9, 16, 53–54, 56–58, 60, 66–67, 70–73, 75, 151, 158
imperialism, American, 86

impressionists, 146
(pan-)Indian identity, 181
individuality, 162–163, 174
*indigenismo*, 181
individuality, 5, 10–11
innovation, 164
Institute of the American Indian Arts, 188–189
integrity, 12, 162
intimacy, 37, 95–97

Jackson-Jarvis, Martha, 186–187
Jacobs, Harriet, 122
James, Joy, 6
jazz, 82, 91
Jehlen, Myra, 199–200
Jessup, Georgia Mills, 194
Jesus, 33, 38, 89, 98, 101, 189
Jim Crow, 148
*jinetera*, 154–155
Johnson, Marie, 235
Jones, Kellie, 120, 140
Jones, Lois Mailou, 185
Jones, Rosalie, 16, 249, 258–263. See *also* Daystar
Jordon, June, xiii
joy, 62, 71–72
Joyce, James, 31
J. Paul Getty Museum, 110
Julien, Isaac, 117, 134

Kachinas, 190
Kahlo, Frida, 183
Kamble, Shantabai, 205
Kant, Immanuel, 5
Kardak, Waman, 205
Kelley, Mary, 135
Kilcup, Karen, 167
Kilpatrick, Anna, 255
Kilpatrick, Frank, 255
King Jr., Martin Luther, 84
Kingsbury, B., 216
Klien, Melanie, 53

## 292 INDEX

knowledge, 5, 15, 64, 66, 83, 118, 240–241, 251
Kossa. *See* clowns
Krigwa ("*Crisis* Guild of Writers and Artists"), 232–234, 242
Kristeva, Julia, 9, 53–57
Kruger, Barbara, 135
Kundera, 73
Kumari, Vijay, 204
Kunti, 208

LaChappelle, David, xii
LaDuke, Winona, 247
La France, Melisse, 99
LaMarr, Jean, 189
lamentation, 213–229. *See also* sadness
Lamm, Kimberly, 10, 11
land, 15–16; —scape, 213–229, 248–263. *See also* place
Langston, John M., 136
language, 8, 15, 26, 29, 33, 57, 68–70, 100, 134, 144, 220, 258
Lanjewar, Jyoti, 202, 206
Lanning, Helen, 235
Laroe, Hector, *"La Fama"* (1974), 86
Latimer, Catherine Allen, 240
Latino(a), 25, 142, 153
Latin American, 142; artists, 182–184 (*see also* individual artists); post-, 143, 158
LeFebvre, Henri, 243
legitimacy, 69, 101
lesbianism, 92, 94, 98, 100–101
Leviticus, 88
libraries, 231–245
Lippard, Lucy, 184
literature, 26, 71, 81
Little Bennie, 92
Little Turtle, Carm, 190
Locke, Alain, 135, 231–232
Lomahaftewa, Linda, 189
López, Yolanda, 182, 184

Lorde, Audre, 8, 9, 14, 71–72, 78, 82, 92
love, 49, 62, 72, 75, 78, 98, 167, 173, 222–223. *See also* desire; passion
lynching, 236

machismo, 26
Māori: 14–15
Madrid, 149, 154
magic, 8, 68–70. *See also* Passion
magical realism, 8, 21–25
*Mahabharat*, 208
Maharashtra Dalit Sahitya Sangh, 199
Makere, 224
Malcolm X, 84, 128
mammies, 135
Manu, 209
mapping, social, 243–244
Marxism, 27–28
Mary Magdalene, 98–99, 101
masculinity, 53, 101
masks, 185, 195
Massey, Doreen, 238, 243
materialism, 43; Anglo 37, 39, 142
matriarchy, 43
medicine, 100, 187–188, 195, 221, 251
melancholy, social, 54–56
memoir, 102
memory (including 'mnemonics'): 16, 214–216, 255
Mendieta, Ana, 183
Mendieta, Eduardo, 11–12
Mesa-Bains, Amalia, 182
Mestizo(a)s, 26, 28, 30, 102, 154
Mitchell, Lofton, 234, 242–243
Mitchell, W.J.T., 135
Mockus, Martha, 10–11
modernism, 162, 166, 179
monogamy, 128
Monson, Siouxsan, 255
morality, 5–6, 72

Morrison, Toni, 8, 9, 60, 68–69, 71, 73–74, 76–78
Morton, Dr. Samuel, 110
mother, -figure, 201–202, 208, 217; -hood, 9, 47, 55, 161
mourning, 223–224
multiculturalism, 147–148
music, 70–72, 82–87, 90–91, 94, 95, 101, 102; epistemological power of, 81; go-go, 92–93; popular, 88
mythology, 146, 228, 256; Christian, 41; origins 172

Nadell, Martha Jane, 135
Naranjo, Michael, 165
Naranjo-Morse, Nora, 166, 169, 189
Narmada Bachao Andolan, 209
National Museum of the American Indian, 179
National Socialist Party, 146
nationalism, transnationalism, 238
Native American women artists, 188–194. *See also* individual artists
nature, natural environment, 186–187, 189, 191–192, 195
Ndegéocello, Meshell, 10–11, 81–102
Neal, Mark Anthony, 94
Nestle, John, 100
New Negro, 117, 137–138
New World, 149
New York, 51, 55
New York Public Library, 15, 16, 231–245
Nietzsche, Friedrich, 77
Nirmala, Darisi Sasi: 207, 209
Niro, Shelley, 189
*nouveau roman*, French, 29
*novios*, 48
Nuremberg, 146

O'Grady, Lorraine, 103, 185
Oliver, Kelly, 7–9
ontology, 8, 12, 42, 45

*Opportunity, The*, 231
oppression, 2–4, 9–10, 26, 53–60, 62–66, 70–71, 95, 110, 112, 140, 184, 206, 210, 248
oral culture and traditions, 219–221, 250
organization, political, 2
origins, myth of, 172, 226–228

Paglia, Camille, 27
palmistry, 185, 187
Pandava brothers, 208
parfleches, 191–192
Papa-tū-ā-nuku (earth mother, Papa), 217, 219–220, 226–228
Paris, 138
Paris Exposition of 1900, 136–137
passing, 236
passion, 49, 59, 61–62, 78; personal, 82
Patkar, Medha, 209
patriarchy, xii, 8–9, 26, 28, 33–34, 43, 49–50, 56, 98, 204, 207, 209
patriotism, xii
Painter, Nell Irving, 127, 128
Pawar, Daya, 206
Pawar, J. V, 199
Pawde, Kumud, 205–206
peace, 173
perception, 4, 12; cultural, 110, 134, 137; "loving perception," 68, 74
performance, 11, 30, 89, 97, 143–145, 147, 149, 151, 153, 156, 158, 248–249
phenomena, 84
phenomenology; of communication, 144. *See also* Heidegger, Martin
philosophy, 145, 147
Phule, Jotiba, 203, 206
phrenology, 109
physiognomy, 109, 111, 116, 118, 137
Pierce, Charles S., 144
piety, 89

Piper, Adrian, 135
place, 7, 14–16, 23, 75, 78, 193, 213–229, 231–245. *See also* space; home; shelter
Plato, 5
play, 61
poetics, 59, 64–65, 68, 71–72, 78
poetry, 11, 55–57, 65, 69, 102
pointillists, 146
Poitras, Jane Ash, 189
Popel, Esther, 235
Pore, Pratibha, 204
pornography, 94
pornoscopia, 151
Porritt, Ruth, 12–13
portraiture, 10, 107–110, 112, 116, 120, 122, 132, 134, 138
postmodernism, 109, 179
postsocialism, 158
pottery, 164–165, 169–170, 173, 186–187
Powhatan, Rose, 189, 192–193
Powell, Richard, 187
Power, 8, 10, 13, 17, 69, 72–73, 77, 101, 155, 168, 170, 179, 187, 257–258, 262–263; erotic, 9, 99; epistemological, 148; imperial, 143, 149, 151; poetic, 67, 71, 78, 92; sexual, 100; Shifting, 47, 50–53; to resist, 48; to see without being seen, 158
powwows, 193, 251
Prince, 82
prostitution, 100, 155, 204
psyche, 53, 55
psychic life, 53, 57–58
psychology, moral, 60
Pueblo philosophy, 161, 165, 167, 179
Puritanism, 15

Quick-to-See Smith, Jaune, 189, 191–192
Quijano, Anibal, 147–148

race, 8, 12, 47, 50–53, 107–111, 115, 120, 124, 134–137, 140–143, 244–245
racism, xii, 2, 8, 10–13, 82, 102–103, 105, 107–108, 112, 136, 184, 188–189, 191, 195;
Raini, Ma, 94
Ranginui-e-tū-nei (Rangi), 226–228
rationality, 5; instrumental, 146
Ram, 207–208
*Ramaya*, 207
Ramirez, Renya, 174
Rani, Swaroopa, 202, 204, 207, 209
Ransom, Rev. Dr. Reverdy C., 136
rape, 156, 204
Rare Essence, 92
Ray, Ethel, 235
Reagen, Toshi, 82
reality, 23, 66, 111, 140; social, 62
realm, 68, 86; aesthetic, 147; of the personal, 94
Reifenstahl, Lenny, 146
Reil, Louis, 260
relationality, 4, 14
religion, 28, 50, 100, 181–183. *See also* Jesus; Christianity; spirituality
Rendon, Marcie, 16, 249–254, 263
repression, 117, 126
resistance, 4, 8, 9, 16, 48, 50, 52–55, 58, 60, 71, 72, 83, 140, 148; erotic, 155; feminist, 94. *See also* domination
respectability, 10, 14
responsibility, 12, 61, 64
revolt, 56–58, 63–65
revolution, 47–50, 55, 56, 86, 87, 154
Rich, Adrienne, 145, 147
Rogue, Alphonse Bertillon, 108
Rose, Cynthia, 26
Rose, Ernestine, 240–242
Roth, Moira, 184
rhythm, 10, 91

Saar, Alison, 185
Saar, Betye, 185
sadness, 12, 173–174. *See also* lamentation
Saeta, Elsa, 31
salsa, 86
Sambos, 135
Sánchez, Cynthia, 182
San Francisco, 145
Sangari, Kumkum, 200–201
Santería, 183, 185, 195
Sapkale, Trayambak, 206
Sartre, 59–61, 64–65
Saussure, Fernand, 144
savitri, 208
Schomberg Center of the New York Public Library, 233, 239–240, 241. *See also* Regina Andrews *and* New York Public Library
science: 19th century, 107
scopic drive, 158
Scott, Clarissa, 235
sculpture, 12
seduction, 96
segregation, 233
Sekula, Allen, 117, 118
self, 1, 12, 15, 75, 77, 82, 84, 86, 117, 137, 145, 174, 206–210
semiotics, 141–145, 158
sensibilities, 4, 5
separatism, 85
sexuality, 25, 102, 107, 129; feminist politics of, 91; lesbian, 94; queer, 88
sex, 92, 110, 134, 154, 155
sexism, xii, 2, 10, 12, 82, 105, 107, 108, 122, 191, 195
Shabri, 207–208
Shaminism, 182, 183, 185
Shange, Ntozake, 2, 8, 9, 59, 60, 67–71, 77, 78
Sharpley-Whiting, T., 6

Shawn, Michelle, 108
Shelly, Percy, 72
shelter, xii–xiii, 4. *See also* home
Shende, Sugandha, 207
Showalter, Elaine, 199
Siddhartha Sahitya Sangh, 199
Simmons, Henry, 236
Simone, Nina, xiii
Simpson, Lorna, 11, 103
Singer, Ed, 190
Sita, 208
slave(s), 70, 75, 127, 142, 154, 156; African American, 110, 137
slavery, 73–77, 90, 110–112, 124, 137, 148, 155, 156, 184
smallpox, 260
Smith, Ailsa, 14–15, 218
Smith, Bessie, 94
Smith-Rosenberg, Carroll, 37
Smith, Shawn Michelle, 108
*Snow White*, 103–105
socialism, 27
sociology, 134
Sofia, the Greek Goddess, 41
somatic semiology, 144, 145
South Carolina, 110
Soul II Soul, 95
sovereignty, white, 156
space, 7, 14–16, 40, 69, 94, 143, 214–218, 231–245; magic, 68; musical, 87; of creativity, 57; psychic, 66, 70; social, 54, 143; time-space, 219. *See also* place; home; shelter
Spain, 149
Spain, Daphne, 240
Spaniards, 30, 154
Spanish court, 149
species, 110
Speer, Albert, 146
Spence, Eulalie, 232
Spillers, Hortense J., 10, 124, 126, 127, 134, 158

spirituality, 9, 13, 16, 28, 29, 43, 44, 181–183, 186–188, 189, 195, 217–218, 221, 223–226, 247–263
stereotypes, 135; black, 83; racial, 138
Stout, Renée, 187
Stowe, Harriet Beecher, 127
strife; economic, 87
subjectivity, 8, 10, 11, 60, 61, 64, 66–68, 95, 108, 126; Cartesian, 147; collective, 112; colonial, 151; human, 146; of the Chicana, 30
subject(s), 66, 75, 94, 107, 111, 112, 146, 147, 214; colonial, 142, 151; desiring, 99; psychoanalytic, 135; raced and gendered, 118, 138; white, 158
sublimation, 9, 54–57
suffering, 12; Christian, 90
surrealism, 182–183
Sweet Honey in the Rock, 82
Swentzell, Ralph, 164
Swentzell, Rina Naranjo, 164, 179
Swentzell, Roxanne, 12, 13, 161–180, 189
symbolic order, 77, 109, 117; of race and gender, 140
syncretism, 2, 12–13, 181–182, 189, 194
Sydney, 149
syntax, 25, 105, 112, 156, 158

*tabula rasa*, 148
Tagg, John, 131–132
Talib Kweli (of Black Star), 87
Tamati Hone Oraukawa, 224
Tangaroa, 227
Tapia, Ernest, 170
Taranaki tribe, 15
Tarot, 185
Te Kahui, 224, 225
Te Rangikaheke, 226
Te Ua Haumene, 224
Te Whetu, 225

*telos*, 29
terror, xii
Tewa, 166, 170, 172
theater, 15–16, 69, 231–263
"The Hottenton Venus" (Saartje Benjamin), 149
*Thelma and Louise*, 40
theory, 3, 6, academic feminist, 102; literary, 5
Tillery, Linda, 88
time, 15, 23, 176, 187, 213–214, 262; time-space, 219 geopolitical, 142, 147. *See also* history
tintypes, 110
Tomek, Ana, 38–39
Tonantzin, 184, 189
tradition(s), 5, 11, 13, 15, 28, 90, 91, 94, 109, 144, 164, 255; academic, 25; literary, 33; of writers, 29; patriarchal, 47
tragedy, xi–xiii
transformation(s), 3, 7, 16, 70–72, 74, 95; feminist, 82; musical, 98; poetic, 64
translation, 8–9
trauma, xi–xiii
Treaty of Waitangi, 15, 214–218
Trelling, Ursala (pseudonym of Regina Andrews), 236
Tremblay, Gail, 189
Trujillo, the Dictator, 47–51
truth, 23, 145–147; in lyrics, 95
Truth, Sojourner, 127, 128
Tsinhahjinnie, Hulleah, 189
Tsuchiya, Tilsa, 182
Tucker, Luella, 235


Uncle Tom, 135

values, 32, 37, 39, 61–62, 68–69, 71, 74, 220; aesthetic, 2–3; patriarchal, 48, 54–55

Van Gogh, 145
Vater, Regina, 183
Velarde, Pablita, 188, 190
victimization, 201
violence, xi–xiii, 31, 94, 135, 156
Vizenor, Gerald, 251
voodoo 149, 185, 187–188, 195
voyeurism, 129

wā (time-space), 219
Walker, Alice, 82, 88
Walker, Rebecca, 91, 100
WalkingStick, Kay, 12, 162, 189, 192
Wallis, Brian, 112
Washington, Booker T., 136–137
Washington D.C., 92
Wasserman, Nadine, 186
war/battle, 223–224
Ward, A., 215
Weaver, Jace, 247, 252, 257
Weems, Carrie Mae, 10, 11, 103–140
Wellman, Kiggo, 92–93, 95
Westerbeck, Colin, 116

Wheeler, Caron, 95, 97–98
White, J., 223
Whitehorse, Emmi 189
whiteness, 69, 70, 92, 103–107, 115, 134
Wiegman, Robyn, 107, 109, 134, 137
Willet, Cynthia, 75–77
Williams, D., 214
Willis, Deborah, 111, 115–117, 128
Wilson, Katherine, 15, 16
Wolf, Naomi, 27
womanhood, 9, 47, 55, 134, 136
*worlding (welten)*, 146–147

Xicanisma, 8–9, 25, 27–28, 42–43
Xicanista, 8, 21, 28–29, 42–43, 45

Yarbro-Bejarano, Yvonne, 25, 30
Yashodhara (Buddha's wife), 205, 208

Zealy T., Joseph, 110

www.ingramcontent.com/pod-product-compliance
Lightning Source LLC
Chambersburg PA
CBHW030129240426
**43672CB00005B/75**